European Yearbook of International Economic Law

EYIEL Monographs - Studies in European and International Economic Law

Volume 18

Series Editors

Marc Bungenberg, Saarbrücken, Germany
Christoph Herrmann, Passau, Germany
Markus Krajewski, Erlangen, Germany
Jörg Philipp Terhechte, Lüneburg, Germany
Andreas R. Ziegler, Lausanne, Switzerland

EYIEL Monographs is a subseries of the European Yearbook of International Economic Law (EYIEL). It contains scholarly works in the fields of European and international economic law, in particular WTO law, international investment law, international monetary law, law of regional economic integration, external trade law of the EU and EU internal market law. The series does not include edited volumes. EYIEL Monographs are peer-reviewed by the series editors and external reviewers.

More information about this subseries at http://www.springer.com/series/15744

Niall Moran

Engagement Between Trade and Investment

The Role of PTIAs

 Springer

Niall Moran
Dublin, Ireland

ISSN 2364-8392   ISSN 2364-8406   (electronic)
European Yearbook of International Economic Law
ISSN 2524-6658   ISSN 2524-6666   (electronic)
EYIEL Monographs - Studies in European and International Economic Law
ISBN 978-3-030-83258-2   ISBN 978-3-030-83259-9   (eBook)
https://doi.org/10.1007/978-3-030-83259-9

This Springer imprint is published by the registered company Springer Nature Switzerland AG.
The registered company address is: Gewerbestrasse 11, 6330 Cham, Switzerland

To mam and dad, for giving me a love of reading and writing and being with me every step of the way. Is mór agam é.

Acknowledgements

This book began as a doctoral thesis, which I defended at Bocconi University, Milan, and was completed during my first year working as a Lecturer at Middlesex University, London. The completion of this book would not have been possible without the encouragement and guidance of my PhD supervisor, colleagues, friends and family during these years.

Firstly, I would like to express my gratitude to my mentor Professor Giorgio Sacerdoti for supervising my thesis and bringing me to Italy with his unique PhD programme in International Economic Law. Your insights shaped and improved my thesis over the course of four and a half years and gave me the belief that it would one day be a book. Thank you.

I am deeply indebted to Professors Claudio Dordi, Anna de Luca and Yane Svetiev for their comments on my thesis as well as the courses I took with them in WTO law and EU economic law during the PhD programme. Other Professors or Visiting Professors at Bocconi have contributed in different ways to the completion of this book. In particular, I would like to thank Professors Alec Stone Sweet, Jürgen Kurtz, Damiano Canale, Leonardo Borlini, Giovanna Adinolfi, Donato Masciandaro, John J. Donohue and Piero Stanig. A special thanks is also due to Professor André Sapir for his classes and welcoming me as a Visiting Researcher at the Université Libre de Bruxelles in 2016.

I would also like to thank my former Heads of Unit Jean-Marc Trarieux and Ieva Lejasisaka for their encouragement with my thesis and for providing me with a working environment that was both incredibly stimulating and that added to the work of this book. Writing a book on Preferential Trade and Investment Agreements seems all the more urgent when you have emerged from a period negotiating one and my time working on the negotiation of TTIP and Mercosur remains a highlight of my professional career. I would like to thank my former colleagues at the Commission Jean Ferrière, Raimondo Serra, Fabienne Alcaraz, Francesco Meggiolaro, Magdalena Miskiewicz, Carlos Coronas-Balsera and Veronica Corella Gomez; as well as my former colleagues at the Council Francis Mangan, Nelius Carey, Jennifer Pickering, Nic Taylor, Órla Ní Chuilleanáin, Tom Stubbs and Róisín Healy. I was privileged to be able to complete this book while lecturing at Middlesex University,

London. I am especially grateful to Professor Laurent Pech for his encouragement of this book and fine stewardship of the School of Law. I am also grateful to my trade law colleagues at Middlesex, Professors Lijun Zhao and Damjan Kukovec, as well as Professor Anthony Cullen, for all of their help and support.

I have had many brilliant teachers over the years and would like to thank Conor Doherty and Paul Bermingham in particular, who taught me so much and are truly two of the best. I would also like to thank Anna-Louise Hinds for introducing me to international trade law during my undergraduate degree and Letizia Raschella-Sergi for her course in WTO law during my LLM.

Finally, I would like to thank my family and friends, for being there for me during these years. To my parents, Enda and Eileen, this book is dedicated to you. To my brother, Thomas and to Alexandra, thank you. To all my friends, in particular, Shane, Phil, Conor, Michael, Shaun and Gethin, thank you.

Contents

Chapter 1
Introduction

1.1 Introduction

International trade and investment are two of the core pillars of international economic law and interaction between these two regimes is examined in this book.[1] As international trade and investment increase in volume and complexity, so too do the demands on the international legal order to put effective rules and enforcement procedures governing the regimes in place.

The trade and investment regimes share the goal of facilitating economic efficiency through international economic activity and complement one another in this regard.

However, despite commonalities, there are major differences between the two regimes. They have developed largely separately in the modern era for historical reasons as well as the differing purposes of the regimes. This book examines the extent of engagement[2] between the regimes and whether these fundamental differences limit engagement between them. It further examines under what circumstances tribunals may refer to the experience of the other regime and what they should bear in mind when making cross-regime references.

The relationship between trade and investment has been memorably compared to that of twins and two sides of the same coin.[3] There are however a series of factors both driving and limiting engagement between the regimes, including the joint

---

[1] See Charnovitz (2011), pp. 3–9; Herdegen (2016), pp. 8–11.

[2] The term 'engagement' is expanded upon in Sect. 1.2.

[3] Broude (2011), p. 20; Di Mascio and Pauwelyn (2008), p. 48. Others are skeptical of whether a "'family reunion' of trade and investment is a realistic and convincing option," Tietje (2013), p. 169. Kurtz compares the relationship to that of a double helix that will "increasingly cohere around that unifying core". Di Mascio and Pauwelyn also describe the two regimes as "bound at the hip", Footer describes foreign investment as "drawn to international trade like a moth to the flame", Puig describes them as "merging", and Van den Broek describes them as operating in "distinct but

© The Author(s), under exclusive license to Springer Nature Switzerland AG 2021
N. Moran, *Engagement Between Trade and Investment*, EYIEL Monographs - Studies in European and International Economic Law 18,
https://doi.org/10.1007/978-3-030-83259-9_1

negotiation of trade and investment chapters in many recent Preferential Trade and Investment Agreements (PTIAs). This question of whether engagement between the trade and investment law regimes is driven by the inclusion of investment chapters in PTIAs, rather than in standalone BITs or other treaties with investment provisions, is the primary question explored in this book. This approach is based on the conviction that the regimes have much in common and that both regimes can take lessons from the experience of the other regime.[4]

1.2   The Meaning of 'Engagement'

The investment law regime is made up of thousands of International Investment Agreements (IIAs)[5] and the awards of tribunals taken under them.[6] IIAs consist of either BITs or PTIAs, which are trade agreements that include an investment chapter. The 'investment law regime' referred to throughout this book refers to the treaties themselves as well as awards and decisions taken under them. They are supplemented by separate or dissenting opinions of tribunal members, which are valuable illustrations of the tensions in interpreting investment treaties.[7]

The trade law regime is made up of the texts of the WTO Agreements, the trade chapters of Preferential Trade Agreements (PTAs) and PTIAs, and dispute settlement reports under regional trade agreements and the WTO's Dispute Settlement Body.[8] When discussing the trade regime, WTO dispute settlement reports are

---

highly parallel universes". See Kurtz (2016), p. 24; Footer (2013), pp. 105–138; Puig (2015), p. 58; Van den Broek (2013), p. 42.

[4]There is a burgeoning literature in this area focusing on the relationship between these two foundational pillars of international economic law. In terms of recent major works in this area, see for example: Kurtz (2016); Hofmann et al. (2013); Behn et al. (2020b); Mitchell et al. (2016); Echandi and Sauvé (2013), pp. 103–173; Sacerdoti et al. (2014); Wagner (2014) etc.

[5]By the end of 2019, 2654 IIAs were in force (3284 IIAs in total minus 349 terminated IIAs). UNCTAD, IIA Issues Note, July 2020, Issue 1, 1.

[6]As of 1 January 2020, the number of known ISDS cases taken under IIAs was 1023. Proceedings had been concluded for 674 of these disputes by this date. UNCTAD, IIA Issues Note, July 2020, Issue 2, pp. 1, 5.

[7]These sources of investment law are complemented by general rules of international law including the customary international law and customary rules of interpretation of public international law.

[8]The trade law regime also encompasses general rules of international law, customary international law, and the customary rules of interpretation of public international law. Article 3.2 of the WTO's Dispute Settlement Understanding states that it seeks to preserve the rights and obligations of Members "in accordance with customary rules of interpretation of public international law". The term Regional Trade Agreements (RTAs) is employed in GATT Article XXIV, however the term PTA is preferred as such agreements do not necessarily denote a geographical proximity.

It is noted that dispute resolution in international trade law has been dominated by the WTO since its establishment in 1995. 596 cases had been initiated under the WTO's dispute settlement system by July 2020, while only two cases were successfully completed under PTAs between 2007 and 2017 (see Chap. 6).

frequently referred to in this book due to the predominance of WTO case law in recent times.[9]

Engagement between trade and investment occurs wherever the content of an investment agreement has a parallel in the trade regime or vice versa. The term 'content' can cover an agreement's preamble, definitions, substantive provisions, exceptions etc. Engagement also occurs in dispute settlement whenever there are cross-regime references by the parties or the tribunal or parallels in the practices or features of dispute settlement. Engagement does not imply convergence and may fall short of this in a given area between the two regimes.

The extent of engagement depends on how closely the content of one regime mirrors the other.[10] As the content of provisions across the two regimes approximates, the more likely parties and tribunals are to invoke and draw upon the law and jurisprudence of the other regime. Parties can subsequently adapt the content of treaties, give binding interpretations, or other forms of interpretative guidance to encourage or discourage cross-regime references by tribunals.

The appropriateness of crossfertilisation of jurisprudence between the two regimes is for tribunals to consider on a case-by-case basis.[11] Two provisions with largely similar wordings that contain important textual differences may have less potential for crossfertilisation than two provisions that share a key word such as "necessary".

Convergence or "points of convergence"[12] may be achieved in certain limited areas between the trade and investment law regimes.[13] Where the contents of provisions approximate, and the contexts are sufficiently similar, the level of engagement may be tantamount to convergence between the two regimes.

---

[9]Where necessary, distinctions are made between the relevance of conclusions for WTO law and their relevance for the trade regime as a whole. It is noted however that disputes under PTIAs would likely see even higher levels of engagement with the investment regime than those at the WTO as investment chapters are part of these agreements.

[10]While quantifying 'degrees' of engagement is generally difficult, this is attempted in Chap. 2 in relation to 120 IIA provisions relating to Preambles and General Exceptions.

[11]Two investment tribunals acknowledged this where they considered but rejected guidance from trade law in the case before them. See *Methanex v United States* and *Merrill & Ring v Canada*, where the tribunals respectively found that it may "derive guidance" from the GATT or interpret a treaty provision "in the light of the meaning" of the GATT, in appropriate cases. See Methanex Corp. v U.S.A, NAFTA/UNCITRAL, Final Award of the Tribunal on Jurisdiction and Merits (2005) Part II Chapter B, Para 6; *Merrill & Ring Forestry LP v. Canada*, ICSID, Award, para 84.

[12]Alford (2014), pp. 37, 60. Alford describes the regimes as having points of convergence and being on "parallel tracks headed in the same direction" with similar but distinct ends.

Wu refers to "select cross-fertilization, rather than true convergence", see Wu (2014), p. 172.

[13]Commentators have referred to this convergence in various ways in the recent academic literature. Broude sees trade and investment as having "strongly converged over the last decade or two", particularly in relation to dispute settlement and the provision of services. Wagner sees "converging trends" in both the commentary and jurisprudence of the two regimes. See Broude (2011), p. 10; Wagner (2014), p. 86.

The concept of engagement is preferred to convergence in this work. Engagement is a more open and flexible concept than convergence. Convergence is not a relative term and it is difficult to speak of degrees of convergence. Full convergence is not possible (or at least desirable without fundamental changes to the regimes) in some areas and when authors speak of partial convergence, the implication remains that full convergence is the destination. The term 'convergence' can also imply binary outcomes (that norms either converge or they do not).[14] This can lead to a premature dismissal of inter-regime engagement based on the misconception that it necessitates disputes being settled by the same methods, in the same forums, or that shared norms should be interpreted in a way that leads to the same results. For these reasons, the concept of engagement is preferred when considering how the regimes interact and how they should interact in this complex area.

When the term convergence is used in relation to the trade and investment law regimes, a distinction should be made between points of convergence or a holistic concept of convergence. While some may view a general concept of convergence as undesirable, or at least difficult to achieve, Alford's idea of points of convergence is much easier to contemplate.[15]

Arguments against convergence have centred on the idea that the two regimes have evolved on different historical trajectories and serve fundamentally different purposes; that investment law governs the relationship between the state and investors while trade law manages state-to-state conflict.[16] The factors that increase and limit engagement are the same factors that affect convergence, with the only difference being the end point described.[17]

The question of whether engagement (or convergence) between the trade and investment law regimes is a good thing *in a general manner* is not answered here. Rather this book takes the stance that engagement between trade and investment is a good thing *when it is appropriate*. Determining the extent of engagement and when it is appropriate to make cross-regime references is the focus of Chaps. 2–7 of this book, and this is done in relation to the areas of substantive provisions, treaty flexibilities and procedural provisions.

---

[14] Some claim that convergence does not imply a destination or "a final point". Nonetheless the more flexible concept of engagement is preferred in this book as the concept of convergence can lead to dichotomous thinking. For Behn et al, convergence and divergence denote an ongoing process, without the necessity of some form of result. They note that while the verb 'converge' implies finality or an end-point, the noun refers to a process without the need of a 'final point'. See Behn et al. (2020a), p. 8.

[15] Alford (2014), pp. 37, 60. Alford describes the regimes as having points of convergence and being on "parallel tracks headed in the same direction" with similar but distinct ends.

[16] Alvarez's arguments are outlined and critiqued in Sect. 4.2.3.

[17] Section 1.4 of this chapter outlines the factors driving and limiting inter-regime engagement.

1.3 Trade and Investment Agreements

This section looks at Preferential Trade and Investment Agreements (PTIAs), International Investment Agreements (IIAs), and the impact of including investment protections within these two types of agreements. The impact of these types of agreements is considered: (1) in general terms; (2) in terms of the evolution of treaty-based investment protection; and (3) in relation to engagement between the trade and investment law regimes.

1.3.1 The Evolution of Preferential Trade and Investment Agreements

Since the Second World War, states have largely pursued investment protection and trade liberalisation separately. Trade and investment provisions were contained in Free Trade Agreements (FTAs) and Bilateral Investment Treaties (BITs) respectively. However trade and investment provisions are increasingly being negotiated simultaneously as part of single agreements known as Preferential Trade and Investment Agreements (PTIAs). This has been described historically as "less a novelty than a return to the basics".[18]

The United States concluded Treaties of Friendship, Commerce and Navigation (FCN) and their precursors extending back to the 1778 Treaty of Amity and Commerce Between The United States and France. Following the end of World War I, trade was by far the most important element of FCN treaties.[19] However, some of these interwar treaties recognised the juridical status of corporations and granted them free access to the courts of law.[20]

Post World War II, FCN treaties emphasised the right of establishment and the promotion of private foreign investment as opposed to trade and shipping.[21] Treaties containing trade and investment rules that could be considered to be first generation PTIAs emerged in this period. These included the United States-Nicaragua FCN

---

[18] Hofmann et al. (2013), p. 14.

[19] Department of State, Office of Public Affairs, Commercial Treaty Program of the United States (Washington: Government Printing Office, 1952), cited in Vandevelde (2017), p. 58.

[20] See e.g. Article XVIII Treaty of Friendship, Commerce and Navigation between the United States of America and the Republic of Liberia, August 8, 1938.

[21] "The change in emphasis is a reflection of the increased foreign investment activities of U.S. businesses following World War II." See Arikaki (1985), p. 344.

Treaty (1956)[22] and the Gabon-Switzerland Trade and Investment Agreement (1972) inter alia.[23]

The modern era of PTIAs began with the conclusion of the North-American Free Trade Agreement (NAFTA) in 1992. The early twenty-first century has seen a surge in the conclusion of Preferential Trade Agreements at the regional level. Where agreements contain both trade and investment provisions, they are deemed to be PTIAs in this book even where the parties refer to an agreement as a BIT, an FTA, or by another name.

Recent PTIAs tend to deal with a wide range of issues, which may be split into three main areas of market access,[24] Non-Tariff Barriers (NTBs), and rules.[25] Investment chapters are part of this third area on rules. 'Rules' may include chapters in economic areas such as intellectual property rights, trade and sustainable development, competition policy, labour, data protection, energy etc. Rules may also encompass chapters in non-economic areas such as anti-corruption and human rights.

The provisions of the investment chapters contained in PTIAs are often similar to those of a BIT. Provisions on dispute settlement may be contained within this chapter or in a separate chapter. PTIAs may also contain other chapters that touch on investment issues, such as chapters on services. A tribunal examining an investment claim under a PTIA may also have to refer to other chapters, such as the Exceptions chapter. Other standard-setting chapters may contain rules affecting investment. These chapters may concern topics such as the environment, labour, transparency and anti-corruption, SMEs, intellectual property, etc.

Modern PTIAs can take many forms and have a number of different parties as signatories. The vast majority of PTIAs considered in this study are bilateral, though

---

[22] The United States-Nicaragua FCN Treaty (1956) contained 22 Articles that are a mix of trade and investment provisions inter alia. E.g. Articles I XVI.1. Article I: "Each Party shall at all times accord equitable treatment to the persons, property, enterprises and other interests of nationals and companies of the other Party." Article XVI: "Products of either Party shall be accorded, within the territories of the other Party, national treatment and most-favored-nation treatment in all matters affecting internal taxation, sale, distribution, storage and use."

[23] The Gabon-Switzerland Trade and Investment Agreement (1972) contains fifteen articles that are a mix of trade and investment provisions. E.g. Article 11 concerns investment protection while Article 3 Switzerland's import regime. Article 3: "Le Gouvernement de la Confédération suisse continue à accorder le même régime libéral que celui existant ce jour à l'importation en Suisse des produits d'origine et de provenance de la République gabonaise."

[24] Market access concerns both agricultural and industrial goods as well as public procurement.

[25] See for example, Report on Parliament's recommendations to the Commission on the negotiations for the Transatlantic Trade and Investment Partnership (TTIP) 1 June 2015; https://www.europarl.europa.eu/doceo/document/A-8-2015-0175_EN.html. Market access is for agricultural and industrial goods as well as public procurement; Non-Tariff Barriers (NTBs) includes TBT and SPS measures, as well as regulatory cooperation.

trilateral, quadrilateral and multilateral PTIAs are also considered. Of the 60 PTIAs examined in Chap. 2, 54 are bilateral, and six contain more than two parties.[26]

These bilateral or trilateral PTIAs are referred to by a variety of names such as Economic Partnership Agreements.[27]

PTIAs of a certain size and that fulfil certain criteria are known as Mega Regional Trade Agreements (MRTAs).[28] These agreements have been described by the World Economic Forum as "deep integration partnerships between countries or regions with a major share of world trade[29] and foreign direct investment (FDI), and in which two or more of the parties are in a paramount driver position, or serve as hubs, in global value chains."[30] By early 2021, the Regional Comprehensive Economic Partnership (RCEP) is the only MRTA to have been signed and which is likely to come into force.[31] After the US withdrawal from TPP in early 2017, the 11 remaining members re-negotiated the Comprehensive and Progressive Agreement for Trans-Pacific Partnership (CPTPP), which entered into force on 20 December 2018. CPTPP is still a PTIA but is no longer a MRTA without the US. It may become a MRTA in the future should the US (or perhaps even China)[32] join the Agreement.

1.3.2   Joint or Separate Negotiations for Trade and Investment

Where parties wish to enhance investment protection and go beyond the trade terms of the WTO Agreements, many are choosing to negotiate PTIAs rather than separate BITs and PTAs. The sequencing of IIA negotiations has at times reflected the

---

[26]These include: USMCA (2018), CPTPP (2018), Central America-Korea FTA (2018), Protocol Pacific Alliance (2014), Central America Mexico (2011), and the Korea-EFTA FTA (2005). Agreements between the EU and one other party, such as CETA, are considered to be bilateral.

[27]E.g. Japan-Mexico EPA. Some of the trilateral PTIAs from this study include: USMCA, ASEAN-Australia-New Zealand FTA, and the China-Japan-South Korea FTA.

[28]See 'Mega-regional Trade Agreements: Game-Changers or Costly Distractions for the World Trading System?', Report of the World Economic Forum's Global Agenda Council on Trade & Foreign Direct Investment (2014).

[29]In order to be considered a MRTA, the Agreement would have to affect 25% of global trade in goods, services and FDI (footnote not in original quote).

[30]'Mega-regional Trade Agreements: Game-Changers or Costly Distractions for the World Trading System?', Report of the World Economic Forum's Global Agenda Council on Trade & Foreign Direct Investment (2014) 13.

[31]Other proposed MRTAs included the original Trans-Pacific Partnership (TPP), the Trade in Services Agreement (TiSA) and the Transatlantic Trade and Investment Partnership (TTIP). TTIP was a proposed PTIA between the EU and the United States for which 16 negotiating rounds took place between 2013 and 2016.

[32]This was hinted at by Chile President Sebastián Piñera on 22 March 2018: https://www.washingtonpost.com/outlook/chiles-new-president-is-concerned-about-donald-trump/2018/03/22/d20e2da0-2d53-11e8-8688-e053ba58f1e4_story.html?utm_term=.7c738e7f28e7.

negotiating strength of the respective parties or the lack of willingness of one side to engage with one of these topics at a given time.[33] In March 2017, India refused to negotiate an investment deal with Canada without broader trade negotiations to "ensure a balanced outcome".[34]

In some instances, an investment agreement may be a precondition for a larger trade agreement. During the George W. Bush administration, BITs were presented as a stepping-stone towards an eventual FTA with the US.[35] The US explicitly required the conclusion of a BIT as part of a six-step programme, "culminating in a free trade agreement" with the US.[36] The EU and industry have described the conclusion of a BIT with China as a precondition, or as a litmus test, for the prospect of a Sino-EU FTA.[37] Wu notes that we appear to be headed to a world where investment agreements with the US and China will be linked to a trade agreement.[38]

The sequencing of negotiations is a key concern for states that view trade and investment agreements as overlapping, interdependent, and essential parts of their international economic law 'programme'. Various factors may determine whether BITs and PTAs are negotiated separately, in parallel, or jointly.

The joint negotiation of trade and investment may seem increasingly common with increased focus on landmark agreements such as CPTPP, CETA and RCEP. However, separate negotiations for trade and investment remain prevalent and the

---

[33] E.g. Brazil did not conclude any BITs in the first 15 years of this century but concluded 13 BITs from 2015 to 2020 (although these do not include ISDS). For the EU-Japan Economic Partnership Agreement, Japan did not wish to include the EU's Investment Court System in the Agreement. See, European Parliamentary Research Service, 'Bilateral trade deal with Japan-largest to date for EU,' PE633.164, page 6, February 2019, available at: https://www.europarl.europa.eu/RegData/etudes/BRIE/2019/633164/EPRS_BRI(2019)633164_EN.pdf.

[34] "The Indian negotiators clearly told the Canadians that both agreements had to be agreed upon simultaneously as only that would result in a balanced outcome," a government official is quoted as saying by the Hindu Business Line. See 'India refuses Canada's proposal of signing investment deal before free trade pact' (March 14, 2017): www.thehindubusinessline.com/economy/policy/india-refuses-canadas-proposal-of-signing-investment-deal-before-free-trade-pact/article9583882.ece. No IIA has been concluded between the parties by April 2021.

[35] See Middle East Free Trade Initiative, 23 June 2004: https://ustr.gov/archive/Document_Library/Fact_Sheets/2003/Middle_East_Free_Trade_Initiative.html.

[36] Mary Jane Bolle, Congressional Report Service, Report for Congress, 'Middle East Free Trade Area: Progress Report' 8 February 2005, 7. These steps included: (1) WTO membership; (2) continuation of GSP; (3) signing of a TIFA; (4) signing a BIT; (5) FTA; (6) trade-capacity building.

[37] See EEAS, EU-China 2020 Strategic Agenda for Cooperation, "Negotiating and concluding such a comprehensive EU-China Investment Agreement will convey both sides' joint commitment towards stronger cooperation as well as their willingness to envisage broader ambitions including, once the conditions are right, towards a deep and comprehensive FTA, as a longer term perspective."; Deutscher Industrie- und Handelskammertag, 'EU-China Investment Agreement: A Checklist,' May 2020, "Only the successfully implemented CAI can pave the way to a comprehensive free trade agreement." See also Deutscher Industrie- und Handelskammertag (DIHK), 'EU-China Investment Agreement: A Checklist'.

[38] Wu (2014), p. 207.

number of concluded BITs far exceeds concluded PTIAs.[39] Nonetheless the joint negotiation of trade and investment agreements remains common and this study looks at a sample of 60 PTIAs concluded from 2005 to 2019, including major agreements such as the EU-Viet Nam IPA (2019), USMCA (2018), Australia-China FTA (2015), as well as those already mentioned.

Negotiating trade and investment separately, but in parallel, is a recent phenomenon that has emerged in light of Opinion 2/15 of the Court of Justice of the European Union (CJEU). On 16 May 2017, the CJEU found that provisions of the EU-Singapore Free Trade Agreement concerning investment protection and ISDS were shared competences between the European Union and its Member States.[40] In response to Opinion 2/15, the EU-Singapore Agreement was split into two agreements, separating trade and investment with the Investment Protection Agreement needing to be ratified by the Member States in line with their national procedures.

It appeared that the structure of EU trade agreements had been reconsidered and that trade and investment would henceforth be negotiated separately. This was confirmed in the European Council's conclusions of May 2018 which noted the Commission's intention to recommend negotiating directives for FTAs covering "exclusive EU competence on the one hand and separate mixed investment agreements on the other".[41] Mixed Agreements require the approval of the European Parliament, European Council, national parliaments, as well as the approval of the regional parliaments of Belgium.[42] Agreements that fall exclusively under EU competence merely require the approval of the European Parliament and the Council.

The EU Council also confirmed in its conclusions of May 2018 that it is for "the Council to decide, on a case-by-case basis, on the splitting of trade agreements".[43] Investment has been noticeably absent in more recent EU agreements and the Council has noted that this "should not set a precedent for the future".[44] While the

---

[39] Investment Policy Hub has a record of 2852 concluded BITS but only 417 concluded PTIAs or Treaties with Investment Provisions (TIPs). Last accessed 26 April 2021.

[40] See Opinion 2/15, *EU-Singapore Free Trade Agreement* (16 May 2017). Other areas found to be shared competences included: "the provisions of Chapters 1 (Objectives and General Definitions), 14 (Transparency), 15 (Dispute Settlement between the Parties), 16 (Mediation Mechanism) and 17 (Institutional, General and Final Provisions) of that agreement, in so far as those provisions relate to the provisions of Chapter 9 and to the extent that the latter fall within a competence shared between the European Union and the Member States."

[41] See European Council Conclusions adopted on 22 May 2018 'New approach on negotiating and concluding EU trade agreements adopted by Council,' p. 3, available on EU Council website, at: https://www.consilium.europa.eu/en/press/press-releases/2018/05/22/new-approach-on-negotiating-and-concluding-eu-trade-agreements-adopted-by-council/.

[42] See European Parliament Briefing, 'Ratification of international agreements by EU Member States,' November 2016. Available at: http://www.europarl.europa.eu/RegData/etudes/BRIE/2016/593513/EPRS_BRI(2016)593513_EN.pdf.

[43] Ibid FN 13, European Council Conclusions adopted on 22 May 2018, p. 3.

[44] Ibid, European Council Conclusions adopted on 22 May 2018, p. 3. These agreements include the EU-Japan EPA and negotiations launched with Australia and New Zealand.

EU has not launched negotiations for investment agreements in parallel to trade negotiations with countries such as Australia, it has been active at the multilateral level where it has been seeking to establish a permanent Multilateral Investment Court with an appeal mechanism.[45]

1.3.3   The Impact of PTAs and IIAs

Before categorising the effects of adding investment chapters to Preferential Trade Agreements, it is important to first briefly outline the effects of PTAs and IIAs in general.

1.3.3.1   PTAs/PTIAs

Deep PTIAs, such as CPTPP, have an impact on trade and investment that can be potentially discriminatory, multilateralising, economic, and systemic.[46] PTAs, such as the EU-Japan EPA, have similar effects but naturally these are restricted to the trade sphere.

For both types of agreements, hard preferences (such as tariff reductions) lead to discriminatory effects, while soft preferences (such as the harmonisation of standards) lead to multilateralising effects. From a global governance perspective, analysts at the ICTSD encourage provisions with a limited risk of discrimination and "with high potential for multilateralization".[47]

In terms of the economic effects of PTAs, there are three central issues to understanding their welfare benefits, including whether they: (1) create or diver trade; (2) increase transaction costs by creating a complex web of agreements; and (3) affect the future course of international trade liberalisation.[48]

---

[45] EU has submitted two papers to UNCITRAL with the aim of establishing a MIC. 115 countries participated in Working Group III's April 2019 meeting on Investor-State Dispute Settlement Reform in what was the first multilateral discussion on ISDS reform since investor claims under modern Investment Agreements began in the 1990s.

[46] See 'Mega-regional Trade Agreements: Game-Changers or Costly Distractions for the World Trading System?', Report of the World Economic Forum's Global Agenda Council on Trade & Foreign Direct Investment (2014) 22–27.

[47] Ibid. 22–23. The report finds that provisions in the areas of SPS, TBT, Regulatory Coherence, e-commerce and anti-corruption/transparency all have a high potential for multilateralization include. Those with a low potential for multilateralization include Tariffs, Services (GATS+), Government Procurement, Labour, Environment, and STE.

[48] The last two of these are also considered under systemic effects below. Johnston and Trebilcock (2013), pp. 252–259.

Johnston and Trebilcock find that the trade creation effects of PTAs predominate over their trade diversion effects.[49] According to a World Economic Forum Report, nearly all PTAs have led to "reverse trade diversion".[50] This means that as a result of a PTA, trade increases with both parties to the agreement and non-parties. However it increases to a greater extent with those that are party to the agreement.

The final types of effects of PTAs are systemic ones. This is a primary area of interest when considering engagement between the trade and investment law regimes and how PTAs affect this. The systemic effects of PTAs include diminishing the WTO's place as a negotiating forum in international economic law, adding to or tidying up the "spaghetti bowl" of PTAs, as well as regulatory convergence, and the impact this may have on developing countries. Whether PTIAs can lead to greater liberalisation is unclear. Marboe concludes that while not necessarily stumbling blocks, PTIAs have at least also the potential to become a vehicle for multilateralisation.[51]

1.3.3.2 The Impact of IIAs

International Investment Agreements have their main impact in the areas of: (1) attracting foreign investment; (2) loss of government policy space; (3) depoliticisation of political disputes; (4) levelling the playing field; and (5) facilitating domestic reforms.[52]

IIAs represent a "broader promise" to foreign investors that the state will extend and safeguard competitive opportunities to them.[53] Although the general aim of IIAs is to promote and protect foreign investment in host states,[54] there is a lack of consensus that IIAs actually attract foreign investment.[55]

Bonnitcha et al. cover 35 studies in their book and a majority find "a positive and statistically significant impact on inward FDI".[56] They found that "studies examining signalling effects seem more likely to find that IIAs have a positive impact".[57] Qualitative as well as quantitative studies in this area have suggested that there is

---

[49] Johnston and Trebilcock (2013), p. 254.

[50] See 'Mega-regional Trade Agreements: Game-Changers or Costly Distractions for the World Trading System?', Report of the World Economic Forum's Global Agenda Council on Trade & Foreign Direct Investment (2014) 8.

[51] Marboe (2013), pp. 240–241.

[52] See Bonnitcha (2017).

[53] See Kurtz (2016), p. 85.

[54] The emphasis on promotion and protection differs among treaties, particularly in relation to whether or not pre or post-establishment rights are granted to investors.

[55] See Hallward-Driemeier (2003), p. 22, which finds "little evidence" that BITs have stimulated additional investment. See also Sauvant and Sachs (2009).

[56] Bonnitcha et al. (2017), p. 159.

[57] Bonnitcha et al. (2017), p. 159.

such an effect.[58] Berger and Busse's 2013 study suggested that agreements that integrate trade and investment disciplines entail significant levels of increases in foreign investment.[59] The study found "strong evidence" that the granting of pre-establishment rights in BITs and PTIAs[60] promotes bilateral FDI. The study also found that where FTAs are limited to trade liberalisation, there is an increase in exports rather than FDI.[61]

A second impact of IIAs concerns policy space and whether overly broad protections lead to regulatory chill.[62] This is the idea that governments are unwilling to take measures in the public interest, for example in areas such as public health or the environment, for fear of cases being taken under IIAs. This has been described as governments being 'prudent' in their action based on risk assessment, rather than chill by Dr. Penelope Ridings before the Waitangi Tribunal.[63] In order to avoid such regulatory chill, states should define precisely what is meant by investment standards such as fair and equitable treatment and indirect expropriation.[64] Host states can take some comfort from the *Philip Morris v. Uruguay* Award concerning plain packaging requirements for tobacco. The tribunal showed deference towards the exercise of a state's police powers and what the state defines as public health issues even under the Switzerland-Uruguay BIT (1991), which did not explicitly refer to public health.[65]

Concerning the depoliticisation of disputes, in theory IIAs avoid the involvement of investors' home states and the turning of disputes into diplomatic incidents. However it is arguable that ISDS does not replace diplomatic protection, but rather

---

[58] E.g. BIICL et al., 'Risk and Return – Foreign Direct Investment and the Rule of Law,' (2015), p. 47, available at www.biicl.org/documents/625_d4_fdi_main_report.pdf (last accessed 9 February 2021). In this study 83% of investors stated that the absence of any investment protection treaty in force between their home state and a state in which they were considering investing affected their decision to invest while 14% stated it had no impact.

See also Shinkman (2007). This *Economist* survey of 602 corporate executives, in which 19% indicated that an investment treaty influenced their investment decisions 'to a very great extent' cited in Bonnitcha et al. (2017), p. 165.

[59] Berger and Busse (2013).

[60] What is referred to as a 'PTIA' in this book, is referred to as a 'RTA with strong investment provisions' in Berger and Busse (2013).

[61] Berger and Busse (2013), p. 12.

[62] See Cotula (2014), pp. 19–31.

[63] WAI-2522 Trans-Pacific Partnership Agreement Inquiry Hearing (held at Wellington, 14–18 March 2016), 420–21.

[64] E.g. CETA Article 8.10 clarifies that breaches of fair and equitable treatment are limited to: "(a) denial of justice in criminal, civil or administrative proceedings; (b) fundamental breach of due process, including a fundamental breach of transparency, in judicial and administrative proceedings; (c) manifest arbitrariness; (d) targeted discrimination on manifestly wrongful grounds, such as gender, race or religious belief; (e) abusive treatment of investors, such as coercion, duress and harassment; or (f) a breach of any further elements of the fair and equitable treatment obligation adopted by the Parties in accordance with paragraph 3 of this Article."

[65] *Philip Morris Brands Sàrl, Philip Morris Products S.A. and Abal Hermanos S.A. v. Oriental Republic of Uruguay*, Award ICSID Case No. ARB/10/7 (2016), para 287. Nonetheless, there was a Concurring and Dissenting Opinion from Co-Arbitrator Gary Born.

complements it.[66] Langford and Behn suggest that investment tribunals may be sensitive to political signals, particularly from powerful states, and that there has been a "significant drop in claimant-investor success" across time.[67] They found suggestive evidence that arbitrators have moderately shifted their behaviour on some types of outcomes, but their empirical evidence indicates that the effect is much greater in the trade regime.[68]

Fourthly, it is questionable whether IIAs 'level the playing field' between foreign and domestic investors. Despite being cited as a core justification in the recent negotiations such as TTIP, where a country has no history of discriminating against foreign investors, this should be treated cautiously.[69]

Lastly, concerning domestic reforms and respect for the rule of law, IIAs should in theory help 'lock in' private property ownership through their expropriation requirements, as well as encouraging sound administrative and judicial processes through FET provisions.[70] However, some empirical studies have shown that this has not been the case or have cast doubt upon this contention.[71]

1.3.4 The Impact of Concluding Investment Chapters Within PTIAs

This book investigates whether investment chapters in PTIAs merely function as BITs transplanted into PTAs, or whether they serve another function, as evidenced by the differences between the texts of these two types of agreements. It has been found that investment chapters in PTIAs "function more like stand-alone BITS" and not as "integral parts of the agreement".[72]

Chapter 2 of this book considers the differences between investment provisions found in the investment chapters of PTIAs and those in stand-alone BITs from an empirical perspective. It finds greater evidence of inter-regime engagement in the 60 PTIAs than in the 60 BITs in relation to 24 provisions identified as evidencing engagement. These differences between the two types of agreements are further considered in Chaps. 3–7 which explore levels of engagement between the regimes,

---

[66] Polanco (2018), p. 230.

[67] Langord et al. (2020), p. 284.

[68] Langord et al. (2020), p. 284.

[69] Bonnitcha (2017), pp. 5–6.

[70] Bonnitcha (2017), pp. 6–7.

[71] See, Ginsburg (2005), pp. 107–123. Jonathan Bonnitcha, 'The Impact of Investment Treaties on Domestic Governance in Myanmar,' (November 8, 2019). Available at SSRN: https://ssrn.com/abstract=3644056.

[72] Gáspar-Szilágyi and Usynin (2020), pp. 41–42. Szilard and Usynin's findings relate to dispute settlement provisions alone.

when cross-regime references are appropriate, and the impact PTIAs have upon engagement for certain key drivers of convergence.[73]

What other factors might explain the differing levels of engagement found in the texts of IIAs? Factors such as sociological factors, the institutional set up of negotiations, and bargaining within the wider context of PTIA negotiations seem to play a role. Engagement may be facilitated by the interaction of negotiators from separate trade and investment backgrounds, who are brought together in the negotiation of a PTIA.

Engagement would also be expected to increase in institutional setups where the same department negotiates the trade and investment chapters of an agreement (compared to setups where separate government departments are in charge of negotiating BITs and PTAs). Having separate departments negotiating trade and investment chapters may not impede engagement where there are frequent interactions between decision-makers in the two departments who are aware of the concerns of both departments. This would seem less likely to arise in the context of a BIT, where the broader context of a deal including multiple trade chapters is absent. For IIAs where the background of the main actors more resembles a traditional WTO background (those with a substantial governmental background), it would also be expected that there would be more inter-regime engagement in these agreements.[74]

PTIAs are wider agreements that cover trade and investment as well as a whole host of 'WTO-extra' issues. The interplay between the various interests at stake is part of a negotiating dynamic where interests may become a bargaining chip as part of a larger deal.[75] This dynamic could impact upon outcomes for the trade and investment regimes and affect inter-regime engagement. Where parties previously disagreed on an element of investor protection, or a way of dispute settlement, the bargaining chip dynamic wasn't in play to the same extent that it is in PTIAs. One way to analyse how bargaining influences the outcome of PTIAs is to examine the differences in the end products of concluded BITs, PTAs and PTIAs.[76]

---

[73]Chapters 3–7 consider the three main categories of provisions (substantive provisions, treaty flexibilities, and procedural provisions). For example, Sect. 1.5 looks at convergence between the dispute settlement mechanisms of the two regimes, in relation to two of the eight provisions found to evidence inter-regime engagement in this area in Sect. 1.2. Section 1.2's empirical study mainly points to the increased engagement for norms in the areas of dispute settlement and treaty flexibilities.

[74]This 'sociological' factor is covered in greater detail in Sect. 1.4.2.3.

[75]See for example: 'Farming risks being used as bargaining chip in EU trade deals,' Farmers Weekly, 18 April 2016; 'Farming must not become TTIP 'bargaining chip', say MEPs' Farmers Weekly, 15 April 2015. Available at: www.fwi.co.uk/business/farming-must-not-become-ttip-bargaining-chip-says-meps.htm, www.fwi.co.uk/business/farming-risks-being-used-as-bargaining-chip-in-eu-trade-deals.htm (last accessed 19 September 2020).

[76]If a country has a consistent practice in its BITs and PTIAs but deviates from this practice in one of its agreements (perhaps with a larger partner), this may be evidence of a concession made by the party. If a country persists with this deviation in its subsequent agreements, it may indicate that it was convinced that this approach is superior, or may just show an attempt at consistency or path dependency.

Wu sees treaty formation as perhaps the trade regime's "greatest influence" on the investment regime.[77] There have been instances where parties would not negotiate a BIT without the inclusion of a wider agreement, and instances where states wouldn't negotiate a PTA without a BIT.[78] The inclusion of investment chapters within PTIAs has been a factor in the proliferation of investment standards where the prospect of broader market access entices countries into making investment commitments.[79] As investment chapters may only represent a single chapter as part of a much larger agreement, this negotiating context may impact the development of investment law.[80] Puig describes the adding of investment chapters to PTAs as a "central mechanism" for convergence as they make the relationship between trade and investment more explicit.[81] Alvarez also acknowledges that PTIAs or 'mixed agreements' may provide more opportunities for "cross-pollination" for adjudicators facing trade or investment questions.[82]

1.4   Factors Driving and Limiting Engagement

This section explores factors driving and limiting inter-regime engagement.[83]

In other instances, the impact of the bargaining chip dynamic may be clearer. It was reported that Canada and Mexico had yielded to US demands on ISDS "as part of a larger bargain" in the renegotiation of NAFTA. See Inside US Trade, 'Canada to propose eliminating ISDS at NAFTA meeting this week; USTR to agree,' available at: https://insidetrade.com/daily-news/sources-canada-propose-eliminating-isds-nafta-meeting-week-ustr-agree (last accessed 19 September 2020). Unfortunately, it is beyond the scope of this book to delve further into this phenomenon.

[77] Wu (2014), p. 206. Wu outlines two instances where investment concessions were made in exchange for trade-related benefits. In one instance, Chile began to accept limitations on the use of performance requirements for better market access. In another instance El Salvador agreed to concessions in relation to remedies and procedural matters in exchange for better market access. Despite these instances, Wu views this practice as being "fairly limited".

[78] This was discussed in Sect. 1.3.2 above in relation to India's refusal to negotiate an investment deal with Canada without broader trade negotiations (2017) and the US and EU policy of presenting BITs as a litmus test or stepping-stone towards an eventual FTA.

[79] See Wu (2014), p. 177.

[80] E.g. USMCA contains 34 chapters.

[81] Puig (2015), pp. 3, 13. The shift of focus from the WTO towards PTIAs as an alternative to global negotiations has been called "minilateralism", which Puig describes as having "propelled further convergence" between the trade and investment law regimes. One of the reasons for the shift of focus away from the WTO as a negotiating forum has been the failure by WTO Members to conclude the Doha Development Round since its launch in 2001.

[82] Alvarez and Brink (2012), pp. 319–362, 361. The authors see this as being the case because PTIAs "present more complex questions of object and purpose".

[83] Kurtz identifies five convergence factors. These include shared legal norms, cross-fertilisation in jurisprudence, interdependence between the regimes, shared jurisdiction, and sociological factors. All five of these factors are considered in either Sects. 1.4 or 1.5 of this chapter. Kurtz (2016), pp. 10–19. Not all commentators agree with these convergence factors. José Alvarez has described

1.4.1   Treaty Provisions Driving Engagement

Chapter 2 operationalises the concept of engagement by coding for 24 elements that evidence engagement between trade and investment across a sample of 120 PTIAs and BITs concluded during the period 2005–19.[84] Of these elements, the following categories of provisions are found: (a) Provisions that represent shared norms between the regimes; (b) Provisions that minimise conflict between the regimes; (c) Provisions that harmonise procedural rules between the regimes; (d) Provisions that refer to the applicability of rules of international (economic) law and the suitability of arbitrators with knowledge of international (trade) law.

1.4.1.1   Provisions That Represent Shared or Similar Norms Between the Regimes

The trade and investment law regimes contain a variety of shared norms that are part of the twin strands making up their "unifying core".[85] Many of these shared legal norms can be seen among these 24 treaty provisions that are found to evidence inter-regime engagement in Chap. 2.[86] Classically, the shared legal terrain between trade and investment encompasses areas such as National Treatment and MFN Treatment. The shared terrain of the two regimes also extends to areas such as General Exceptions. Tribunals interpret these shared norms in dispute settlement systems that often contain some degree of harmonisation of procedural rules. This core of shared norms provides abundant evidence of engagement between the two regimes.

Within these norms, there are shared standards such as 'likeness' and less favourable treatment. Despite their similarities, such standards may be interpreted differently at the WTO and under IIAs due to factors including the different treaty contexts of the provisions. There may also be different categories of a shared norm. Concerning general exceptions, Kurtz categorises three types of exceptions clauses, including those with explicit, implicit, and thin commonalities between the regimes.[87] An example of explicit engagement is the direct incorporation of

---

them as "not reflecting the reality of 25 years of case law" where references to trade law have, in his view, been minimal in investment law jurisprudence. See José Alvarez's presentation on the 'Boundaries of Investment Arbitration,' NYU School of Law, 11 December 2019 (34m20). Available at: https://www.youtube.com/watch?v=iEaQ09dUBI8&ab_channel=WilmerCutlerPickeringHaleandDorrLLP-InternationalArbitrationLibrary.   Alvarez's views are explored in detail in Sect. 4.2.3.

[84] For a discussion of these 24 elements, see Sect. 2.2.2.

[85] Kurtz (2016), p. 24.

[86] Kurtz refers to shared legal norms and "micro norms" as a convergence factor between the trade and investment law regimes. Kurtz (2016), pp. 10–11.

[87] Kurtz characterises these exceptions clauses as being evidence of: (1) deep integration by incorporation by reference; (2) those modelled from the law of the WTO; and (3) those that evidence thin commonality. Kurtz (2016), pp. 193–212.

GATT Article XX or GATS Article XIV. Implicit engagement may be seen in investment agreements that include clauses modelled on WTO law, and both of these evidence high levels of engagement between the regimes.[88] Thin commonalities may arise where agreements contain exceptions sharing more limited common elements with the other regime.

1.4.1.2 Provisions That Minimise Conflict Between the Regimes

Treaty drafters may minimise conflict between the trade and investment regimes in a number of ways. Two examples coded for in Chap. 2 include expropriation articles that provide an exemption for measures that are TRIPS compatible and references to performance requirements that provide exemptions for measures compatible with TRIMS. As negotiators consciously minimise conflict between the regimes, the potential for inter-regime engagement becomes greater, or at least does not decrease.

1.4.1.3 Provisions That Harmonise Procedural Rules Between the Regimes

Engagement between the trade and investment law regimes can be seen in increasingly similar procedural rules. As seen in Chap. 2, many recent IIAs provide for rules that were previously more commonly seen in trade law and public international law. These rules include provisions for transparency in proceedings, the allowance of *amicus curiae* submissions from third parties, more robust conflict of interest provisions for adjudicators, and potentially more robust appeal procedures. As procedural rules between the regimes approximate, the barriers to tribunals and the parties to disputes making cross-regime references decrease.

1.4.1.4 Provisions That Refer to the Applicability of Rules of International Law and the Suitability of Arbitrators with Knowledge of International (Trade) Law

These provisions are usually included in the dispute settlement section of investment chapters.[89] The meaning of *applicable* rules of international law is unclear. Does it mean any rule of international law invoked during proceedings that is of significance

---

[88] This study categorises two additional types of engagement for general exceptions including provisions that protect against arbitrary and discriminatory measures, and exceptions within articles on performance requirements. See Sect. 2.3.3 for a more detailed account of these five types of General Exceptions provisions.

[89] E.g. Japan-Kazakhstan BIT (2014), Article 17.15: "An arbitral tribunal established under paragraph 4 of this Article shall decide the issues in dispute in accordance with this Agreement and applicable rules of international law."

to a claim or is it limited to those with a "direct bearing on investment"?[90] Principles of international law, possibly including those relevant to international trade law, may inform decisions relating to disputes under the agreement where the tribunal deems them applicable.

Similarly, the inclusion of a reference to the suitability of arbitrators with knowledge of international trade law is an acknowledgement by the parties of the overlap and potential for engagement between the two regimes. The implication of including arbitrators with knowledge of trade law is that this knowledge may be useful when deciding disputes and considering norms that overlap between the two regimes under the agreement.[91]

1.4.2 Other Factors Driving Engagement

As well as shared legal norms, there are additional factors driving engagement between trade and investment law. These factors include the fact that the regimes are interdependent and often have shared negotiations, jurisdiction and communities.

1.4.2.1 Overlapping Jurisdiction

State measures can give rise to claims that fall within the jurisdiction of both the trade and investment law regimes and there have been several instances of parallel proceedings being brought at the WTO and under IIAs.[92] Examples in recent times have included the Softwood Lumber,[93] High Fructose Corn Syrup disputes[94] and proceedings arising out of Australia's Tobacco Plain Packaging Act.[95] Breaches of

---

[90] Schreuer (2014), pp. 16–17.

[91] An example of such a provision is found in Article 24.2 of the Canada-China BIT (2012): "Article 24 Arbitrators (...) 2. Arbitrators shall: (a) have expertise or experience in public international law, international trade or international investment rules, or the resolution of disputes arising under international trade or international investment agreements;"

[92] For a comprehensive account of parallel proceedings at the WTO and under IIAs, see Alford (2014), pp. 44–50. For analysis of relevant recent case law, see Kurtz (2016), pp. 13–15. Kurtz outlines instances of shared jurisdiction in trade remedies, plain packaging of tobacco, and its potential in the renewable energy sector.

[93] *United States-Final Dumping Determination on Softwood Lumber from Canada,* WT/DS 264; *Canfor Corporation v. United States of America,* Decision on Preliminary Question, 6 June 2006.

[94] *Mexico-Anti-Dumping Investigation of High-Fructose Corn Syrup (HFCS) from the United States* WT/DS 132; *Mexico-Taxes on Soft Drinks and Other Beverages* WT/DS 308; *Cargill, Inc. v. Mexico,* ICSID Case No. ARB(AF)/05/2, Award, 18 Sep. 2000.

[95] *Australia-Certain Measures Concerning Trademarks, Geographical Indications and Other Plain Packaging Requirements Applicable to Tobacco Products and Packaging,* WT/DS 467; *Philip Morris Asia Limited v. The Commonwealth of Australia,* UNCITRAL, PCA Case No. 2012-12.

international trade standards have formed the basis for investment claims and this has further blurred the lines between the regimes.[96]

In other instances, investment tribunals have considered import and export bans in NAFTA cases such as *SD Myers v. Canada* and *Apotex v. United States*. These cases may traditionally have been viewed as trade disputes to be taken under Article XI GATT or its equivalents in regional agreements.[97] Puig notes that under recent agreements, States are enforcing provisions aimed at protecting FDI and private parties are enforcing trade breaches in investment arbitration.[98]

Investment protection clauses in IIAs may provide a remedy for states and parties that can be an alternative to proceedings at the WTO, or that can operate concurrently to proceedings at the WTO. If it is deemed more effective or expedient, states may shift away from taking actions at the WTO and encourage industry affected by measures to litigate under IIAs.[99]

This overlap in jurisdiction between the trade and investment law regimes has the potential to increase engagement as tribunals may be required to look across the aisle when parallel proceedings are taking place. Looking to proceedings in the other regime may be useful in terms of seeing the pleadings of the parties as well as the findings of the relevant tribunal. In *Canfor v. US*, the NAFTA tribunal had regard to WTO proceedings where the US categorised a measure as a "payment programme" rather than as a trade remedy. In view of this categorisation, the tribunal found that it had jurisdiction to consider whether the measure breached investor rights under NAFTA Chapter 11.[100] In light of recent case law, Kurtz concludes that it is "often practically impossible to simply ignore the factual and legal issues" in the other regime.[101] Treaty drafters should consider the desirability of parallel proceedings and the circumstances where it is or is not desirable to have concurrent claims at the WTO and under IIAs.

---

[96]Mercurio (2015), p. 242. In this regard, Mercurio also refer to *Eli Lilly and Company v. Canada*, UNCITRAL, ICSID Case No. UNCT/14/2.

[97]One such trade case has been taken under Article 306 of the EU-Ukraine Association Agreement. This case is based on a breach of Article 35 of the Agreement concerning Import and Export Restrictions.

[98]Puig (2015), p. 38. Puig cites the cases of *Pope & Talbot, SD Myers* and *ADF Group v. United States*.

[99]If the potential relief under the investment chapter of the PTIA is deemed to be greater, international economic law could see a shift towards disputes such as these being litigated under PTIAs rather than at the WTO.

[100]See Kurtz (2016), p. 13, referring to *Canfor Corp and Terminal Forest Products Ltd. v. United States of America*, Decision on Preliminary Question (UNCITRAL, 6 June 2006).

[101]Kurtz (2016), pp. 14–15. Kurtz takes the first example of *Canfor v. US*, where investor rights under NAFTA Chapter 11 clashed with state rights under the anti-dumping provisions in Chapter 19. The tribunal found that the claim related entirely to trade remedies except for one part of the US scheme, which it had identified as a "payment programme" in WTO proceedings. A second example of looking across the aisle is given in the Mexico High Fructose Corn Syrup case where the Mexican authorities breached their NAFTA obligations in reaction to a legal ruling in the WTO.

1.4.2.2 Interdependence Between the Regimes

Trade and foreign investments can be strict substitutes, particularly where an investor is looking for a way to circumvent a high-tariff wall.[102] The EU has referred to the need to strengthen policy coherence between trade and investment since they are "increasingly complementary, independent and intertwined in today's global economy."[103] FDI has however become a complement to cross-border trade because of reduced tariff levels globally and the increasing importance of Global Supply Chains (GSCs) for consumers and Global Value Chains (GVCs) for businesses. Multinational Companies (MNCs) locate different parts of the production process in different countries with a view to reducing overall cost. This necessitates foreign investment and results in increased trade in intermediate goods and services, which now account for over 70% of global trade.[104] Between 1999 and 2014 income associated with GVCs doubled.[105]

GSCs & GVCs depend on unrestricted trade and investment. If state measures restrict the import and export of goods and services, this impacts on the viability of an investment in that state as part of a GSC/GVC. If state measures restrict how investments can operate by obliging them to source inputs locally for example, this impacts on the import of goods and services that can no longer be used as inputs and ultimately impacts on exports if the operation of the investment is affected.

PTIAs involve the coupling of trade and investment issues as part of a single agreement. Agreements that cover interdependent areas such as trade and investment can facilitate greater policy coherence for states and greater certainty for economic operators.

PTIAs also allow states to define in a single agreement the boundaries as to what constitutes a claim under the trade regime and under the investment regime. The possibility for foreign states and parties to strategically consider whether it is best to seek remedies under trade or investment law illustrates the interdependency of the two regimes, but this can be limited with careful treaty drafting.

---

[102] Kurtz (2016), pp. 15–17.

[103] WTO Trade Policy Review of The European Union, 6 November 2017, WT/TPR/M/357/Add.1, p. 24, where the EU further stated: "The EU is supportive of initiatives aimed at making international trade and investment rules more integrated and global. In this respect, the EU endorses the work done by the G20 Trade and Investment Working Group, in particular the enhanced G20 policy coordination on investment issues which has led to the adoption of the Guiding Principles on Investment Policymaking. In the longer term, we support the incorporation of investment rules into the WTO, as an opportunity to simplify and update the current web of bilateral agreements to set up a clearer, more legitimate and more inclusive system."

[104] 'Global Value Chains: Challenges, Opportunities, and Implications For Policy,' OECD, WTO and World Bank Group (2014) 7; OECD, Trade Policy Brief, Trade Policy Implications of Global Value Chains, February 2020.

[105] 'Global Value Chains: Challenges, Opportunities, and Implications for Policy,' OECD, WTO and World Bank Group (2014) 7.

1.4.2.3 Sociological Factors

Engagement has been facilitated by the interaction of actors of the two 'different epistemic communities' including negotiators, adjudicators and scholars acting as expert witnesses between the two regimes.[106] Sociological factors drive engagement where the "movement of actors" in the trade and investment law regimes results in increased engagement, or minimised inter-regime conflict.[107]

Previously, it was the texts of agreements and tribunal reports that attracted the greater scrutiny in the literature on convergence. However, there is now a focus on the negotiation process of trade and investment agreements. This increased scrutiny has been a result of the focus on the TTIP negotiations and in particular negotiations of the United Kingdom's withdrawal from the European Union.[108]

The utility of having adjudicators who are familiar with WTO law and jurisprudence has long been recognised in investment agreements. Those who adjudicate trade and investment agreements can facilitate or potentially exclude engagement between the two regimes. The dispute settlement mechanisms of IIAs have also turned to the WTO or former WTO adjudicators where the parties cannot reach agreement on adjudicators.[109]

PTIA negotiators are important potential facilitators of engagement between the two regimes. In terms of facilitating engagement, the importance of the PTIA negotiating framework depends on the degree of integration and interaction between departments.

Negotiators draft trade and investment provisions at the same time, with the relevant negotiators consulting and influencing each other during the process to some extent, or at the very least to the extent that the chief negotiator is aware of the contents of the trade and investment provisions. Where separate government departments are in charge of negotiating BITs and FTAs, inter-regime conflict can still be minimised where there are frequent interactions between decision-makers in the two

---

[106]Hofmann et al. (2013), p. 15.

[107]Kurtz (2016), p. 19.

[108]See for example, Grossman (2016); Dhingra et al. (2017), pp. S22–S30; Sampson (2016).

[109]E.g. Article 3.29.6 of the EU-Singapore IPA sets out: "Should the list provided for in paragraph 1 of Article 3.44 (Lists of Arbitrators) not be established at the time required pursuant to paragraph 3, the chairperson shall be selected by lot from among former Members of the WTO Appellate Body, who shall not be a person of either Party."

In the Singapore-Sri Lanka FTA (2018), drafters provide for a role for the Director-General of the WTO where Parties fail to agree a Chairperson. Annex 16-B, 20 provides that: "If the Parties fail to agree on the need to replace the chairperson, any Party may request that such matter be referred to a neutral third party. If the Parties are unable to agree on a neutral third party, such matter shall be referred to the Director-General of the WTO whose decision on the need to replace the chairperson shall be final. If the neutral third party or the Director-General of the WTO as the case may be decides that the original chairperson did not comply with the requirements of the Code of Conduct, the Parties shall agree on the replacement. If the Parties fail to agree on a new chairperson, the Director-General of the WTO shall, at the request of any Party, select the new chairperson within twenty (20) days of the request."

departments and these decision-makers are aware of the concerns of both departments.

This potential to facilitate engagement is a factor of proximity and the timing of negotiations (whether they take place concurrently). The more closely key decision-makers work together, the greater the potential to facilitate engagement. There is less opportunity for facilitating engagement in institutional setups where PTAs and BITs are negotiated by separate departments with fewer interactions. Where a trade agreement and an investment agreement are not negotiated concurrently, even less engagement would be expected in such a setting.

One example of negotiators minimising inter-regime conflict is the carving out of compulsory licencing from expropriation guarantees. Such carve-outs acknowledge that actions in one regime could trigger problems in another. Recent negotiators of PTIAs have tried to avoid hard conflicts such as these, thereby minimising system friction.[110]

By way of example, the US Department of State, when negotiating BITs, should seek input from the USTR in order to minimise conflict with the trade regime, and vice versa if the USTR is negotiating a FTA. Where the US negotiates a PTIA such as TTIP, these interactions tend to happen to some degree as the chief negotiator is aware of the potentially conflicting elements in the trade and investment chapters.

In this author's view, the persons in the three positions of chief investment negotiator, chief negotiator, and signing official have the greatest potential to impact upon engagement between trade and investment. One might imagine that the chief investment negotiator would have the greatest potential to impact upon engagement, and that the signing official might not be involved in such technical matters. However, the signing official sets the overall course for negotiations. To take the example of the EU, the drive to include ICS in negotiations in recent years did not primarily come from the chief investment negotiator but rather from the level of the signing official.

In the case of investment chapters and agreements, where the background of the main actors more resembles a traditional WTO background (those with a substantial governmental background), the more inter-regime engagement there is likely to be in agreements. In the case of the EU, negotiators responsible for investment texts tend to come from the trade department (DG TRADE) and would thus be expected to be sensitive to potential conflicts with the trade regime.[111] Where investment negotiators are working within a Department of Trade, and are drawn from workers within such a Department, it can be expected that the negotiated investment outcomes in a

---

[110] E.g. Australia-Chile FTA, Article 10.11: Expropriation and Compensation: (. . .) 5. This Article does not apply to the issuance of compulsory licences granted in relation to intellectual property rights in accordance with the TRIPS Agreement, or to the revocation, limitation, or creation of intellectual property rights, to the extent that such revocation, limitation, or creation is consistent with Chapter 17 (Intellectual Property).

[111] See for example, European Commission, Civil Society Dialogue, 'Update on the Transatlantic Trade and Investment Partnership (TTIP) – First Negotiation Round,' Available at: http://trade.ec.europa.eu/doclib/docs/2013/july/tradoc_151656.pdf (last accessed 11 February 2021).

PTIA would take trade concerns on board to a greater extent than would be the case for a BIT and PTA negotiated by separate departments particularly if the negotiations were conducted non-concurrently.[112]

1.4.3 Factors Limiting Engagement

International trade agreements and investment treaties share many similar norms and standards, but also have pronounced differences. These include the historical separation of the regimes, as well as differences in purpose, standing, remedies, the possibility of appeal, and the centralisation of dispute settlement.

The historical separation of trade and investment post World War II dates to the failure of the Havana Charter and has led to many of the differences between the regimes that are evident today. The different paths and functions of the regimes have had a "long-lasting impact on the formal characteristics" of the frameworks regulating trade and investment.[113] The failure of the International Trade Organization (ITO) to come into existence set back any prospect of a 'merged' field of trade and investment, notwithstanding the fact that the language used in respect of investment in the Havana Charter was merely "hortatory".[114] For decades to come, the GATT (1947) regulated international trade. The GATT's focus on trade in goods was expanded with the establishment of the WTO in 1995. The WTO Agreements regulate international trade in a much broader manner, with investment featuring prominently in its Agreements on services (GATS) and investment (TRIMS). Mode 3 of the GATS covers services supplied through commercial presence and it is seen as the first multilateral investment liberalisation treaty.[115]

Given the failure to conclude a multilateral agreement on foreign investment, a vast network of investment treaties regulating foreign investment developed in the aftermath of the Second World War.[116] The first BIT was concluded in 1959 and ten European countries had concluded BITs by 1966.[117] Sovereignty concerns shaped the structure of investment agreements before the Multilateral Agreement on Investment (MAI)[118] and attempts to bring such negotiations to the WTO were blocked by

---

[112] The effect of bringing together trade and investment negotiators when negotiating PTIAs could be the subject of a separate study, but is beyond the scope of this chapter.

[113] Puig (2015), p. 11.

[114] For an account of the separation of trade and investment, see Broude (2011) see in particular, Section 2: 'Degrees of Separation: A Narrative of the Trade/Investment Divide'.

[115] Newcombe and Paradell (2009), p. 55.

[116] It has proven difficult to multilateralise investment commitments in the past for various reasons. See Kurtz (2014).

[117] See Kurtz (2016), p. 43.

[118] Kurtz (2014), p. 726.

developing countries.[119] Developed countries attempted to conclude a MAI among themselves at the OECD but substantial progress could not be made.[120] This lack of progress at the multilateral level has largely been mirrored at the WTO, which has succeeded in concluding just one multilateral agreement since its inception in 1995.[121]

A major difference between the regimes is the integrated nature of dispute settlement at the WTO compared to the dispersed nature of dispute settlement under IIAs.

WTO Members have tended to litigate at the WTO rather than under the Dispute Settlement Mechanisms (DSMs) of PTAs for various reasons. These include the high levels of trust in the WTO dispute settlement system, the relative predictability of the system, the enforceability of WTO awards, and the reputational damage the offending Member may suffer if it is seen to be violating its WTO commitments. While the WTO was to the fore as a settler of disputes and enforcer of the WTO texts, regional trade agreements have been the primary forum for negotiating and shaping the evolution of trade rules since the turn of the century.[122]

The possibility of appeal is another area of difference between the dispute settlement systems of the two regimes. Investment awards have not traditionally been subject to appeal except on very limited grounds. The WTO had a standing Appellate Body from 1995 to 2019 but this has been defunct since 11 December 2019. Mexico and 93 other Delegations launched a joint proposal on 5 December 2019 to start the AB selection processes but this was blocked by the US as the systemic concerns that had led to it blocking appointments "remained unaddressed".[123]

This previously fundamental difference between the regimes may now be reversing as work on the formation of a Multilateral Investment Court (MIC) is underway at UNCITRAL.[124] It must also be noted that a multi-party interim appeal arrangement (MPIA) has been notified to the WTO. This arrangement provides for a formal two-step dispute settlement system for the 24 WTO Members that have signed up to

---

[119] See Cho (2004), p. 219.

[120] Kurtz (2014), p. 765. During the negotiations of the MAI, the Chair asked countries to table their exceptions at the outside to aim for the highest level of liberalisation, but this led to many being tabled by the liberal, developed states.

[121] The Trade Facilitation Agreement entered into force on 22 February 2017. The Doha Development Round was launched by WTO Members in 2001 but failed to make any progress on investment and indeed any other areas until "the page was turned" in 2015. See Opening statement by Hon. Joshua Setipa, Chairman of the ACP Ministers of Trade Meeting and Minister of Trade & Industry of Lesotho, 20 October 2015, Brussels.

[122] As an example of this, see Wu (2016), pp. 53–58. This paper gives an overview of three areas where new trade rules were agreed upon in the proposed text of TPP.

[123] Minutes of Meeting, WTO Dispute Settlement Body, WT/DSB/M/438, 18 December 2019, paras 5–5.7; Dispute Settlement Body, Communication on Appellate Body appointments, 8 December 2019, WT/DSB/W/609/Rev.19.

[124] See UNCITRAL, Report of Working Group III (Investor-State Dispute Settlement Reform) on the work of its resumed 39th session, 10 December 2020.

it by early 2021.[125] Related to the fact that the WTO has had a standing Appellate Body is its permanent secretariat. The investment law regime has had no equivalent to date and investment agreements usually provide for ad hoc arbitration, whereby tribunals carry out their functions without the help of a secretariat.

Regional agreements have taken an importance that goes beyond negotiation and their adjudicatory functions are likely to be of increasing importance in light of the recent cessation of the functioning of the WTO's Appellate Body. Even before this issue arose, there were question marks over the ability of the WTO to deal with its heavy workload.

Fundamentally, the regimes share certain commonalities of purpose, such as the protection of foreign products, services and investments from discrimination; the trade regime has done this by combatting protectionism and ensuring compliance with negotiated concessions. The investment regime has focused on protecting investments through the granting of enforceable rights to investors in treaties. While these complementary purposes could in theory drive engagement, it is the differences in the "normative orientations" and underpinnings of the regimes are seen as obstacles to increased engagement between the regimes.[126] Wu describes the WTO regime as being designed to promote a rules-based system and to manage state-to-state conflict, while the investment law regime "at its heart, is about promoting and vindicating the rights of non state actors and providing an expedited legal outlet for private conflicts."[127] Wu sees "true convergence" as undesirable as both regimes are reluctant to converge towards the normative orientation of the other regime.[128] The regimes undoubtedly have different normative orientations and the inter-state character of dispute settlement at the WTO is a fundamental difference compared to ISDS. Investment treaties give foreign investors standing and are directly enforceable by investors. However, the disputes that come before tribunals of the two regimes are often similar (and can verge on identical) and the questions asked by tribunals are often similar. It is in these instances that cross-regime references are of primary utility and where instances of the "select cross-fertilization" may occur.[129]

Another major difference between the regimes concerns remedies. Investment treaties give rise to damages. Monetary damages are not available as a remedy at the

---

[125] See WTO website, 'Statement on a mechanism for developing, documenting and sharing practices and procedures in the conduct of WTO disputes,' 30 April 2020, JOB/DSB/1/Add.12, as well as addenda 13 & 14, and JOB/DSB/1/Add.12/Suppl.6 for Ecuador, Nicaragua and Macao who have subsequently joined.

[126] Wu (2014), p. 172.

[127] Wu (2014), p. 209.

[128] Wu (2014), p. 209.

[129] Wu (2014), pp. 172, 208.

WTO, which focuses on the removal or modification of infringing measures and the right to retaliate via the suspension of benefits while implementation is pending.[130]

While the interaction of actors facilitates engagement, the different backgrounds of adjudicators remains one of the fundamental differences between the regimes. Trade officials and lawyers, who often have backgrounds as government officials, have heavily influenced the trade regime, while the role of private parties and lawyers who come from a commercial arbitration background has been more pronounced in investment law.[131] While 88% of appointed panellists at the WTO had a "substantial government background", 76% had a private sector background at ICSID.[132]

One of the difficulties with such data is that it does not necessarily distinguish between BITs and PTIAs. Of the 674 concluded treaty-based ISDS cases, only 69 of them were taken under PTIAs (10.2%).[133] Thus, while it might be true that 76% of panellists have had a private sector background at ICSID, this may not be true under PTIAs, particularly ones based on the EU's Investment Court System where the states draw up a permanent roster.[134]

This distinction of the different backgrounds of actors extends to the governmental departments that negotiate agreements. Different outcomes can be expected where investment negotiations are conducted (1) in parallel with trade negotiations, and (2) by departments that are aware of the concerns of their trade counterparts and

---

[130]Temporary remedies can be applied pending withdrawal or modification of the measure, including compensation and the suspension of concessions or other obligations. See Van den Bossche and Zdouc (2017), p. 458.

[131]See Sect. 6.3.1 on 'Divergence Factors' and the backgrounds of adjudicators. Although 40% of the Appellate Body Members appointed between 1995 and 2015 have served as ICSID arbitrators, there are only 13 overlaps in appointments of the 396 individuals who were ICSID arbitrators and 251 appointed as WTO panellists. While 88% of appointed panellists at the WTO had a "substantial government background", 76% had a private sector background at ICSID.

One of the difficulties with such data is that it does not necessarily represent the situation under PTIAs. Rather it is based on the entirety of treaty-based ISDS cases without distinguishing between BITs and PTIAs. Of the 514 concluded cases taken at ICSID, only 34 were taken under PTIAs (6.6%). Of the 674 concluded treaty-based ISDS cases, only 69 of them were taken under PTIAs (10.2%). Of these 69 cases taken under PTIAs, 64 of them were taken under NAFTA and the CAFTA-DR FTA. These agreements were concluded in 1992 and 2004 respectively. Thus, while it might be true that 76% of panellists have had a private sector background at ICSID, this may not be true under modern PTIAs, particularly ones based on the EU's Investment Court System where the states draw up a permanent roster.

[132]Pauwelyn (2015), p. 11. It is noted that the number of WTO panelists with a government background was found to be 74% in a concurrent study. See Johannesson and Mavroidis (2015), pp. 685, 688.

[133]591 disputes were taken under BITs or the ECT, and 14 other under instruments. Note: Investment tribunals tend to be made up of ICSID and ad hoc arbitral tribunals established under UNICTRAL rules. This was compiled with reference to UNCTAD Investment Policy Hub database based on data available on 4 August 2020, available at https://investmentpolicy.unctad.org/investment-dispute-settlement/.

[134]This is discussed in greater detail in Sect. 6.3.

vice versa.[135] US trade negotiations have traditionally been conducted by the USTR and investment negotiations by the Department of State. In the UK, the Foreign and Commonwealth Office (FCO) has traditionally conducted investment negotiations[136] rather than the Department of Trade and Industry (DTI).[137]

These differences in standing, remedies, the possibility of appeal are significant systemic differences between the regimes. Any tribunal drawing upon the jurisprudence of the other regime when interpreting an agreement must be mindful of them, as well as differences in the purpose and content of treaties. The extent to which these differences should limit the making of cross-regime references when interpreting a shared legal norm is considered in a general manner in the next section (1.5) as well as in greater depth in Chaps. 3–7 in relation to a number of key norms.[138]

1.5   Cross-Regime References in Trade and Investment Disputes

References by tribunals to external sources can benefit the legal regimes concerned and promote coherence across public international law. They can be made in a variety of ways, including by reference to the VCLT or general principles of law, because of the express incorporation of provisions from one regime into another, with reference to shared norms and standards, or the common derivation of provisions.

Comparative law has been described as the most potent influence on Western legal development as a whole;[139] borrowing has been described as the main way law changes.[140] Cross-fertilisation between the regimes may occur without an explicit cross-regime reference and this may be in a conscious or unconscious manner.[141]

---

[135] As noted above in Sect. 1.4.2, there is less opportunity for facilitating engagement in institutional setups where PTAs and BITs are negotiated by separate departments and where a trade agreement and an investment agreement are not negotiated concurrently, even less engagement would be expected.

[136] Walter (2000), pp. 9–11.

[137] In the case of the UK it should be borne in mind that trade negotiations were conducted by the European Union on behalf of the UK from when it joined the EU in 1973 until it left on 31 January 2020. This was in accordance with Article 207 Treaty on the Functioning of the European Union (TFEU), formerly Article 133 Treaty establishing the European Community (TEC).

[138] Chapter 3—national treatment, MFN treatment, likeness, less favourable treatment; Chapter 4—treaty exceptions; Chapter 5—preambles; Chapter 6—provisions on appellate mechanisms; Chapter 7—*amicus curiae* briefs.

[139] Watson (1978), p. 318.

[140] Watson (1978), p. 321.

[141] This has been referred to as 'legal common sense' cross-fertilisation. See Cook (2020), p. 210.

Even where there are fundamental differences between the regimes, if there is an abundance of jurisprudence in a particular area that has scarcely been dealt with by the other regime, tribunals may consider how a norm has been interpreted in the other regime. Tribunals may also refer to the approaches undertaken in other areas of international law where there are serious concerns about the approach taken by previous tribunals in relation to a similar set of questions.[142]

1.5.1 WTO Law Influence in Investment Law & Vice Versa

It has been more common for investment law tribunals to look to WTO law than the other way around. Although the frequency of references has been uneven, it has not been unidirectional. The potential for the trade regime to influence investment treaties can be seen in the treaty texts via references to the trade regime and also shared standards and legal norms such as likeness and national treatment. Notable instances of investment tribunals drawing on the jurisprudence of the trade law regime include interpretations of national treatment provisions such as the approach of the tribunal in *SD Myers v. Canada*. The tribunal endorsed a competition-based approach to likeness. In doing so, it referred to WTO jurisprudence while taking into account contextual differences between the regimes.[143]

The tribunal in *Continental Casualty v. Argentina* also drew upon the experience of the trade regime in dealing with treaty exceptions when interpreting the concept of necessity.[144] This 'common derivation approach' was based on the fact that the US-Argentina BIT's non-precluded measures article was derived from similar articles in US FCN treaties, which in turn were inspired by GATT Article 1947. This link was deemed to be sufficient for the tribunal to consider the jurisprudence developed under the GATT as a source of guidance when interpreting a norm common to all three of the treaties.

The tribunal in *Occidental v. Ecuador* rejected the relevance of trade law jurisprudence as being "not specifically pertinent".[145] It underlined the fact that disputes under investment treaties involve exporters and trade law involves imported products and based on this, it found that the purposes of national treatment in the two regimes are "opposite".[146]

---

[142] E.g. This would be the case for investment tribunals interpreting Article XI of the US-Argentina BIT in the aftermath of the CMS Annulment Committee.

[143] *SD Myers, Inc. v Government of Canada*, NAFTA/UNCITRAL Tribunal, 1st Partial Award and Separate Opinion, IIC 249 (2000), paras 243–251.

[144] *Continental Casualty Company v. The Argentine Republic*, Award ICSID Case No. ARB/03/9, IIC 511 (2008), paras 189–195.

[145] *Occidental Petroleum Corp. v. The Republic of Ecuador*, Final Award, UNCITRAL Arbitration, London Court of International Arbitration Case No. UN 3467 (2004), para. 175.

[146] *Occidental Petroleum Corp. v. The Republic of Ecuador*, Final Award, UNCITRAL Arbitration, London Court of International Arbitration Case No. UN 3467 (2004), paras. 174–5.

The tribunals in *Methanex* and *Merrill & Ring* considered but ultimately rejected the relevance of trade law principles in relation to likeness. In *Methanex v. United States*, the tribunal found that it may "derive guidance" from legal reasoning developed in GATT and WTO jurisprudence on likeness.[147] Ultimately it was not persuaded as to the relevance of GATT jurisprudence and underlined the intent of the drafters to create "distinct regimes for trade and investment".[148] The tribunal noted that the drafting parties were fluent in GATT law and incorporated it "when they wished to do so" (i.e. in other chapters of NAFTA).[149]

In *Merrill & Ring v Canada*, the tribunal followed a similar approach to *Methanex* and found that the investor must be compared to log producers subject to the same regime rather than producers in other provinces, this being the comparator in the most "like circumstances".[150] The tribunal did not exclude the possibility of a contextual interpretation of a treaty provision in the light of provisions of other treaties such as the GATT, *in appropriate cases*.[151] However Canada "persuasively argued" that log exporters in British Columbia were the appropriate comparator. Canada argued that 'in like circumstances' should not be interpreted in the light of the GATT because Article 1102 reflects a specific understanding and intent of the parties and should be read on its own terms.[152]

These cross-regime references have all been the subject of some criticism. Kurtz claims that misuse of WTO law in *Occidental* and *Methanex* has been the controlling factor for critical inconsistency in investment law jurisprudence leading to "wildly inconsistent outcomes" in cases.[153] The approach of the tribunal in *Continental Casualty* has also been criticised by Alvarez and Brink.[154]

Generally speaking, the influence of trade law on investment law has been described as "relatively limited" and largely confined to general exceptions and instances of imported jurisprudence that remain an anomaly.[155] Despite these claims, it must be borne in mind that the "heavy activation" of these dispute settlement systems only occurred in the late 1990s.[156] The five awards discussed above range from 2002 to 2010.

---

[147] Methanex Corp. v U.S.A, NAFTA/UNCITRAL, Final Award of the Tribunal on Jurisdiction and Merits (2005) Part II Chapter B, para 6.

[148] Methanex Corp. v U.S.A, NAFTA/UNCITRAL, Final Award of the Tribunal on Jurisdiction and Merits (2005) Part IV Chapter B, para 35.

[149] Methanex Corp. v U.S.A, NAFTA/UNCITRAL, Final Award of the Tribunal on Jurisdiction and Merits (2005) Part IV Chapter B, para 30.

[150] *Merrill & Ring Forestry LP v. Canada*, ICSID, Award, para 71.

[151] *Merrill & Ring Forestry LP v. Canada*, ICSID, Award, para 84.

[152] *Merrill & Ring Forestry LP v. Canada*, ICSID, Award, para 91.

[153] Kurtz (2009), p. 6. Kurtz (2016), p. 18.

[154] Alvarez and Brink (2012), pp. 319–362; see Chap. 4 for discussion of this case.

[155] Wu (2014), p. 206.

[156] Kurtz (2016), p. 18.

Investment law tribunals have also turned to WTO law jurisprudence in other areas such as in relation to procedural matters,[157] references to rules of treaty interpretation,[158] and in cases where parallel proceedings have made it all but a necessity for tribunals to take into account the proceedings and findings before the other regime.[159]

Instances of WTO tribunals referring to the findings of investment tribunals are rarer.

In *U.S.-Stainless Steel*, the Appellate Body referred to the findings of an investment tribunal when addressing the question of consistency of jurisprudence.[160]

In *China-Rare Earths*, the Panel referred to the ruling in *MTD v. Chile*.[161] The Panel considered the investment tribunal's interpretation of fair and equitable treatment in its interpretation of the term "even-handedness". Both of these investment

---

[157] The tribunal in *Methanex v. United States* looked to the practice of the WTO's Appellate Body before finding that it would accept *amicus curiae* submissions. The tribunals in *Marvin Feldman v. Mexico* and *Thunderbird Gaming v Mexico* both referred to the Appellate Body Report in *United States-Measures Affecting Imports of Woven Wool Shirts and Blouses from India* (1997) in relation to the burden of proof lying with the party who asserts a fact.

[158] The tribunal in *Telefónica v. Argentina* referred to the Appellate Body Report in *Japan-Alcoholic Beverages-II*, in relation to the meaning of subsequent practice under VCLT Article 31.3(b). *Telefónica v. Argentina,* Decision of the Tribunal on Objections to Jurisdiction, ICSID Case No. ARB/03/20, FN73.

[159] See *United States-Final Dumping Determination on Softwood Lumber from Canada,* WT/DS 264; *Canfor Corporation v. United States of America,* Decision on Preliminary Question, 6 June 2006. In *Canfor v Mexico,* the tribunal found that: "While the conduct of the United States before the WTO and the findings of WTO Panels and its Appellate Body have no binding effect upon this Tribunal, they constitute relevant factual evidence which the Tribunal can and should appropriately take into account, especially in the case of positions advocated by the United States before the WTO that amount to admissions against interest for purposes of this NAFTA case." (para 327). See also *Mexico-Anti-Dumping Investigation of High-Fructose Corn Syrup (HFCS) from the United States* WT/DS 132; *Mexico-Taxes on Soft Drinks and Other Beverages* WT/DS 308; *Cargill, Inc. v. Mexico,* ICSID Case No. ARB(AF)/05/2, Award, 18 Sep. 2000; *Archer Daniels Midland Company and Tate & Lyle Ingredients Americas, Inc. v. The United Mexican States,* ICSID Case No. ARB (AF)/04/5; In the *Archer v Daniels* Award, the tribunal referred to the WTO decision finding that the tax was discriminatory. (para 190).

[160] Appellate Body Report, *United States-Final Anti-Dumping Measures on Stainless Steel from Mexico,* WT/DS344/AB/R, para. 160. The Appellate Body referred to *Saipem S.p.A. v. The People's Republic of Bangladesh,* ICSID IIC 280 (2007), p. 20, para. 67, which states that "[t]he Tribunal considers that it is not bound by previous decisions. At the same time, it is of the opinion that it must pay due consideration to earlier decisions of international tribunals. It believes that, subject to compelling contrary grounds, it has a duty to adopt solutions established in a series of consistent cases. It also believes that, subject to the specifics of a given treaty and of the circumstances of the actual case, it has a duty to seek to contribute to the harmonious development of investment law and thereby to meet the legitimate expectations of the community of States and investors towards certainty of the rule of law."

[161] *China-Measures Related to the Exportation of Rare Earths, Tungsten and Molybdenum,* Panel Report, WT/DS431/R, WT/DS432/R and WT/DS433/R, 26 March 2014, para 7.319; referring to *MTD Equity Sdn. Bhd. and MTD Chile S.A. v. Republic of Chile,* ICSID Case No. ARB/01/7, Award on Merits, para 13.

cases were referred to in footnotes of these Reports. Aside from the adjudicators, the disputing parties in WTO proceedings have referred to the decisions of investment law tribunals in their pleadings in various disputes.

At the WTO, the use of cross-regime references to date has been described as filling procedural gaps and helping to interpret the meaning of terms.[162] Although WTO tribunals have shown reluctance to make such references, this need not be the case. The role of external authorities is not stipulated in the WTO Agreements and their influence is under the control of the adjudicator.[163] WTO tribunals have made some references, particularly to the ICJ, in line with the VCLT and relying on the principle of systemic integration provided for in Article 31(3)(c) of the VCLT. The VLCT provides a legal basis for considering the findings of IIA tribunals in WTO disputes.

1.5.2   References to WTO Law in Disputes Under Other Chapters of PTIAs

This section considers four disputes taken under other PTAs or the non-investment chapters of PTIAs. All four of these referred to WTO law in some manner, while none of them referred to investment disputes.

Between 2007 and 2016, only two cases were successfully completed under PTAs or the non-investment chapters of PTIAs.[164] *Costa Rica v. El Salvador*[165] and *Guatemala-Issues Relating to the Obligations Under Article 16.2.1(a) of the CAFTA-DR* were both taken under CAFTA-DR (Dominican Republic-Central America FTA).[166] The former concerned non-compliance with import obligations and the latter a labour dispute.[167] Where disputes have taken place in relation to the labour or trade chapters of PTIAs, they have taken WTO law into account.

---

[162] Pauwelyn (2003), pp. 997–998.

[163] Zang (2017), p. 292.

[164] See Vidigal (2017), pp. 927–950, 928; See also Foreign Trade Information System (SICE), Trade Policy Developments, Central America – Dominican Republic – United States (CAFTA), Documents relating to the CAFTA-DR Dispute Settlement.

[165] Informe Final del Grupo Arbitral, *Costa Rica vs El Salvador-Tratamiento Arancelario a Bienes Originarios de Costa Rica*, 18 November 2014 (CAFTA-DR/ARB/2014/CR-ES/17).

[166] Final Report of the Panel, *Guatemala-Issues Relating to the Obligations Under Article 16.2.1 (a) of the CAFTA-DR* (2017).

[167] See *Costa Rica v El Salvador*, para 4.1.(iii).

In the Guatemala Labor Panel Report[168] the tribunal said it would take WTO law into account "where appropriate"[169] and this was found to be the case in relation to party submissions that "relied heavily" on WTO panel and Appellate Body reports. The panel found WTO precedent "helpful" concerning the submission of evidence[170] and "minimally useful" in interpreting CAFTA-DR Article 16.2[171] on the enforcement of labour laws.[172]

In *Costa Rica v. El Salvador*, the Panel referred to WTO law case law when considering the requirements for the establishment of a panel. It referred to the requirement of the Appellate Body that a summary of the legal basis of the complaint be provided as well as the articles claimed to have been violated.[173]

When considering the object and purpose of CAFTA-DR, the Panel observed that there are two mechanisms for dealing with "unfair competition" including anti-dumping or countervailing measures both under the WTO Agreements and in line with Article 8.8 CAFTA-DR.[174]

There have also been two recent disputes under EU Agreements, including Panel Reports in relation to a Ukrainian export ban on wood, and labour practices under the EU-Korea Free Trade Agreement. *Ukraine-Wood Products*[175] concerned an export ban, which was challenged under Article 35 of the EU-Ukraine Association

---

[168] This case was taken under Chapter 16 (Labor) of the Free Trade Agreement between Central America, the Dominican Republic and the United States of America (CAFTA). Costa Rica referred to WTO case law in its submission, claiming that although certain aspects were not included in the request for the establishment of the Panel, that they could be considered because they have a clear link with the measure and the basis of the dispute. The Panel found that the allegation of non-compliance within Article 4.15 CAFTA-DR was not within its mandate. Informe Final del Grupo Arbitral, *Costa Rica vs El Salvador-Tratamiento Arancelario a Bienes Originarios de Costa Rica*, 18 November 2014, 4.98–99.

[169] Final Report of the Panel, *Guatemala-Issues Relating to the Obligations Under Article 16.2.1 (a) of the CAFTA-DR* (2017), para 69.

[170] See Annex 2: Ruling on Request for Extension of Time to File Initial Written Submission and on the Treatment of Redacted Evidence, para 47.

[171] Article 16.2: Enforcement of Labor Laws 1. (a) A Party shall not fail to effectively enforce its labor laws, through a sustained or recurring course of action or inaction, in a manner affecting trade between the Parties, after the date of entry into force of this Agreement.

[172] Final Report of the Panel, *Guatemala-Issues Relating to the Obligations Under Article 16.2.1 (a) of the CAFTA-DR* (2017), para 189.

[173] Informe Final del Grupo Arbitral, *Costa Rica vs El Salvador-Tratamiento Arancelario a Bienes Originarios de Costa Rica*, 18 November 2014, para 4.41. Appellate Body Report, *United States-Countervailing and Anti-dumping Measures on Certain Products from China*, WT/DS449/AB/R, adopted 22 July 2014, para 4.17. The Panel determined that the measure was properly identified in accordance with Article 20.6.1 CAFTA-DR Informe, para 4.59.

[174] Informe Final del Grupo Arbitral, *Costa Rica vs El Salvador-Tratamiento Arancelario a Bienes Originarios de Costa Rica*, 18 November 2014, para 4.226.

[175] Final Report, *Restrictions applied by Ukraine on exports of certain wood products to the European Union*, 11 December 2020.

Agreement (AA).[176] Article 35 incorporates GATT Article XI and makes it "an integral part" of the Agreement. Article 36 of the AA incorporates Articles XX and XXI of GATT 1994 and its interpretative notes, which are also an integral part of the Agreement.

The Panel found that Article 35 of the AA incorporates Article of the GATT 1994 "as a whole"[177] and that the two Articles "impose identical obligations".[178] The Panel recalled that Article 320 of the AA required that Article 35 be interpreted in a way that is "consistent with any relevant interpretation established in rulings of the WTO Dispute Settlement Body".[179] Thus it found that it was not necessary to show that a measure has the actual effect of restricting exports as this would "create a significant divergence" between GATT Articles XI:1 and Article 35 of the AA.[180] It found the export bans to be incompatible with Article 35 of the AA.[181]

It then considered whether the export bans could be justified under GATT Article XX, applicable by virtue of Article 36 of the AA. The Panel found the 2005 export ban was justified under GATT Article XX(b) and that it was compliant with the Article's chapeau.[182]

The Panel then found the 2015 temporary export ban was not justified under GATT Article XX(g). This subparagraph covers measures related to "the conservation of exhaustible natural resources *if such measures are made effective in conjunction with restrictions on domestic production or consumption.*" The Panel noted that this notion demands real restrictions on domestic production to reinforce and complement restrictions on international trade.[183] Ukraine had a cap on domestic consumption, which was well in excess of actual consumption. The Panel found that this confirmed that the ban does not protect trees "in the absence of an effective domestic consumption cap" and that the ban did not meet the requirements of

---

[176] Article 35 (Import and Export Restrictions) of the Agreement, along with Article 34 (National Treatment), make up Section 3 of the Agreement on Non-Tariff Measures. The two Articles incorporate GATT Article XI and III respectively and make them "an integral part of the Agreement".

[177] Final Report, *Restrictions applied by Ukraine on exports of certain wood products to the European Union*, 11 December 2020, paras 185–191.

[178] Final Report, *Restrictions applied by Ukraine on exports of certain wood products to the European Union*, 11 December 2020, para 204.

[179] Final Report, *Restrictions applied by Ukraine on exports of certain wood products to the European Union*, 11 December 2020, para 204.

[180] Final Report, *Restrictions applied by Ukraine on exports of certain wood products to the European Union*, 11 December 2020, para 205.

[181] Final Report, *Restrictions applied by Ukraine on exports of certain wood products to the European Union*, 11 December 2020, para 218.

[182] Final Report, *Restrictions applied by Ukraine on exports of certain wood products to the European Union*, 11 December 2020, para 373.

[183] Final Report, *Restrictions applied by Ukraine on exports of certain wood products to the European Union*, 11 December 2020, para 455.

Article XX(g).[184] As the measure was incompatible with Article XX(g), it was not necessary to investigate whether it met the requirements of Article XX's chapeau.[185]

The dispute under the EU-Korea FTA concerned Trade and Sustainable Development (TSD) obligations and was the first such dispute taken by the EU.

The Panel found that the EU's request did not seek to use TSD for protectionist purposes referring to the Declaration of the 1996 World Trade Organisation (WTO) Ministerial Conference held in Singapore in 1996, which accepted that the promotion of core ILO labour standards should not be construed as protectionism *per se*.[186]

The Panel in this proceeding under Article 13.15 of the FTA considered the relationship between TSD and trade. It found that complaints were not limited to trade-related aspects of labour, but this does not mean that the Panel Request refer to matters which have no connection to trade.[187] The Panel noted that the Agreement was drafted to "create a strong connection between the promotion and attainment of fundamental labour principles and rights and trade".[188] As the 'floor' of labour rights is an integral component of the system the parties are committed to, "national measures implementing such rights are therefore inherently related to trade".[189]

1.5.3 References to Public International Law in Trade and Investment Disputes

This section looks at cross-regime references made by trade and investment law tribunals in the wider field of public international law (PIL) and the basis for making them, as this in turn informs our understanding of how the regimes relate to each other.[190] The trade and investment law regimes are not self-contained but rather form

---

[184] Final Report, *Restrictions applied by Ukraine on exports of certain wood products to the European Union*, 11 December 2020, paras 463–465.

[185] Final Report, *Restrictions applied by Ukraine on exports of certain wood products to the European Union*, 11 December 2020, para 469.

[186] Report of the Panel of Experts, *Proceeding Constituted under Article 13.15 of the EU-Korea Free Trade Agreement*, 20 January 2021, para 87. "We reject the use of labour standards for protectionist purposes, and agree that the comparative advantage of countries, particularly low-wage developing countries, must in no way be put into question." Singapore World Trade Organisation Ministerial Declaration, WT/MIN(96)/DEC, 18 December 1996.

[187] Report of the Panel of Experts, *Proceeding Constituted under Article 13.15 of the EU-Korea Free Trade Agreement*, 20 January 2021, para 94. The complaints concerned measures based on Article 13.4.3 (Multilateral Labour Standards and Agreements).

[188] Report of the Panel of Experts, *Proceeding Constituted under Article 13.15 of the EU-Korea Free Trade Agreement*, 20 January 2021, para 95.

[189] Report of the Panel of Experts, *Proceeding Constituted under Article 13.15 of the EU-Korea Free Trade Agreement*, 20 January 2021, para 95.

[190] Public international law is the set of rules that is generally accepted in relations between States and its sources are reflected in Article 38 of the Statute of the International Court of Justice. Article 38.1. "The Court, whose function is to decide in accordance with international law such disputes as

part of the wider field of public international law as recognised in Article 42(1) of the ICSID Convention and DSU Article 3(2), at the WTO.[191]

Where the ordinary meaning of a term is elusive, tribunals may look to the wider context of public international law and how other tribunals have dealt with shared or similar legal norms.

Article 31(3)(c) VCLT tells us that when interpreting treaties, "any relevant rules of international law applicable in the relations between the parties" shall be taken into account. This article "gives expression to the objective of systemic integration", which governs all treaty interpretation.[192] Article 31(3)(c) concerns external sources that are relevant to treaty interpretation, including other treaties, customary rules, or general principles of law.[193]

Douglas tells us that "rules" within the meaning of the VCLT is best understood as "any legal norms" including principles and that tribunals should be able to extract principles to aid treaty interpretation.[194] The regimes may find it useful to look to the interpretations of other tribunals because of their "recognized pedigree".[195]

Trade and investment agreements often contain general concepts or principles of international law[196] and the reason for this is that their content can evolve over time

---

are submitted to it, shall apply: a. international conventions, whether general or particular, establishing rules expressly recognized by the contesting states; b. international custom, as evidence of a general practice accepted as law; c. the general principles of law recognized by civilized nations; d. subject to the provisions of Article 59, judicial decisions and the teachings of the most highly qualified publicists of the various nations, as subsidiary means for the determination of rules of law."

[191] Article 42(1) ICSID states that the Tribunal "shall apply the law of the Contracting State party to the dispute (including its rules on the conflict of laws) and such rules of international law as may be applicable." DSU Article 3(2) states that the dispute settlement system "serves to preserve the rights and obligations of Members under the covered agreements, and to clarify the existing provisions of those agreements in accordance with customary rules of interpretation of public international law. Recommendations and rulings of the DSB cannot add to or diminish the rights and obligations provided in the covered agreements." See also United Nations Report of the Study Group of the International Law Commission: 'Fragmentation of International Law: Difficulties Arising From The Diversification And Expansion Of International Law' (2006); and Campbell et al. (2007).

[192] International Law Commission, Conclusions of the work of the Study Group on the Fragmentation of International Law: Difficulties arising from the Diversification and Expansion of International Law (2006), paras 17–18.

[193] International Law Commission, Conclusions of the work of the Study Group on the Fragmentation of International Law: Difficulties arising from the Diversification and Expansion of International Law (2006), para 18.

[194] Douglas (2009), p. 86.

[195] Watson (2013), p. 607.

[196] E.g. Annex A, Model US BIT: "Customary International Law: The Parties confirm their shared understanding that "customary international law" generally and as specifically referenced in Article 5 [Minimum Standard of Treatment] and Annex B [Expropriation] results from a general and consistent practice of States that they follow from a sense of legal obligation. With regard to Article 5 [Minimum Standard of Treatment], the customary international law minimum standard of treatment of aliens refers to all customary international law principles that protect the economic rights and interests of aliens."

through interpretative practices and so the instrument can adapt to changing realities without requiring constant amendment.[197]

Tribunals in the investment regime have been more willing to rely on PIL in terms of defining the substantive rights of parties. References to PIL have been made when elucidating the meaning of standards such as fair and equitable treatment, or when importing treaty exceptions.[198] When the ordinary meaning of a broad provision such as FET is unclear, despite the tribunal having regard to its context, object, and purpose, recourse to principles of PIL may be necessary. Douglas asks how else are such standards to be interpreted if not by reference to relevant principles of international law?[199] The subjective notions of individual tribunals are not preferable.

Investment tribunals have frequently referred to the jurisprudence of the ECtHR in areas such as proportionality analysis and the margin of appreciation.[200] Alvarez acknowledges that it is "inconceivable" that such cross-regime references would cease to occur, given the "textual and normative similarities" of the two regimes.[201]

WTO tribunals regularly refer to non-WTO instruments in their reports.[202]

Article 3(2) of the DSU provides for dispute settlement to preserve the rights and obligations of Members and to clarify them "in accordance with customary rules of interpretation of public international law." While this opens the door to a role for PIL, the next sentence adds: "the DSB cannot add to or diminish the rights and obligations provided in the covered agreements." Nonetheless tribunals may still refer to non-WTO instruments in line with the VCLT. Article 31.3(c) VCLT allows adjudicators to take account of "any relevant rules of international law" between the parties.[203]

The Panel in *Thai-Cigarettes* found that the Appellate Body "extensively" relied on general principles of international law to interpret members' obligations.[204]

---

[197] Douglas (2009), p. 88. Douglas compares this to the interpretation of general concepts in a constitution and the longevity this brings.

[198] Section 2.2.2 details the relationship between FET and the requirements of customary international law. Tribunals have looked to international law when interpreting treaty exceptions in case such as *CMS v. Argentina*. See *CMS Gas Transmission Company v. Argentine Republic*, Award ICSID Case No. ARB/01/08, IIC 303 (2005), para 315. "The Tribunal, like the parties themselves, considers that Article 25 of the Articles on State Responsibility adequately reflect the state of customary international law on the question of necessity."

[199] Douglas (2009), p. 87.

[200] See Sweet (2010), p. 47; Arato (2014), p. 545.

[201] Alvarez (2017), p. 95.

[202] For a thorough account of PIL in Appellate Body decisions, see Cook (2015).

[203] The Appellate Body has taken international instruments or customary international law into account on this basis. Where tribunals have referred to non-WTO instruments, it has generally been to support an interpretation arrived at "on the basis of the text, context and purpose of the provision at issue". Cook (2015), p. 65. Cook adds that "there is no case in which a WTO adjudicator has justified its interpretation of a WTO provision expressly and primarily on the basis of Article 31(3) (c)."

[204] Panel Report, *Thailand-Customs and Fiscal Measures on Cigarettes from the Philippines*, WT/DS371/R, FN1760.

Pauwelyn has described the use of "non-WTO law" or the making of cross-regime references by WTO Panels and the AB as fulfilling two main functions: (1) interpreting the meaning of terms in the WTO agreement; and (2) filling procedural gaps in areas where the WTO agreement is silent.[205]

The Appellate Body referred to public international law in *US-Gasoline*,[206] its first case, where it acknowledged that the "General Agreement is not to be read in clinical isolation from public international law".[207] It also referred to the rules of general international law on state responsibility in *US-Cotton Yarn*[208] in relation to the calculation of appropriate countermeasures. In *US-Shrimp*, the Appellate Body made reference to international conventions and instruments in determining the definition of 'exhaustible natural resources'.[209]

WTO tribunals have also referred to the case law and practice of the ICJ or its predecessor, the PCIJ. In *India-Patents,* the Appellate Body referred to the PCIJ's findings in *Certain German Interests in Polish Upper* Silesia in relation to municipal law.[210] More recently, in *Russia-Traffic in Transit*, the Panel cited six ICJ cases in its Report in relation to jurisdiction.[211] The Panel recalled that tribunals have inherent jurisdiction deriving from the exercise of their adjudicative function.[212] The Panel further found that the phrase "which it considers" in the chapeau of GATT Article XXI(b) does not apply to the subparagraphs of XXI(b) and is not "totally" self-judging.[213] Concerning Russia's argument that the invocation of Article XXI's

---

[205] Pauwelyn (2003), pp. 997–998. Examples of where the WTO Agreement is silent are burden of proof, standing, representation before Panels, the retroactive application of treaties or error in treaty formation.

[206] Appellate Body Report, *United States-Standards for Reformulated and Conventional Gasoline*, WTO doc. WT/DS2/AB/R, 29 April 1996.

[207] Appellate Body Report, *United States-Standards for Reformulated and Conventional Gasoline*, WTO doc. WT/DS2/AB/R, 29 April 1996, p. 17.

[208] Appellate Body Report, *United States-Transitional Safeguard Measure on Combed Cotton Yarn from Pakistan,* WT/DS192/AB/R, para 120. The Appellate Body applied the general principle of proportionality as found in Article 51 of the International Law Commission Draft Articles on State's Responsibility.

[209] *United States-Import Prohibition of Certain Shrimp and Shrimp Products*, WT/DS58/AB/R, para 130.

[210] See Appellate Body Report, *India-Patent Protection for Pharmaceutical and Agricultural Chemical Products,* WTO doc. WT/DS50/AB/R, paras 64–66; referring to PCIJ case *Certain German Interests in Polish Upper Silesia (Germany v. Poland),* [1926], Series A, No. 7.

[211] Panel Report, *Russia-Traffic in Transit*, WT/DS512/R, 5 April 2019, Section 7.5.3.

[212] Section 7.5.3. See also, FN144, which refers to: (1) International Court of Justice, Preliminary Objections, Case Concerning the Northern Cameroons, (*Cameroon v. United Kingdom*) (1963) ICJ Reports, p. 15; (2) International Court of Justice, Questions of Jurisdiction and/or Admissibility, Nuclear Tests Case, (*Australia v. France*) (1974) ICJ Reports, p. 253.

[213] See para 7.102 of the Report and FN156, which refers to: (1) International Court of Justice, Merits, Case Concerning Oil Platforms, (*Islamic Republic of Iran v. United States of America*) (2003) ICJ Reports, p. 161; and (2) International Court of Justice, Merits, Case of Military and Paramilitary Activities in and Against Nicaragua, (*Nicaragua v. United States of America*) (1986) ICJ Reports, p. 14.

Security Exceptions involves a "political question" and as such is non-justiciable, the Panel cited the ICJ, which has found that "as long as the case before it. . .turns on a legal question capable of a legal answer," it has a duty to take jurisdiction. On this point the ICJ decisions in *Certain Expenses of the United Nations*[214] and *Prosecutor v. Tadić*[215] were cited.[216]

There are also instances where non-WTO law, rules or standards are explicitly provided for under WTO rules (e.g. *Codex Alimentarius* standards referred to in the SPS Agreement[217]). In such instances, non-WTO law may, on the merits, prevent a breach of WTO rules.[218]

1.5.4 Making Cross-Regime References

Cross-regime references are a potent tool in the development of the law and in ensuring its coherence. There are few regimes more ripe for such references than trade and investment law, two of the core pillars of international economic law, described as twins separated at birth when the International Trade Organization failed to come into being in 1948. Claims for breach of their respective agreements require consideration of whether there has been a breach of standards that may be common to the two regimes, which may then be defended under exceptions provisions that are similar or common to the regimes.

When considering the jurisprudence of another regime in relation to a shared norm, any lessons drawn by tribunals must take into account the wider context of international law and fundamental differences between the regimes. Trade and investment tribunals must have regard for the regimes' different origins, goals, treaty texts, institutional structures, procedures, and remedies. They must consider the

---

[214] International Court of Justice, Advisory Opinion, *Certain Expenses of the United Nations*, (United Nations) (1962) I.C.J. Reports, p. 151.

[215] International Criminal Tribunal for the Former Yugoslavia, Decision on the Defence Motion for Interlocutory Appeal on Jurisdiction, *Prosecutor v. Tadić*, (1995), Case No IT-94-1-A.

[216] Panel Report, *Russia-Traffic in Transit*, WT/DS512/R, 5 April 2019, see para 7.103 and FN183.

[217] E.g. Article SPS Article 12.3: "3. The Committee shall maintain close contact with the relevant international organizations in the field of sanitary and phytosanitary protection, especially with the Codex Alimentarius Commission, the International Office of Epizootics, and the Secretariat of the International Plant Protection Convention, with the objective of securing the best available scientific and technical advice for the administration of this Agreement and in order to ensure that unnecessary duplication of effort is avoided."

[218] See Pauwelyn (2003), pp. 997–1030 and 1020–1028. This article outlines areas where non-WTO law may preclude breach, including: (1) non-WTO defences explicitly incorporated into the WTO system; (2) violations permitted pursuant to dispute settlement under another treaty (e.g. breaches of the ILO's Forced Labour Convention); (3) violations permitted pursuant to another treaty (e.g. obligations under the WHO FCTC); (4) violations permitted under another treaty, where violation of that treaty is required.

differences between the regimes that may justify different, tailored or nuanced approaches in the context of the particular regime where it is being applied.

If the two regimes are not self-contained and are to look beyond themselves, there is arguably no more appropriate regime for the trade regime to look to than investment law, and vice versa. Coherence between the trade and investment law regimes depends on the degree to which judicial communication exists and the regimes allow the "integration of alien legal sources".[219] Trade law tribunals already draw upon public international law as an interpretative instrument.

But what are the limiting principles on the extent to which the jurisprudence of the other regime ought to be considered? When tribunals compare shared norms between the regimes, they must explain their reasons for doing so,[220] and consider the following differences between the regimes and the treaties themselves: (1) textual differences; (2) contextual differences; (3) the differing purposes of agreements; and (4) systemic differences.[221]

1.5.4.1 Textual and Contextual Differences

Differences of text and context are not an insurmountable obstacle to borrowing or drawing on the jurisprudence of another agreement; it is for this reason that adjudicators at the WTO have interpreted national treatment under the TBT Agreement with reference to case law developed under the GATT.[222] When interpreting a shared norm, any attempt to draw upon the jurisprudence of the other regimes must be done with due regard to the textual and contextual differences between treaties. There are variances in the language and construction of articles that must be considered when interpreting a treaty.

---

[219] Lanyi and Steinbach (2017), pp. 61–85.

[220] E.g. ICISD Convention, Article 52.1(e) provides a ground for annulment where "the award has failed to state the reasons on which it is based".

[221] Where trade and investment law have shared or similar legal norms, Kurtz emphasises four primary considerations when comparing these shared legal norms, including: textual differences, contextual differences, systemic differences, and differences in remedy structures. See Kurtz (2016), pp. 85–94. This section considers remedies structures as part of the systemic differences between the regimes.

[222] See for example, Panel Report, *United States-Measures Affecting the Production and Sale of Clove Cigarettes*, WT/DS406/R, paras 7.81–83. See also Appellate Body Report, *United States-Measures Affecting the Production and Sale of Clove Cigarettes*, WT/DS406/AB/R, adopted on 24 April 2012, paras 104–121; Panel Report, *United States-Certain Country of Origin Labelling (COOL) Requirements*, WT/DS384/R and WT/DS386/R, adopted on 23 July 2012, paras. 7.252–7.256; Appellate Body Report, *United States-Certain Country of Origin Labelling (COOL) Requirements*, WT/DS384/AB/R and WT/DS386/AB/R, adopted on 23 July 2012, paras. 270–71; Panel Report, *United States-Measures Concerning the Importation, Marketing and Sale of Tuna and Tuna Products*, WT/DS381/R, adopted on 13 June 2012, paras 7.213–7.252; and Appellate Body Report, *United States-Measures Concerning the Importation, Marketing and Sale of Tuna and Tuna Products*, WT/DS381/AB/R, adopted on 13 June 2012, para 209.

GATT Article III can be seen as a grandmother provision for national treatment in the WTO Agreements as it has been the most litigated national treatment provision before the WTO's Dispute Settlement Body. When interpreting other national treatment provisions under the other WTO Agreements, tribunals have considered the jurisprudence under GATT Article III.[223]

There are important textual and contextual considerations for tribunals considering the previous findings of tribunals under the GATT. The text of GATT Article III:1 sets out the purpose of the provision. The context for interpreting Article III is also shaped by the presence of GATT Article XX (General Exceptions). When determining national treatment under the TBT Agreement, there is no expression of the purpose of the provision akin to GATT Article III:1, and no General Exceptions provision. Nonetheless, the Appellate Body has interpreted likeness under the TBT Agreement in a way that was based on the competitive relationship between products.[224] In *US-Clove Cigarettes*, the AB found that the context provided by Article 2.1, the TBT Agreement, and by GATT Article III:4 supported this approach.[225] In relation to less favourable treatment, the Appellate Body considered whether the detrimental impact from the measure "stems exclusively from a legitimate regulatory distinction".[226] This is a different test to the one undertaken under GATT Article III and was based on the context and object and purpose of the TBT Agreement.[227] Under GATT Article III, the defending party can contest a finding of less favourable treatment under the General Exceptions of GATT Article XX. The TBT has no equivalent provision and enquiries concerning regulatory purpose such as those carried out under Article XX are done within Article 2.1 itself. Regulatory purpose has also been part of the inquiry of the national treatment provision under NAFTA Article 1102, where similarly there is no general exceptions article. Given these

---

[223] Ibid.

[224] Appellate Body Report, *United States-Measures Affecting the Production and Sale of Clove Cigarettes*, WT/DS406/AB/R, adopted on 24 April 2012, para 156. "In contrast, we have concluded that the context provided by Article 2.1 itself, by other provisions of the *TBT Agreement*, by the *TBT Agreement* as a whole, and by Article III:4 of the GATT 1994, as well as the object and purpose of the *TBT Agreement*, support an interpretation of the concept of "likeness" in Article 2.1 that is based on the competitive relationship between and among the products and that takes into account the regulatory concerns underlying a technical regulation, to the extent that they are relevant to the examination of certain likeness criteria and are reflected in the products' competitive relationship."

[225] Appellate Body Report, *United States-Measures Affecting the Production and Sale of Clove Cigarettes*, WT/DS406/AB/R, adopted on 24 April 2012, para 156.

[226] Appellate Body Report, *United States-Measures Affecting the Production and Sale of Clove Cigarettes*, WT/DS406/AB/R, adopted on 24 April 2012, para. 174.

[227] Appellate Body Report, *United States-Measures Affecting the Production and Sale of Clove Cigarettes*, WT/DS406/AB/R, adopted on 24 April 2012, para 181. The tribunal did acknowledge that it found "previous findings by the Appellate Body in the context of Article III:4 of the GATT 1994 to be instructive in assessing the meaning of "treatment no less favourable", provided that the specific context in which the term appears in Article 2.1 of the TBT Agreement is taken into account. Similarly to Article III:4 of the GATT 1994, Article 2.1 of the TBT Agreement requires WTO Members to accord to the group of imported products treatment no less favourable than that accorded to the group of like domestic products." (para 180).

structural similarities, a tribunal interpreting less favourable treatment in a national treatment claim under the WTO's TBT Agreement may have greater recourse to certain findings in NAFTA cases such as *SD Myers v. Canada*[228] rather than findings in cases under the GATT. Thus the same approach was used in relation to likeness, despite the textual differences between GATT Article III:4 and TBT Article 2.1, but a different approach was taken to less favourable treatment in view of the different contexts of the provisions.

1.5.4.2   The Differing Purposes of Agreements

Tribunals interpret the ordinary meaning of treaty terms "in their context and in the light of its object and purpose".[229] When interpreting treaty provisions, the text and structure of provisions are important, but so too is the object and purpose of an agreement.[230] The closer the textual similarity, the closer the structural set up, and the more the objects and purposes of the treaties are aligned, the greater the potential to invoke and draw upon the law and jurisprudence of the other regime.

Engagement was said earlier to be appropriate when the structure and wording of provisions lend themselves to this in light of the purpose of the treaties at issue; but to what extent should differences in the purposes of two regimes block the making of a cross-regime reference? Consider a national treatment provision in the investment chapter of a PTIA, that (1) refers to 'treatment no less favourable' (2) being accorded to investors 'in like situations', and (3) this is to be interpreted in light of an exceptions chapter that directly incorporates GATT Article XX.[231] Should tribunals be able to draw upon the jurisprudence of cases from the trade regime when interpreting such provisions? To what extent should the different purposes of these Agreements affect the legal tests used in relation to provisions with such similar texts and structures?

---

[228] The tribunal in *SD Myers v. Canada* adopted a competition-based approach to likeness and so a tribunal in the trade regime may more readily refer to it.

[229] VCLT Article 31(1).

[230] For a general description of the differences in the regimes' purposes, rather than one relating to cross-regime references, see Sect. 1.4.3.

[231] E.g. CETA Article 8.6: "National treatment 1. Each Party shall accord to an investor of the other Party and to a covered investment, treatment no less favourable than the treatment it accords, in like situations to its own investors and to their investments with respect to the establishment, acquisition, expansion, conduct, operation, management, maintenance, use, enjoyment and sale or disposal of their investments in its territory. 2. The treatment accorded by a Party under paragraph 1 means, with respect to a government in Canada other than at the federal level, or, with respect to a government of or in a Member State of the European Union, treatment no less favourable than the most favourable treatment accorded, in like situations, by that government to investors of that Party in its territory and to investments of such investors."

The Exceptions Chapter of CETA also incorporates the GATT explicitly and the GATS implicitly (CETA Article 28.3.1.)

Might these differing purposes prevent such references in the case of (2), but not (3)?

Where a state concludes a PTIA and a BIT with two different countries in quick succession, where the substantive provisions are largely similar but the object and purpose of the agreement are substantially different, to what extent should these differences in purposes affect the tribunal's interpretation?[232]

Consider the Colombia-Canada FTA and Colombia-Turkey BIT, where the first two sections of the national treatment article of the Colombia-Canada FTA[233] are almost identical to those of the combined national treatment and MFN article of the Colombia-Turkey BIT.[234] The only difference relates to the scope of the articles, but both cover the expansion and sale or disposal of investments.[235] This question of interpreting provisions with similar texts and structures but differing objects and purposes is the subject of Chap. 5.

1.5.4.3 Systemic Differences

Differences in standing, remedies and the possibility of appeal and treaty exit are key systemic differences between the regimes.[236] Any tribunal referring to the

---

[232] Chapter Two outlines instances where states have concluded a PTIA and BIT in a short space of time, where the substantive provisions are largely similar, but where the strength of the reference to the right to regulate is at different ends of the spectrum. E.g. Colombia concluded an FTA with Canada in 2008, which scored a 5 on this scale from 0 to 5. It subsequently concluded BITs with Japan (2011), Singapore (2013) and Turkey (2014), which scored 2, 0 and 1 respectively on this scale.

[233] "Article 803: National Treatment: 1. Each Party shall accord to investors of the other Party treatment no less favourable than that it accords, in like circumstances, to its own investors with respect to the establishment, acquisition, expansion, management, conduct, operation and sale or other disposition of investments in its territory. 2. Each Party shall accord to covered investments treatment no less favourable than that it accords, in like circumstances, to investments of its own investors with respect to the establishment, acquisition, expansion, management, conduct, operation and sale or other disposition of investments in its territory."

[234] "Article 5: National Treatment and Most-Favoured-Nation Treatment: 1. Each Contracting Party shall accord to investor of the other Contracting Party treatment no less favorable than that it accords, in like circumstances, to its own investors with respect to the expansion, management, maintenance, operation, enjoyment, extension and sale or disposal of their investments in its territory. 2. Each Contracting Party shall accord investments of investors of the other Contracting Party, once established, treatment no less favorable than that it accords, in like circumstances, to investments of its own investors with respect to the expansion, management, maintenance, operation, enjoyment, extension and sale or disposal of their investments in its territory."

[235] The former covers establishment, acquisition, and conduct in relation to the investment, while the latter covers the maintenance and enjoyment of the investment (although different words are used in places, there is overlap between some of these different concepts).

[236] For a general description of these systemic differences, rather than one relating to cross-regime references, see Sect. 1.4.3.

jurisprudence of the other regime when interpreting an agreement must be mindful of these systemic differences, as well as differences in the purpose and content of treaties.

Exit from the WTO is constrained to a far greater degree than exit from IIAs.

This "permanency" of the WTO needs to be considered when deciding how flexibly to interpret IIAs.[237] IIAs frequently provide for the possibility of the parties exiting, renegotiating or issue binding interpretations of the agreement. Alvarez seems to suggest that the reaction of the parties may well be to exit the treaty but parties may also have recourse to the treaty's joint interpretation facility or to amend the treaty, depending on the treaty text. A further consideration in this area in relation to PTIAs, is the reluctance some parties may have to exit a treaty, where the overall package is beneficial to them, but they would terminate the investment agreement if it were a standalone agreement.

For Alvarez, cross-regime borrowing could lead parties to exit treaties, and he has warned against "drawing facile conclusions" from the trade regime where exit is constrained.[238] Even where provisions are phrased identically, as has been the case with PTIA provisions that have directly incorporated provisions such as GATT XX/XXI, converging outcomes should not be presumed. Alvarez notes that this is because the structure of dispute settlement matters.[239]

These considerations all impact upon whether or not a cross-regime reference is appropriate; but where tribunals face similar sets of facts (perhaps due to overlapping jurisdiction)[240] and ask similar questions (due to shared norms and standards) in interpreting a provision, there may be good reasons to look to and draw upon the experience of the other regime.

These considerations merely highlight the degree of caution tribunals should exercise when drawing upon the jurisprudence of another regime. While some view the potential for cross-fertilisation as being limited,[241] Zang categorises judicial communication as a "middle ground" on the continuum between resistance and convergence.[242] The dispersed investment system offers a laboratory in which to theorize about communication and when it is appropriate. Likewise, the trade and investment regimes should not be isolated and occasions for informed dissent may

---

[237] Alvarez and Brink (2012), pp. 319–362, 351.

[238] Alvarez and Brink (2012), pp. 319–362, 351–352. The tribunal in *Continental Casualty v. Argentina* referred to GATT jurisprudence when interpreting whether a measure was 'necessary'. *Continental Casualty Company v. The Argentine Republic*, Award ICSID Case No. ARB/03/9, IIC 511 (2008), para 198.

[239] See Alvarez (2020), p. 311.

[240] Investment cases concerning import bans such as *SD Myers v. Canada* and *Apotex v. United States* are very similar to trade cases.

[241] Wu is of the view that cross-regime borrowing "may seem appealing at first, but it often may turn out to be inappropriate because of fundamental differences between the regimes". See Wu (2014), p. 208.

[242] Zang (2017), p. 274.

lead to a more sophisticated system.[243] Tribunals may, with caution, refer to or draw upon the jurisprudence of another regime.

1.6 Aims and Structure

1.6.1 Aims

This study examines the role played by PTIAs in facilitating increased engagement between the trade and investment law regimes. It charts areas of engagement between the two regimes both empirically (Sect. 1.2) and in relation to the question of when engagement is appropriate, and to what extent it is appropriate for certain key drivers of convergence (Sects. 1.3–1.5).

This study tests a series of hypotheses relating to PTIAs and engagement. It examines whether engagement is increasing over time and in relation to three main categories of provisions. The main question considered is whether engagement between the trade and investment regimes increases when parties conclude PTIAs rather than BITs, by analysing the frequency and content of provisions evidencing engagement in the texts of concluded IIAs.

This question is broken down into three sub-parts: (1) for the sample of IIAs contained in this study, is there evidence that the conclusion of PTIAs compared to BITs has resulted in increased levels of engagement between the trade and invest-ment law regimes? (Sect. 1.2); (2) is there evidence of increased levels of engage-ment between the trade and investment law regimes in relation to key areas such as preambles, nondiscrimination provisions, treaty exceptions, and dispute settlement mechanisms? (Sects. 1.3–1.5); and (3) is there evidence that the conclusion of PTIAs compared to BITs gives greater scope to tribunals to draw upon the jurisprudence of the other regime and make cross-regime references? (Sects. 1.2–1.5).

This is the first such study examining the effect of concluding PTIAs compared to BITs on engagement between the trade and investment law regimes based on empirical evidence.

This book examines whether the conclusion of PTIAs results in increased engagement as well as the nature of this engagement. Where parties conclude agreements that cover both trade and investment within a single agreement, Chap. 2 outlines the extent to which this results in increased engagement both between the regimes and over several periods of time for the set of Agreements covered.

---

[243] See Ziegler (2013), p. 176. The laboratory analogy quoted by Ziegler is from a paper by Bjorklund and Nappert (2011).

1.6.2 Structure

This introduction has introduced and defined key concepts as well as setting out the main research questions of this study. Section 1.2 conducts an empirical analysis of levels of engagement in PTIAs and BITs and a series of hypotheses are tested against a sample of 120 IIAs (60 PTIAs and 60 BITs). The presence of 24 provisions evidencing engagement is measured across these 120 Agreements. The presence of six of these provisions that are identified as being of particular importance to inter-regime engagement is then measured. In each instance, it is demonstrated that for the set of 120 Agreements in this study, there is more evidence of engagement in PTIAs than in BITs for the set of agreements as a whole, as well as in each of the three main categories of provisions.

Sections 1.3–1.5 examine key provisions in light of the empirical conclusion that PTIAs result in increased levels of engagement between the trade and investment law regimes for these agreements. These provisions are divided into three areas: host state flexibility, dispute settlement, and substantive provisions. For each of these norms and features, the following questions were considered: (1) the extent of inter-regime engagement; (2) the utility and practice of making references to the experience of the other regime; and (3) engagement and the role of PTIAs.

Sections 1.3 and 1.4 concern substantive protections and the flexibilities relating to them found within trade and investment agreements. Section 1.5 looks at shared provisions relating to dispute settlement. It makes the case that where the regimes share similar procedural and institutional features, this brings the regimes closer together.

References

Alford R (2014) The convergence of International Trade and Investment Arbitration. Santa Clara J Int Law 12(1)

Alvarez JE (2017) The use (and misuse) of European Human Rights Law in Investor-State Dispute Settlement. In: Ferrari F (ed) The impact of EU law on International Commercial Arbitration. JurisNet, LLC, p 95. https://papers.ssrn.com/sol3/papers.cfm?abstract_id=2875089. Last accessed 22 July 2020

Alvarez JE (2020) Epilogue: 'Convergence' is a many-splendored thing. In: Behn D, Gáspár-Szilágyi S, Langford M (eds) Adjudicating trade and investment law: convergence or divergence? Cambridge University Press, p 311

Alvarez JE, Brink T (2012) Revisiting the necessity defense: Continental Casualty v. Argentina. In: Yearbook on international investment law & policy. Oxford University Press

Arato J (2014) The margin of appreciation in international investment law. Va J Int Law 54:545

Arikaki EA (1985) Appendix 1: Treaties of friendship, commerce and navigation and their treatment of service industries. Mich J Int Law 7(1):344

Behn D, Gáspár-Szilágyi S, Langford M (2020a) Assessing convergence in international economic disputes – a framework. In: Behn D, Gáspár-Szilágyi S, Langford M (eds) Adjudicating trade and investment law: convergence or divergence? Cambridge University Press, p 8

Behn D, Gáspár-Szilágyi S, Langford M (eds) (2020b) Adjudicating trade and investment law: convergence or divergence? Cambridge University Press

Berger A, Busse M (2013) Do trade and investment agreements lead to more FDI? Accounting for key provisions inside the Black Box. International Economics and Economic Policy

Bjorklund AK, Nappert S (2011) Beyond fragmentation. UC David Legal Studies Research Paper No. 243

Bonnitcha J (2017) Assessing the impacts of investment treaties: overview of the evidence. International Institute for Sustainable Development Report

Bonnitcha J, Poulsen LS, Waibel M (2017) The political economy of the investment regime. Oxford University Press

Broude T (2011) Investment and trade: the "Lottie and Lisa" of international economic law? International Law Forum of the Hebrew University of Jerusalem Law

Campbell M et al (2007) International Investment Arbitration: substantive principles. Oxford University Press

Charnovitz S (2011) What is international economic law? J Int Econ Law 14(1):3–9

Cho S (2004) A bridge too far: the fall of the fifth WTO Ministerial Conference in Cancún and the future of trade constitution. J Int Econ Law 7:219

Cook G (2015) A digest of WTO jurisprudence on public international law concepts and principles. Cambridge University Press

Cook G (2020) The use of object and purpose by trade and investment adjudicators: convergence without interaction. In: Behn D, Gáspár-Szilágyi S, Langford M (eds) Adjudicating trade and investment law: convergence or divergence? Cambridge University Press, p 210

Cotula L (2014) Do investment treaties unduly constrain regulatory space? Questions of International Law, 19–31

Dhingra S, Ottaviano G, Sampson T (2017) A hitch-hiker's guide to post-Brexit trade negotiations: options and principles. Oxf Rev Econ Policy 33(S1):S22–S30

Di Mascio NA, Pauwelyn J (2008) Nondiscrimination in trade and investment treaties: worlds apart or two sides of the same coin? Am J Int Law, 48

Douglas Z (2009) The international law of investment claims. Cambridge University Press

Echandi R, Sauvé P (eds) (2013) Part II of 'Prospects in International Investment Law and Policy'. Cambridge University Press, pp 103–173

Footer M (2013) On the laws of attraction: examining the relationship between foreign investment and international trade. In: Echandi R, Sauvé P (eds) Prospects in international investment law and policy. Cambridge University Press, pp 105–138

Gáspár-Szilágyi S, Usynin M (2020) Investment chapters in PTAs and their impact on adjudicative convergence. In: Behn D, Gáspár-Szilágyi S, Langford M (eds) Adjudicating trade and investment law: convergence or divergence? Cambridge University Press, pp 41–42

Ginsburg T (2005) International substitutes for domestic institutions: bilateral investment treaties and governance. Int Rev Law Econ 25:107–123

Grossman GM (2016) The purpose of trade agreements. NBER Working Paper 22070

Hallward-Driemeier M (2003) Do bilateral investment treaties attract foreign direct investment? Only a bit – and they could bite. World Bank Policy Research Working Paper WPS3121, p 22

Herdegen M (2016) Principles of international economic law, 2nd edn. Oxford University Press, Oxford, pp 8–11

Hofmann R, Tams CJ, Schill S (2013) Preferential trade and investment agreements: from recalibration to reintegration. Nomos, Baden, p 15

Johannesson L, Mavroidis PC (2015) Black Cat, White Cat: the identity of WTO judges. J World Trade 49:685, 688

Johnston AM, Trebilcock MJ (2013) The proliferation of preferential trade agreements: the beginning of the end of the multilateral trading system? In: Hofmann R, Tams CJ, Schill SW (eds) Preferential trade and investment agreements: from recalibration to reintegration. Nomos, Baden

Kurtz J (2009) The use and abuse of WTO law in Investor–State Arbitration: competition and its discontents. EJIL Volume 20, 6

Kurtz J (2014) A general investment agreement in the WTO? Lessons from Chapter 11 Of NAFTA and the OECD Multilateral Agreement on investment. Univ Pa J Int Law 23(4) Art. 3

Kurtz J (2016) The WTO and international investment law: converging systems. Cambridge University Press

Langord M, Creamer CD, Behn D (2020) Regime responsiveness in international economic disputes. In: Behn D, Gáspár-Szilágyi S, Langford M (eds) Adjudicating trade and investment law: convergence or divergence? Cambridge University Press, p 284

Lanyi PA, Steinbach A (2017) Promoting coherence between PTAs and the WTO through systemic integration. J Int Econ Law 20:61–85

Marboe I (2013) Bilateral free trade and investment agreements: 'Stumbling Blocks' or 'Building Blocks' of multilateralism? In: Hofmann R, Tams CJ, Schill SW (eds) Preferential trade and investment agreements: from recalibration to reintegration. Nomos, Baden, pp 240–241

Mercurio B (2015) Safeguarding public welfare? Intellectual property rights, health and the evolution of treaty drafting in international investment agreements. J Int Dispute Settlement 6 (2):242

Mitchell A, Heaton D, Henckels C (2016) Non-discrimination and the role of regulatory purpose in international trade and investment law. Edward Elgar Publishing

Newcombe A, Paradell L (2009) Law and practice of investment treaties: standards of treatment, vol 55. Kluwer Law International

Pauwelyn J (2003) How to win a World Trade Organization dispute based on non-World Trade Organization Law? J World Trade 37(6)

Pauwelyn J (2015) The rule of law without the rule of lawyers? Why investment arbitrators are from Mars, trade panelists are from Venus. AJIL, 11

Polanco R (2018) The return of the home state to Investor-State Disputes: bringing back diplomatic protection? Cambridge University Press, p 230

Puig S (2015) The merging of international trade and investment law. Berkeley J Int Law 33:1

Sacerdoti G, Acconci P, De Luca A, Valenti M (2014) General interests of host states in international investment law. Cambridge University Press

Sampson T (2016) Four principles for the UK's Brexit trade negotiations. CEP Brexit Analysis

Sauvant KP, Sachs LE (2009) 'The effect of treaties on foreign direct investment: bilateral investment treaties, double taxation treaties, and investment flows. Oxford University Press

Schreuer C (2014) Jurisdiction and applicable law in investment treaty arbitration. McGill J Dispute Resolution 1(1):16–17

Shinkman M (2007) 'The investors' view: economic opportunities versus political risks in 2007–11. In: Kekiz L, Sauvant K (eds) World Investment Prospects to 2011: foreign direct investment and the challenge of political risk. The Economist Intelligence Unit, London

Sweet AS (2010) Investor-State Arbitration: proportionality's new frontier. Law Ethics Hum Rights 4:47

Tietje C (2013) Perspectives on the interaction between international trade and investment regulation. In: Echandi R, Sauvé P (eds) Prospects in international investment law and policy. Cambridge University Press, p 169

Van den Bossche P, Zdouc W (2017) The law and policy of the World Trade Organisation, text cases and materials, 4th edn. Cambridge University Press, p 458

Van den Broek N (2013) WTO litigation, investment arbitration and commercial arbitration. Kluwer Law International, p 42

Vandevelde KJ (2017) The first bilateral investment treaties, U.S. postwar friendship, commerce and navigation treaties. Oxford University Press, p 58

Vidigal G (2017) Why is there so little litigation under free trade agreements? Retaliation and adjudication in international dispute settlement. J Int Econ Law 20(4):927–950, 928

Wagner M (2014) Regulatory space in international trade law and international investment law. Univ Pa J Int Law 36(1):86

Walter A (2000) British investment treaties in South Asia: current status and future trends. Report Prepared for the International Development Center of Japan, 9–11

Watson A (1978) Comparative law and legal change. Camb Law J 37(2)

Watson A (2013) The birth of legal transplants. Georgia J Int Comp Law 41:607

Wu M (2014) The scope and limits of trade's influence in shaping the evolving international investment regime. In: Douglas Z, Pauwelyn J, Vinuales JE (eds) The foundations of international investment law. Oxford University Press

Wu M (2016) The "China, Inc." challenge to global trade governance. Harv Int Law J 57:1001–1063

Zang M (2017) Shall we talk? Judicial communication between the CJEU and WTO dispute settlement. EJIL 28(1)

Ziegler AR (2013) Is it necessary to avoid substantive and procedural overlaps with other agreements in IIAs? In: de Mestral A, Lévesque C (eds) Improving international investment agreements. Routledge, p 176

Part I
Empirical Study

Chapter 2
An Empirical Analysis of Levels of Engagement in PTIAs and BITs

2.1 Introduction

This chapter introduces various provisions that evidence engagement between the trade and investment law regimes. It provides an empirical analysis of engagement between the trade and investment law regimes using data from 120 Bilateral Investment Treaties (BITs) and Preferential Trade and Investment Agreements (PTIAs) signed between 2005 and 2019. This empirical analysis is used to test two main hypotheses: (1) that there is greater evidence of engagement between trade and investment in PTIAs compared to BITs; and (2) that there is evidence of increasing engagement between the regimes over time.[1]

Section 2.2 outlines how engagement is measured and the aims and means of this study. It looks at the treaties selected for inclusion in this study and the methodology behind their selection. It then outlines each of the 24 treaty provisions selected in this study.

Section 2.3 tests whether PTIAs are increasing engagement between the regimes by comparing the frequency of provisions that evidence engagement across 120 BITs and PTIAs. It gives the results of the study for all 24 provisions showing that there is more evidence of engagement in PTIAs than in BITs and that there is evidence of increasing engagement between trade and investment over time. It then considers the results of the study in relation to six key provisions, demonstrating that for these too, there is more evidence of engagement in PTIAs compared to BITs and that this is increasing over time.[2]

---

[1] This is tested specifically in relation to five time periods: (1) 2005–06; (2) 2007–08; (3) 2009–11; (4) 2013–16 and (5) 2017–19.

[2] These six provisions are divided evenly across the three major categories of provisions: host state flexibility, dispute settlement, and substantive provisions.

© The Author(s), under exclusive license to Springer Nature Switzerland AG 2021
N. Moran, *Engagement Between Trade and Investment*, EYIEL Monographs -
Studies in European and International Economic Law 18,
https://doi.org/10.1007/978-3-030-83259-9_2

This chapter then tests whether engagement is increasing over time by analysing the frequency of provisions evidencing engagement across five different time periods between 2005 and 2019.

2.2   Measuring Engagement Between PTIAs & BITs

This section outlines how engagement is measured in this study. It looks at the treaties selected for inclusion and the methodology behind their selection. It then outlines each of the 24 treaty provisions selected in this study and the reason for their selection.

24 provisions evidencing engagement were selected and their prevalence is coded across 60 BITs and 60 PTIAs. This study codes the prevalence of provisions evidencing engagement between the two regimes in BITs and PTIAs concluded during the 2005–19 period. It then provides analysis based on the frequency of these provisions across the 120 Agreements featured in this study.

2.2.1   Case Selection

A criterion for selection in this study was that each agreement had to contain an investment chapter containing an investor-state dispute settlement mechanism. Dispute settlement is one of the three main categories this empirical study is divided into and so analysis of the data would have been incomplete if some of the agreements did not contain one of the major categories. As a result, some of the conclusions of this study are more relevant to International Investment Agreements (IIAs) containing an investor-state dispute settlement mechanism. Furthermore, only BITs with at least one party that has concluded a PTIA including ISDS have been selected to ensure there is some overlap between the parties concluding the two types of agreements examined. The last four BITs signed each year were chosen for each year covered by this study, where the texts are available on the UNCTAD International Investment Agreement database. Where the same party has concluded more than one of the most recently signed BITs in a given year, only one was considered in order to keep the sample more general. The same party may feature more than once in a given year where there is not a sufficient number of other BITs that have been concluded between other parties. A party to a BIT featured a maximum of five times for this analysis in order to avoid the results being overly reflective of the treaty preferences of any individual state. Only treaties that have been uploaded to the UNCTAD database by September 2020 have been considered in this study.[3]

As there are fewer PTIAs than BITs, the sample of PTIAs is less evenly spread over the 2005–19 period.[4] For example, for the year 2012, no PTIA fit the criteria for inclusion at the time of the finalisation of this study.[5] Other PTIAs that included ISDS and were concluded between 2005 and 2019 did not feature in this study for reasons including: (1) ensuring the various time periods featured equally; (2) minimising the number of times a party featured, etc.[6]

IIAs are typically referred to by their date of entry into force throughout this book. However, for the empirical section of this study, treaties are categorised by their year of signature, which is the date of interest in this section. Thus, while a treaty may be referred to as US-Argentina BIT (1994) elsewhere in this book, this agreement is labelled the US-Argentina BIT (1991) for this chapter.

---

[3]For the period of 2005–15, only IIAs that have come into force were selected. This criterion was relaxed for the period 2016–19 as there were too few treaty texts available at the time of the finalisation of this study for this to be respected, while respecting the other criteria set out above.

As of 9 September 2020, the following Agreements are yet to enter into force: Armenia-Singapore (2019); EU-Viet Nam IPA (2019); EU-Singapore IPA (2018); CETA (2016); Iran-Nicaragua BIT (2019); Belarus-Uzbekistan BIT (2019); Burkina Faso-Turkey BIT (2019); Japan-Jordan BIT (2018); Kazakhstan-Singapore BIT (2018); UAE-Uruguay BIT (2018); Cambodia-Turkey BIT (2018); Ethiopia-Qatar BIT (2017); Turkey-Uzbekistan BIT (2017); Colombia-UAE BIT (2017); and the Morocco-Nigeria BIT (2016).

[4]To facilitate a comparison of different time periods, a minimum of ten IIAs have been included for each time period: (1) 2005–06; (2) 2007–08–14; (3) 2009–11; (4) 2013–16; and (5) 2017–19. The selection of some IIAs was based on the availability of the treaty text at the time this study was initially compiled in 2016.

[5]This empirical study was finalised in September 2020. There was no text available on the UNCTAD database at the time of this finalisation for a PTIA containing an investment chapter with an investor-state dispute settlement mechanism. The UNCTAD database describes some agreements concluded in 2012 as 'Other IIA' but these do not qualify as PTIAs for the following reasons: (1) No investment chapter: EU-Vietnam Framework PCA, Colombia-EU-Peru FTA, EU-Iraq Cooperation Agreement; (2) No ISDS: Australia-Malaysia FTA, GCC-US Framework Agreement; (3) Not a PTIA: China-Japan-Korea trilateral investment agreement; (4) Text not available: GCC-Peru Framework Agreement.

Certain other PTIAs for which the text was available were not included in this study. Given the limited number of PTIAs including ISDS, the main criteria for selection were: (1) availability of the treaty text at the time of this study; and (2) minimising the number of IIAs from a given year.

[6]PTIAs concluded by Colombia, Peru and Korea fit the criteria but were excluded from the analysis to keep the sample more diverse. These agreements included: Chile-Colombia FTA (2006), Chile-Colombia FTA (2006), Colombia-Panama FTA (2013), Colombia-Honduras FTA (2013), Colombia-Costa Rica FTA (2013), Colombia-Korea FTA (2013), Chile-Peru FTA (2006), Canada-Peru FTA (2008), Panama-Peru FTA (2011), Costa Rica-Peru FTA (2011), Mexico-Peru FTA (2011), Honduras-Peru FTA (2015), India-Korea CEPA (2009) and the Korea-New Zealand FTA (2015).

2.2.2 Operationalising Engagement

Engagement in IIAs is operationalised in this study by coding for 24 treaty provisions that evidence engagement across 120 IIAs. 60 PTIAs and 60 BITs that were signed during the period 2005–19 are surveyed in this study. The 24 provisions considered are divided into three categories, which include host state flexibility, dispute settlement, and substantive provisions.

2.2.2.1 Host State Flexibility

The eight IIA provisions coded under this heading include: (a) agreements that refer to WTO law in their preamble; (b) preambles balancing investment promotion with other regulatory objectives; (c) treaty exceptions; (d) exceptions for health or environmental measures; (e) expropriation articles featuring TRIPS exceptions; (f) expropriation articles that refer to public policy objectives; (g) performance requirements articles that refer to WTO law; and (h) capital withdrawal safeguards.

Agreements Referring to WTO Law in Their Preamble

Preambles set out the object and purpose of a treaty. The Vienna Convention states that treaties shall be interpreted in good faith and in the light of its object and purpose.[7] The content of a preamble applies to the entirety of a treaty. In the case of a BIT, the content of the preamble is likely to be more specific to investment concerns than in a PTIA, as the subject matter for BITs is more restricted than for PTIAs.

The rights and obligations of the parties under the WTO Agreement are expressly referred to in the preambles of some IIAs. The importance given to an objective in the preamble can be seen in the parties' choice of phrasing in outlining their level of commitment to it. The phrase most commonly used in relation to the WTO Agreement is that the parties, "Building on" these rights, have agreed as follows.

Such a reference appeared in 57/60 PTIAs (95%) contained in this study, while only featuring in the Chile-Hong Kong BIT (2016). Although it has not been the case that references to the WTO Agreement have been common in standalone investment agreements, this may change in the future. Negotiations for the EU-Singapore

---

[7]Article 31.1 VCLT states that a treaty shall be interpreted "in good faith in accordance with the ordinary meaning to be given to its terms in the context of the treaty and in the light of its object and purpose".

Investment Protection Agreement were concluded in April 2018[8] and its preamble refers to the parties respective rights and obligations under the WTO Agreement.[9]

In the case of a PTIA, the necessity of including a reference to WTO law is much more apparent as there are trade chapters as well as investment chapters within the agreement. However, the inclusion of a reference to WTO law in the preamble may be seen as informing not only the trade chapters of an agreement but also the investment chapter. Reference to the WTO Agreements in the preamble of a PTIA increases the potential for engagement between the trade and investment law regimes. This is because a party to an investment dispute can claim that building on WTO rights and obligations is one of the objects and purposes of the agreement.

Given the potential of such references to facilitate inter-regime engagement, this is a clear example of an area where PTIAs exhibit greater potential engagement than BITs.

Preambles Balancing Investment Promotion with Other Regulatory Objectives

IIA preambles increasingly recognise the need to balance the promotion and protection of investment with the pursuit of other public policy objectives. These provisions featured in 48/60 PTIAs (80%) and 30/60 BITs surveyed as part of this study.

Provisions referring to the right to regulate, sustainable development, and environmental preservation are all considered to balance these competing rights. Reference to other public policy objectives such as a general desire to "improve living standards"[10] or "reduce poverty"[11] were excluded from the analysis in this study. One reason for this is that it is unclear whether raising living standards or reducing poverty is facilitated more by increasing investment protection or by giving the parties more regulatory space.

---

[8]Investment Protection Agreement Between The European Union And Its Member States, Of The One Part, And The Republic Of Singapore, Of The Other Part. See European Commission Press Release of 18 April 2018: 'European Commission proposes signature and conclusion of Japan and Singapore agreements,' available at: http://trade.ec.europa.eu/doclib/press/index.cfm?id=1826.

[9]"(. . .) BUILDING on their respective rights and obligations under the WTO Agreement and other multilateral, regional and bilateral agreements and arrangements to which they are party, in particular, the EUSFTA (. . .) Have Agreed as follows:"

[10]E.g. Kazakhstan-Macedonia FTA, "AGREEING that a stable framework for investment will maximize effective utilization of economic resources and improve living standard".

[11]E.g. Peru-US FTA "PROMOTE broad-based economic development in order to reduce poverty and generate opportunities for sustainable economic alternatives to drug-crop production."

The right to regulate,[12] sustainable development,[13] and environmental preservation[14] are shared concerns of trade and investment law. Tribunals have considered these concepts in WTO and investment law jurisprudence and may interpret them in establishing the object and purpose of an agreement. In doing so, tribunals may have regard to how provisions with similar wordings have been interpreted in the other regime, where appropriate.

Incorporation of Treaty Exceptions

Treaty exceptions were selected as they are commonly found in trade and investment agreements and they represent one of the clearest areas for potential interaction between the regimes. Investment treaties have incorporated WTO-based exceptions in a number of ways and the interpretation of these provisions is a fertile ground for cross-fertilisation of jurisprudence. Treaty Exceptions featured in 59/60 PTIAs and 28/60 BITs surveyed as part of this study

Four categories of 'treaty exceptions' were categorised in this chapter, which were given different weightings based on their potential to impact engagement between the regimes. These categories are expanded on in Chap. 4 and include exceptions explicitly modelled on WTO law (weighting = 1), exceptions implicitly modelled on WTO law (1), exceptions thinly connected to WTO law (0.66), and exceptions within articles on performance requirements (0.25). Exceptions provisions modelled on, or closely connected to, those at WTO include both general exceptions and essential security exceptions.

Article Providing an Exception for Health or Environmental Measures

General exceptions for environmental or health measures have been quite common in IIAs featuring in 45/60 PTIAs and 20/60 BITs surveyed as part of this study. The

---

[12] A typical phrasing of a reference to the promotion of sustainable development in a PTIA reads as follows: "REAFFIRMING their right to pursue economic philosophies suited to their development goals and their right to regulate activities to realise their national policy objectives;"—India Singapore Comprehensive Economic Cooperation Agreement (2005).

[13] A typical phrasing of a reference to the promotion of sustainable development in a PTIA reads as follows; "The Government of the United States of America and the Government of the Republic of Peru, resolved to: IMPLEMENT this Agreement in a manner consistent with environmental protection and conservation, promote sustainable development, and strengthen their cooperation on environmental matters;"—Peru US FTA, 2009.

[14] A typical phrasing of a reference to the environmental preservation in a PTIA reads as follows; "IMPLEMENT this Agreement in a manner consistent with environmental protection and conservation, promote sustainable development, and strengthen their cooperation on environmental matters; PROTECT and preserve the environment and enhance the means for doing so, including through the conservation of natural resources in their respective territories;"—US-Panama TPA (2007).

wording of these exceptions can be quite broad and these provisions may be included in addition to General Exceptions explicitly or implicitly incorporating GATT Article XX or GATS Article XIV. Similarly to treaty exceptions, articles providing an exception for such measures represent a clear area for potential interaction between the trade and investment law regimes, given the wealth of jurisprudence in these areas in the trade regime.

Article 10.15 of the New Zealand-Malaysia FTA (2009) contains a typical phrasing of an article providing an exception for health or environmental measures:

> Investment and Environment: Nothing in the Chapter shall be construed to prevent a Party from adopting, maintaining or enforcing any measure otherwise consistent with this Chapter that it considers appropriate to ensure that investment activity in its territory is undertaken in a manner sensitive to environmental concerns.

This wording is quite strong in ensuring the right to regulate of the parties.[15] Provisions such as these facilitate inter-regime engagement for agreements that do not incorporate GATT/GATS General Exceptions in particular.[16] The Canada-Honduras FTA (2013) is an example of a weaker phrasing of this exception whereby the parties merely recognise that it is inappropriate to relax regulatory standards in these areas.[17]

Expropriation Articles That Feature TRIPS Exceptions

An exception for the issuance of compulsory licences that comply with the WTO's TRIPS Agreement featured in 48/60 PTIAs (80%) and 16/60 BITs (26.6%) in this study. The New Zealand-Taiwan ECA (2013) contains an example of an article that provides that expropriation provisions do not apply in relation to compulsory licences that are TRIPS compliant.[18] These provisions were given as an example

---

[15] The New Zealand-Malaysia FTA explicitly incorporates GATT Article XX and GATS Article XIV.

[16] This was the case for seven of the PTIAs and eight of the BITs included in this study, e.g. the Guatemala-Peru FTA (2011). Article 12.8 of Guatemala-Peru FTA is almost identical to Article 10.15 of the New Zealand-Malaysia FTA: "2. Nada en este Capítulo se interpretará en el sentido de impedir que una Parte adopte, mantenga o haga cumplir cualquier medida por lo demás compatible con este Capítulo, que considere apropiada para asegurar que las inversiones en su territorio se efectúen tomando en cuenta inquietudes en materia ambiental."

[17] Article 10.15: Health, Safety and Environmental Measures: "The Parties recognize that it is inappropriate to encourage investment by relaxing domestic health, safety or environmental measures. Accordingly, a Party should not waive or otherwise derogate from, or offer to waive or otherwise derogate from, those measures to encourage the establishment, acquisition, expansion or retention in its territory of an investment of an investor. If a Party considers that the other Party has offered this encouragement, it may request discussions with the other Party and the two Parties shall enter into discussions with a view to avoiding any such encouragement."

[18] See New Zealand-Taiwan ECA (2013), Chapter 12, Article 13 (5): "This Article does not apply to the issuance of compulsory licenses granted in relation to intellectual property rights in accordance with the TRIPS Agreement, or to the revocation, limitation or creation of intellectual property

in Chap. 1 of provisions that minimise conflict between the regimes. The inclusion of provisions of this sort in investment agreements shows that treaty drafters are cognisant of the effects IIAs can have on the parties' obligations in the trade regime. Provisions such as these have been described as tools for "managing potential conflicts" between investment treaty law and WTO law.[19]

Expropriation Articles That Refer to Public Policy Objectives

Expropriation provisions in investment agreements may feature an exception for measures taken in furtherance of public welfare in areas such as health or the environment. Such an exception may be contained within the investment chapter itself or as an Annex. These exceptions featured in 40/60 PTIAs and 21/60 BITs (35%) surveyed as part of this study.

Expropriation is one of the fundamental protections provided in IIAs and exceptions in areas such as public health and the environment give rise to potential engagement between the regimes, given the wealth of jurisprudence in these areas in the trade regime.

Such provisions may provide an exception to claims for indirect expropriation or expand on the requirement that expropriations be carried out in the public interest and in the pursuit of a legitimate regulatory purpose.[20] The articles may include a non-exhaustive list of policy objectives that may justify expropriation.[21] Where exceptions potentially cover direct expropriation, this approach risks going too far and potentially allowing states to avoid their obligation to pay adequate compensation in cases of expropriation.[22]

---

rights, to the extent that such issuance, revocation, limitation, or creation is consistent with Chapter 10 (Intellectual Property)."

[19] See Kurtz J (2016), p. 11.

[20] Annex I, 3 of the Canada-Burkina Faso (2015) provides an example of the phrasing of an article providing a public welfare exception for indirect expropriation: "A non-discriminatory measure or series of measures of a Party designed and applied to protect legitimate public welfare objectives, such as health, safety and the environment, does not constitute indirect expropriation, except in rare circumstances, such as when a measure or a series of measures is so severe in the light of its purpose that it cannot be reasonably considered as having been adopted and applied in good faith."

[21] Annex 9B(c)(ii) of the Korea-Peru FTA (2010) provides a non-exhaustive list of policy objectives that may justify expropriation: "Except in rare circumstances, such as, for example, when a measure or series of measures have an extremely severe or disproportionate effect in light of its purpose, non-discriminatory regulatory actions by a Party that are designed and applied to protect legitimate public welfare objectives, such as public health, safety, the environment, and real estate policy measures (for example, measures to improve the housing conditions for low-income households), do not constitute indirect expropriations[FN1]." The footnote states: "For greater certainty, the list of "legitimate public welfare objectives" in subparagraph (c)(ii) is not exhaustive."

[22] See Kurtz (2016), p. 185.

Performance Requirements Articles That Refer to WTO Law

Performance requirements are conditions imposed upon foreign investors that are often explicitly trade distorting (such as domestic content requirements). The WTO Agreement on Trade-Related Investment Measures (TRIMs) disciplines the use of performance requirements and many IIAs do likewise.

Articles on performance requirements that refer to WTO law featured in 40/60 PTIAs and 8/60 BITs (13.3%) surveyed in this study. References to the WTO either come by way of these articles reaffirming TRIMS obligations or exceptions specific to the article that are often implicitly based on WTO law.

These exceptions are specific to this article alone unlike many other exceptions seen above that are general exceptions and apply to the entire agreement. Many of these 'specific exceptions' are based on Article 8.3 of US Model BIT.[23] This article draws heavily on the wording of GATT Article XX and GATS Article XIV. Although the wordings are similar, they are not identical and tribunals would have to be careful of these differences of wording and context.

Performance requirements articles may also reaffirm the parties' TRIMS obligations, e.g. Article 9 Canada-China BIT (2012) and Article 92 of the Malaysia-Pakistan FTA (2007) provide succinct references to WTO law in their Articles on Performance Requirements.[24] These articles directly incorporate the provisions of the TRIMS.[25]

Capital Withdrawal Safeguard

Articles providing for capital withdrawal safeguards featured in 34/60 PTIAs (56.6%) and 24/60 BITs (40%) surveyed as part of this study. These articles allow host states to limit the transfer of funds in the case of balance of payments difficulties

---

[23] Article 8.3 of US Model BIT (2012): "(a) Nothing in paragraph 2 shall be construed to prevent a Party from conditioning the receipt or continued receipt of an advantage (...) in its territory (...) (c) Provided that such measures are not applied in an arbitrary or unjustifiable manner, and provided that such measures do not constitute a disguised restriction on international trade or investment, paragraphs 1(b), (c), and (f), and 2(a) and (b), shall not be construed to prevent a Party from adopting or maintaining measures, including environmental measures: (i) necessary to secure compliance with laws and regulations that are not inconsistent with this Treaty; (ii) necessary to protect human, animal, or plant life or health; or (iii) related to the conservation of living or non-living exhaustible natural resources."

[24] Article 92 of the Malaysia-Pakistan FTA (2007): "1. For the purposes of this Chapter, the Parties reaffirm their commitments to the Agreement on Trade-Related Investment Measures in Annex 1A to the WTO Agreement (hereinafter referred to as "TRIMS") and hereby incorporate the provisions of the TRIMS, as may be amended, as part of this Chapter. 2. A Party shall, upon notification by the other Party, promptly convene consultations with the other Party on any matter relating to this Article that affects the other Party's investors and their investments."

[25] TRIMs applies GATT Exceptions in its Article 3, Exceptions: "All exceptions under GATT 1994 shall apply, as appropriate, to the provisions of this Agreement."

in a manner akin to that provided for in GATS Article XII and GATT Article XII (Restrictions to Safeguard the Balance of Payments). These capital withdrawal safeguard provisions are "best characterised as safeguard measures" rather than as general exceptions to provisions providing for the free transfer of funds.[26] They allow host states to restrict transfers in certain circumstances, such as in the case of balance of payments difficulties. This approach of providing for an unrestricted right to transfer funds was called into question as a result of Malaysia's success in imposing capital controls during the 1997–98 Asian Financial Crisis.[27]

Such provisions are a shared legal norm with the trade law regime and have the potential to facilitate inter-regime engagement. Some of these provisions in IIAs, including Article 21.5 of the China-Korea FTA (2015), directly refer to the WTO Agreement.[28] Article 100 of the Malaysia-Pakistan FTA (2007) notes that "financial services" shall have the same meaning as in the Annex on Financial Services to the GATS. Article 12 of the Canada-China BIT (2012) does not refer to the WTO, but like the WTO Agreement, provides for the need to be consistent with the Articles of Agreement of the IMF.[29]

The GATS requires the complete liberalisation of transfers and payments except under the circumstances envisaged in GATS Article XII. Article XII allows for restrictions on capital flows in the case of "serious balance-of-payments and external financial difficulties or threat thereof". WTO Members can also impose restrictions on capital flows at the request of the IMF in line with GATS Article XI. Any restrictions must comply with certain conditions, such as being carried out in a temporary and non-discriminatory manner.[30]

---

[26] Newcombe and Paradell (2009), p. 415.

[27] In response to this crisis, South Korea, Thailand and Indonesia followed IMF programmes which relied on liberalising financial markets and undergoing structural reforms. Malaysia imposed capital controls, which led to a hostile reaction from the IMF but ultimately to a quicker recovery. See Kaplan and Rodrik (2002).

[28] Article 21.5: "Where the Party is in serious balance of payments and external financial difficulties or threat thereof, it may, in accordance with the WTO Agreement and consistent with the Articles of *Agreement of the International Monetary Fund*, adopt measures deemed necessary."

[29] "4. (a) Nothing in the Agreement shall be construed to prevent a Contracting Party from adopting or maintaining measures that restrict transfers when the Contracting Party experiences serious balance of payment difficulties, or the threat thereof, provided that such measures: o (i) are of limited duration, applied on a good-faith basis, and should be phased out as the situation calling for imposition of such measures improves; o (ii) do not constitute a dual or multiple exchange rate practice; o (iii) do not otherwise interfere with an investor's ability to invest, in the territory of the Contracting Party, in the form chosen by the investor and, as relevant, in local currency, in any assets that are restricted from being transferred out of the territory of the Contracting Party; o (iv) are applied on an equitable and non-discriminatory basis; o (v) are promptly published by the government authorities responsible for financial services or central bank of the Contracting Party; o (vi) are consistent with the *Articles of Agreement of the International Monetary Fund* done at Bretton Woods on 22 July 1944; and o (vii) avoid unnecessary damage to the commercial, economic and financial interests of the other Contracting Party."

[30] GATS Article XII: 2: "The restrictions referred to in paragraph 1: (a) shall not discriminate among Members; (b) shall be consistent with the Articles of Agreement of the International Monetary

2.2.2.2   Dispute Settlement

The eight IIA provisions coded under this heading include those relating to:
(a) *amicus curiae* submissions; (b) transparency in proceedings; (c) conflict of
interest provisions for arbitrators; (d) arbitrators' knowledge of international
(trade) law; (e) the establishment of an appellate mechanism; (f) review of dispute
settlement; (g) 'applicable rules' of international law; and (h) binding interpretations.

Amicus curiae Submissions

Provisions that authorise tribunals to accept *amicus curiae* submissions featured in
28/60 PTIAs (46.66%) and 6/40 BITs (15%) surveyed as part of this study. These
provisions are examples of provisions that harmonise procedural rules between the
regimes, at least to some extent.

WTO tribunals may look for information from relevant sources in line with DSU
Article 13.[31] The ICSID Arbitration Rules and UNCITRAL Transparency Rules set
out criteria for *amicus* submissions and IIA provisions on *amicus* submissions often
reflect these rules. Criteria may include that submissions assist the Tribunal, are
within the scope of the dispute, come from parties with a significant interest in the
arbitration, and that there is a public interest in the subject-matter of the arbitration.[32]

Transparency in Proceedings

Articles that provide for transparency in proceedings featured in 31/60 PTIAs
(51.66%) and 8/60 BITs (13.33%) in this study. This is a further example of a

---

Fund; (c) shall avoid unnecessary damage to the commercial, economic and financial interests of
any other Member; (d) shall not exceed those necessary to deal with the circumstances described in
paragraph 1; (e) shall be temporary and be phased out progressively as the situation specified in
paragraph 1 improves."

[31] Article 13: Right to Seek Information: "1. Each panel shall have the right to seek information and
technical advice from any individual or body which it deems appropriate. However, before a panel
seeks such information or advice from any individual or body within the jurisdiction of a Member it
shall inform the authorities of that Member. A Member should respond promptly and fully to any
request by a panel for such information as the panel considers necessary and appropriate. Confidential information which is provided shall not be revealed without formal authorization from the
individual, body, or authorities of the Member providing the information. 2. Panels may seek
information from any relevant source and may consult experts to obtain their opinion on certain
aspects of the matter. With respect to a factual issue concerning a scientific or other technical matter
raised by a party to a dispute, a panel may request an advisory report in writing from an expert
review group. Rules for the establishment of such a group and its procedures are set forth in Annex
4."

[32] See for example Article 836.4 Canada-Peru FTA (2008). This can be compared to the lengthier
Article 831 of the Canada-Colombia FTA (2008), including Annex 831.

provision that harmonises procedural rules between the regimes. Transparency has been a major concern for critics of the investment regime since the early 2000s.[33] The fact that WTO dispute settlement hearings have taken place behind closed doors has also led to doubts among certain civil society groups about the unbiased and fair nature of proceedings.[34] At the WTO, only recently have some hearings been opened to the general public via delayed broadcast at the request of the participants.[35]

For the purpose of this study, ISDS proceedings are deemed transparent if: (1) certain key documents have to be made available to the public, including awards and party submissions; and (2) hearings are open to the public. A typical phrasing of an article providing for transparency in investment disputes is found in the Colombia-US FTA (2006):

> 1. Subject to paragraphs 2 and 4, the respondent shall, after receiving the following documents, promptly transmit them to the non-disputing Parties and make them available to the public: . . .(b) the notice of arbitration; (c) pleadings, memorials, and briefs submitted to the tribunal by a disputing party. . .(e) orders, awards, and decisions of the tribunal.

> 2. The tribunal shall conduct hearings open to the public and shall determine, in consultation with the disputing parties, the appropriate logistical arrangements. However, any disputing party that intends to use information designated as protected information in a hearing shall so advise the tribunal. The tribunal shall make appropriate arrangements to protect the information from disclosure.[36]

Avoidance of Any Conflict of Interest for Arbitrators

Articles providing for the avoidance of a conflict of interest for arbitrators featured in 28/60 PTIAs (46.66%) and 11/60 BITs (18.33%) in this study. WTO procedural rules also seek to avoid any conflict of interest for tribunal members as provided for in DSU Article 8.2 and Article 17.3.[37] Inter-regime engagement is facilitated where procedural rules such as these are harmonised between the two regimes.

Under IIAs, conflict of interest provisions may be given a simple formulation such as in the Canada-Côte d'Ivoire BIT (2014). Article 25.2 provides that arbitrators "shall be independent of, and not be affiliated with or take instructions from, a Party." Variations on these provisions include allowing the parties to waive the

---

[33] Bonnitcha et al. (2017), p. 248.

[34] Ehring (2008), p. 1023.

[35] See for example, WTO website 'Registration opens for public viewing of oral hearing in "US — Tax Incentives" appeal': https://www.wto.org/english/news_e/news17_e/hear_ds487_16jun17_e. htm (last accessed 28 April 2021).

[36] Colombia-US FTA (2006), Article 10.21: Transparency of Arbitral Proceedings.

[37] DSU Article 8.2: "Panel members should be selected with a view to ensuring the independence of the members, a sufficiently diverse background and a wide spectrum of experience."

DSU Article 17.3: "The Appellate Body shall comprise persons of recognized authority, with demonstrated expertise in law, international trade and the subject matter of the covered agreements generally. They shall be unaffiliated with any government. (. . .) They shall not participate in the consideration of any disputes that would create a direct or indirect conflict of interest."

conflict of interest requirement for a potential arbitrator or stipulating that a "usual place of residence" is sufficient for an arbitrator to be deemed to be affiliated to a party.[38]

There appears to be a trend of these provisions becoming more detailed and stringent over time. EUSIPA Article 3.11 provides that tribunal members shall be chosen amongst persons "whose independence is beyond doubt" and they shall refrain from "acting as counsel, party-appointed expert or party-appointed witness in any pending or new investment protection dispute under this or any other agreement or domestic law."

Reference to Arbitrators' Knowledge of International Law or International Trade Law

Articles referring to an arbitrator's knowledge of public international law or international trade law featured in 19/60 PTIAs (31.66%) and 11/60 BITs (18.33%) surveyed as part of this study. This provision was chosen as it explicitly recognises that the IIA in question is part of the wider context of public international law and that tribunals are required to resolve disputes in accordance with applicable rules of international law. These applicable rules of international law include Article 31.3 (c) of the VCLT, which provides for the taking into account of "any relevant rules of international law applicable in the relations between the parties".

Provisions that require tribunal members to have knowledge of international trade law acknowledge the proximity of the regimes, the overlaps in certain norms, and the potential for lessons to be drawn from the other regime. As such, the inclusion of these references may be an expression of the desire of the parties for the possibility of trade principles to be included in the analysis of the chapter's provisions. The obvious implication of including arbitrators with knowledge of trade law is that this knowledge may be useful when deciding disputes and considering norms that overlap between the two regimes under the agreement.

A typical example of the phrasing of a provision referring to arbitrators' knowledge of public international law and/or international trade law is found in the Colombia-Singapore BIT (2013): "5. Arbitrators shall: (a) have experience or expertise in public international law, international trade law or international investment law".[39]

Variations on these provisions include the requirement that arbitrators have experience of "the resolution of disputes arising under international trade or

---

[38] E.g. Article 106.9 of the Japan-Thailand BIT (2007) provides: "Unless the disputing parties agree otherwise, the third arbitrator shall not be of the same nationality as the disputing investor, nor be a national of the disputing Party, nor have his or her usual place of residence in the Area of either of the Parties, nor be employed by either of the disputing parties at the time of his or her appointment."

[39] This is a translation from the original Spanish, which states: "5. Los árbitros deberán: (a) tener experiencia o experticia en derecho internacional publico, Derecho Comercial Internacional o derecho internacional de las inversiones".

international investment agreements"[40] or expertise in the specific subject matter of the dispute.[41] Such a formulation broadens the field of potential arbitrators for disputes and includes expertise of international trade law where this would be relevant to the dispute.

Provision Providing for an Appellate Mechanism or Contemplating One

Articles providing for the addition of an appellate mechanism featured in 19/60 PTIAs (31.66%) and 0/60 BITs surveyed as part of this study. Appellate mechanisms have great potential to facilitate engagement between the regimes. Engagement was defined as encompassing parallels in the *features* of tribunals and the addition of appellate mechanisms pushes the regimes in this direction. Appellate mechanisms increase the parallels in the institutional features of tribunals (despite the current paralysis of the WTO's Appellate Body), which encompass the rules and procedures of the two regimes.[42] The appellate mechanism of the EU's Investment Court System is modelled on the WTO's appeal system and the European Commission has described it as "operating on similar principles to the WTO Appellate Body".[43]

Of the 19 IIAs in this study containing provisions contemplating the establishment of an appellate mechanism, ten contain wording that closely resembles Article 28.10 of the United States Model BIT (2004). Nine of these contain either the

---

[40] See Article 9.21.2 of the Korea-Vietnam FTA (2015).

[41] Article 30.4 of the Colombia-Japan BIT (2011). "In appointing the arbitrators, the disputing parties consider that arbitrators of a Tribunal should have expertise and competence in the fields of international public law, the law on foreign investment or the subject-matters of the investment dispute arisen between the disputing parties."

[42] The similarities between the appeal mechanisms of the trade and investment regimes, whether there is a case for greater similarities between these mechanisms, and the role of PTIAs in this regard, is explored in greater detail in Chap. 5.

[43] European Commission—Press release: Commission proposes new Investment Court System for TTIP and other EU trade and investment negotiations, Brussels, 16 September 2015: http://europa.eu/rapid/press-release_IP-15-5651_en.htm.

United States or Peru as a party.[44] Other provisions specify timelines for the commencement of negotiations for the establishment of an appellate mechanism.[45]

A further type of provision in this area is that found in CPTPP (2018), which emphasises transparency of proceedings before any appellate mechanism.[46] This structure is replicated in the Australia-Peru FTA (2018).

Three IIAs in this study provide for the establishment of an appellate mechanism, including CETA, EUSIPA and EUVIPA. The EU's ICS marks a move away from ISDS and introduces a system with a permanent roster of tribunal members with the necessary qualifications for appointment to judicial office.[47] Recent EU Agreements provide for bilateral appellate tribunals and that the parties shall pursue a "multilateral investment tribunal and appellate mechanism for the resolution of investment

---

[44] The US is party to five of these Agreements, and Peru is party to the other four, all of which were concluded subsequent to the Peru-US FTA (2006). The Argentina-Chile FTA (2017) is also included but the wording here is slightly different.

See United States Model BIT (2004), Article 28.10: "If a separate, multilateral agreement enters into force between the Parties that establishes an appellate body for purposes of reviewing awards rendered by tribunals constituted pursuant to international trade or investment arrangements to hear investment disputes, the Parties shall strive to reach an agreement that would have such appellate body review awards rendered under Article 34 in arbitrations commenced after the multilateral agreement enters into force between the Parties."

Another agreement includes the Taiwan-Nicaragua FTA (2006), which Nicaragua concluded less than 2 years after signing CAFTA-DR (2004), to which the US is a party.

[45] Article 9.23 of Australia-China FTA (2015) provides: "Appellate Review: Within three years after the date of entry into force of this Agreement, the Parties shall commence negotiations with a view to establishing an appellate mechanism to review awards rendered under Article 9.22 in arbitrations commenced after any such appellate mechanism is established. Any such appellate mechanism would hear appeals on questions of law."

The Canada-Korea FTA provides that the parties "shall consider whether to establish a bilateral appellate body" within three years. It provides for a "bilateral appellate body or similar mechanism". Annex 8-E, Possibility of a Bilateral Appellate Mechanism provides. The Canada-Korea FTA (2014) was concluded in the aftermath of the Korea-US FTA (2007). It contemplates setting up an appellate mechanism but with different wording to KORUS. Canada-Korea FTA (2014), Annex 8-E: "Within three years after the date this Agreement enters into force, the Parties shall consider whether to establish a bilateral appellate body or similar mechanism to review awards rendered pursuant to Article 8.42 in arbitrations commenced after they establish the appellate body or similar mechanism." The wording of the Australia-China FTA (2015) provision is similar to that of the Canada-Korea FTA. The Australia-United States FTA (2004) entered into force in 2005 but didn't contain a provision contemplating an appellate mechanism.

[46] CPTPP Article 9.23.11: "In the event that an appellate mechanism for reviewing awards rendered by investor-State dispute settlement tribunals is developed in the future under other institutional arrangements, the Parties shall consider whether awards rendered under Article 9.29 (Awards) should be subject to that appellate mechanism. The Parties shall strive to ensure that any such appellate mechanism they consider adopting provides for transparency of proceedings similar to the transparency provisions established in Article 9.24 (Transparency of Arbitral Proceedings)."

[47] See CETA Article 8.27.4: "The Members of the Tribunal shall possess the qualifications required in their respective countries for appointment to judicial office, or be jurists of recognised competence. They shall have demonstrated expertise in public international law. It is desirable that they have expertise in particular, in international investment law, in international trade law and the resolution of disputes arising under international investment or international trade agreements."

disputes".[48] As seen with the US Model BIT, where influential actors on push for the inclusion of provisions such as these, they can propagate and be included in the agreements of other parties.

A final variation includes the Central America-Korea FTA (2018), which succinctly states "The Parties by mutual agreement may consider whether to establish a bilateral appellate body or similar mechanism to review awards rendered under Article 9.27."[49]

Provision Providing for Review of Dispute Settlement

Articles providing for the review of dispute settlement featured in 60/60 PTIAs and 37/60 BITs (61.66%) surveyed as part of this study. These provisions often provide formal mechanisms that have the potential to bring about greater parallels in the features and practices of tribunals. These provisions may also be used to decrease engagement or entrench the separation of the regimes where the parties reconsider their treaty obligations.[50]

Some Agreements provide for the establishment of a Committee on Investment with functions including the ability "to review the implementation of this Chapter" and to "consider any other matters related to this Chapter".[51] Canadian Agreements tend to specify the powers of the Committee. For example, Article 824.2 of the Canada-Peru BIT (2006) states: "The Commission shall have the power to make rules supplementing the applicable arbitral rules and may amend any rules of its own making. Such rules shall be binding on a Tribunal established under this Section, and on individual arbitrators serving on such a Tribunal."[52] Recent Agreements often make it easier for review of dispute settlement by the parties through the creation of formal mechanisms for this process.

The final provisions of IIAs often contain a provision for agreeing amendments to them. These are counted as providing for review of dispute settlement. An example of such a provision is Article 24.02 of the Taiwan-Nicaragua FTA (2006), which states, "The Parties may agree on any amendment or addition to this Agreement." At the WTO, Article X of the Marrakesh Agreement concerns Amendments.[53]

---

[48] See e.g. CETA Article 8.28 and 8.29.

[49] Central America-Korea FTA (2018), Article 9.21.10.

[50] Where parties have renegotiated the content of IIAs, it has been found that these renegotiated agreements tend to leave host governments with less regulatory space than the initial agreements. See Broude et al. (2018), p. 14.

[51] AANZFTA, Chapter 11, Article 17.3 (b) & (c).

[52] See also Article 10.23.2 of the Canada-Honduras FTA (2013), and Article 822.2 of the Canada-Colombia FTA (2008).

[53] Marrakesh Agreement, Article X: "1. Any Member of the WTO may initiate a proposal to amend the provisions of this Agreement or the Multilateral Trade Agreements in Annex 1 by submitting such proposal to the Ministerial Conference. The Councils listed in paragraph 5 of Article IV may also submit to the Ministerial Conference proposals to amend the provisions of the corresponding

Reference to 'Applicable Rules of International Law'

Articles referring to 'Applicable rules of international law' as governing the agreement featured in 37/60 PTIAs (61.66%) and 26/60 BITs (43.33%) in this study. Such provisions facilitate engagement by recognising that investment agreements are situated within the wider context of international law and requiring tribunals to resolve disputes in accordance with the applicable rules. They provide for the possibility of principles of international law to be included in the analysis of the chapter's provisions.

These provisions typically provide that disputes should be decided in accordance with the text of the Agreement and rules of international law, while maintaining the right of the parties to give authoritative interpretations on provisions.[54] These applicable rules of international law include customary international law, general principles of law, and customary rules of interpretation of international law.[55]

Even where IIAs omit such references to international law, tribunals may turn to public international law where the meaning of terms is not sufficiently clear.[56] However, where such recognition is made, it facilitates cross-regime references, recognises the proximity of the regimes, the overlaps in certain norms, and the potential for lessons to be drawn from the other regime. This is particularly the case where WTO law is explicitly mentioned. This is the case in the Rules of Interpretation for EUVIPA, which state that the panel shall take into account "any relevant interpretation established in rulings of the WTO Dispute Settlement Body".[57]

Multilateral Trade Agreements in Annex 1 the functioning of which they oversee. Unless the Ministerial Conference decides on a longer period, for a period of 90 days after the proposal has been tabled formally at the Ministerial Conference any decision by the Ministerial Conference to submit the proposed amendment to the Members for acceptance shall be taken by consensus. Unless the provisions of paragraphs 2, 5 or 6 apply, that decision shall specify whether the provisions of paragraphs 3 or 4 shall apply. If consensus is reached, the Ministerial Conference shall forthwith submit the proposed amendment to the Members for acceptance. If consensus is not reached at a meeting of the Ministerial Conference within the established period, the Ministerial Conference shall decide by a two-thirds majority of the Members whether to submit the proposed amendment to the Members for acceptance. Except as provided in paragraphs 2, 5 and 6, the provisions of paragraph 3 shall apply to the proposed amendment, unless the Ministerial Conference decides by a three-fourths majority of the Members that the provisions of paragraph 4 shall apply."

[54] See for example, Chile-Japan EPA (2007), Article 93: Governing Law "1. Subject to paragraph 2, when a claim is submitted to arbitration under this Section, a Tribunal shall decide the issues in dispute in accordance with this Agreement and applicable rules of international law."

[55] E.g. VCLT Article 31.3(c), which provides for the taking into account of "any relevant rules of international law applicable in the relations between the parties".

[56] Sacerdoti (2004), pp. 24–25.

[57] EU-Vietnam IPA Article 3.21 Rules of Interpretation: "The arbitration panel shall interpret the provisions referred to in Article 3.2 (Scope) in accordance with customary rules of interpretation of public international law, including those codified in the Vienna Convention on the Law of Treaties, done at Vienna on 23 May 1969 (hereinafter referred to as the "Vienna Convention"). The arbitration panel shall also take into account relevant interpretations in reports of panels and of the Appellate Body adopted by the Dispute Settlement Body under Annex 2 of the WTO Agreement

Ability of the Parties to Issue Binding Interpretations of the Agreement

Articles that give the parties the authority to issue 'binding interpretations' of IIA provisions featured in 40/60 PTIAs and 8/60 BITs (13.33%) surveyed as part of this study. This has the potential to impact upon engagement between the trade and investment regimes as the parties can use such interpretations to encourage (or discourage) interpretations that facilitate inter-regime engagement. Binding interpretations may then influence a tribunal's readiness to look to the other regime when interpreting the provisions of an agreement.

Interpretations of IIAs may be given in line with provisions such as CPTPP Article 27.2.2: "The Commission may: . . .(f) issue interpretations of the provisions of this Agreement." Interpretations of the WTO Agreement may be made under Article IX:2 of the Marrakesh Agreement on 'Decision-Making', which sets out the authority to adopt interpretations.[58]

In practice, binding interpretations of IIAs are rare.[59] The NAFTA Free Trade Commission (FTC) issued a binding interpretation on 31 July 2001 in response to what it considered to be an expansive interpretation of the Fair and Equitable Treatment standard in *Pope & Talbot v. Canada*.[60] The tribunal had found that the fairness element of FET adds to the minimum standard of treatment. The FTC then issued its interpretation equating the two standards. Newcombe notes that although tribunals have accepted this binding interpretation, the approach has been criticised with claimants arguing that the interpretation amounted to an unauthorised amendment to NAFTA and was therefore beyond the FTC's authority.[61] The scope of the

---

(hereinafter referred to as "DSB"). The reports and rulings of the arbitration panel cannot add to or diminish the rights and obligations of the Parties provided for in this Agreement."

See also EU-Singapore IPA, Article 3.42 Rules of Interpretation: "The arbitration panel shall interpret the provisions referred to in Article 3.25 (Scope) in accordance with customary rules of interpretation of public international law, including those codified in the Vienna Convention on the Law of Treaties. Where an obligation under this Agreement is identical to an obligation under the WTO Agreement, the arbitration panel shall take into account any relevant interpretation established in rulings of the WTO Dispute Settlement Body (hereinafter referred to as "DSB"). The rulings of the arbitration panel cannot add to or diminish the rights and obligations provided in the provisions referred to in Article 3.25 (Scope)."

[58] On binding interpretations, see the Appellate Body Reports for *US-Clove-Cigarettes* pages 91–93 and *US-Gambling* para 211.

Article IX: 2: The Ministerial Conference and the General Council shall have the exclusive authority to adopt interpretations of this Agreement and of the Multilateral Trade Agreements. In the case of an interpretation of a Multilateral Trade Agreement in Annex 1, they shall exercise their authority on the basis of a recommendation by the Council overseeing the functioning of that Agreement. The decision to adopt an interpretation shall be taken by a three-fourths majority of the Members. This paragraph shall not be used in a manner that would undermine the amendment provisions in Article X.

[59] Gáspar-Szilágyi and Usynin (2020), p. 49. The authors note that these powers tend to be underused and may politicise disputes.

[60] Newcombe and Paradell (2009), p. 273.

[61] See Newcombe and Paradell (2009), pp. 272–274.

minimum standard of treatment remains ambiguous however and the tribunal in *Saluka v. Czech Republic* noted that any differences between them "may well be more apparent than real".[62]

Szilard and Usynin conclude that binding interpretations may lead to some convergence between the regimes due to the "interpretive function of treaty bodies" such as Joint Committees.[63] Where committees are responsible for entire agreements, it can be argued that this "might lead to more coherence and convergence in the implementation and interpretation of these rules when they are handled under one institutional roof".[64]

2.2.2.3 Substantive Provisions

The eight IIA provisions coded under this heading include those relating to: (a) national treatment; (b) MFN treatment; (c) likeness; (d) less favourable treatment; (e) fair and equitable treatment; (f) FET with a reference to customary international law; (g) expropriation; (h) the free transfer of funds. Some additional norms are then considered.

National Treatment

National treatment provisions aim to ensure that products, services, investments and items of intellectual property are not discriminated against once they have crossed a border. It is a relative standard whereby the treatment afforded to investors and foreign exporters is compared to that given to their domestic competitors.

A national treatment provision featured in all of the PTIAs and 58/60 BITs (96.66%) surveyed as part of this study. National treatment is a shared legal obligation of the trade and investment law regimes and it is the second most common provision to feature in this study.

The China-Portugal BIT (2005) contains a simple phrasing of a national treatment provision: "Each Party shall accord to investments and activities associated with such investments by the investors of the other Party treatment no less favourable than

---

[62] *Saluka Investments B.V. v. The Czech Republic*, UNCITRAL, Partial Award (2006) para 291: "Whatever the merits of this controversy between the parties may be, it appears that the difference between the Treaty standard laid down in Article 3.1 and the customary minimum standard, when applied to the specific facts of a case, may well be more apparent than real. To the extent that the case law reveals different formulations of the relevant thresholds, an in-depth analysis may well demonstrate that they could be explained by the contextual and factual differences of the cases to which the standards have been applied."

[63] Gáspar-Szilágyi and Usynin (2020), p. 47.

[64] Ibid 48.

that which it accords to the investments and associated activities by its own investors."[65]

Within PTIAs, national treatment provisions may feature across a variety of chapters. For example, in the China-Korea FTA (2014), a national treatment provision provided substantive rights for parties in four chapters including those on Market Access For Goods (2), Trade In Services (8), Financial Services (9), and Investment (12). It may also feature in Chapters on Intellectual Property.[66] Unlike MFN provisions, national treatment provisions tend not to be subject to exceptions for RTAs, tax matters etc. as the context often doesn't necessitate such exceptions.

Most-Favoured-Nation Treatment

Most-favoured-nation (MFN) treatment and national treatment are the two core standards that aim to ensure non-discrimination in international trade and investment law. MFN treatment is a relative standard involving comparisons with domestic counterparts to ensure non-discriminatory treatment. MFN provisions are a shared legal norm of the trade and investment law regimes. Such shared provisions represents common ground between the two regimes and facilitate inter-regime engagement by tribunals.

The MFN standard featured in 55/60 PTIAs (91.66%) and 58/60 BITs (96.66) surveyed as part of this study. As well as featuring in the vast majority of the agreements in this study, MFN provisions have been the subject of much litigation at the WTO and under IIAs. Tribunals have used MFN provisions to import provisions from other treaties, which may also facilitate inter-regime engagement. The potential for such engagement as a result of MFN provisions is even clearer where no exception for dispute settlement is contained in the MFN provision.

Some MFN provisions combine MFN and national treatment in a single provision,[67] while others are standalone.[68] MFN provisions are frequently subject to exceptions. Article 12.4 of the China-Korea FTA provides exceptions for Regional Trade Agreements, dispute settlement in other investment agreements, as well as

---

[65] China-Portugal BIT (2005), Article 3.2 (Treatment of Investment).

[66] E.g. Canada-Korea FTA (2014) Article 16.6.

[67] E.g. Article 4.2 of the Jordan-Thailand BIT (2005) (Treatment of Investments) "Each Contracting Party shall in its territory accord investors of the other Contracting Party, as regards management, maintenance, use, enjoyment or disposal of their investments, treatment not less favourable than that which it accords to its own investors or investors of any third State, whichever is more favourable."

[68] E.g. Article 12.4 of the China-Korea FTA (2015): "1. Each Party shall in its territory accord to investors of the other Party and to covered investments treatment no less favourable than that it accords in like circumstances to investors of any non-Party and to their investments with respect to investment activities and the matters relating to the admission of investment in accordance with paragraph 2 of Article 12.2."

aviation, fisher and maritime matters.[69] These exceptions mean that the same treatment does not have to be extended to the other party where preferential treatment is accorded to a third party on the basis of such an arrangement. Taxation is another area that is frequently the subject of an exception in MFN provisions.

Although this study primarily focuses on MFN provisions within the investment chapters of PTIAs, MFN provisions may feature in a variety of other chapters in PTIAs. For example, in the Canada-Korea FTA (2014), an MFN provision featured in chapters including those on Market Access For Goods (2), Cross-Border Trade In Services (9) and Financial Services (10). To give an example of one such provision, the Trade in Services chapter of the India-Singapore FTA (2005) contains an MFN provision that allows the parties to request treatment no less favourable than that provided in any subsequent agreement with a non-Party on trade in services.[70] The EU-Singapore IPA (2018) does not contain a standard MFN provision but rather includes it as part of its "Compensation for Losses" Article.[71]

Like Circumstances

Likeness is a shared concept of the trade and investment law regimes. This concept is shared terrain for the regimes featuring in 59/60 PTIAs (98.33%), 31/60 BITs (51.66%), and across the WTO Agreements. Likeness is frequently interpreted by tribunals at the WTO and under IIAs and is a fertile ground for engagement between the two regimes. In IIAs, the concept of likeness appears in national treatment

---

[69] See Article 12.4 of the China-Korea FTA (2015): "2. Paragraph 1 shall not be construed so as to oblige a Party to extend to investors of the other Party and covered investments any preferential treatment resulting from its membership of: (a) any customs union, free trade area, monetary union, similar international agreement leading to such union or free trade area, or other forms of regional economic cooperation; (b) any international agreement or arrangement for facilitating small scale trade in border areas; or (c) any bilateral and multilateral international agreements involving aviation, fishery and maritime matters including salvage. 3. It is understood that the treatment accorded to investors of any non-Party and to their investments as referred to in paragraph 1 does not include treatment accorded to investors of any non-Party and to their investments by provisions concerning the settlement of investment disputes between a Party and investors of any non-Party that are provided for in other international agreements."

[70] India-Singapore FTA (2005): "Article 7.6: Review Of Most Favoured Nation Commitments: If, after this Agreement enters into force, a Party enters into any agreement on trade in services with a non-Party, it shall give consideration to a request by the other Party for the incorporation herein of treatment no less favourable than that provided under the aforesaid agreement. Any such incorporation should maintain the overall balance of commitments undertaken by each Party under this Agreement."

[71] Article 2.5.1: "Covered investors of one Party whose covered investments suffer losses owing to war or other armed conflict, revolution, a state of national emergency, revolt, insurrection or riot in the territory of the other Party shall be accorded by that Party, as regards restitution, indemnification, compensation or other settlement, treatment no less favourable than that accorded by that Party to its own investors *or to the investors of any third country*, whichever is more favourable to the covered investor concerned. (Emphasis added)

provisions, MFN provisions, and occasionally in other provisions such as dispute settlement provisions[72] and in relation to establishment rights.[73] To establish a breach of many national treatment and MFN clauses in trade and investment law, a complainant must show that their product, service or investment is receiving discriminatory treatment compared to a 'like' domestic producer, supplier of services, or investment. What constitutes 'likeness' varies across Agreements and regimes. While the GATT and GATS refer to like products and services, IIAs tend to refer to investors 'in like circumstances'.[74] Interpretations of likeness depend on the wording of provisions and the context of the agreement as a whole. As such, tribunals must be careful when looking to interpretations of the standard under other agreements.

All 90 of the Agreements in this study containing the concept of likeness feature it in a non-discrimination provision. In relation to likeness, the wordings of these provisions tend to be quite homogenous referring to the obligation to treat investors of the other Party no less favourably than the treatment accorded 'in like circumstances' to its own investors or to the investors of any non-Party.

Less Favourable Treatment

Typically, the second requirement for demonstrating breach of national treatment or MFN treatment is to show that a good, service or investment has received less favourable treatment compared to their domestic counterpart(s).

While a likeness test is often contained in the wording of these provisions, less favourable treatment is nearly always contained in agreements across the trade and investment law regimes. The concept of less favourable treatment featured in 60/60 PTIAs and 59/60 BITs (98.33%) in this study, making it the single most common

---

[72] Article 20 of the Korea-EFTA FTA (2005) provides an example of a test for like circumstances outside of non-discrimination provisions. The Agreement incorporates an exceptions clause, which draws strongly on the construction of GATT Article XX. The chapeau of the article is identical to that of GATT Article XX (mutatis mutandis) except instead of prohibiting discrimination "between countries where the same conditions prevail", it prohibits discrimination "between States where like conditions prevail" (as opposed to 'between countries where the same conditions prevail' under GATT Article XX).

[73] A second example of an atypical likeness test found in this study is found in Article II.2 of the St Vincent & the Grenadines-Taiwan BIT (2009) which grants establishment and acquisition rights "on a basis no less favourable than that which, in like circumstances, it permits such acquisition or establishment by: (a) its own investors or prospective investors; or (b) investors or prospective investors of any third state." Both the Korea-EFTA FTA (2005) and the St Vincent & the Grenadines-Taiwan BIT (2009) also contain the concept of likeness in non-discrimination provisions.

[74] E.g. Article 10.3.1 of the Peru-US FTA (2006) "Each Party shall accord to investors of another Party treatment no less favourable than that it accords, in like circumstances, to its own investors with respect to the establishment, acquisition, expansion, management, conduct, operation, and sale or other disposition of investments in its territory."

provision. What constitutes less favourable treatment varies across agreements and the regimes despite its largely homogenous wording.

GATT Article III and GATS Article XVII refer to the obligation to accord 'treatment no less favourable' than [each Member] accords to its own services etc. Similarly, IIAs often state that the Parties shall accord 'treatment no less favourable' than it accords, in like circumstances, to its own investors.[75] IIAs occasionally give examples of what may constitute less favourable treatment under national treatment and MFN provisions.[76]

Fair and Equitable Treatment

The standard of fair and equitable treatment (FET) is widespread in investment agreements and featured in 57/60 PTIAs (95%) and 57/60 BITs in this study. Fair and equitable treatment is an absolute standard meaning investors do not need to seek a comparator to show breach of an Agreement.

Article 4.1 of the Bahrain-Mexico BIT (2012) is an example of a typical phrasing of the FET standard in an investment treaty: "4.1. Each Contracting Party shall accord to investments of investors of the other Contracting Party treatment in accordance with customary international law, including fair and equitable treatment and full protection and security. 2. For greater certainty: (a) the concepts of "fair and equitable treatment" and "full protection and security" do not require treatment in addition to or beyond that which is required by the customary international law minimum standard of treatment of aliens".

The drafting of FET provisions varies considerably across IIAs with some agreements including it as an independent standard while others provide for FET as part of the minimum standard of treatment. As seen above, articles may pair the FET standard with other standards, such as 'full protection and security'. The FET standard is often contained in a provision concerning the 'Minimum Standard of Treatment'.

The relationship between FET and the minimum standard of treatment can be a complicated one. Uncertainty as to the scope of FET led to the NAFTA Free Trade

---

[75] E.g. Australia-Chile FTA (2008), Article 10.3.1 (National Treatment): "Each Party shall accord to investors of the other Party treatment no less favourable than that it accords, in like circumstances, to its own investors with respect to the establishment, acquisition, expansion, management, conduct, operation, and sale or other disposition of investments in its territory."

[76] Article 3(2) of the Germany-Pakistan BIT (2009) gives the following examples, which are subject to several public policy exceptions: "The following shall, in particular be deemed 'treatment less favorable': unequal treatment in the case of restrictions on the purchase of raw or auxiliary materials; of energy or fuel or of means of production or operation of any kind, unequal treatment in the case of impeding the marketing of products inside or outside the country, as well as any other measures having similar effects. Measures that have to be taken for reasons of public security and order, public health or morality shall not be deemed 'treatment less favorable'."

Commission issuing a binding interpretation of NAFTA Article 1105 equating FET with the minimum standard of the treatment.

The scope of the terms 'fair', 'equitable' and 'treatment' can be ambiguous when no other guidance is offered to tribunals. Article 2.4 of the EU-Singapore Investment Protection Agreement (2018) gives considerable guidance to tribunals in relation to some of the key interpretative questions surrounding FET.[77] This Article elucidates

---

[77] Article 2.4 Standard of Treatment: "1. Each Party shall accord in its territory to covered investments of the other Party fair and equitable treatment[1] and full protection and security in accordance with paragraphs 2 to 6. 2. A Party breaches the obligation of fair and equitable treatment referenced in paragraph 1 if its measure or series of measures constitute: (a) denial of justice[2] in criminal, civil and administrative proceedings; (b) a fundamental breach of due process; (c) manifestly arbitrary conduct; (d) harassment, coercion, abuse of power or similar bad faith conduct. 3. In determining whether the fair and equitable treatment obligation, as set out in paragraph 2, has been breached, a Tribunal may take into account, where applicable, whether a Party made specific or unambiguous representations[3] to an investor so as to induce the investment, that created legitimate expectations of a covered investor and which were reasonably relied upon by the covered investor, but that the Party subsequently frustrated[4]. 4. The Parties shall, upon request of a Party or recommendations by the Committee, review the content of the obligation to provide fair and equitable treatment, pursuant to the procedure for amendments set out in Article 4.3 (Amendments), in particular, whether treatment other than those listed in paragraph 2 can also constitute a breach of fair and equitable treatment. 5. For greater certainty, "full protection and security" only refers to a Party's obligation relating to physical security of covered investors and investments. 6. Where a Party, itself or through any entity mentioned in paragraph 7 of Article 1.2 (Definitions), had given a specific and clearly spelt out commitment in a contractual written obligation[5] towards a covered investor of the other Party with respect to the covered investor's investment or towards such covered investment, that Party shall not frustrate or undermine the said commitment through the exercise of its governmental authority[6] either: (a) deliberately; or (b) in a way which substantially alters the balance of rights and obligation in the contractual written obligation unless the Party provides reasonable compensation to restore the covered investor or investment to a position which it would have been in had the frustration or undermining not occurred. 7. A breach of another provision of this Agreement, or of a separate international agreement, does not establish that there has been a breach of this Article."

---

[1] Treatment in this Article includes treatment of covered investors which directly or indirectly interferes with the covered investors' operation, management, conduct, maintenance, use, enjoyment and sale or other disposal of their covered investments.

[2] For greater certainty, the sole fact that the covered investor's claim has been rejected, dismissed or unsuccessful does not in itself constitute a denial of justice.

[3] For greater certainty, representations made so as to induce the investments include the representations made in order to convince the investor to continue with, not to liquidate or to make subsequent investments.

[4] For greater certainty, the frustration of legitimate expectations as described in this paragraph does not, by itself, amount to a breach of paragraph 2, and such frustration of legitimate expectations must arise out of the same events or circumstances that give rise to the breach of paragraph 2.

[5] For the purposes of this paragraph, a "contractual written obligation" means an agreement in writing, entered into by a Party, itself or through any entity mentioned in paragraph 7 of Article 1.2 (Definitions), with a covered investor or a covered investment whether in a single instrument or multiple instruments, that creates an exchange of rights and obligations, binding both parties.

[6] For the purposes of this Article, a Party frustrates or undermines a commitment through the exercise of its governmental authority when it frustrates or undermines the said commitment

on the meaning of FET by setting out the types of measures that may result in a breach of FET and the factors a tribunal may take into account in determining whether there has been a breach.

While the FET standard does not have a direct trade law equivalent, it does impact upon engagement as it gives rise to considerations for tribunals in relation to shared legal concepts of the trade and investment law regimes. For example, a tribunal considering a case under Article 2.4 of the EU-Singapore Investment Protection Agreement could look at how concepts such as due process,[78] arbitrary conduct,[79] and legitimate expectations[80] have been dealt with in the trade regime.

Kurtz argues that the FET standard also has a "potential, albeit loose" commonality with WTO law in cases where a state relies on scientific inquiry in assessing risk regulation.[81] Unlike investment law, the WTO has advanced methodologies for dealing with claims based on scientific inquiry under the WTO's SPS Agreement.

Kurtz contends that certain types of measures could be examined using a science-based approach and that WTO law could be a useful comparator for investment tribunals in this respect.[82] Tribunals should offer a "structured, rigorous and process-driven methodology" when assessing breach and that a "baseline" that builds on WTO law would do just that.[83]

FET with a Reference to Customary International Law

The FET standard has been coupled with a reference to customary international law in many investment agreements including 47/60 PTIAs (78.33%) and 28/60 BITs (46.66%) in this study.

Some wordings, such as Article 4 of the Japan-Colombia BIT merely link FET to customary international law: "1. Each Contracting Party shall in its Area accord to investments of investors of the other Contracting Party treatment in accordance with customary international law, including fair and equitable treatment and full protection and security."

---

through the adoption, maintenance or non-adoption of measures mandatory or enforceable under domestic laws.

[78] WTO law has considerable jurisprudence on due process. See Cook (2015), Chapter 6: Due Process. Cook reports that "due process" has been referred to over 2300 times in 189 different WTO reports, awards and decisions (p. 107).

[79] What constitutes arbitrary conduct is considered in WTO law in areas such as the chapeau of GATT Article XX/GATS XIV which protects against measures applied in a manner which would constitute "arbitrary or unjustifiable discrimination".

[80] 'Legitimate expectations' were considered by the Panel and Appellate Body in *India-Patents (US)*. See AB Report para 45.

[81] Kurtz (2016), p. 137.

[82] Kurtz (2016), p. 144.

[83] Kurtz (2016), p.167.

Other wordings make it clear that the FET standard does not go beyond what is required under customary international law.[84] Article 11.5 on the Minimum Standard of Treatment in the Korea-US FTA (2007) makes this point clearly: "1. Each Party shall accord to covered investments treatment in accordance with customary international law, including fair and equitable treatment and full protection and security. 2. For greater certainty, paragraph 1 prescribes the customary international law minimum standard of treatment of aliens as the minimum standard of treatment to be afforded to covered investments. The concepts of 'fair and equitable treatment' and 'full protection and security' do not require treatment in addition to or beyond that which is required by that standard, and do not create additional substantive rights(. . .)."

Where such a reference to customary international law is made, it moves the FET standard away from the types of inquiries seen above (such as inquiries into due process, arbitrary conduct, and legitimate expectations) and towards the type of treatment investors can expect under customary international law. Interpretations under CIL may be narrower than those based on treaty obligations and reduce the scope for inter-regime engagement in the abovementioned areas. On the other hand, engagement may increase where interpretations under customary international law are of similar relevance to the trade regime (e.g. what constitutes an arbitrary measure).

Expropriation

Provisions protecting investors against expropriation are core elements that feature in the vast majority of investment agreements including 59/60 PTIAs (98.33%) and 59/60 BITs surveyed as part of this study.[85]

---

[84] E.g. Article 10.10 of the New Zealand-Malaysia FTA (2009) on the Minimum Standard of Treatment: "1. Each Party shall accord to covered investments fair and equitable treatment and full protection and security. 2. For greater certainty: (a) fair and equitable treatment requires each Party not to deny justice in any legal or administrative proceedings; (. . .) (c) the concepts of "fair and equitable treatment" and "full protection and security" do not require treatment in addition to or beyond that which is required under customary international law, and do not create additional substantive rights."

[85] Article 11 of the Japan-Iraq BIT (2012) is an example of a provision on Expropriation and Compensation: "1. Neither Contracting Party shall expropriate or nationalise investments in its Area of investors of the other Contracting Party or take any measure equivalent to expropriation or nationalisation (hereinafter referred to as "expropriation") except: (a) for a public purpose; (b) in a non-discriminatory manner; (c) upon payment of prompt, adequate and effective compensation pursuant to paragraphs 2, 3 and 4; and (d) in accordance with due process of law and Article 5. 2. The compensation shall be equivalent to the fair market value of the expropriated investments at the time when the expropriation was publicly announced or when the expropriation occurred, whichever is the earlier. The fair market value shall not reflect any change in value occurring because the expropriation had become publicly known earlier. 3. The compensation shall be paid without delay and shall include interest at a commercially reasonable rate, taking into account the length of time until the time of payment. It shall be readily realisable and freely transferable, and shall be freely

Expropriation is one of the fundamental protections provided in IIAs and exceptions in areas such as public health and the environment give rise to potential engagement between the regimes, given the wealth of jurisprudence in these areas in the trade regime.

Expropriation is not a shared legal norm of the trade and investment law regimes. However, similar to the Fair and Equitable Treatment standard, it has some analogues in the trade regime such as the requirements that expropriations be nondiscriminatory and in line with due process.[86]

Two of the provisions in the category of 'Host State Flexibilities' depend on there being an expropriation provision in the agreement. As seen above, an increasingly common feature of expropriation provisions is to include an exception for: (1) TRIPS compliant compulsory licences; and (2) measures taken in furtherance of public welfare objectives. It is on this basis that the inclusion of expropriation provisions is deemed to facilitate inter-regime engagement.

Claims for indirect expropriation often expand on the requirement that expropriations be carried out in the public interest and in the pursuit of a legitimate regulatory purpose.[87] Tribunals may find that certain measures are not expropriatory where they are designed and applied to protect legitimate public welfare objectives, such as health, safety and the environment.[88]

---

convertible into the currency of the Contracting Party of the investors concerned and into freely usable currencies, at the market exchange rate prevailing on the date of expropriation. 4. Without prejudice to the provisions of Article 17, the investors affected by expropriation shall have a right of access to the courts of justice or administrative tribunals or agencies of the Contracting Party making the expropriation to seek a prompt review of the investors' case and the amount of compensation in accordance with the principles set out in this Article."

[86] Expropriation law generally imposes four conditions: (1) it must be for a public purpose; (2) it must be nondiscriminatory; (3) it must be compensated with prompt, adequate and effective compensation; and (4) it must be conducted in line with due process.

[87] See FN21. FN21 states: Annex I, 3 of the Canada-Burkina Faso (2015) provides an example of the phrasing of an article providing a public welfare exception for indirect expropriation: "A non-discriminatory measure or series of measures of a Party designed and applied to protect legitimate public welfare objectives, such as health, safety and the environment, does not constitute indirect expropriation, except in rare circumstances, such as when a measure or a series of measures is so severe in the light of its purpose that it cannot be reasonably considered as having been adopted and applied in good faith."

[88] See FN22. FN22 states: Annex 9B(c)(ii) of the Korea-Peru FTA (2010) provides a non-exhaustive list of policy objectives that may justify expropriation: "Except in rare circumstances, such as, for example, when a measure or series of measures have an extremely severe or disproportionate effect in light of its purpose, non-discriminatory regulatory actions by a Party that are designed and applied to protect legitimate public welfare objectives, such as public health, safety, the environment, and real estate policy measures (for example, measures to improve the housing conditions for low-income households), do not constitute indirect expropriations[FN1]." The footnote states: "For greater certainty, the list of "legitimate public welfare objectives" in subparagraph (c)(ii) is not exhaustive."

Free Transfer of Funds

It is a fundamental concern for foreign investors that they are able to transfer funds relating to their investment into and out of host states. Provisions relating to the free transfer of funds are quite prevalent in IIAs and featured in 49/60 PTIAs (81.66%) and 58/60 BITs (96.66%) in this study.

Articles in early IIAs often provided for the unrestricted right to transfer funds. As seen above in the category 'Host State Flexibilities', many modern IIAs now contain capital withdrawal safeguard provisions that allow host states to restrict transfers in certain circumstances, such as in the case of balance of payments difficulties.

Such provisions are a shared legal norm with the trade law regime and have the potential to facilitate engagement between the trade and investment law regimes. The GATS requires the complete liberalisation of transfers and payments but for a few circumstances.[89] WTO Members can however impose restrictions on capital flows in the case of balance of payment difficulties or at the request of the IMF.[90] Any restrictions must comply with certain conditions, such as being carried out in a temporary and non-discriminatory manner.[91]

Article 6 of the Guatemala-Russia BIT (2013) is an example of a provision on the Free Transfer of Payments: "1. In accordance with the legislation of its State each Contracting Party shall guarantee to investors of the other Contracting Party a free transfer abroad of payments related to their investments, and shall include in particular: a) returns; b) funds in repayment of loans and credits recognized by both Contracting Parties as investments, as well as accrued interest; c) proceeds from the partial or full liquidation or sale of investments; d) compensation, indemnification or other settlements referred to in Articles 4 and 5 of the present Agreement; e) wages and other remunerations received by investor and nationals of the State of the latter Contracting Party who have the right to work in the territory of the State of the former Contracting Party in relation to the investments.

2. The transfer of payments referred to in paragraph 1 of this Article shall be made without undue delay in a freely convertible currency at the rate of exchange applicable on the date of the transfer pursuant to the foreign exchange legislation of the State of the Contracting Party in the territory of which the investments are made."

---

[89] GATS XI:1 provides that: "Except under the circumstances envisaged in Article XII, a Member shall not apply restrictions on international transfers and payments for current transactions relating to its specific commitments."

[90] GATS Article XI: 2. Article XII of the GATS allows for restrictions on capital flows in the case of "serious balance-of-payments and external financial difficulties or threat thereof".

[91] GATS Article XII: 2: "The restrictions referred to in paragraph 1: (a) shall not discriminate among Members; (b) shall be consistent with the Articles of Agreement of the International Monetary Fund; (c) shall avoid unnecessary damage to the commercial, economic and financial interests of any other Member; (d) shall not exceed those necessary to deal with the circumstances described in paragraph 1; (e) shall be temporary and be phased out progressively as the situation specified in paragraph 1 improves."

Articles covering free transfer of payments related to investments typically contain: (1) a list of items covered; and (2) that this be without undue delay in a freely convertible currency at the rate of exchange applicable on the date of the transfer. Additional elements may include: (1) exceptions allowing a delay where the host state is ensuring compliance with tax matters; and (2) an exception in the event of serious balance of payments difficulties, external financial difficulties, economic sanctions etc.

Additional Norms

As well as the above eight provisions, Annex 1 includes a ninth column in the 'substantive provisions' section recording any additional norm found in the sample of 120 IIAs that evidences engagement between the two regimes. These additional norms are not included in the data analysis of Sect. 2.3. Their prevalence across the IIAs in this study can however be seen in Annex 1.

Additional norms that evidence increased engagement between the trade and investment law regimes were found in 23/60 PTIAs (38%) and 15/60 BITs. These norms were not added to the empirical analysis as a study of 24 provisions split evenly into three categories was favoured. Further considerations included the fact that some of these provisions did not evidence engagement to the same extent as the 24 provisions included. Others were less prevalent or were only included in the agreements of a limited number of countries.

These additional norms found in the PTIAs and BITs of this study included provisions relating to: (1) references to TRIPS or (multilateral) intellectual property agreements outside of those mentioned in Sect. 2.2.2.1;[92] (2) the conformity of measures taken pursuant to decisions under Article IX and X of the WTO

---

[92] This group includes provisions referring to the permissibility of derogations from IIA obligations in a manner consistent with TRIPS, e.g. Article 10.9.4 of the Canada-Honduras FTA (2013): "In respect of intellectual property rights, a Party may derogate from Articles 10.4, (National Treatment) 10.5 (MFN Treatment) and subparagraph 1(f) of 10.7 (Performance Requirements - transfer technology) in a manner that is consistent with the TRIPS Agreement and with the waivers to the TRIPS Agreement adopted pursuant to Article IX of the WTO Agreement."

This group also includes provisions concerning the compliance of the IIA with TRIPS and other (multilateral) Intellectual Property Agreements, e.g. Article 9.12.4 of the Korea-Vietnam FTA (2015): "Nothing in this Chapter shall be construed to derogate from the rights and obligations under international agreements in respect of protection of intellectual property rights to which the Parties are party, including the TRIPS Agreement and other treaties concluded under the auspices of the World Intellectual Property Organization."

Other provisions include those on non-conforming measures referring to TRIPS, e.g. Article 12.7.3 of the Guatemala-Peru FTA (2011), articles excluding the extension of favourable treatment accorded through multilateral Intellectual Property Agreements, e.g. Article 22 on Intellectual Property Rights of the Japan-Peru BIT (2008), and articles providing that the agreement does not affect Intellectual Property Agreements already signed, e.g. Article 8.3 of the Libya-Spain BIT (2007).

Agreement;[93] (3) panels not being able to 'add to or subtract from' the parties' rights;[94] and (4) limiting commitments to WTO levels.[95]

2.3   Results

2.3.1   Results for the Entire Set of Agreements

Section 2.3 tests two hypotheses; the first is that PTIAs are increasing engagement between the trade and investment law regimes (H1) and the second is that engagement is increasing over time (H2).

H1:   **that PTIAs are increasing engagement between the trade and investment law regimes**

This section examines:

1. How frequently provisions that indicate engagement feature in PTIAs compared to BITs in the treaties examined (Fig. 2.1);
2. How many provisions indicating engagement feature on average in PTIAs compared to BITs for every year from 2005 to 2019 (Fig. 2.2);
3. How frequently provisions in the three categories of host state flexibility, dispute settlement, and substantive provisions occur each year from 2005 to 2019.

Figure 2.1 looks at the how often each of the 24 provisions featured across the sample of 60 PTIAs and 60 BITs.

Figure 2.1 shows that on average the PTIAs in this study contain more provisions that indicate engagement than the BITs.

---

[93] E.g. Article IX.8 of the Canada-Slovakia BIT (2010): "Any measure adopted by a Contracting Party in conformity with a decision adopted, extended or modified by the World Trade Organization pursuant to Articles IX:3 or IX:4 of the WTO Agreement shall be deemed to be also in conformity with this Agreement. An investor purporting to act pursuant to Article X (Settlement of Disputes between an Investor and the Host Contracting Party) of this Agreement may not claim that such a conforming measure is in breach of this Agreement."

[94] E.g. Article 64 on the 'Functions of Arbitral Panel' of the China-Pakistan FTA (2006), which is reminiscent of Article 3.2 of the WTO's DSU. Article 64 states: "The arbitral panel, in their findings and recommendations, cannot add to subtract from or alter the rights and obligations provided in this Agreement."

[95] E.g. Article 3.5 of the Guatemala-Russia BIT (2013): "Without prejudice to the provisions of Articles 4 (Expropriation), 5 (Compensation for Losses) and 8 (ISDS) of the present Agreement, neither of Contracting Parties is committed by the present Agreement to accord a treatment more favourable than the treatment granted by each Contracting Party in accordance with their obligations under the Marrakesh Agreement establishing the World Trade Organization (the WTO Agreement) signed on 15 April 1994, including the obligations of the General Agreement on Trade in Services (GATS), as well as in accordance with any other multilateral arrangements concerning the treatment of investments to which the State of the both Contracting Parties are parties."

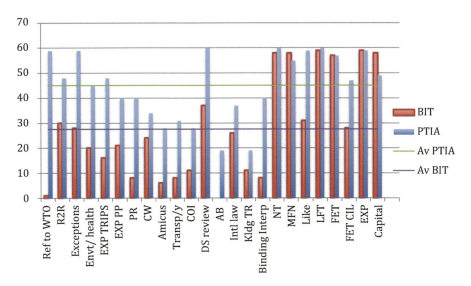

Fig. 2.1 Overview on how often each of the 24 provisions featured across the sample of 60 PTIAs and 60 BITs

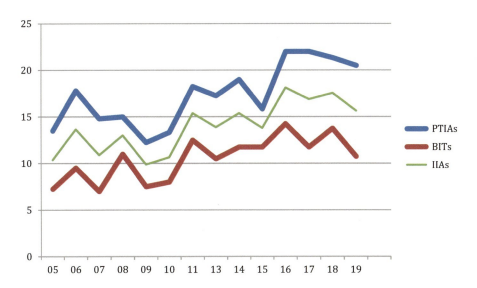

Fig. 2.2 Frequency of provisions evidencing engagement in PTIAs and BITs in the sample of IIAs for every year (except 2012) from 2005 to 2019

The average provision featured 45 times in the 60 PTIAs surveyed.

The average provision featured 27.6 times in the 60 BITs surveyed.

The following table shows how often provisions featured *on average* for the Agreements as a whole, as well as for the three main categories of provisions. It also

Table 2.1 Overview on how often provisions featured on average for the Agreements as a whole, as well as for the three main categories of provisions

	Agreements as a whole (/60)	Host State Flexibility (/60)	Dispute Settlement (/60)	Substantive Provisions (/60)
PTIAs	45 (75%)	46.75 (77.9%)	32.75 (47.85%)	55.75 (92.92%)
BITs	27.625 (46%)	18.5 (30.83%)	13.375 (22.29%)	51 (85%)
Percentage increase	62.9%	154%	144.8%	9.3%

shows the percentage increase in the frequency of provisions in PTIAs compared to BITs.

Table 2.1's first column shows an average of 63% more provisions evidencing engagement in PTIAs compared to BITs for the agreements as a whole.[96] There are significantly higher levels of engagement for host state flexibilities and dispute provisions, while there are marginal levels of increased engagement for substantive provisions.

Annex 1 also shows that the average PTIA contained 16.95 provisions evidencing engagement. The average BIT contained 10.55 provisions evidencing engagement.

Figure 2.2 looks at the frequency of provisions evidencing engagement in PTIAs and BITs in the sample of IIAs for every year (except 2012)[97] from 2005 to 2019.

Figure 2.2 shows that provisions indicating engagement are more frequent in PTIAs compared to BITs in the treaties examined for every year from 2005 to 2019.

H1:   as demonstrated in Figs. 2.1 and 2.2, and Tables 2.1, there is more evidence of engagement in PTIAs than in BITs for the set of agreements as a whole, as well as in each of the three main categories of provisions.

H2:   that engagement is increasing over time

This section considers whether there is increasing engagement in PTIAs compared to BITs over five periods of time. It does so by examining whether there are more provisions that evidence engagement in 2007–08 compared to 2005–06 (T2 compared to T1) etc. The time ranges were selected to ensure as even a distribution of IIAs for each time period as possible.

---

[96] As provisions evidencing engagement are 154% more frequent in category 1, and 144% more frequent in category 2, one might expect that the overall for the 3 categories would be greater than 63%. It must be remembered however, that the provisions in category 3 occurred with significantly greater frequency in the 120 Agreements of this study, as can be seen in Fig. 2.1, and as a result the percentage for the Agreements as a whole is lower than one might expect given the differences for categories 1 and 2.

[97] For the year 2012, there was no text available on the UNCTAD database at the time of the finalisation of this study for a PTIA containing an investment chapter with an investor-state dispute settlement mechanism.

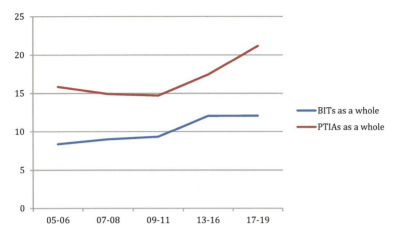

Fig. 2.3 Frequency of provisions evidencing engagement in PTIAs and BITs in the sample of IIAs for five time periods from 2005 to 2019

Table 2.2 Levels of Engagement for the three main categories of provisions in PTIAs compared to BITs over five periods of time

PTIAs	05–06	07–08	09–11	13–16	17–19	Overall increase from T1 to T5
Host state flexibilities	5.9	5.8	6.27	6.14	6.82	15.6%
Dispute settlement provisions	3.76	3.27	3.27	4.71	6.63	76%
Substantive provisions	7.23	7.63	7.27	7.42	7.7	6.5%
BITs	05–06	07–08	09–11	13–16	17–19	Overall increase from T1 to T5
Host state flexibilities	1	1.25	2.5	3.06	3.08	208%
Dispute settlement provisions	1.25	1.5	1.08	2.75	1.66	32.8%
Substantive provisions	6.375	6.5	6.66	6.875	7.25	13.7%

This section examines: (1) whether engagement is increasing over time in PTIAs and BITs for the agreements as a whole (Fig. 2.3); and (2) whether engagement is increasing over time in the three categories of host state flexibility, dispute settlement, and substantive provisions.

Figure 2.3 looks at the frequency of provisions evidencing engagement in PTIAs and BITs in the sample of IIAs for five time periods from 2005 to 2019.

Figure 2.3 shows a general but uneven trend of increasing engagement over time.

While engagement for PTIAs dipped marginally from T1 to T3 (8%), it increased significantly from T3 to T5 (44%). Engagement for BITs rose in each of the time periods, with an overall increase of 44% from T1 to T5.

Table 2.2 looks at the levels of engagement for the three main categories of provisions (host state flexibilities, dispute settlement, and substantive provisions) in PTIAs compared to BITs over five periods of time. It examines whether there are more of these provisions in 2007–08 compared to 2005–06 (T2 compared to T1) etc. The time ranges were selected to ensure as even a distribution of IIAs for each time period as possible. For the three categories, the average amount of provisions evidencing engagement is considered.

There is a higher prevalence of provisions that indicate engagement in PTIAs for all three categories and in all of the five time periods considered.

For the 15-year period, in terms of host state flexibilities, the average number of provisions per treaty is 6.2 for PTIAs and 2.42 for BITs.

For dispute settlement provisions, the average number of provisions per treaty is 4.33 for PTIAs and 1.78 for BITs

Finally, for substantive provisions, the average number of provisions per treaty is 7.45 for PTIAs and 6.8 for BITs.

H2:   as demonstrated in Fig. 2.3, there is a general trend of increasing engagement over time for both PTIAs and BITs. From T1 to T5, the frequency of provisions evidencing engagement increased by 33.7% for PTIAs and 44% for BITs.

2.3.2 Conclusions for the Entire Set of Agreements

This section demonstrated that there is more evidence of engagement in PTIAs than in BITs for the set of agreements as a whole, as well as in the three categories of provisions (Hypothesis 1).

Table 2.1 showed that there is an average of 63% more provisions evidencing engagement in PTIAs compared to BITs for the agreements as a whole. In terms of the three main types of provisions, there was 154% more provisions evidencing engagement for the category 'Host State Flexibility', 144% for the category 'Dispute Settlement' and 9% for the category 'Substantive Provisions'.

Figure 2.2 showed that there is a higher prevalence of provisions that indicate engagement in PTIAs compared to BITs in the treaties examined for every year from 2005 to 2019.

Hypothesis 2 was then tested and it was demonstrated that there is a general but uneven trend of increasing engagement over time.

Table 2.2 demonstrated that there is a higher prevalence of such provisions for each of the time periods across the three categories of provisions.

While engagement for PTIAs dipped marginally from T1 to T3 (8%), it increased significantly from T3 to T5 (44%). Engagement for BITs rose in each of the time periods, with an overall increase of 44% from T1 to T5.

2.3.3 Summary

There is a clear difference in the potential for engagement between older-style BITs that have an unmitigated focus on creating favourable conditions for investment and more recent PTIAs that directly refer to the WTO in their preamble, substantive obligations, exceptions, and dispute settlement provisions. This greater potential for engagement is borne out in the data for this sample of 60 BITs and 60 PTIAs.

This chapter tested two main hypotheses, including: (1) whether there is greater evidence of engagement between trade and investment in PTIAs than in BITs (H1); and (2) whether there is evidence of increasing engagement between the regimes over time (H2). Section 2.3.1 tested these hypotheses in relation to 24 provisions evidencing engagement between the regimes. For Hypothesis 1, it was demonstrated that there is more evidence of engagement in PTIAs than in BITs for the set of agreements as a whole, as well as in each of the three categories of provisions.

For Hypothesis 2, it was demonstrated that there is more evidence of engagement in T5 than in T1, for the agreements as a whole, and for each of the three categories of provisions. While the level of engagement decreased for certain periods (e.g. T1–T3 for PTIAs), there is a clear trend of increased engagement over time as evident in Fig. 2.3. Thus, for this study's sample at least, it can be concluded that there are greater levels of inter-regime engagement present in the PTIAs compared to the BITs.

References

Bonnitcha J, Poulsen LS, Waibel M (2017) The political economy of the investment regime. Oxford University Press, p 248

Broude T, Haftel Y, Thompson A (2018) Who cares about regulatory space in BITs? A comparative international law approach. In: Roberts A, Verdier P-H, Versteeg M, Stephan PB (eds) Comparative international law. Oxford University Press, p 14

Cook G (2015) A digest of WTO jurisprudence on public international law concepts and principles. Cambridge University Press

Ehring L (2008) Public access to dispute settlement hearings in the World Trade Organization. J Int Econ Law 11(4):1023

Gáspar-Szilágyi S, Usynin M (2020) Investment chapters in PTAs and their impact on adjudicative convergence. In: Behn D, Gáspár-Szilágyi S, Langford M (eds) Adjudicating trade and investment law: convergence or divergence? Cambridge University Press
Kaplan E, Rodrik D (2002) Did the Malaysian capital controls work? In: Edwards S, Frankel J (eds) Preventing currency crises in emerging markets. The University of Chicago Press for the NBER
Kurtz J (2016) The WTO and international investment law: converging systems. Cambridge University Press
Newcombe A, Paradell L (2009) Law and practice of investment treaties: standards of treatment. Kluwer Law International
Sacerdoti G (2004) Investment arbitration under ICSID and UNCITRAL rules: prerequisites, applicable law, review of awards. ICSID Rev 19(1):24–25

Part II
Substantive Provisions

Chapter 3
Nondiscrimination Provisions

The four standards of national treatment, MFN treatment, likeness, and less favourable treatment are presented in a single chapter here. This is because of their interconnected nature and the fact that conclusions concerning the interpretation of one of these standards may directly impact interpretations of another.

3.1 Introduction

Non-discrimination is a cornerstone of the trade and investment regimes and is expressed in the foundational concepts of national treatment and the Most-Favoured-Nation (MFN) principle. National treatment and MFN provisions aim to prevent nationality-based discrimination. National treatment aims to ensure imported products, services, items of intellectual property, investors and investments are not discriminated against vis-à-vis their domestic counterparts, while MFN obligations prohibit WTO Members and host states discriminating among these categories.[1] National treatment and MFN treatment are relative standards in that they compare the treatment given to foreign exporters and investors operating in the host state to the treatment afforded to their domestic counterparts.

Nondiscrimination is one of the main instruments of international economic law used in the pursuit of trade liberalisation. It serves both political and economic purposes, quelling tensions in international relations as well as preventing market inefficiencies.[2] In the trade context, nondiscrimination provisions aim to ensure that products and services, items of intellectual property are not discriminated against

---

[1] See, Van den Bossche (2008). Note: this is expressed slightly differently in the fourth edition (2017).
[2] See Diebold (2010), pp. 15–17.

© The Author(s), under exclusive license to Springer Nature Switzerland AG 2021
N. Moran, *Engagement Between Trade and Investment*, EYIEL Monographs -
Studies in European and International Economic Law 18,
https://doi.org/10.1007/978-3-030-83259-9_3

once they have crossed a border. These provisions aim to ensure that foreign products and services are treated no less favourably than their like domestic counterparts. In the investment context, nondiscrimination provisions aim to ensure that investors and investments are not discriminated against and are treated no less favourably than their like domestic counterparts.

Nondiscrimination provisions are shared legal obligations that feature prominently across the trade and investment law regimes. National treatment provisions were found in 118/120 treaties surveyed in Chap. 2, while MFN provisions featured in 113/120. Within PTIAs, nondiscrimination provisions may feature across a variety of chapters.[3] This chapter looks at the extent to which engagement[4] already exists between the two regimes in terms of nondiscrimination provisions, whether this should influence tribunals, and whether PTIAs have any kind of an impact on this engagement.

3.2 Nondiscrimination Provisions in the Trade and Investment Law Regimes

3.2.1 National Treatment

The stages in a national treatment claim are common to the trade and investment law regimes. There are typically four stages when a tribunal treats a claim under a national treatment provision. Firstly, the claimant must identify a domestic comparator, before secondly proving that they are in 'like circumstances'. Thirdly, it must be demonstrated that less favourable treatment has been accorded to the product, service or investment.[5] The fourth step, may involve the state attempting to justify the differences in its treatment of investors based on treaty exceptions.

While national treatment has not always been as important as other standards in BITs, the fact that protection from discrimination has always featured in IIAs shows that it has always been a concern for parties.[6] As domestic standards for the treatment

---

[3] For example, in the China- Korea FTA (2014), a national treatment provision provided substantive rights for parties in four chapters including those on Market Access For Goods (Chap. 2), Trade In Services (8), Financial Services (9), and Investment (12). National treatment provisions have also featured in Chapters on Intellectual Property. E.g. Canada- Korean FTA (2014) Article 16.6.

[4] Engagement between trade and investment law was described in Chap. 1 as occurring wherever the content of one of the regimes has a parallel in the other or wherever there are cross-regime references in dispute settlement or parallels in the practices of tribunals.

[5] The Total tribunal found that the complainant must demonstrate that it received less favourable treatment "as compared to the treatment granted to the specific local investor or the specific class of national comparators." *Total v. Argentina*, Decision on Liability, ICSID Case No. ARB/04/01 (2010) para. 212.

[6] The initial inclusion of national treatment may have been an attempt to go beyond the Calvo doctrine. The Calvo doctrine was popularised in Latin American States in the late nineteenth and early twentieth centuries. The doctrine provides that aliens should not receive treatment that is more

of investment have risen and developed countries have begun concluding investment agreements *inter se*, national treatment has gained in importance in IIAs.[7]

National treatment articles are extremely common in IIAs and are found across the WTO Agreements.[8] National treatment provisions in IIAs often feature the four abovementioned elements. Notwithstanding these features, national treatment provisions are still heterogeneous in IIAs and as a result it can be "difficult to distil general principles" about national treatment in the investment context.[9] There are also instances of BITs that do not contain national treatment provisions.[10] The features of national treatment provisions in the trade and investment regimes as well as how they have been interpreted are now considered.

3.2.1.1 National Treatment Provisions in the Trade Regime

National treatment features in the three main WTO Agreements—GATT, GATS and TRIPS, and is a core discipline of trade law. It also features in the TBT Agreement, SPS Agreement, TRIMS Agreement, the Anti-Dumping Agreement, and in both of the currently active Plurilateral Agreements. The varying national treatment provisions have been treated differently in dispute settlement at the WTO, which reflects the varied wordings found throughout the WTO Agreements.

In terms of the rest of the trade regime, the trade chapters of PTIAs tend to incorporate WTO provisions, e.g. Article 34 of the EU- Ukraine Association Agreement.[11] This section examines GATT Article III and some of the differences in the construction of national treatment provisions found across the WTO Agreements.

---

favourable than that accorded to nationals. See Newcombe and Paradell (2009) Chapters 1 & 4; Di Mascio and Pauwelyn (2008), p. 68.

[7] Di Mascio and Pauwelyn (2008), pp. 66–69.

[8] Agreements featuring National Treatment include: GATT Article III, GATS Article XVII, TRIPS Article 3, TRIMS Article 2, TBT Article 2.1, The SPS Agreement Annex C. 1(a) and in the Agreement on Implementation of Article VI of the GATT '94 (the Anti-Dumping Agreement) Article 2.6. The two plurilateral agreements that are still active both contain National Treatment provisions (Agreement on Public Procurement Article IV, Agreement on Trade in Civil Aircraft Article 4.3).

[9] Di Mascio and Pauwelyn (2008), p. 66.

[10] See for example, Argentina-Sweden BIT (1991).

[11] A recent trade dispute involving Ukraine's wood export ban was taken under the EU—Ukraine Association Agreement. The export ban was alleged to breach Article 35 (Import and Export Restrictions) of the Agreement. This Article, along with Article 34 (National Treatment), make up Section 3 of the Agreement on Non-Tariff Measures. The two Articles incorporate GATT Article XI and III respectively and make them "an integral part of the Agreement". See Final Report, *Restrictions applied by Ukraine on exports of certain wood products to the European Union*, 11 December 2020.

The GATT

GATT Article III can be seen as a grandmother provision for national treatment in the WTO Agreements. This is because it has been the most litigated national treatment provision before the WTO's Dispute Settlement Body. When interpreting other national treatment provisions under the other WTO Agreements, tribunals have considered the jurisprudence under GATT Article III.[12]

GATT Article III's jurisprudence has been shaped by what has been described as its "complicated textual set-up".[13] GATT Article III:1 indicates the overall telos or purpose of Article III which is to prevent measures being applied that afford "protection to domestic production".[14] Subparagraphs 2 and 4 deal with the key areas of taxation and regulation but are constructed differently so that the way the Article's objective is implemented differs for the different provisions.

To establish a breach of Article III: 4, a complainant must show that the product being discriminated against is 'like' a domestic product. Once likeness is established, the complainant must then show that the imported product receives less favourable treatment than its domestic comparator. The following two questions are central considerations for tribunals in national treatment cases: (1) the comparators relied upon in likeness analysis; and (2) what constitutes less favourable treatment under national treatment provisions.

In terms of the first of these questions, under the WTO Agreements, the word 'likeness' is accorded many meanings. Its meaning in a given context depends on how the accordion is "stretched and squeezed" as it was put by the Appellate Body in the *Japan- Alcoholic Beverages II.*[15]

In order to demonstrate less favourable treatment, the entire group of imported goods must be treated less favourably than the entire group of domestically produced goods.[16] These questions are considered in detail in Sects. 3.2.3 and 3.2.4 of this chapter. If a breach of a Member's national treatment obligations is established, the

---

[12] See, for example, Appellate Body Report, *United States—Measures Affecting the Production and Sale of Clove Cigarettes*, WT/DS406/AB/R, adopted on 24 April 2012, Appellate Body Reports, *United States—Certain Country of Origin Labelling (COOL) Requirements*, WT/DS384/AB/R and WT/DS386/AB/R, adopted on 23 July 2012, and Appellate Body Report, *United States—Measures Concerning the Importation, Marketing and Sale of Tuna and Tuna Products*, WT/DS381/AB/R, adopted on 13 June 2012.

[13] Kurtz (2009), p. 754.

[14] Article III:1 states that measures "should not be applied to imported or domestic products so as to afford protection to domestic production." This is a statement of the aim of GATT's national treatment Article, which is to avoid protectionism. The Appellate Body has found that the test for this should be objective rather than subjective. In practical terms, this means that the Appellate Body has regard to the effects of internal measures and doesn't consider the purpose of the measure under Article III:1.

[15] Appellate Body Report, *Japan—Taxes on Alcoholic Beverages II*, WT/DS8/AB/R, WT/DS10/AB/R, WT/DS11/AB/R, adopted 1 November 1996, page 21.

[16] Di Mascio and Pauwelyn (2008), p. 66.

Member may then defend its measure under the General Exceptions of GATT Article XX.

Other WTO Agreements

While GATS is broadly similar to the GATT, this is not the case for other WTO Agreements such as the TBT and SPS Agreements. This section briefly considers the differences in these Agreements in turn.

GATS Article XVII concerns national treatment and provides that: "[E]ach Member shall accord to services and service suppliers of any other Member, in respect of all measures affecting the supply of services, treatment no less favourable than that it accords to its own like services and service suppliers". This treatment only applies to sectors listed in the Member's Schedules.[17] GATS Article XIV provides for General Exceptions that are broadly similar to those in GATT Article XX.

The architecture of the TBT Agreement is significantly different to that of the GATT and GATS. Both its national treatment and MFN protections are laid down in Article 2.1 of the TBT Agreement. Members shall ensure that in respect of technical regulations, products imported from the territory of any Member shall be accorded treatment no less favourable than that accorded to like products of national origin and to like products originating in any other country. TBT Agreement Article 2 provides the equivalent of GATT Article XX or GATS Article XIV. It contains a list of legitimate objectives including national security, human and animal health, the environment, as well stating how measures should be applied:

> Members shall ensure that technical regulations are not prepared, *adopted or applied with a view to or with the effect of* creating unnecessary obstacles to international trade. For this purpose, technical regulations shall not be more trade-restrictive than necessary to fulfil a legitimate objective, taking account of the risks non-fulfilment would create.

The italicised words above indicate that the intention and the effects of measures are to be considered by tribunals. The SPS Agreement is similar to the TBT Agreement. SPS Agreement Article 2.3 contains both national treatment and MFN protection, combined with wording aimed at ensuring measures do not "arbitrarily or unjustifiably discriminate" between Members. Article 2.3 is supplemented by SPS Agreement Article 5.5, which elaborates on the importance of the consistency of measures and relevant factors to be considered by Tribunals.

3.2.1.2 National Treatment Provisions in the Investment Regime

The construction of national treatment provisions varies between different International Investment Agreements. These differences in the wordings of national

---

[17] GATS Article XVII.1.

treatment provisions affect the coherence of the interpretation of this norm across international investment law.[18] There are four stages that are common in national treatment claims under IIAs, and these are similar to those under the trade regime.[19]

National treatment clauses contain a variety of elements, some of which may not be present in some IIAs. These include: (i) whether or not they grant establishment rights into the host state; (ii) whether they apply to investors as well as investments; (iii) whether a comparator is specified, e.g. one in a "like situation" or "similarly-situated"; (iv) whether the national treatment clause appears in the same article as the MFN provision. The granting of establishment rights is seen a major dividing line between different IIAs. The right of establishment remains within the discretion of the host state.[20] Early BITs signed by the US and Canada typically provided for rights for investors during the pre-establishment phase.[21] These BITs grant access to the host's market on the same terms as those enjoyed by national investors.[22] BITs concluded by the US are far-reaching in terms of granting market access and liberalising domestic markets for its investors.

A second category of agreements include those concluded by European countries, inter alia, that only cover what are known as post-establishment or post-entry rights.

---

[18] Another reason for a potential lack of coherence in the interpretation of national treatment under investment treaties is the lack of an Appellate Body, such as in the WTO system, whose role it is to give unity and coherence to the body of law as a whole.

[19] These stages include (1) identifying a domestic comparator, (2) proving that they are in 'like circumstances', (3) demonstrating that less favourable treatment has been accorded to the investor or investment, and finally (4) consideration of host state justifications for the measure in question.

[20] UNCTAD 'International Investment Agreements: Key Issues' UNCTAD/ITE/IIT/2004/10 (Vol. I), page 9.

[21] States may or may not permit the admission of goods and services into their territory. While restrictions on the admission of goods have decreased considerably in recent decades, this has not happened to the same extent for investment. One motivation for such restrictions is the potential harm of the ownership of a country's productive resources by foreign investors. This is still a cause for concern among EU Member States in 2020. See Regulation (EU) 2019/452 of the European Parliament and of the Council of 19 March 2019 establishing a framework for the screening of foreign direct investments into the Union, PE/72/2018/REV/1. See also Guerin, S.S., 'Do the European Union's bilateral investment treaties matter? The way forward after Lisbon,' Centre for European Policy Studies Working Document No. 333 (2010) 2.

[22] The US- Ecuador BIT is an example of this approach. Article II states: "Each Party shall permit and treat investment...". The word 'permit' guarantees pre-establishment rights. A notable feature of Article II and other pre-establishment treaties is that it is subject to the right of each Party "to make or maintain exceptions falling within one of the sectors or matters listed in the Protocol to this Treaty". This provision was a standard draft for the US and is exactly the same as the text of the much-litigated US- Argentina BIT.

These BITs operate a system of negative scheduling whereby everything is covered unless it is expressly excluded from the protocol. Even for the US, their assurance to investors that they will not enjoy fewer rights than other investors is subject to a protocol with reservations and exceptions. Sacerdoti sees this as a strategy that "requires a list of exceptions" and could only be pursued by a country like the US. Sacerdoti (2000), p. 109. Under the WTO Agreements for example, Members subscribe to a positive listing system whereby they commit to liberalise in areas listed in their schedule of concessions.

These rights may only be exercised once an investment has already been established within a host state. In order for an investment to be established, it has to conform with and be "in accordance with domestic laws".[23]

The tribunal in *Total v. Argentina* summarised the stages of a national treatment.[24] The complainant must (i) identify the local subject for comparison; (ii) prove that the claimant-investor is in like circumstances with the identified preferred national comparator(s); and (iii) demonstrate that it received less favourable treatment."[25] This sequence of analysis was employed in this dispute under the France-Argentina BIT (1993) and has been employed elsewhere. At this point, the burden of proof shifts to the defendant, and there is a fourth step in the analysis where the host state may attempt to justify the differences in its treatment of investors.

This section now considers the national treatment provisions of a series of more recent PTIAs featured in this study, aiming to highlight the nuance of these articles. The texts of the national treatment provisions for the China—Korea FTA (2015)[26] and the Australia—China FTA (2015)[27] are drafted quite differently. China

---

[23] E.g. Article 2 of Bolivia—Netherlands BIT (1994): Either Contracting Party shall, within the framework of its law and regulations, promote economic cooperation through the protection in its territory of investments of nationals of the other Contracting Party. Subject to its right to exercise powers conferred by its laws or regulations, each Contracting Party shall admit such investments. See also: Denmark- Argentina BIT (1995) & France- Argentina BIT (1993).

[24] *Total v. Argentina*, Award & Dissenting Opinion, ICSID Case No. ARB/04/01 (2013).

[25] *Total v. Argentina*, Award & Dissenting Opinion, ICSID Case No. ARB/04/01 (2013) para 212.

[26] Article 12.3: National Treatment 1. Each Party shall in its territory accord to investors of the other Party and to covered investment treatment no less favorable than that it accords in like circumstances to its own investors and their investments with respect to investment activities. 2. Paragraph 1 shall not apply to non-conforming measures, if any, existing at the date of entry into force of this Chapter maintained by each Party under its laws and regulations, or—119—any amendment or modification to such measures, provided that the amendment or modification does not decrease the conformity of the measure as it existed immediately before the amendment or modification. Treatment granted to covered investment once admitted shall in no case be less favorable than that granted at the time when the original investment was made. 3. Each Party shall take, where applicable, all appropriate steps to progressively remove all the non-conforming measures referred to in paragraph 2.

[27] Article 9.3: National Treatment 1. Australia shall accord to investors of China treatment no less favourable than that it accords, in like circumstances, to its own investors with respect to the establishment, acquisition, expansion, management, conduct, operation and sale or other disposition of investments in its territory. 2. China shall accord to investors of Australia treatment no less favourable than that it accords, in like circumstances, to its own investors with respect to the expansion, 1 management, conduct, operation and sale or other disposition of investments in its territory. 3. Australia shall accord to covered investments treatment no less favourable than that it accords, in like circumstances, to investments of its own investors with respect to the establishment, acquisition, expansion, management, conduct, operation and sale or other disposition of investments in its territory. 4. China shall accord to covered investments treatment no less favourable than that it accords, in like circumstances, to investments of its own investors with respect to the expansion, management, conduct, operation and sale or other disposition of investments in its territory.

concluded both agreements in the same year and they both feature the typical four stages of national treatment provisions.[28]

There are however differences in the two Agreements. National treatment under the investment chapter of the China- Korea FTA does not apply to non-conforming measures, although it is agreed that steps will be taken to "progressively remove" any such measures. The Australia—China FTA is unusual and sets out separate clauses for Australia and China in terms of the scope of national treatment for investors and investments. The wording to these provisions is identical except for this scope.[29]

CETA contains the first investment chapter of a concluded PTIA negotiated by the EU. CETA's investment chapter resembles the NAFTA approach to national treatment and includes a provision for "treatment no less favourable than the most favourable treatment accorded, in like situations, by that government to investors".[30] Therefore, it seems likely that under EU investment chapters findings of less favourable treatment will be based on a comparison with any one domestic investor rather than the class of domestic investors as a whole. This standard of the "most favourable treatment" is however absent from other EU Agreements such as EUSIPA.[31]While there are differences between these national treatment provisions, they are not far apart along the spectrum of potential national treatment provisions in IIAs. The Model BITs of Norway and India illustrate the broad spectrum of what can be contained in the national treatment provisions of IIAs. These Model BITs were published in 2015 and illustrate the starting points for IIA negotiations for these countries.

Article 3 of Norway's Draft Model BIT contains a national treatment provision referring to likeness, less favourable treatment, and the purpose of a measure.[32] Where measures bear a "reasonable relationship to rational policies", they are justifiable. The attachment of a list of policy exceptions to a national treatment clause in an investment treaty brings clarity to the public policy exceptions envisaged by the contracting parties. Beyond the specific exceptions in Article 3, there are also General Exceptions in Article 24, which covers a series of familiar grounds.[33]

---

[28]Under both Articles an investor must identify a domestic comparator and show 'likeness', it must demonstrate less favourable treatment, and finally both Agreements contain treaty exceptions under which the host state can defend a measure.

[29]Australian investors and investments are covered in relation to the "expansion,[1] management, conduct, operation and sale or other disposition of investments in its territory." Chinese investors and investments are covered in relation to "establishment, acquisition, expansion, management, conduct, operation and sale or other disposition of investments in its territory."

[30]CETA Article 8.6.

[31]E.g. EUSIPA Article 2.3.

[32]The purpose of the provision is contained in a footnote, which provides a list of policy exceptions to the national treatment clause including the "protection of public health, human rights, labour rights, safety and the environment".

[33]". . .[N]othing in this Agreement shall be construed to prevent a Party from adopting or enforcing measures necessary: i. to protect public morals or to maintain public order;[4] ii. to protect human,

Chapter I, Article 4 of India's Draft Model BIT[34] could be seen as diluting the principle of national treatment and calling into question its effectiveness. Article 4.2–4.3 adds three controversial concepts to national treatment.[35] Article 4.2 states that a breach will only occur if the challenged measure constitutes "intentional and unlawful discrimination" based on nationality. This has been described as overly vague and would lead to enforcement issues.[36] Article 4.3 provides that representatives of the government at a local and regional level would not be deemed to be representing the state of India and as such a national treatment claim couldn't be brought against their acts.[37] This would also be against principles of customary international law.[38] The Model BIT contains no provision for fair and equitable treatment, which makes a strong national treatment provision all the more necessary.

---

animal or plant life or health; iii. to secure compliance with laws and regulations that are not inconsistent with the provisions of this Agreement; iv. for the protection of national treasures of artistic, historic or archaeological value; or v. for the protection of the environment."

[34] Model Text for the Indian Bilateral Investment Treaty (2015) available at: https://www.mygov.in/sites/default/files/master_image/Model%20Text%20for%20the%20Indian%20Bilateral%20Investment%20Treaty.pdf (last accessed 25 August 2020).

[35] Article 4: National Treatment

4.1 Each Party shall not apply to Investments, Measures that accord less favourable treatment than that it accords, in like circumstances,[2] to domestic investments with respect to the management, conduct, operation, sale or other disposition of Investments in its territory.

4.2 A breach of Article 4.1 will only occur if the challenged Measure constitutes intentional and unlawful discrimination against the Investment on the basis of nationality.

4.3 This Article shall not apply to any Law or Measure of a Regional or local Government.

2 The requirement of "like circumstances" recognizes that States may have various legitimate reasons for distinguishing between investments including, but not limited to, (a) the goods or services consumed or produced by the Investment; (b) the actual and potential impact of the Investment on third persons, the local community, or the environment, (c) whether the Investment is public, private, or state-owned or controlled, and (d) the practical challenges of regulating the Investment. The factors and determinations used by the Host State to distinguish between Investors and Investments are to be given substantial deference by any tribunal constituted under Article 14.5 or Article 15.2.

[36] The Society for Research in Law, 'Suggestions And Comments In Response To Model Text For The Indian Bilateral Investment Treaty,' *First SRIL International Research Initiative* (2015) 19.

[37] If, for example, the state of Florida grants special treatment to Floridian investors that is not extended to investors from other states, should this treatment be extended to foreign investors under the national treatment principle? One view is that less favourable treatment is unqualified. Furthermore, treaties should apply to an entire territory. The opposing view is that national treatment looks to nationality-based discrimination, which is not present here. NAFTA incorporates the former view while the 2004 US Model BIT incorporates the latter. Given the ambiguity here, negotiators should make their choice explicit within treaties.

[38] International Law Commission's Articles on Responsibility of States for Internationally Wrongful Acts Article IV.

3.2.1.3 Interpreting National Treatment Provisions

Interpreting National Treatment at the WTO

The national treatment test under GATT Article III:4 was articulated for the first time in *EC- Asbestos*.[39] This case involved France's import ban of chrysotile, a known carcinogen and form of asbestos that was produced in Canada. The Panel concluded that France had violated GATT Article III:4 and that chrysotile and non-asbestos based construction products were like products. In their view, to consider health risks under Article III:4 was not appropriate and would be to "nullify" the effect of Article XX(b).[40] This approach would guarantee market access subject to the defendant being able to find a non-protectionist justification under Article XX.

The Panel in *EC-Asbestos* reiterated that the approach outlined in *The Report of the Working Party on Border Tax Adjustments* should be followed. This approach consists of applying four criteria which include: (i) properties, nature and quality of the products; (ii) the end use of products; (iii) consumers' tastes and habits; and (iv) the tariff classification of the products, if this is sufficiently detailed. There are risks in using tariff bindings that are too broad as a measure of product 'likeness'.

The Appellate Body (AB) reversed the Panel's findings that the products were like. The AB found that Articles III and XX "are distinct and independent provisions" and so a measure may be deemed unjustifiable for public health reasons under both.[41] This may imply less frequent recourse to Article XX(b), but considerations of health reasons under Article III do not deprive Article XX (b) of its *effet utile*. Article XX(b) would only be deprived of its *effet utile* if it could not serve to allow a Member to "adopt and enforce" measures "necessary to protect human … life or health".[42] The AB found that this was not the case as different inquiries are made under the different Articles.

In a somewhat controversial reversal of this position, the Appellate Body clarified in *EC—Seal Products* that "treatment no less favourable" only refers to a detrimental impact on competitive opportunities for imported products. There is no need to consider the regulatory purpose of the measure in Article III:1 separately. Consideration of the purpose of a measure is now confirmed to be reserved exclusively for Article XX. *EC—Seal Products* clarified that Article III:4 deals with the trade impact of measures only. This method makes is easier to establish prima facie breach of Article III, and the purpose of a measure only comes into play during the defence of a

---

[39] Appellate Body Report, *European Communities - Measures Affecting Asbestos and Asbestos-Containing Products*, WT/DS/135/AB/R, adopted on 5 April 2001.

[40] See Panel Report, *European Communities – Measures Affecting Asbestos and Asbestos-Containing Products*, WT/DS/135/R, adopted on 5 April 2001, paras 3.450 and 3.512 for the respective quotation marks.

[41] Appellate Body Report, *European Communities – Measures Affecting Asbestos and Asbestos-Containing Products*, WT/DS/135/AB/R, adopted on 5 April 2001, para 115.

[42] Appellate Body Report, *European Communities – Measures Affecting Asbestos and Asbestos-Containing Products*, WT/DS/135/AB/R, adopted on 5 April 2001, para 115.

measure under a General Exceptions provision. This interpretative method could prove problematic to follow in WTO jurisprudence for a number of reasons. Firstly, the number of defences available under Article XX is limited and was drawn up in 1947. Secondly, the burden of proof is shifted to the defendant who must show they fall within the exception. Thirdly, Article XX is difficult to comply with. Indeed, in only two of the first twenty GATT Article XX claims to come before the Appellate Body (*EC—Asbestos* & *US—Shrimp II*), were the measures taken deemed compliant with the WTO Agreements.[43]

The separation of Article III and XX is arguably fundamental to the sound operation of the national treatment principle in the GATT in line with the *EC—Asbestos* finding that they are distinct and independent provisions. Lastly, WTO Agreements such as TRIPS and the TBT Agreement do not contain General Exceptions. As such the purpose of measures are considered under the National Treatment provisions, as was done in *EC—Asbestos*. Thus, if the purpose of a measure can only be considered under the General Exceptions to the GATT or GATS, this creates two separate strains of WTO jurisprudence for national treatment. The role of regulatory purpose and the stage at which tribunals should consider it in their analysis is one of the major interpretative questions surrounding nondiscrimination provisions. The jurisprudence has been inconsistent in this regard and Sects. 3.2.3 and 3.2.4 go into greater depth in the areas of likeness and less favourable treatment respectively.

Interpreting National Treatment Under IIAs

The key tasks for tribunals when interpreting national treatment provisions include: how interpreting likeness affects interpretations of less favourable treatment, and how both of these stages should inform tribunals' interpretations of treaty exceptions.

Differences in the wording of national treatment provisions in early IIAs such as the US-Argentina BIT and NAFTA have affected how tribunals have interpreted these provisions.[44] The treaties set different standards of comparison between domestic and foreign investors under the Agreements. A restrictive approach to the likeness test was found under the NAFTA in *Methanex v. United States*, while the tribunal in *Occidental v. Ecuador* took a far broader approach where differential treatment in matters of tax was prohibited between different sectors of the economy. Under the US-Ecuador BIT, Article II mentions treatment "no less favourable than that accorded in like situations to investment or associated activities of its own national or companies". Unlike the NAFTA, it contains no mention of "most favourable treatment" which makes it harder to satisfy the less favourable treatment criterion. Sections 3.2.3 and 3.2.4 go into greater depth in the areas of likeness and less favourable treatment respectively.

---

[43] See Moran (2017), pp. 3–21.
[44] See Schill (2009), p. 78.

3.2.2 Most-Favoured Nation Treatment

This section considers the main features of Most-Favoured Nation (MFN) provisions in the trade and investment law regimes and the main interpretative questions under them.

3.2.2.1 MFN Provisions in the Trade and Investment Regimes

In the trade regime, MFN is a mechanism for the automatic removal of distortions that would otherwise hamper comparative advantage.[45] It provides a multiplier effect assuring that any advantage accorded to one WTO Members spreads throughout the multilateral system.[46] The main MFN provisions in the WTO Agreements include GATT Article I:1, GATS Article II, and TBT Article 2.1. These provisions are supplemented by other "MFN-like treatment" found in, for example, the chapeau of GATT Article XX.[47]

GATT Article I:1 provides that with respect to certain measures[48] *"any advantage, favour, privilege or immunity granted by any contracting party to any product originating in or destined for any other country shall be accorded immediately and unconditionally to the like product originating in or destined for the territories of all other contracting parties"* (emphasis added). Article I.1 covers advantages granted to any other country and not just other WTO Members. Article I:1 is not concerned with less favourable treatment, but rather the legal standard is expressed as an obligation to extend 'any advantage granted by a Member to any product... to the 'like product' originating in or destined for all other Members.'[49]

The main interpretative questions that stem from this provision concern the types of measures covered, what constitutes 'like products', 'advantage', and what it means that treatment is accorded 'unconditionally'. Article I:1 is concerned with prohibiting discriminatory measures and equality of competitive opportunities. For

---

[45] Matsushita (2015), p. 158.

[46] Matsushita (2015), p. 158.

[47] See Van den Bossche and Zdouc (2017), p. 715. The chapeau of GATT Article XX provides that "measures are not applied in a manner which would constitute a means of arbitrary or unjustifiable discrimination between countries where the same conditions prevail".

[48] This broad array of measures at the beginning of Article I:1 includes: "With respect to customs duties and charges of any kind imposed on or in connection with importation or exportation or imposed on the international transfer of payments for imports or exports, and with respect to the method of levying such duties and charges, and with respect to all rules and formalities in connection with importation and exportation, and with respect to all matters referred to in paragraphs 2 and 4 of Article III..."

[49] Appellate Body Report, *European Communities – Measures Prohibiting the Importation and Marketing of Seal Products*, WT/DS400/AB/R and WT/DS401/AB/R, adopted on 18 June 2014, para 5.81.

breach of GATT Article I to be found, neither discriminatory intent nor trade effects need be demonstrated.

MFN treatment is also an obligation in relation to services and GATS Article II:1 provides: "With respect to any measure covered by this Agreement, each Member shall accord immediately and unconditionally to services and service suppliers of any other Member treatment no less favourable than that it accords to like services and service suppliers of any other country." There are three interpretative questions to be answered in relation to this provision. These concern: (1) 'like' services and service suppliers; (2) less favourable treatment; and (3) measures falling within the scope of Article II:1.

A final MFN provision considered is TBT Agreement Article 2.1, which provides: "Members shall ensure that in respect of technical regulations, products imported from the territory of any Member shall be accorded treatment no less favourable than that accorded to like products of national origin and to like products originating in any other country." Article 2.1 covers both MFN treatment and national treatment. The TBT Agreement contains no General Exceptions Article unlike the GATT and GATS.

As with the trade regime, the aim of MFN provisions in the investment regime is to prevent discrimination and ensure equality of competitive opportunities. MFN provisions are extremely common in IIAs but there are significant variations in their wording. These variations often relate to whether or not the following elements are included: (i) establishment rights; (ii) exceptions to MFN treatment (these may be in the areas of taxation, regional agreements etc.). Aside from these specific exceptions contained with article, general exceptions may also be applicable to MFN provisions; (iii) a comparator (e.g. 'like circumstances'); (iv) an exclusion for dispute resolution; (v) a reference to both investors and investments.

Exceptions to MFN provisions for the purposes of taxation and regional agreements are less common in recent agreements. One example of such a provision can be found in Article 3 of the BLEU (Belgium-Luxembourg Economic Union)- Korea BIT (2006).[50] More recent PTIAs tend to be quite comprehensive with regard to covering the above elements, with CETA Article 8.7 referring to all of them, while CPTPP Article 9.5 contains all but one (exceptions). Article 1103 NAFTA refers only to elements (i), (iii) and (v) and this approach is replicated in the USMCA.

---

[50] "Article 3 (. . .) 3. Pareil traitement ne s'étendra pas aux privilèges accordés par l'une ou l'autre Partie Contractante aux investisseurs d'Etats tiers, en vertu de sa participation ou de son association actuelle ou future à une union douanière ou économique, un marché commun ou une zone de libre échange ou à un accord international analogue.

4. Les dispositions des paragraphes 1 et 2 du présent article ne pourront être interprétées comme obligeant une Partie contractante à étendre aux investissements des investisseurs de l'autre Partie contrac- tante le bénéfice de tout traitement, préférence ou privilège résultant de tout accord ou arrangement international concernant principalement ou exclusivement l'imposition, notamment tout accord tendant à éviter la double imposition." Under IIAs, MFN treatment concerns the treatment of investments.

3.2.2.2 Interpreting MFN Provisions

Interpreting MFN Treatment at the WTO

At the WTO, MFN treatment extends any advantage accorded to any product immediately and unconditionally to all like products of other Members. A series of key Appellate Body interpretations of the MFN standard are now considered.

The Appellate Body confirmed in *Canada- Autos* that GATT Article I:1 covers not only *de jure* discrimination, but also "in fact", or de facto, discrimination.[51] This dispute concerned the duty-free imports of vehicles by certain manufacturers. Eligibility was set out in an origin-neutral manner, but in practice imports were only from companies related to importers.[52] The AB has found that in determining de facto discrimination, panels must scrutinise the "design, architecture, revealing structure, operation, and application of the technical regulation at issue".[53] The measure at issue in *EC- Seal Products* is an example of one failing this test, where the design and structure of the measure detrimentally affected the conditions of competition between the parties.[54] The Panel concluded that the EC's exception for indigenous communities excluded the vast majority of seal products from Canada and Norway while "virtually all domestic seal products qualify".[55]

The main interpretative questions that stem from GATT Article I.1 include which measures are covered, what constitutes 'like products', 'advantage', and what it means that treatment is accorded 'unconditionally'.[56] These last two questions can be considered to replace the 'less favourable treatment' requirement. Indeed, GATS Article II:1 sets out criteria that are similar in some respects, (likeness and whether a measure is covered), but asks whether less favourable treatment was accorded instead of the final two criteria.[57]

---

[51] Appellate Body Report, *Canada — Certain Measures Affecting the Automotive Industry*, WT/DS139/AB/R, para 78.

[52] Appellate Body Report, *Canada — Certain Measures Affecting the Automotive Industry*, WT/DS139/AB/R, para 71.

[53] See Appellate Body Report, *United States — Measures Affecting the Production and Sale of Clove Cigarettes*, WT/DS406/AB/R, adopted on 24 April 2012, para 182.

[54] Appellate Body Report, *European Communities – Measures Prohibiting the Importation and Marketing of Seal Products*, WT/DS400/AB/R and WT/DS401/AB/R, adopted on 18 June 2014, para 5.95.

[55] Panel Report, *European Communities – Measures Prohibiting the Importation and Marketing of Seal Products*, WT/DS400/R and WT/DS401/R, para 7.608.

[56] GATT Article I:1 provides that with respect to certain measures, "any advantage, favour, privilege or immunity granted by any contracting party to any product originating in or destined for any other country shall be accorded immediately and unconditionally to the like product originating in or destined for the territories of all other contracting parties".

[57] GATS Article II.

GATT Article I.1 covers a broad range of measures but not an unlimited range.[58] It applies to both fiscal and non-fiscal border measures.[59] MFN only applies for 'like' products and services. As will be seen in Sect. 3.2.3, likeness is interpreted differently across the WTO Agreements as the accordion is "stretched and squeezed". A major interpretative question is whether the regulatory purpose of a measure should be considered when determining likeness.

The next question involves whether or not a measure grants "any advantage" in comparison with other WTO Members. *EC—Bananas III* demonstrates the wide array of measures that may constitute an advantage.[60] The AB in *Canada—Autos* emphasised the use of the term 'any advantage' applied to 'any product', rather than some advantages applied to some products, which seems to permit construing what constitutes an advantage in broad terms. The AB found that Canada had granted an advantage to some products from some Members that had not been extended to all other Members.[61]

Advantages must be granted to all like products 'immediately and unconditionally'.

In *EC—Seal Products*, the AB found that GATT Article I is concerned with protecting expectations of equal competitive opportunities but does not prohibit a Member attaching conditions to the granting of an advantage. Rather it prohibits conditions that have a *detrimental impact on the competitive opportunities* for like imported products from any Member.[62]

---

1. With respect to any measure covered by this Agreement, each Member shall accord immediately and unconditionally to services and service suppliers of any other Member treatment no less favourable than that it accords to like services and service suppliers of any other country.
2. A Member may maintain a measure inconsistent with paragraph 1 provided that such a measure is listed in, and meets the conditions of, the Annex on Article II Exemptions.
3. The provisions of this Agreement shall not be so construed as to prevent any Member from conferring or according advantages to adjacent countries in order to facilitate exchanges limited to contiguous frontier zones of services that are both locally produced and consumed.

[58] See *EC- Commercial Vessels* (2005) para 7.83, where the AB found that measures covered by GATT Article III: 8 (b) fall outside the application of GATT Article III: 2 & 4. Thus these measures also fall outside the scope of GATT Article I.1, which refers to customs duties and charges..."with respect to all matters referred to in paragraphs 2 and 4 of Article III". Measures covered under GATT Article XXIV: 3 (a) with respect to frontier traffic are also not covered by GATT Article I.1.

[59] Panel Report, *European Communities – Regime for the Importation, Sale and Distribution of Bananas, Complaint by Ecuador*, WT/DS27/R/ECU, adopted 25 September 1997, para 7.188–7.193.

[60] See *EC- Bananas (Ecuador)* Panel para 7.188–7.241. One such advantage was the absence of a licence allocation based on activity functions for ACP countries, which meant the procedural and administrative requirements for imports differed for non-ACP countries. The Panel found that "substantially more data must be maintained and submitted to show entitlement to a licence" and so the ACP position was considered as an advantage. (para 7.221).

[61] Appellate Body Report, *Canada — Certain Measures Affecting the Automotive Industry*, WT/DS139/AB/R, para 79–81.

[62] Appellate Body Report, *European Communities – Measures Prohibiting the Importation and Marketing of Seal Products*, WT/DS400/AB/R and WT/DS401/AB/R, adopted on 18 June 2014, para 5.88.

In terms of less favourable treatment under the GATS, the AB has found that this involves an assessment of whether a measure modifies the conditions of competition in favour of the services of another Member.[63]

Interpreting MFN Treatment under IIAs

Under IIAs, MFN treatment concerns the treatment of investments.[64] Where MFN provisions are invoked under one of the thousands of IIAs, disputes can be divided into four areas.[65] These include: (1) those concerning cases where more favourable substantive treatment has been granted to an investor of a third country; (2) provisions used to claim a general treatment not provided in the 'basic treaty'[66]; (3) MFN as a basis for disregarding limitations to treatment provided in the 'basic treaty'. This concerns whether an investor can look to a more favourable expression of a standard such as fair and equitable treatment in treaties with third countries and limit unfavourable elements in the treaty in question;[67] and (4) dispute settlement provisions, and whether ISDS provisions from agreements with third countries can be invoked. This possibility has proved controversial and is explicitly excluded from recent agreements such as CPTPP.[68]

Beyond these different categories, tribunals are generally faced with two main interpretative questions when applying MFN provisions. These concern determining whether the relevant investor or investment is 'in like circumstances', and whether they have received treatment less favourable than their third country counterparts (these topics are the subject of the next sections). The tribunal in *Parkerings v. Lithuania*[69] considered these questions in relation to the revocation of a permit to design, build and operate a "modern integrated parking system" due to environmental and cultural concerns.[70] Parkerings claimed that a Dutch firm, had obtained

---

[63] Appellate Body Report, *Argentina – Measures Relating to Trade in Goods and Services*, WT/DS453/AB/R, adopted 9 May 2016, para 6.111.

[64] MFN provisions have also been used to import treatment not covered in a particular IIA (such as Fair and Equitable Treatment), as well as procedural provisions generally concerning ISDS.

[65] See Sacerdoti and Moran (forthcoming 2022).

[66] *Bayindir v. Pakistan* is an example of this occurring, where the FET provisions of the Turkey-Switzerland BIT was imported on the basis of a MFN provision.

[67] See *Asian Agricultural Products Ltd. (AAPL) v. Sri Lanka*, where the claimant sought to apply the full protection and security clause in the case of a civil disturbance (which that BIT excluded) because another BIT of Sri Lanka did not set this out. The tribunal rejected this claim on the merit but did not rule out that such a better treatment could be imported.

[68] CPTPP Article 9.5.3: "For greater certainty, the treatment referred to in this Article does not encompass international dispute resolution procedures or mechanisms, such as those included in Section B (Investor-State Dispute Settlement)."

[69] *Parkerings Compagniet AS v. Lithuania*, ICSID Case No. ARB/05/8, Award, 11 September 2007.

[70] *Parkerings Compagniet AS v. Lithuania*, ICSID Case No. ARB/05/8, Award, 11 September 2007, para 51.

more favourable treatment with respect to the building of a parking complex in violation of the MFN provision of the Lithuania–Norway BIT (1992).[71] The tribunal found that for the investors to be in like circumstances, Parkerings must be a foreign investor in the same economic or business sector as the Dutch firm Pinus Proprius.[72] For a determination of less favourable treatment, the two investors must be treated differently due to a state measure. However such treatment would be acceptable if a State's legitimate objective justifies such different treatment.[73]

The tribunal found that the investors were not in like circumstances because Parkering's investment was larger and "extended significantly more into the Old Town" of Vilnius, a sensitive heritage area.[74] The tribunal found the Municipality's revocation was "justified by various concerns", notably those of a historical, archaeological and environmental nature.[75] The tribunal considered factors such as environmental concerns in its determination of 'likeness'. This is a novel approach that allows the regulatory purpose of a measure to be factored into likeness analysis and has no precedent in GATT or in investment cases.[76]

3.2.3   Likeness

This section considers the concept of likeness in its various wordings, and how it has been interpreted in the trade and investment law regimes. Likeness is usually included in provisions that aim to prevent nationality-based discrimination. Breach of these provisions can be found where a claimant can show that it is in a like situation to a domestic investor or that its service or product is like a domestic counterpart.

---

[71] It is noted that Article IV provides no express basis for comparison i.e. wording such as 'in like circumstances'.

Article IV Most favoured Nation Treatment

1. Investments made by Investors of one Contracting Party in the Territory of the other Contracting Party, as also the Returns therefrom, shall be accorded treatment no less favourable than that accorded to investments made by Investors of any third state.

[72] *Parkerings Compagniet AS v. Lithuania*, ICSID Case No. ARB/05/8, Award, 11 September 2007, para 371.

[73] *Parkerings Compagniet AS v. Lithuania*, ICSID Case No. ARB/05/8, Award, 11 September 2007, para 371. The introductory paragraph to para 371 implies that LFT is a requirement for the investors to be 'in like circumstances', a novel approach which is not elaborated upon and is unlikely to be replicated elsewhere.

[74] *Parkerings Compagniet AS v. Lithuania*, ICSID Case No. ARB/05/8, Award, 11 September 2007, para 392.

[75] *Parkerings Compagniet AS v. Lithuania*, ICSID Case No. ARB/05/8, Award, 11 September 2007, para 396.

[76] See Sacerdoti and Moran (forthcoming 2022).

The concept of likeness typically appears in national treatment and MFN provisions across the two regimes, but has also featured in provisions such as those concerning general exceptions, establishment rights,[77] and dispute settlement provisions.[78]

Nondiscrimination provisions are based on the idea that like cases should be treated in the same way and so the scope of likeness is fundamental to determining what constitutes a breach of these norms. To make a prima facie claim for breach of a national treatment or MFN provision, a complainant must identify an investor in like circumstances compared to which it has received less favourable treatment. In some cases where likeness was not expressly mentioned in the treaty provision, the need for a comparator has been deemed to be inherent in national treatment provisions.[79]

This chapter looks at the scope for crossfertilisation between the trade and investment law regimes in this area. While 'likeness' may seem a fertile ground for engagement, the systems differ in that investment law focuses on the individual over the group and tribunals have looked beyond the competition-based approach that has characterised trade jurisprudence. The types of enquiries may also differ under IIAs where "broader comparisons" of the treatment of investors may be carried out than those under the GATT.[80]

---

[77] See the St Vincent and the Grenadines- Taiwan BIT (2010). Under the Agreement, establishment rights are accorded on a basis no less favourable than that, which "in like circumstances" is granted, to the host state's nationals or those of any third state. Article II, 3: "Each Contracting Party shall permit establishment of a new business enterprise or acquisition of an existing business enterprise or a share of such enterprise by investors or prospective investors of the other Contracting Party on a basis no less favourable than that which, in like circumstances, it permits such acquisition or establishment by: (a) its own investors or prospective investors; or (b) investors or prospective investors of any third state."

[78] The General Exceptions article in the EFTA-Korea Investment Agreement (2006) also covers discrimination between "States where like conditions prevail". EFTA-Korea Investment Agreement (2006), Article 20: "Exceptions- Subject to the requirement that such measures are not applied in a manner which would constitute a means of arbitrary or unjustifiable discrimination between States where like conditions prevail, or a disguised restriction on investors and investments, nothing in this Agreement shall be construed to prevent the adoption or enforcement by any Party of measures: (a) necessary to protect public morals or to maintain public order; (b) necessary to protect human, animal or plant life or health; or the environment; or (c) necessary to secure compliance with laws and regulations which are not inconsistent with the provisions of this Agreement."

[79] See Total v. Argentina, Decision on Liability, ICSID Case No. ARB/04/1, para 213. "In view of the above, the Tribunal concludes that the absence of the term "like" in Article 4 of the BIT is not decisive since this element is inherent in an evaluation of discrimination." There is an inherent need for a comparator when interpreting national treatment provisions. However, this is not to say that the wording has no effect on interpretation. Indeed, the tribunal in Occidental v. Ecuador viewed the wording as instructive in terms of differentiating the national treatment norm in the investment context from its trade context.

[80] Mitchell et al. (2016), p. 36.

3.2.3.1 Likeness in the Trade & Investment Regimes

The flexible concept of likeness varies across the WTO Agreements, appearing in the GATT, GATS, TBT, SPS and SCM Agreements.[81] The Agreements generally refer to 'like products' or 'like services', and this is particularly the case in relation to nondiscrimination provisions.[82]

This section focuses on likeness under the GATT, with references to other Agreements.[83] In the context of trade in goods, a complainant may establish 'likeness' by demonstrating that a measure distinguishes between products based exclusively on origin.[84] Scope for such a presumption has been found to be more limited under the GATS as there is "greater complexity" in trade in services.[85]

The objective of GATT Article III: 1 is to prevent measures being applied so as to afford "protection to domestic production". Subparagraphs 2 and 4 concern taxation and regulation respectively but are constructed differently so that the Article's objective, as expressed in III: 1, is implemented differently for the two provisions. To establish a breach of a national treatment provision, a complainant must establish likeness with a domestic product and that the imported product has received less favourable treatment than its domestic comparator. If a breach is established prima facie, the Member may then defend its measure under treaty exceptions, usually under GATT Article XX. The extent of the competitive relationship necessary

---

[81] See Iacovides (2016), p. 125, Table 3.1, which documents 76 references to likeness across these Agreements.

[82] 'Like commodities' and 'like merchandise' are also referred to under the GATT 1947 in Article VI on Anti-dumping and Countervailing Duties and in Article VII on Valuation for Customs Purposes respectively. In Annex 2 to the Agreement on Agriculture, which concerns exemptions for reductions commitments for domestic support, Article 8 refers to a "natural or like disaster".

[83] GATT Article III has been the most litigated national treatment provision at the WTO and tribunals have referred to the jurisprudence under GATT Article III when interpreting other national treatment provisions elsewhere in the WTO Agreements. See, for example, Appellate Body Report, *United States — Measures Affecting the Production and Sale of Clove Cigarettes*, WT/DS406/AB/R, adopted on 24 April 2012, Appellate Body Reports, *United States — Certain Country of Origin Labelling (COOL) Requirements*, WT/DS384/AB/R and WT/DS386/AB/R, adopted on 23 July 2012, and Appellate Body Report, *United States — Measures Concerning the Importation, Marketing and Sale of Tuna and Tuna Products*, WT/DS381/AB/R, adopted on 13 June 2012.

[84] In relation to GATT Article III:2. see Panel Reports Argentina—Hides and Leather, para. 11.168; China – Auto Parts, para. 7.216. In relation to GATT Article III:4, see Panel Reports, *Argentina— Import Measures*, para. 6.274; *Canada—Autos*, para. 10.74; *Canada—Wheat Exports and Grain Imports*, para. 6.164; *China—Publications and Audiovisual Products*, para. 7.1447; *India—Autos,* para. 7.174; *Thailand—Cigarettes (Philippines)*, para. 7.661; *Turkey—Rice*, paras. 7.214–7.216; *US—FSC (Article 21.5—EC)*, paras. 8.132–8.135.

[85] This is for two reasons: (1) likeness under the GATS involves consideration of both the service and the service supplier. Not only does it have to be shown that the origin-based distinction applies to the service, but also the service supplier; and (2) GATS Article XXVIII(f), (g), and (k) through (n) indicate the possible complexities of determining origin and whether a distinction is exclusively based on this reason. These complexities limit the scope of presumption although it doesn't render it inapplicable. See Appellate Body Report, *Argentina—Measures Relating to Trade in Goods and Services*, WT/DS/453/AB/R, adopted on 9 May 2016, paras. 6.36–6.41.

between products for them to be considered 'like' cannot be considered in the abstract and must be determined on a case-by-case basis.[86] The analogy of an accordion that "stretches and squeezes" as different provisions are applied has been used to explain the different meaning of 'likeness' under the WTO Agreements.[87] The most narrow of these meanings is in the term "identical" founding in the Article 2.6 of the Anti-Dumping Agreement or in the standard for likeness laid down in *Methanex v, U.S.A* under the NAFTA Agreement. This is followed by Article III:2, sentence one, which was deemed to be "narrowly squeezed" by the Appellate Body in the *Japan- Alcohol*.[88] Next is Article III:4, which was deemed by the Appellate Body in *EC-Asbestos* to be a larger group than that of "like" products under III: 2. Finally, likeness is construed most broadly for Directly Competitive or Substitutable (DCS) products under GATT Article III: 2, second sentence. The Appellate Body found in the *Korea- Alcoholic Beverages*[89] that potential competition from overseas markets that has been stifled hitherto is relevant in determining whether two products are DCS, which would entail an even broader meaning.

Although competition is a central element of the trade law analysis of likeness,[90] it is not the only element. The SPS Agreement is not concerned with the comparability of products but with "the comparability of risks".[91] As a result, 'like' products causing dissimilar risks (externalities) are not subject to non-discriminatory treatment and can legitimately be regulated differently under the SPS.

Table 3.1 The application of a potentially discriminatory climate change tax

	Rural	Urban
Drinks sector	Coastal brewery (FI)	*City drinks (FI) & downtown beverages*
Flowers sector	Farmers' flowers	*Metro flowers*
Renewables sector	Green turbines (FI)	Versatile turbines

---

[86] Van den Bossche (2008), p. 356.

[87] Appellate Body Report, *Japan – Taxes on Alcoholic Beverages II*, WT/DS8/AB/R, WT/DS10/AB/R, WT/ DS11/AB/R, adopted 1 November 1996, page 21. Indeed, even within provisions, the 'accordion of likeness' may have different meanings, also page 21.

[88] Appellate Body Report, *Japan – Taxes on Alcoholic Beverages II*, WT/DS8/AB/R, WT/DS10/AB/R, WT/ DS11/AB/R, adopted 1 November 1996, page 21.

[89] Appellate Body Report, *Korea – Taxes on Alcoholic Beverages II*, WT/DS75/AB/R, WT/DS84/AB/R, adopted 17 February 1999, para 137. "But if another market displays characteristics similar to the market at issue, then evidence of consumer demand in that other market may have some relevance to the market at issue."

[90] See Di Mascio and Pauwelyn (2008), p. 64 where it is stated: The Appellate Body's approach to likeness analysis can be "summed up" by the word competition.

[91] Panel Report, *European Communities – Measures Concerning Meat and Meat Products (Hormones)*, WT/DS26/R, 18 Aug. 1997, at para. 8.176. See also Schebesta and Sinopoli (2018), pp. 125–126.

The SPS Agreement refers to likeness in Annex C on Control, Inspection and Approval Procedures.

The preamble to the WTO Agreement refers to sustainable development and other non-market objectives behind the WTO Agreement. Consequently, Mitchell et al. find it "unduly narrow" to focus on competition alone.[92] They make the compelling case that if the Appellate Body were to "recognise that the purposes of the WTO Agreement, GATT and TBT Agreements extend beyond equality of competitive conditions", it would "enable the Appellate Body to articulate what kinds of discrimination are relevant, that is, to articulate a normative basis for its non-discrimination analysis".[93]

For investment agreements, where reference is made to a comparator in nondiscrimination provisions, 'in like circumstances' is the most common phrasing. Variations such as 'in like situations' are also found.[94] Other IIAs contain no such phrasing and it has been found that the need for a comparator is inherent in the concept of discrimination.[95] Even if a comparator is inherent, the wording of an IIA may affect treaty interpretation. In *Occidental v. Ecuador*, the claimant argued that the standard of national treatment was not qualified by the reference to 'in like situations' in the Ecuador-Spain BIT and that under the MFN provision of the Ecuador- United States BIT it was entitled to this "less restrictive treatment".[96] The tribunal found these arguments to be convincing.[97]

As seen in the commentary to the Draft Consolidated Text of the Negotiating Group on the Multilateral Agreement on Investment, those that opposed the inclusion of the concept of likeness found it to be "unnecessary and open to abuse", while its advocates were of the view that "the comparative context should be spelled out" and comparisons should be "on the basis of characteristics that are relevant".[98]

How a tribunal defines likeness is central to "mapping the ambit of the operation" of national treatment provisions.[99] In this regard, the presence or absence of terms such as 'like' or 'similar' etc. is likely to be less important than "how tribunals characterise the subjects".[100]

---

[92] Mitchell et al. (2016), p. 131.

[93] Mitchell et al. (2016), p. 132.

[94] E.g. Article 87 of the Agreement On Free Trade And Economic Partnership Between Japan And The Swiss Confederation: "Each Party shall accord to investors of the other Party and to their investments, in relation to their investment activities, treatment no less favourable than that it accords, in like situations, to its own investors and to their investments." (emphasis added) See also US Argentina BIT (1994).

[95] See *Total v. Argentina*, Decision on Liability, ICSID Case No. ARB/04/1, para 213. See also Mitchell et al. (2016), p. 65.

[96] *Occidental Exploration and Production Company v. The Republic of Ecuador*, Final Award, 1 July 2004, LCIA Case No. UN3467, para 170.

[97] *Occidental Exploration and Production Company v. The Republic of Ecuador*, Final Award, 1 July 2004, LCIA Case No. UN3467, para 173.

[98] OECD, Negotiating Group on the Multilateral Agreement on Investment (MAI), DAFFE/MAI (98)8/REV1, 11.

[99] Kurtz (2009), p. 752.

[100] Newcombe and Paradell (2009), pp. 159–161.

The test for likeness has allowed investment tribunals to balance investor interests against public policy concerns, which includes "a list far broader than the exceptions in GATT Article XX."[101] The regulatory objectives of a measure have been brought within the text of certain recent IIAs. The fact that the regulatory purpose of a measure is considered during the likeness stage has been made explicit in the national treatment provisions of some recent IIAs. E.g. CPTPP's states: "For greater certainty, whether treatment is accorded in "like circumstances" under Article 9.4 (National Treatment) or Article 9.5 (Most-Favoured-Nation Treatment) depends on the totality of the circumstances, including whether the relevant treatment distinguishes between investors or investments on the basis of legitimate public welfare objectives." There are no General Exceptions to this chapter and this clarification introduces an assessment as to the state's regulatory purpose to the test for likeness.[102]

3.2.3.2 Interpreting Likeness

Interpreting Likeness at the WTO

This section summarises key interpretations of the concept of 'likeness' at the WTO.

Japan—Alcoholic Beverages II[103]

This claim was brought in response to Japan's Liquor Tax Law, which established a system of internal taxes for liquors based on their categorisation. The Appellate Body found that the tax violated GATT Article III:2. It found that vodka and shochu share physical characteristics, were subject to the same tariff schedule, and that Japan had failed to produce evidence that the two products were not like. The AB referred to the criteria for determining likeness first formulated by the GATT's Contracting Parties in 1970.[104] The AB found that tariff bindings risked including a wide range of products calling into question its usefulness as a reliable criterion for determining likeness.[105] It acknowledged the nuance of likeness and stated that

---

[101] Di Mascio and Pauwelyn (2008), p. 83. The authors compare likeness analysis under investment agreements to Article XX defences at the WTO.

[102] Kurtz refers to this as a "purpose-based test", see 'Kurtz (2014), pp. 276–277.

[103] *Japan- Taxes on Alcoholic Beverages II*, WT/DS8/R, WT/DS10/R, WT/DS11/R.

[104] The Report of the Working Party on Border Tax Adjustments formulated the following criteria: (1) The product's end-uses in a given market; (2) Consumers' tastes and habits; and (3) The product's properties, nature and quality; (4) The tariff classification of the products if this is sufficiently detailed.

[105] Appellate Body Report, *Japan – Taxes on Alcoholic Beverages II*, WT/DS8/AB/R, WT/DS10/AB/R, WT/ DS11/AB/R, adopted 1 November 1996, page 22.

Panels can only apply their "best judgement in determining whether products are 'like'".[106]

EC—Asbestos[107]

This dispute concerned France's ban on white asbestos. The Canadian government argued that its use could be restricted and that the ban did not extend to domestic noncarcinogenic products used to insulate buildings claiming this was a violation of GATT Article III: 4. The Panel found the ban was justified under GATT Article XX (b). The Appellate Body upheld the ban but reversed the Panel's findings that the products (asbestos and cement-based products) were like products.

The AB emphasised that GATT Articles III and XX "are distinct and independent provisions" to be interpreted separately.[108] The Appellate Body found that health risks associated with a product may be relevant in a consideration of likeness under GATT Article III:4.[109] It found that evidence of health risks can be evaluated under the criteria of physical properties and consumers' tastes and habits.[110]

EC—Seal Products[111]

The EU seal regime banning the importation of seal products was contested in this dispute.[112] Norway claimed certain exceptions to the ban were discriminatory. The EU defended the ban under GATT Article XX(a) with this ban on seal products being considered necessary to protect public morals.

This dispute settled the longstanding question over the role of regulatory purpose in inquiries under GATT Article III.[113] *EC—Seal Products* emphasised the economic purpose of GATT Article III and "definitively established" that detrimental impact is sufficient for breach of Article III with other regulatory purposes being

---

[106]The Appellate Body acknowledged, this involves an "unavoidable element of individual, discretionary judgement". Page 20–21.

[107]Panel Report, *European Communities – Measures Affecting Asbestos and Asbestos-Containing Products*, WT/DS/135/R, adopted on 5 April 2001.

[108]Appellate Body Report, *European Communities – Measures Affecting Asbestos and Asbestos-Containing Products*, WT/DS/135/AB/R, adopted on 5 April 2001, para 115.

[109]Appellate Body Report, *European Communities – Measures Affecting Asbestos and Asbestos-Containing Products*, WT/DS/135/AB/R, adopted on 5 April 2001, para 113.

[110]Appellate Body Report, *European Communities – Measures Affecting Asbestos and Asbestos-Containing Products*, WT/DS/135/AB/R, adopted on 5 April 2001, para 113.

[111]Appellate Body Report, *European Communities – Measures Prohibiting the Importation and Marketing of Seal Products*, WT/DS401/AB/R, adopted on 18 June 2014.

[112]See Regulation 1007/2009 of 16 September 2009 on trade in seal products, OJ 2009 L 286/36.

[113]See Ming Du (2015). "After *EC – Seal Products*, the long- standing controversy on whether Article III:4 itself affords policy space for a WTO Member to consider Article XX-like policy rationale is over."

irrelevant.[114] For the AB, the fact that "a Member's right to regulate is accommodated under Article XX, weighs heavily against an interpretation of Articles I:1 and
III:4 that requires an examination of whether the detrimental impact of a measure on
competitive opportunities for like imported products stems exclusively from a
legitimate regulatory distinction."[115] Under the TBT Agreement, tribunals have
considered the regulatory purpose of a measure in its analysis of less favourable
treatment. *EC—Seal Products* has set the jurisprudence on "diametrically opposed
paths" under the GATT and the TBT Agreement.[116] Arguably these different
interpretative paths are necessary in light of the absence of general exceptions to
the TBT Agreement. Kurtz has described this as a "crude disparate impact approach"
that could problematically lock parties into a list of policies that may remain static
for decades.[117] The AB denied that there is an imbalance between the scope of the
right to regulate under TBT Article 2.1 and the GATT and highlighted the lack of
concrete examples of a legitimate objective that could fall under TBT Article 2.1 but
wouldn't fall within the scope of GATT Article XX.[118]

When considering the relevant measure under GATT Article XX, the AB found
that the EU had not demonstrated that the EU seal regime complied with Article
XX's chapeau. The EU had not made "comparable efforts" to allow Canadian Inuits
to qualify for the IC exception in contrast to its efforts in relation to Greenlandic
Inuits. Furthermore, to comply with the Regulation, the requirement for a certificate
from a recognised body was found to entail a "significant burden".[119] The AB
corrected the Panel's finding that applying the same legal test as was applied to
Article 2.1 of TBT Agreement was appropriate in analysing Article XX's chapeau,
finding the Panel should have given further explanation as to why it was relevant and
applicable.[120]

---

[114] Mitchell et al. (2018), p. 116. Arato, Claussen, & Heath argue that now, in the light of the
pandemic, may be the time to "resuscitate the view" that trade adjudicators should consider
regulatory aims when interpreting likeness for goods and services; Julian Arato (2020), p. 8.

[115] Appellate Body Report, *European Communities – Measures Prohibiting the Importation and
Marketing of Seal Products*, WT/DS400/AB/R and WT/DS401/AB/R, adopted on 18 June 2014,
para 5.125.

[116] Mitchell et al. (2018), p. 174.

[117] Kurtz (2016), p. 179.

[118] [U]nder the TBT Agreement, the balance between the desire to avoid creating unnecessary
obstacles to international trade under the fifth recital, and the recognition of Members' right to
regulate under the sixth recital, is not, in principle, different from the balance set out in the GATT
1994, where obligations such as national treatment in Article III are qualified by the general
exceptions provision of Article XX. Para 5.127-8.

[119] Appellate Body Report, *European Communities – Measures Prohibiting the Importation and
Marketing of Seal Products*, WT/DS400/AB/R and WT/DS401/AB/R, adopted on 18 June 2014,
para 5.337.

[120] Appellate Body Report, *European Communities – Measures Prohibiting the Importation and
Marketing of Seal Products*, WT/DS400/AB/R and WT/DS401/AB/R, adopted on 18 June 2014,
para 5.310–5.315. It has been noted that the EU can comply with the AB's findings by removing the
exception for indigenous communities. Ironically this would be more trade restrictive and would not

Argentina—Financial Services

Following *EC- Seals*, the regulatory purpose of a measure is considered exclusively under GATT Article XX and it appears that this is also the case under the GATS.[121]

The Appellate Body clarified in *Argentina—Financial Services* that likeness "serves the same purpose" in the context of both trade in goods and trade in services, which is to determine whether the products are in a competitive relationship. The AB endorsed employing the same criteria to determine likeness "provided that they are adapted as appropriate to account for the specific characteristics of trade in services".[122]

Interpreting Likeness in IIAs

This section summarises three approaches to interpreting 'likeness' under IIAs, before considering interpretations of the regulatory purpose of measures. Determining likeness has proved to be a complex interpretive question for investment tribunals. In national treatment claims, an investor must typically make a prima facie case that it is in like circumstances with a domestic investor and that it has received less favourable treatment from the host state.[123]

Tribunals have found that the elements that make up likeness depend upon the "facts of a given case",[124] the "legal context and the specific circumstances of any individual case",[125] and taking into account "all the circumstances of each case".[126] These differing formulations have led to a range of domestic comparators being used for the purposes of likeness. These approaches to determining the relevant comparator have been criticised as "scant, brief and barely reasoned".[127] This claim is now examined in relation to three approaches that have been employed by tribunals, including what are called here (1) the narrow approach; (2) the broad approach; and (3) the economic sector or competition-based approach.

---

benefit Canada or its indigenous population. Catti de Gasperi, G, 'Case Note and Comment on European Communities – Measures Prohibiting the Importation and Marketing of Seal Products,' WTO case law in 2014, It. YIL 24:395–430 (2015).

[121] Appellate Body Report, *Argentina – Measures Relating To Trade In Goods And Services*, WT/DS453/AB/R, adopted 9 May 2016, para 6.31.

[122] Appellate Body Report, *Argentina – Measures Relating To Trade In Goods And Services*, WT/DS453/AB/R, adopted 9 May 2016, para 6.31.

[123] While this is also the case for MFN provisions, national treatment provisions are the focus of this section.

[124] *Pope & Talbot Inc. v Government of Canada*, NAFTA/ UNCITRAL, Tribunal Damages Award IIC 195 (2002) Award on Merits para 75.

[125] *Total v. Argentina*, Award & Dissenting Opinion, ICSID Case No. ARB/04/01 (2013) para 210.

[126] *SD Myers, Inc. v Government of Canada*, NAFTA/ UNCITRAL Tribunal, 1st Partial Award and Separate Opinion, IIC 249 (2000) para 244.

[127] Mitchell et al. (2016), p. 66.

The Narrow Approach

The tribunal in *Methanex v. U.S.A* employed a 'narrow approach' to identifying the proper comparator. In this case, methanol and ethanol were competing products that were treated differently. The tribunal found that this was not discriminatory as there was an identical domestic investment that received the same level of treatment. The The tribunal followed a methodology that examined comparators that were similar "in all relevant respects".[128] The tribunal found that it would be "perverse" to ignore such an identical comparator and to use comparators that were less 'like'.[129] Looking for an identical comparator may present difficulties given the many possible differences between operators in terms of their size, structure etc. The tribunal found that where there is no identical counterpart, it may look "farther afield and expand the scope of domestically-owned comparators."[130]

It is unclear how this approach would be applied as part of the regulatory context approach, for which the comparator need not even be a competitor.[131] The narrow approach also "runs the risk of excluding swathes" of discriminatory conduct from the scope of national treatment.[132] This problem with the narrow approach would be critical in situations an investor receives less favourable treatment, but so too does a minor, identical domestic firm. A non-identical competitor receives preferential treatment but is not deemed 'like' as the more identical competitor is the one in like circumstances.

The Broad Approach

The tribunal in *Occidental v. Ecuador* applied a 'broad approach' in identifying the proper comparator. Ecuador argued that the appropriate comparator was other oil producers that were not entitled to receive a VAT refund. The purpose of national treatment provisions is to combat discrimination based on nationality and as the domestic oil producer Petroecuador was treated similarly, Ecuador argued that the policy was applied in a nondiscriminatory manner. The purpose of VAT refunds is to ensure unchanged conditions of competition, a goal that is only relevant to producers

---

[128] *Methanex Corp. v U.S.A,* Final Award of the Tribunal on Jurisdiction and Merits (UNCITRAL, 3 August 2005) Part IV- Chapter B- page 9- paragraph 16.

[129] *Methanex Corp. v U.S.A,* Final Award of the Tribunal on Jurisdiction and Merits (UNCITRAL, 3 August 2005) Part IV- Chapter B- page 9- paragraph 17.

[130] *Methanex Corp. v U.S.A,* Final Award of the Tribunal on Jurisdiction and Merits (UNCITRAL, 3 August 2005) Part IV - Chapter B, Para 15.

[131] Even an 'identical' domestic counterpart might not necessarily be in like circumstances where assessing the purpose of the measure is a key component of this determination. Under this approach, differential treatment of identical investors may still be justified and two investors with different characteristics may be in an identical situation. See Newcombe and Paradell (2009), pp. 159–170, see also footnote 77.

[132] Kurtz (2009), p. 769. Several authors point out that this approach fails to capture certain types of discrimination: Di Mascio and Pauwelyn (2008) 85; Kurtz (2016), p. 100; and Newcombe and Paradell (2009), pp. 165–169.

in the same sector. Occidental claimed that other companies involved in the export of goods were the appropriate comparator.

The tribunal rejected Ecuador's arguments as the purpose of national treatment "is to protect investors as compared to local producers, and this cannot be done by addressing exclusively the sector in which that particular activity is undertaken."[133]

The tribunal never addressed the question of whether or not the discrimination was nationality based. The tribunal stated that it compared Occidental to all domestic exporters as "no exporter ought to be put in a disadvantageous position as compared to other exporters".[134]

At issue here, is the question of whether competition is a necessary condition for likeness or whether flowers and oil can be considered together.[135] The reasoning in the award assumes that the de facto discrimination between Occidental and other exporters was based on nationality, without considering whether the flower and seafood exporters were foreign or domestically owned.[136] Criticism of the Occidental award and the question of whether investors from different sectors should be treated in the same way in certain regulatory circumstances is the subject of the next section.

The Economic Sector or Competition-Based Approach

The economic sector approach is in between the broad and narrow approaches used by the tribunals in *Occidental* and *Methanex*. This test was used in *Pope & Talbot v. Canada*, where the tribunal stated that the first step in national treatment analysis is essentially a comparison of whether the investments are in the same business or economic sector.[137] The tribunal found that where there is a difference in treatment between investors in the same economic sector, there is a presumptive violation of national treatment.[138]

---

[133] *Occidental Exploration and Production Company v. The Republic of Ecuador*, Final Award, 1 July 2004, LCIA Case No. UN3467, para 173.

[134] *Occidental Exploration and Production Company v. The Republic of Ecuador*, Final Award, 1 July 2004, LCIA Case No. UN3467, para 176.

[135] Allowing for such broad comparators in likeness analysis is described as "seemingly absurd" by Di Mascio and Pauwelyn. See 'Nondiscrimination in Trade and Investment Treaties: Worlds Apart or Two Sides of the Same Coin?' *American Journal of International Law* (2008) 85. The authors find that the test applied in Occidental was "truer to the objectives" of national treatment in investment than the narrow approach used by the tribunal in Methanex. This is because it focused on the "absence of any legitimate reason to distinguish" between investments in the different sectors (e.g. the oil and flower sectors).

[136] A further consideration is the fact that Petroecuador was state-owned and as such any tax rebate would be revenue neutral. See Newcombe and Paradell (2009), p. 165.

[137] *Pope & Talbot Inc. v Government of Canada*, Tribunal Report, Award on the Merits of Phase 2, (UNCITRAL, 10 April 2001), para 78.

[138] *Pope & Talbot Inc. v Government of Canada*, Tribunal Report, Award on the Merits of Phase 2, (UNCITRAL, 10 April 2001), para 78.

The tribunal in *SD Myers v. Canada* endorsed a competition-based approach to likeness and found: "The concept of 'like circumstances' invites an examination of whether a non-national investor complaining of less favourable treatment is in the same "sector" as the national investor. The tribunal takes the view that the word "sector" has a wide connotation that includes the concepts of "economic sector" and "business sector"."[139]

This test was applied in *Levy de Levi v. Peru*,[140] which involved an allegedly discriminatory bank bailout programme. The tribunal found that BNM was not in like circumstances with three beneficiaries of the programme as BCP and Banco Wiese were the first and second-largest banks in Peru.[141] Banco Latino was similar in size to BNM but the tribunal distinguished it from BNM based on its "far-reaching network of individual depositors".[142] This finding raises the question of whether and in what situations the size of an investment should be a decisive factor in determining likeness.[143] This dispute demonstrates that the economic sector approach can give rise to similar problems to those seen with the first two tests. The economic sector was arguably drawn too narrowly in this case where BNM bank was not deemed to be like the other banks because of its size and portfolio composition.[144] It is also possible to imagine the economic sector test being drawn in an overly broad manner.

In *Mercer v. Canada* the investor established that it was treated differently to other self-generating pulp mills in the same sector. However, the tribunal found that other pulp mills "whilst ostensibly comparators" were not in like circumstances. Their different treatment was explained on the basis of their individual circumstances under the Power Authority's "consistent application" of its methodology.[145] The tribunal compared Mercer's treatment to that of other pulp mills and agreed with

---

[139] *SD Myers, Inc. v Government of Canada*, NAFTA/ UNCITRAL Tribunal, 1st Partial Award and Separate Opinion, IIC 249 (2000) para 250.

[140] Agreement concluded between the Republic of Peru and the Republic of France on the Promotion and Reciprocal Protection of Investments (1996).

[141] They accounted for 44% of loans and 51% of deposits in the country. BNM represented 4% of loans and 2% of deposits.

[142] *Levy de Levi v. Republic of Peru*, (ICSID Case No. ARB/10/17) Final Award, para 398.

[143] *Levy de Levi v. Republic of Peru*, (ICSID Case No. ARB/10/17) Final Award, para 398.

[144] The dissenting opinion of Prof. Joaquín Morales Godoy described the finding as "grotesque" as the banks "performed the same functions as the other identified banks, that is, they provided similar financial services, had a similar growth rate, and took similar risks. In addition, they also had the same corporate clients as well as individual customers". *Levy de Levi v. Republic of Peru*, (ICSID Case No. ARB/10/17) Dissenting Opinion of Prof. Joaquín Morales Godoy, para 186.

The defendant submitted that the "most comparable" bank was NBK Bank and that this would be the appropriate reference for comparing the treatment of BNM. The tribunal did not address this point. The market segment of the banks, including size and portfolios, was decisive for the tribunal in determining entities in similar circumstances. See *Levy de Levi v. Republic of Peru*, (ICSID Case No. ARB/10/17) Respondent's Counter-Memorial on the Merits, paras 379 to 385.

[145] *Mercer International Inc. v. Government of Canada*, Award ICSID Case No. ARB(AF)/12/3 (2018) para 7.45.

Canada's expert witness that differences in the electricity purchase contracts were the result of differences in the mills' individual circumstances.[146] The tribunal found that the Power Authority could enter into arrangements with mills but this does not mean that every investor "is entitled to precisely the same arrangements" relating to the treatment of its investment as are agreed with other investors.[147] Thus, although investors may be operating within the same industry, for the purpose of a specific regulatory treatment, differences in the individual circumstances of the investors may entitle the regulator to treat them differently.

Newcombe has criticised this presumptive violation of national treatment where there is a difference in the treatment of investors in the same economic sector as establishing too low a threshold to establish a prima facie case.[148] Investors may be in the same economic sector but this approach often fails to reflect the regulatory differences between the investments or investors. Newcombe suggests that it would be preferable that the claimant must find an appropriate comparator and "demonstrate how it is in comparable circumstances in light of the purpose of the measure at issue."[149]

---

[146]Dr. Rosenzweig confirmed that: "This difference, however, does not constitute an inconsistent methodology, but rather reflects the differences in contractual obligations of the mills. The critical difference is that, during the years leading up to the 2009 EPA, Skookumchuck's operational decisions were influenced by its contract that committed it to sell generation from its plant. Because the obligations under the 1997 EPA would be disappearing, actual generation at Skookumchuck would have been an inappropriate baseline for its GBL as it would not have accurately represented what was truly incremental generation to be incentivized in the 2009 EPA. It was therefore necessary to base Skookumchuck's GBL on a model of the amount of [redacted] as the parties agreed it would, considering the economic conditions at the time absent an EPA. In contrast, Celgar never had a contract with BCH, [i.e. BC Hydro] it self-supplied essentially all of its load, and its operations in 2007 represented current normal self-generation in the absence of a contract.

In conclusion, both Celgar's and Tembec's GBLs were set following a consistent BCH methodology. The differences in the details of how each mill's GBL was calculated are explained by the unique circumstances of the mill (such as a prior EPA with BCH), and reflect a consistent application of BCH's GBL methodology."

[147]*Mercer International Inc. v. Government of Canada*, Award ICSID Case No. ARB(AF)/12/3 (2018) para 7.37.

[148]Newcombe and Paradell (2009), p. 163.

[149]Newcombe and Paradell (2009), p. 163. This question of the competition-based approach versus the regulatory context approach is the subject of the next section (III.3).

3.2.3.3 The Role of Competition in Likeness Analysis

The Competition-Based Approach V. the Regulatory Context Approach

Interpreting nondiscrimination provisions often requires tribunals to go through a series of stages that are common to both trade and investment law.[150] As outlined above, the competition-based approach (CB approach) is clearly the preferred approach in the trade context. The regulatory context approach (RC approach) is a second approach, which has been taken by investment tribunals when interpreting nondiscrimination provisions.

The RC approach favours the idea that likeness extends beyond competition in the investment context. For proponents of the RC approach, determining the appropriate comparator "cannot be divorced" from the reasons for the treatment in question.[151] Unlike in the trade regime, a competitive relationship is not seen as necessary so long as the regulatory circumstances of the investors or investments are sufficiently similar.[152] Competition may still be a factor in many likeness analyses, but in certain circumstances, it is the regulatory circumstances that are decisive. Investment differs from trade as it has a "much broader impact on society" given the broad array of regulations that may affect investment.[153] Under the regulatory context approach, the tribunal must take into account the regulatory purpose of the treatment when identifying the relevant subject for comparison.[154] There are circumstances that warrant "discrepant regulation" of competitors just as there are circumstances that would warrant equal regulation of noncompetitors.[155] Di Mascio & Pauwelyn give the example of a clothes and toy manufacturer, who could expect the same treatment under a chemical regulation.[156]

The role of competition in likeness analysis is one of the most controversial questions concerning likeness and IIAs. Supporters of the competition-based approach argue that the risk of overreach is "exponentially higher" where likeness

---

[150]These questions concern likeness and finding the appropriate comparator, whether less favourable treatment has been accorded, and whether the state can justify the differences in the treatment based on treaty exceptions.

[151]Newcombe and Paradell (2009), p. 163.

[152]Di Mascio and Pauwelyn (2008), p. 89. Pauwelyn elaborates that competition is not the core test, and that "assessments of national treatment in investment treaties may also lead to comparisons between investors that are not even competitors".

[153]Di Mascio and Pauwelyn (2008), p. 81.

[154]Newcombe gives the example of a measure that aims to reduce urban pollution, where the applicable comparator may be "other emitters in the geographical area, rather than a direct competitor in the same sector that operates in a less environmentally sensitive area". Newcombe and Paradell (2009), p. 163.

[155]See e.g. Di Mascio and Pauwelyn (2008), p. 81.

[156]Di Mascio and Pauwelyn (2008), p. 81. There is also a question of whether such claims should be taken under national treatment provisions or as a breach of fair and equitable treatment.

goes beyond competitive relationships.[157] The award in *Occidental* is cited as an example of this overreach.[158] The tribunal extended its interpretation of likeness beyond competition and did not consider any justification for this measure in its award.[159]

A similar approach was followed in *Bilcon v. Canada*, where the investor was denied permission to construct a quarry and marine terminal. Bilcon argued that the tribunal should consider all enterprises affected by the environmental assessment process to be in like circumstances.[160] The tribunal found that while this "might be correct", it was not necessary to decide the case. LFT had already been determined in relation to domestic projects that were extremely similar to that of the claimant and so an approach to likeness that extended beyond competition was not necessary to decide the case.[161] In the absence of such a close domestic comparator, it appears that the tribunal was sympathetic to the regulatory context approach and would have sought such a comparator.

Regulators must indeed be mindful that wherever a measure treats companies or sectors differently, they must be able to justify it on public policy grounds. Mitchell et al. contend that extending likeness beyond competition "conflates the question of the comparator" with the question of whether there has been LFT, rendering this area unpredictable.[162] However, extending likeness beyond competition to consider regulatory purpose serves a very different purpose to considering regulatory purpose under the LFT standard. It seeks to capture measures that protect domestic operators in similar regulatory circumstances to investors. The problem with considering the regulatory purpose of a measure at the LFT stage of the analysis, as per the Mitchell approach, is that it may already be too late to capture the relevant discriminatory behaviour. This is illustrated in Table 3.1 below.

---

[157] Kurtz (2016), p. 125. Mitchell et al. contend that the competition-based approach is "justifiable", citing Kurtz's definition of protectionism that refers to those "competing with foreign investors". "It follows that the determination of the comparator must be an inquiry into whether the foreign investor has received LFT compared to domestic actors with which it competes." Mitchell et al. (2016).

[158] See Newcombe and Paradell (2009), pp. 169–170. There were failings in the Occidental approach, which included the following: of course, tribunals applying the regulatory context approach need not repeat these failings.

[159] The pleadings in the case are not publicly available and it is unclear whether Ecuador provided rationales for the distinction.

[160] *Bilcon v Canada*, Award on Jurisdiction and Liability, para 694.

[161] *Bilcon v Canada*, Award on Jurisdiction and Liability. Some of the proposed comparison cases specifically involved quarry and marine terminal export projects that had the potential to affect a local community (para 696). On this point, Canada stated that "it is the circumstances underlying the way in which Canada treats two investors that are determinative of whether or not treatment was accorded in like circumstances . . . including consideration of a State's policy objectives in according the treatment in question", para 655.

[162] Mitchell et al. (2016), pp. 78–79.

For Mitchell et al., at the likeness stage of the inquiry, regulatory purpose can at most provide *evidence of important differences* between investors.[163] However for proponents of a broader approach, this could be the role that competition plays. While competition may be neither necessary nor sufficient to show likeness, it has an *evidential role* in showing discrimination. Where a foreign investor is treated differently to a domestic counterpart, the fact that they are in competition may explain this treatment. However this does not mean that competition is necessitated in every instance. Where tribunals have followed the competition-based approach, tribunals have also considered other factors.[164]

An Example

Table 3.1 presents an abstract example of a potentially discriminatory measure outlining the differing outcomes where a tribunal applies the competition-based approach and regulatory context approach. This example is based on a national treatment claim.[165] A hypothetical climate change tax exempts certain industries and only applies in urban areas. Would such a tax discriminate against foreign investors?[166] The tax would apply to the companies in Table 3.1 whose names are in italics.

There are several stages to a tribunal's analysis under nondiscrimination provisions. The analysis involves: (a) considering the domestic comparator and whether they are 'in like circumstances'; (b) whether less favourable treatment has been accorded to the investor or investment;[167] (c) whether the state can justify these differences in treatment based on the regulatory purpose of a measure. This

---

[163] Mitchell et al. (2016), p. 89.

[164] In *Grand River v. United States*, the legal regime was found to be the compelling factor. In *Archer Daniels* the tribunal found that "all circumstances" must be considered to identify the appropriate comparator. In *Feldman v. Mexico*, the company was found to be in like circumstances with cigarette reseller-exporters but not cigarette producer-exporters as there were rational bases for treating them differently. The tribunal found that firms reselling/exporting cigarettes were in like circumstances while those that merely produced cigarettes were not. It was acknowledged that there are "at least some rational bases for treating" these investors differently including discouraging smuggling, protecting intellectual property rights inter alia.

In *SD Myers*, while competition was considered, the tribunal found that the concept of like circumstances "invites an examination of whether a non-national investor complaining of less favourable treatment is in the same "sector" as the national investor." Para 250.

[165] This example is based on a national treatment claim. Although MFN treatment could be the relevant standard here, the four companies not labelled as foreign investors (FI) are considered to be domestic investors rather than investors from third countries.

[166] Examples of factors that could result in measures being applied in a discriminatory way include e.g. location (urban v. rural), size of company (SMEs versus larger companies), environmental protection (carbon taxes), public safety, the prohibition of grey market sales, and economic sector (a digital tax).

[167] The tribunal in *Total v. Argentina* found that the complainant must demonstrate that it received less favourable treatment "as compared to the treatment granted to the specific local investor or the

interpretative stage may take place when interpreting the substantive provision itself or under treaty exceptions.

These stages present a series of interpretative questions for tribunals.

(i) Concerning likeness, the tribunal's determination of the role of competition in its analysis is probably the most fundamental and controversial question in this area. The tribunal must decide whether a competitive relationship is necessary for a finding of likeness, or whether this concept extends beyond competition.

In relation to this fictional measure, following the competition-based approach, City Drinks, the foreign investor, is in like circumstances with both Coastal Brewery and Downtown Beverages. In an approach that focuses on the regulatory context of investors, City Drinks is in like circumstances with Central Beverages, Bright Flowers and Versatile Turbines, but is no longer in like circumstances with Coastal Brewery. In line with the regulatory context approach, tribunals must take into account the regulatory purpose of the treatment.[168]

(ii) Concerning less favourable treatment, the tribunal must consider whether the effect of the measure constitutes LFT. Under the competition-based approach, City Drinks, the foreign investor, is in like circumstances with both Coastal Brewery and Downtown Beverages. It has not been treated less favourably than Downtown Beverages, but has been treated less favourably than Coastal Brewery. Thus this treatment of City Drinks satisfies the effects-based test.

Under the regulatory context approach, City Drinks is in like circumstances with Central Beverages, Bright Flowers and Versatile Turbines. It has not been treated less favourably than Central Beverages or Bright Flowers, but has been treated less favourably than Versatile Turbines.

Depending on the construction of the treaty, the tribunal may face a second interpretative question of whether a legitimate regulatory purpose should prevent a finding of LFT. This would be the case for agreements that do not contain general exceptions that apply to their investment chapter (e.g. NAFTA).[169]

(iii) in relation to the regulatory purpose of the measure, the two approaches have led to different comparators. The CBA leads to City Drinks being compared to a rural rival from the same sector, while the RC approach leads to a comparison with a non-competitor in the same regulatory context. When considering the

---

specific class of national comparators." *Total v. Argentina*, Decision on Liability, ICSID Case No. ARB/04/01 (2010) para. 212.

[168] Newcombe gives the example of a measure that aims to reduce urban pollution, where the applicable comparator may be "other emitters in the geographical area, rather than a direct competitor in the same sector that operates in a less environmentally sensitive area". Newcombe and Paradell (2009), p. 163. Di Mascio & Pauwelyn give the example of a clothes and toy manufacturer, who could expect the same treatment under a chemical regulation. There is also a question of whether such claims should be taken under national treatment provisions or as a breach of fair and equitable treatment.

[169] See Sect. 3.2.4 below, or Table 3.2 in Sect. 3.3.1 for a summary.

regulatory purpose of the measure, a tribunal would likely find that there is a legitimate reason for the differential treatment afforded to City Drinks in both instances.[170] While the two approaches arrive at the same conclusion, the stark contrast between them is clear. Such a measure may legitimately distinguish between City Drinks and a rural drinks company as well as an urban renewables company.

However, if the fictional measure were implemented in a protectionist manner and did *not* apply to Metro Flowers, this discriminatory purpose would not be captured by the competition-based approach. This would be particularly concerning where certain industries are dominated by foreign investors and measures can be selectively applied to non-competitors. Likewise, if this tax were to be levied on Coastal Brewery (FI), but no other rural operators, it would also fail to be captured by the competition-based approach. Both of these discriminatory purposes would be captured by the regulatory purpose approach. The problem with the regulatory context approach is that comparisons can be made to a company in any other industry, which could lead to overreach by tribunals.

3.2.4 Less Favourable Treatment

3.2.4.1 LFT in the Trade Regime and Investment Regimes

What constitutes 'less favourable treatment' (LFT) varies across agreements and the two regimes despite the largely homogenous wording of this standard. The treatment received by a product, investment etc., is compared to that of a domestic or third country counterpart. In IIAs, the LFT standard is also extremely common in nondiscrimination provisions and was found in 119/120 IIAs in Chap. 2. Under IIAs, less favourable treatment tends to arise in the forms of the application of laws, regulations, procedures or policies or the action of state officials.[171]

At the WTO, the obligation to accord treatment no less favourable is found in the text of the nondiscrimination provisions of four of the WTO Agreements including the GATT, GATS, TBT, and TRIPS Agreements.[172] In the trade regime, treatment no less favourable was interpreted as calling for effective equality of opportunities for imported products in respect of "the application of laws, regulations and

---

[170]The differences in examining the regulatory purpose of a measure under the LFT standard compared to a general exceptions provision are considered in Sect. 3.2.4.

[171]See Newcombe and Paradell (2009), p. 184.

[172]This standard of treatment is found in GATT Article III (National Treatment), GATS Article II (MFN Treatment), GATS Article XVII (National Treatment), TBT Article 2.1 (MFN and National Treatment), and TRIPS Article 3 (National Treatment).

requirements" etc.[173] In *US- Section 337*, importers were found to have received less favourable treatment as there were different administrative and court procedures for patent infringements.[174] Since this dispute, Panels and the Appellate Body have consistently emphasised this point when interpreting 'treatment no less favourable'.[175]

Two fundamentally different and inconsistent ways of identifying less favourable treatment have been used in the trade and investment law regimes. The first is a "diagonal test", which tests whether there are any imports receiving less favourable treatment than any like domestic products. The second is called the "asymmetric impact test", which compares in aggregate both domestic sub-groups with both foreign sub-groups. The treatment received by imports is only less favourable than that accorded to like domestic goods if the burden arising from the measure is heavier for imports than for domestic goods.[176]

In the trade regime, a measure gives rise to less favourable treatment when the entire group of imported goods is treated less favourably than the entire group of domestically produced goods.[177] In *US—Gasoline*, a measure was applied in a manner that was less favourable to importers.[178] In this case, domestic gasoline refiners were allowed to use individual baselines to determine compliance with the Clean Air Act of 1990 while importers were required to use the baseline prescribed by statute.[179] This was found not to provide equality of opportunity for importers.

Tribunals have adopted both approaches in the investment regime.[180] National treatment provisions typically refer to treatment no less favourable than accorded to "its own investors and their investments".[181] Kurtz describes the usage of the plural as "critical" to interpreting LFT and that on this basis the most favoured domestic

---

[173] Panel Report, *United States - Section 337 Of The Tariff Act of 1930*, L/6439 - 36S/345, adopted on 7 November 1989, paras. 5.11–5.14.

[174] The Panel's interpretation was that non-discriminatory treatment required equality of opportunities for importers to comply with laws or regulations. Panel Report, *United States - Section 337 Of The Tariff Act of 1930*, L/6439 - 36S/345, adopted on 7 November 1989, paras. 5.11–5.12.

[175] See for example Panel Report, *United States — Standards for Reformulated and Conventional Gasoline*, WT/DS2/R, adopted on 20 May 1996, paragraph. 6.10.

[176] See Ehring, Lothar, 'De Facto Discrimination in WTO Law: National and Most-Favored-Nation Treatment – or Equal Treatment?' *Jean Monnet Working Paper* 12/01, 3–4.

[177] Di Mascio and Pauwelyn (2008), p. 66.

[178] Appellate Body Report, *United States — Standards for Reformulated and Conventional Gasoline*, WT/DS2/AB/R, adopted on 20 May 1996.

[179] An individual refinery baseline represents the average quality of gasoline produced and sold by that refinery. See Energy Information Administration, 'Refiners Switch to Reformulated Gasoline Complex Model,' page 4: https://www.eia.gov/outlooks/steo/special/pdf/rfg1.pdf

[180] Compare for example, *Marvin Feldman v. Mexico*, Award (2002) para 185, and *Pope & Talbot*, Award on the Merits (2002) para 68.

[181] References to LFT than "that which it accords to investments" of its own national or those of any third State are also in the following BITs: UK- Ethiopia BIT Article 3, Mexico- Korea BIT Article 3, Switzerland- Kenya BIT Article 4.2, Taiwan- Grenadine BIT Article 3.1.

investor reading cannot be applied to such provisions.[182] These provisions direct the tribunal to a group-based approach rather than focusing on individual investors.[183] Nonetheless, NAFTA Article 1102.3 refers to "treatment no less favorable than the most favorable treatment accorded" despite also referring to investments in the plural.[184] The most favoured investor standard has prevailed in this conflict and has been the approach of successive tribunals. Absent a requirement for intent, this approach sets a "very low burden" for breach in a system that already confers broad rights.[185] Recent agreements such EUSIPA and CPTPP maintain references to "investors" in the plural but do not contain the most favoured investor standard, which opens the door to the asymmetric impact test.[186]

3.2.4.2 Interpreting LFT

This section considers how the less favourable treatment standard has been interpreted in the trade and investment law regimes in relation to two questions with a substantial bearing on inter-regime engagement: (a) Whether subjective discriminatory intent plays a role in this determination or whether an objective, effects-based test is sufficient; and (b) the type of link needed between a measure and its aim.[187]

The Effects of a Measure v. Discriminatory Intent

The question of whether the LFT standard is concerned exclusively with the objective effects of a measure, or whether, and to what extent, subjective discriminatory intent plays a role has been interpreted broadly similarly in the trade and investment law regimes. Given the difficulty of establishing the intent of a regulator

---

[182] Kurtz (2016), p. 112.

[183] See Kurtz (2016), p. 113.

[184] Article 1102: "3. The treatment accorded by a Party under paragraphs 1 and 2 means, with respect to a state or province, treatment no less favorable than the most favorable treatment accorded, in like circumstances, by that state or province to investors, and to investments of investors, of the Party of which it forms a part."

[185] Kurtz (2016), p. 115.

[186] EUSIPA Article 2.3.1. refers to "treatment no less favourable than the treatment it accords, in like situations, to its own investors and their investments". CPTPPP Article 9.4.1 refers to "treatment no less favourable than that it accords, in like circumstances, to its own investors".

[187] Section 3.3.1. considers four approaches in relation to measures taken for legitimate regulatory purposes and whether they should prevent findings of LFT. These include approaches whereby measures that accord LFT in the pursuit of a legitimate objective are prohibited: i. In every circumstance (at least in a *prima facie* sense); ii. When the discrimination does not stem exclusively from a legitimate regulatory distinction; iii. When discrimination is the state's dominant purpose in adopting the measure; or iv. When discrimination is more than a *de minimis* factor in adopting the measure.

(particularly for investors), there is significant authority for an effects-based approach that may be buttressed by evidence of subjective intent. Subjective intent is neither necessary nor sufficient to establish LFT, but may signify a 'smoking gun' in certain circumstances (e.g. the responsible minister clearly stating the protectionist intent of a measure).

At the WTO, the question of whether the test for less favourable treatment is objective or subjective has been interpreted under the GATT, GATS, TBT and SPS Agreements. This question has been treated differently under the GATT compared to the other Agreements because of the its textual set up and the presence of Article III:1.

The authority for an effects-based test was established in *Japan—Alcoholic.*

Beverages II and the Appellate Body subsequently confirmed this approach.[188] The AB applied an objective effects-based test where the focus was on the "design, the architecture and the revealing structure of a measure".[189] The tribunal in *Chile— Alcoholic Beverages* found that the subjective intentions of legislators were not accessible to them but that they were pertinent to the extent that they were given "objective expression" in the legislation.[190]

Subjective intent has however been referred to in buttressing effects-based assessments. In *Canada—Periodicals*, the AB found that the measure's design and structure was to protect domestic industry. The AB relied on statements in a pre-legislative report that the tax's objective was to protect domestic industry.[191] Similarly, in *Mexico—Soft Drinks,* a legislator declared that the purpose of a tax was to protect the national sugar industry.[192] The Panel's findings, which were subsequently confirmed by the AB, noted that the AB had advised not to place too much weight on subjective intention but that in their view it "should not be totally disregarded".[193] The primary inquiry has been, and should be, an objective

---

[188] *Japan— Taxes on Alcoholic Beverages II,* WT/DS8/AB/R. WT/DS10/AB/R, WT/DS11/AB/R (1996) pages 29–31. See for example *Chile— Taxes on Alcoholic Beverages,* WT/DS87/AB/R & WT/DS110/AB/R (1999) para 62, quoting the previous decision.

[189] Japan—Taxes on Alcoholic Beverages II, WT/DS8/AB/R (1996) page 29.

[190] Chile—Taxes on Alcoholic Beverages, WT/DS87/AB/R & WT/DS110/AB/R (1999) para 62.

[191] Appellate Body Report, *Canada – Certain Measures Concerning Periodicals*, WT/DS31/AB/R, adopted 30 July 1997, page 30.

[192] In the investment case Corn Products v Mexico, the panel expressed doubts concerning:

"[R]emarks of individual members of the Mexican Congress about the purpose of the legislation. We have doubts about the extent to which such comments can legitimately be treated as evidence of the intent of the Legislature as a whole, let alone of the State itself, in imposing a measure of this kind, although we do not need finally to decide that point. Para 137

[193] Para 8.91. This finding was subsequently quoted in the Award in *Archer Daniels v. Mexico* (2007).

effects-based test. Where there is evidence of subjective intent, of the nature of *Canada—Periodicals*, this may lend weight to the tribunal's other findings.[194]

In investment law, proof of protectionist intent is neither a necessary nor a sufficient condition for a finding of LFT.[195] Tribunals have generally demonstrated similar scepticism towards subjective intent. Investment law tribunals such as those in *Feldman & Bayindir* have endorsed an objective effects-based test that does not look to the subjective intent of the host state. In *Feldman v. Mexico*, the tribunal was prepared to assume that the differential treatment was based on nationality and that the subjective intention need not be shown "explicitly".[196]

In *Bayindir v. Pakistan*, the tribunal endorsed the Feldman approach and noted that the text of the Article II(2) of the Pakistan- Switzerland BIT supported this (presumably based on the lack of any mention of a subjective approach).[197] The tribunal in *Occidental* noted that it was convinced that discrimination was not the intent of the host state but that LFT was the "result of the policy enacted."[198]

Some tribunals have emphasised the importance of subjective intent to some degree. The *Archer Daniels* and *Methanex* tribunals gave stronger endorsements of intent, while other tribunals, such as that of *SD Myers,* have found that intent is a factor to be taken into account when considering whether there has been a breach of Article 1102.

In *Archer Daniels v. Mexico*, the tribunal reviewed the intent of the measure and found that it was to protect the domestic cane sugar industry.[199] There was nothing in the text of the measure to suggest it was a countermeasure as had been claimed. This was preceded by a reference to the WTO Panel Report in *Mexico—Soft Drinks*,

---

[194] Mitchell et al. are of the view that there has been a failure of the AB to clarify the significance of subjective intent and whether, on its own, it could establish 'protective application' under GATT III:1. Such a clarification would be welcome, but the AB has been quite categorical that the objective effects-based test is the primary subject of inquiry and that subjective intent, while it may be referred to, is a secondary inquiry with a merely buttressing effect. Mitchell et al. (2016), pp. 105–106.

[195] Newcombe and Paradell (2009), pp. 174–175. For Mitchell et al., the concept of the subjective desires of legislators goes beyond the 'regulatory purpose' of a measure as they define it. Mitchell et al. (2016), p. 103. The effects of a measure come within Mitchell's definition of regulatory purpose: 'Regulatory purpose encompasses a measure's actual and objectively ascertainable and rational intended effects'. If regulatory purpose encompasses the effects of a measure, the regulatory purpose must be considered in an effects-based approach to determining less favourable treatment.

[196] *Marvin Roy Feldman Karpa v. Mexico*, NAFTA Tribunal Award, ICSID Case No. ARB(AF)/99/1 (2002), 16 December 2002, para 181.

[197] *Bayindir Insaat Turizm Ticaret Ve Sanayi A.S. v. Pakistan*, Award ICSID Case No. ARB/03/29 (2009) para 390. Article II(2): "Each Party shall accord to these investments, once established, treatment no less favourable than that accorded in similar situations to investments of its investors or to investments of investors of any third country, whichever is the most favourable."

[198] *Occidental Exploration and Production Company v. The Republic of Ecuador*, LCIA Case No. UN3467, Final Award, 1 July 2004, para 177.

[199] *Archer Daniels v. Mexico,* ICSID Case No. ARB (AF)/04/5 Award, 21 November 2007, para 142.

which found that the measure "does not seem to be an unintended effect, but rather an intentional objective".[200]

The tribunal in *Methanex* found that it must be demonstrated that California "intended to favour domestic investors by discriminating against foreign investors".[201] In *Pope & Talbot,* the tribunal found that the approach proposed in the parties' submissions tends to "excuse discrimination that is not facially[202] directed at foreign owned investments".[203] In other words, where intent is not apparent, no discrimination should be found. The tribunal also found that differences in treatment "will presumptively violate" Article 1102(2) unless they are connected to rational government policies.[204]

In *Thunderbird Gaming v. Mexico*, the tribunal found that it was not expected that Thunderbird show that any LFT was motivated because of nationality.[205] No less favourable treatment was found in this dispute. The policies in question were directed at both Mexican and non-Mexican gambling operations and as such "one cannot talk of discrimination" or the subjective intentions of the regulators.[206]

Requiring an investor, or even a government, to demonstrate the subjective intention of a regulator seems excessive. Where there is evidence of discrimination however, it should be considered and form part of the analysis, supplementing an effects-based test. A moderate approach to subjective intent such as this was taken in *SD Myers v. Canada*, where intent was recognised to be an important factor but "not necessarily decisive...if the measure in question were to produce no adverse effect".[207] In *SD Myers*, the tribunal found that factors to be considered included the effect of a measure and whether, on its face, it favours nationals (and thus contains a discriminatory objective). The tribunal found that this should be

---

[200] *Archer Daniels v. Mexico,* ICSID Case No. ARB (AF)/04/5 Award, 21 November 2007, para 141.

[201] *Methanex Corp. v U.S.A*, NAFTA/ UNCITRAL, Final Award of the Tribunal on Jurisdiction and Merits (2005) Part IV Chapter B, para 12. Part IV of the Report also stated, somewhat confusingly, that a demonstration of "malign intent" is not required. *Methanex Corp. v U.S.A*, NAFTA/ UNCITRAL, Final Award of the Tribunal on Jurisdiction and Merits (2005) Part IV Chapter B, para 1.

[202] *Pope & Talbot Inc. v Government of Canada*, NAFTA/UNCITRAL, Tribunal Damages Award IIC 195 (2002). 'Facially' refers to treatment that is not discriminatory on the face of it, or in a *prima facie* sense.

[203] *Pope & Talbot Inc. v Government of Canada*, NAFTA/ UNCITRAL, Tribunal Damages Award IIC 195 (2002) para 79.

[204] *Pope & Talbot Inc. v Government of Canada*, NAFTA/ UNCITRAL, Tribunal Damages Award IIC 195 (2002) para 78.

[205] *International Thunderbird Gaming Corporation v. The United Mexican States*, UNCITRAL, Arbitral Award, 26 January 2006, para 177.

[206] *International Thunderbird Gaming Corporation v. The United Mexican States*, UNCITRAL, Arbitral Award, 26 January 2006, para 181.

[207] *SD Myers, Inc. v Government of Canada*, NAFTA/ UNCITRAL Tribunal, 1st Partial Award and Separate Opinion, IIC 249 (2000) para 254.

determined in the context of all the facts.[208] The tribunal did not make a finding as to whether effect on its own could ground a finding.

LFT, Nexus Requirements, and the Appropriate Standard of Review

The link between a measure and its regulatory purpose may be set at several levels of exigency in order for it to be found not to discriminate. When considering the regulatory purpose of a measure at the LFT stage, should the measure be merely *related to* a legitimate aim or should it be necessary, or even indispensable, in achieving its purpose? There is a risk that if the nexus requirement is set at a level that is less than rigorous, discriminatory treatment may be too easily excluded from treaty protection.[209]

Exceptions articles set out explicitly the required level of connection between a measure and its objective via nexus requirements.[210] These exceptions may apply to the entire treaty (general) or to a single provision (specific).[211] Regulatory purpose may also be considered as part of the inquiry into less favourable treatment, the difference being that the required relationship between the measure and its aims is not made explicit in the treaty text.

In the absence of treaty guidance, what level of link should tribunals look for between a measure and its aims? Mitchell et al. consider three possibilities in this area, the first two of which are deemed "viable" options[212] for the investment regime: (1) a rational or reasonable connection test; (2) necessity analysis; and (3) proportionality analysis.

---

[208] *SD Myers, Inc. v Government of Canada*, NAFTA/ UNCITRAL Tribunal, 1st Partial Award and Separate Opinion, IIC 249 (2000) paras 252–253.

[209] The nexus requirements of general exceptions articles such as GATT Article XX are analysed separately in Chap. 4. This section focuses on the appropriate standard of review for National Treatment provisions that do not include General or Specific Exceptions.

[210] See e.g. Article 2.3.3 EU-Singapore IPA, GATT Article XX. The italicised words of Article 9.8 Australia- China FTA highlight the nexus requirements: General Exceptions

1. For the purposes of this Chapter and subject to the requirement that such measures are not applied in a manner which would constitute arbitrary or unjustifiable discrimination between investments or between investors, or a disguised restriction on international trade or invest- ment, nothing in this Agreement shall be construed to prevent a Party from adopting or enforcing measures: (a) *necessary to* protect human, animal or plant life or health; (b) *necessary to* ensure compliance with laws and regulations that are not inconsistent with this Agreement; (c) *imposed for the protection of* national treasures of artistic, historic or archaeological value; or (d) *relating to* the conservation of living or non-living exhaust- ible natural resources (. . .).

[211] Article 2.3.3 EU-Singapore Investment Protection Agreement qualifies the National Treatment provision (it is noted that there is no MFN Article) and sets out the appropriate nexus requirement for a series of regulatory purposes within the National Treatment Article.

[212] Mitchell et al. (2016), p. 4.

Where a measure needs to merely *relate to* its objective, the nexus requirement risks not being rigorous enough in prohibiting discriminatory measures. A measure may be related to a legitimate regulatory purpose, but taking a broader view, its implementation may be primarily motivated by protectionist intent.[213] Examination of whether a measure is rationally connected to a legitimate objective is a "valid starting point" when examining LFT under IIAs.[214] However, it needs to be supplemented because of the wide range of discriminatory measures that would not be captured because of a tangential link to a legitimate regulatory objective.

Mitchell et al. find necessity analysis to be an adequate means of balancing the needs of capturing discriminatory treatment and preserving the right to regulate.[215] The authors emphasise that necessity analysis must be "appropriately deferential" and allow sufficient leeway to the state. This is unsurprising given how narrowly certain tribunals have interpreted the concept of necessity under Article 25 ARSIWA.

The core of necessity analysis has been described as the deployment of a least-restrictive means (LRM) test, whereby the adjudicator ensures that the measure does not curtail the right any more than is necessary for the government to achieve its stated goals.[216] In practice, tribunals do not invalidate a measure simply because they can find one less restrictive alternative. Rather, most courts check to see that the government did not refuse one or more less restrictive alternatives that were reasonably available.[217]

In trade law, the Appellate Body clarified its approach to necessity under GATT Article XX in *Korea—Beef*, where a "process of weighing and balancing a series of factors" is undertaken.[218] These factors include: (1) the importance of the interest; (2) the extent to which the measure contributes to the realisation of the end pursued; and (3) the impact of the law or regulation on imports or exports. The Appellate

---

[213] Mitchell et al. suggest that this was likely the case in *GAMI v. Mexico*. Mitchell et al. (2016), pp. 87–88, FN239.

[214] Mitchell et al. (2016), p. 160.

[215] Mitchell et al. (2016), p. 163. The authors emphasise that necessity analysis must be "appropriately deferential" and allow sufficient leeway to the state.

[216] Stone Sweet and Mathews (2008), p. 76.

[217] Stone Sweet to Alvarez (5). In contrast to necessity analysis that refers to Article 25 ARSIWA, the tribunal in *Continental Casualty* used the process to resolve a conflict between a rights claim and a non-precluded measures provision. The tribunal elicited one positive principle regarding necessity, which was that the necessity of a measure should be determined by the weighing and balancing of (usually) three factors including the importance of the measure, its contribution to the ends pursued and the restrictiveness imposed by the measure. The tribunal further elicited one negative principle regarding necessity, which was that a measure would not be deemed necessary if a "less inconsistent alternative measure, which the member State concerned could reasonably be expected to employ is available". *Continental Casualty Company v. The Argentine Republic*, Award ICSID Case No. ARB/03/9, IIC 511 (2008) para 195.

[218] This analysis was carried out under GATT Article XX (d), which explicitly states that Members may adopt or enforce measures "necessary to secure compliance with laws or regulations which are not inconsistent with the provisions of this Agreement."

Body subsequently stated that in order for a measure to be considered necessary, it should be "apt to make a material contribution" to its achievement.[219]

Proportionality analysis (PA) is an alternative way of establishing whether there is an appropriate link between a measure and its aims. PA is a multi-stage adjudicative process used by tribunals to settle competing rights claims.[220] The initial stages of suitability and necessity closely resemble the tests above. For PA's third stage, balancing *stricto sensu*, the adjudicator weighs the benefits of the act against the costs incurred by infringement of the right, in order to decide which side shall prevail.[221] Defenders of PA view it as a general principle of law that has diffused globally and provides a coherent framework for settling competing rights claims.[222]

Several authors find that proportionality analysis grants too much discretion to adjudicators.[223] Wagner describes PA as entailing an "inherent power shift" towards tribunals, while Mitchell et al. deem it unworkable in the area of less favourable treatment.[224] While there are legitimate concerns that PA grants too much discretion to tribunals, PA does provide a useful analytical framework for trade and investment tribunals. PA could play a role in instances where measures are rationally connected to their objectives, where there is no alternative that meets this objective to the same extent, but the gains of the measure are outweighed by the infringements of other rights.

---

[219] Appellate Body Report, *Brazil – Measures Affecting Imports of Retreaded Tyres*, WT/DS332/AB/R, adopted 17 December 2007. The AB found that it would be difficult for a panel to find that measure necessary unless it is satisfied that the measure is apt to make a material contribution to the achievement of its objective (para 150).

[220] In its fully developed form, proportionality analysis contains four steps; the first concerns whether the government has the legitimacy to take such a measure; the second considers the suitability of the means in attaining the ends; the third step looks at the necessity of the measure where the "core" is an LRM test; if the first three criteria are fulfilled, the last step involves balancing by the judge where she weighs the benefits of the act against the cost of the infringement. This is a condensed description of Stone Sweet's description of Proportionality Analysis in 'Proportionality Balancing and Global Constitutionalism,' Stone Sweet and Mathews (2008), p. 76.

[221] See Stone Sweet and Della Cananea (2014), pp. 4–5.

[222] Stone Sweet discusses the diffusion of proportionality analysis and how it has "been recognized as an unwritten general principle of law by many of the world's most powerful national and international courts" including the ECJ, ECtHR, WTO AB and in investment tribunals. "In the international investment field, nothing precludes the recognition of norms of due process of law as general principles under Article 38(1)(c) of the ICJ Statute." Stone Sweet and Della Cananea (2014), pp. 18 & 26.

[223] Kurtz is sceptical of balancing that involves "complex value-laden and empirical judgments." In his view, the lack of an appellate mechanism in investment law also makes the LRM test a "better institutional fit". Kurtz (2016), pp. 201–202.

Henckels describes how the *Tecmed* tribunal used proportionality analysis *stricto sensu* without its prior analytical stages and this gives a tribunal "extremely broad discretion" 107.

[224] Wagner (2014), p. 68.

For Mitchell et al., proportionality analysis is unworkable because balancing tests involve "a question of value judgement that gives an undesirable degree of discretion to adjudicators". Mitchell et al. (2016), pp. 163–165.

An illustration of the benefits of this approach is found in the 2004 Israeli Supreme Court case *Beit Sourik*.[225] This case involved a separation fence intended to impede terrorist activity.[226] The proposed route required land seizures. A unanimous Supreme Court panel found that the route was suitable and that no alternative route could provide the same level of security. However, the gains in security as opposed to a less intrusive alternative were found to be insufficient to justify the infringement.[227] While this case falls outside of trade and investment law, its implications are clear. A measure may have a rational aim and achieve its objective well, but its implementation may also have a disproportionate impact on competing rights. The competing rights at stake in *Beit Sourik* are property rights, which are frequently at stake in investment disputes. If a measure has a legitimate aim, and there is no alternative that meets this objective to the same extent, proponents of PA believe tribunals should be able to consider the fact that the implementation of this measure *disproportionately* affects other rights under the trade or investment regime.

3.3 Nondiscrimination Provisions and Engagement

This section now considers the extent of engagement between the two regimes, as well as the role of PTIAs, and the appropriateness of drawing on WTO law for guidance in deciding investment law disputes and vice versa. First, this section looks at the stage at which the regulatory purpose of a measure be considered and the implications of this for inter-regime engagement.

3.3.1 At What Stage Should the Regulatory Purpose of a Measure Be Considered?

A critical question in this area of inter-regime engagement is the stage at which the regulatory purpose of a measure is considered under nondiscrimination provisions.

The purpose of a measure can be considered at the stage of: (a) likeness; (b) less favourable treatment; and/ or (c) treaty exceptions. Table 3.2 attempts to provide a quick guide to the various possibilities under the two regimes.

The purpose of a measure may be considered at more than one (or even all) of these stages. Before addressing the merits and demerits of considering regulatory

---

[225] See Stone Sweet 132–138 for a discussion of proportionality analysis before the Israeli Supreme Court. *Beit Sourik Village Council v. Government of Israel* [2004] IsrSC 58(5) 807, translated in ISR. L. REP. 264 (2004). HCJ 2056/04.

[226] Translated opinion HCJ 2056/04 *Beit Sourik Village Council v. Government of Israel*, Para B1 https://versa.cardozo.yu.edu/opinions/beit-sourik-village-council-v-government-israel

[227] ISR. L. REP. 264, 308-09 (2004). Id. para. 61.

Table 3.2 the stage at which the regulatory purpose of a measure is considered[a]

IIAs		WTO	
The likeness stage			
Yes (RCA)	No (CBA)	No (CBA)	
The LFT stage			
Yes (all)	No (possibly occidental)	Yes (*EC—Asbestos, clove-cigarettes*)	No (*EC—Seal products*)
The exceptions stage			
Yes (e.g. CETA)[b]	No (e.g. NAFTA)	Yes (GATT/GATS)	No (TBT)

[a]The Regulatory Context Approach and Competition-Based Approach are referred to as 'RCA' and 'CBA'
[b]See Article 28.3, where general exceptions apply to the provisions for non-discriminatory treatment and the establishment of investment

purpose at each stage, a comment relating to the investment regime is made in terms of the impact of these considerations on inter-regime engagement. As may be clear, the various pathways in Table 3.2 can lead to considerations for tribunals that are very similar or that have little in common.[228]

Under IIAs, if regulatory purpose is considered at the likeness stage, this likely reduces engagement. This was referred to as the regulatory context approach (RC approach) in the last section. Under the RC approach, likeness extends beyond the competition-based approach, the favoured approach at the WTO.

If regulatory purpose is considered at the LFT stage, this is more facilitative of engagement. This was certainly the case under the *EC—Asbestos* strand of jurisprudence and is in line with current decisions under the TBT Agreement. Where regulatory purpose is considered at the exceptions stage, this may facilitate engagement to the greatest extent. While this traditionally would not have been the case, the current jurisprudence under the GATT post *EC—Seal Products* finds that the purpose of a measure may only be looked to at the exceptions stage.

3.3.1.1 Consideration of Regulatory Purpose at the Likeness Stage

Under the RC approach, a competitive relationship is not seen as necessary so long as the regulatory circumstances of the investors or investments are sufficiently similar.

This approach is contrasted with the competition-based approach (CB approach), which is the approach of choice at the WTO. As concluded above, there are

---

[228]The most similar pathway would involve investment tribunals embracing the CBA, before considering regulatory purpose both at the stage of LFT and the exceptions stage. This would entail very similar considerations to trade tribunals in *EC—Asbestos*. Alternatively, adopting the RCA before considering purpose exclusively under the LFT stage is a pathway that would minimise engagement.

arguments for both approaches, but the RC approach is far less conducive to engagement than the CB approach.

Under this approach, where a measure distinguishes between investors based on a legitimate regulatory purpose, those investors may not be in like circumstances. The burden shifts to the host state to show there was a legitimate regulatory purpose behind the discrimination and to reverse the finding of likeness. Likeness based on economic sector can be rebutted where there is a reason to distinguish investors for regulatory purposes.[229]

The regulatory purpose of the treatment must be taken into account in establishing breach of national treatment provisions in investment agreements. The only dispute that perhaps goes against this idea is *Occidental v. Ecuador*.

In *Feldman v. Mexico*,[230] the company was found to be in like circumstances with cigarette reseller-exporters but not cigarette producer-exporters as there were "rational bases" for treating them differently.[231] The tribunal found that firms reselling or exporting cigarettes were in like circumstances while those merely producing cigarettes were not. It was acknowledged that there are "at least some rational bases" for treating these investors differently including discouraging smuggling, protecting intellectual property rights inter alia.[232]

In *Cargill v. Mexico*, the tribunal found that like circumstances is not determined in the abstract but rather "by reference to the rationale for the measure that was being challenged." Indeed in respect of other measures, the mills in GAMI and the lumber producers in Pope & Talbot "could have been found to be in 'like circumstances'." Thus the question is whether investors are in "like circumstances" *with respect to the particular measure in question.*[233]

Kurtz advocates that competition should be a condition of likeness. Kurtz's view is that the aim of investment agreements is to facilitate capital flows and that while operating in a host state investors are "usually and naturally operating in some form of competition with domestic actors".[234] Any tribunal that ignores competition should address the "serious risk of political failure" in constructing their preferred approach.[235]

For Pauwelyn every major interpretation has rejected the trade law emphasis on "alteration of the conditions of competition" in favour of one that focuses on whether discrimination is based upon nationality rather than some other policy reason ("the

---

[229] See for example, *Windstream Energy LLC v. Government of Canada*, Award PCA Case No. 2013-22 (2016).

[230] *Marvin Feldman v. Mexico*, (ICSID Case No. ARB(AF)/99/1).

[231] Di Mascio and Pauwelyn (2008), p. 74.

[232] *Marvin Roy Feldman Karpa v. Mexico*, NAFTA Tribunal Award, ICSID Case No. ARB(AF)/99/1 (2002), 16 December 2002, paras 170-71.

[233] See *Mercer International Inc. v. Government of Canada*, Award ICSID Case No. ARB(AF)/12/3 (2018) para 7.21.

[234] Kurtz (2016), pp. 96–97.

[235] Kurtz (2016), p. 97.

regulatory context test").[236] Kurtz disagrees that investment tribunals have rejected the competition-based approach.

In *Corn Products v. Mexico*, the tribunal concluded that the products were "interchangeable and indistinguishable" for end-users and were therefore in like circumstances.[237] While the tribunal did not consider the regulatory purpose of a measure, it is important to remember that Mexico did not defend the measure on this basis.[238]

3.3.1.2 Consideration of Regulatory Purpose at the LFT Stage

If a measure taken for a legitimate regulatory purpose also has a discriminatory effect, should it be permitted? At the WTO, the jurisprudence has been inconsistent in relation to the question of whether a discriminatory measure (i.e. one that accords less favourable treatment), which is appropriately connected to a legitimate objective, is prohibited.[239] This section considers four approaches in relation to measures taken for legitimate regulatory purposes and whether they should prevent findings of LFT. These approaches consider the level of discrimination permissible in pursuit of a legitimate objective. Measures that accord LFT in the pursuit of a legitimate objective may be prohibited:

(i) In every circumstance (at least in a *prima facie* sense);
(ii) When the discrimination does not stem exclusively from a legitimate regulatory distinction;
(iii) When discrimination is the state's dominant purpose in adopting the measure; or
(iv) When discrimination is more than a *de minimis* factor in adopting the measure.[240]

---

[236] Di Mascio and Pauwelyn (2008), pp. 75–76.

[237] *Corn Products International, Inc. v. United Mexican States,* Decision on Responsibility (redacted version) ICSID Case No. ARB (AF)/04/1, 15 January 2008, para 126.

[238] *Corn Products International, Inc. v. United Mexican States,* Decision on Responsibility (redacted version) ICSID Case No. ARB (AF)/04/1, 15 January 2008, para 125: Mexico raised three factors which, it claimed, militated against CPI and the sugar producers being in like circumstances: (1) the fact that the price for sugar was regulated, whereas that for HFCS was not, (2) the fact that Mexican sugar was to a significant extent denied access to the United States market during the relevant period, whereas there was no barrier to trade in HFCS across the US-Mexican border, and (3) the fact that the trade association of which CPI was a member had lobbied in the United States against increasing the amount of Mexican sugar which could be imported into the United States.

[239] See Section A.III.2 of this chapter.

[240] As stated above, consideration of regulatory purpose at the LFT stage may facilitate engagement to a considerable extent. This would be the case to varying degrees under approaches 2–4.

The Detrimental Impact Approach

This approach prohibits consideration of the regulatory purpose of a measure at the LFT stage. The Appellate Body followed this approach in *EC—Seal Products* where it established that detrimental impact alone is sufficient to establish breach of GATT Article III. A Member's right to regulate "is accommodated under Article XX" (GATT). Under this approach, where it is established that a measure is discriminatory, it will always be prohibited under GATT Article III. This measure may then be justified under Article XX. This approach relies on a comprehensive exceptions article similar to GATT Article XX. However, this approach has serious limitations. No investment tribunal appears to have adopted this approach.[241]

Discrimination Stemming Exclusively from a Legitimate Purpose

This approach has been taken at the WTO under the TBT Agreement. At first, it seems to be overly demanding of the defending state or host state in the investment context. However, the Appellate Body has interpreted the "stemming exclusively" standard rather flexibly.

In *US—Clove Cigarettes*, the Appellate Body found that detrimental effect on competition is inconsistent with TBT Article 2.1 "unless it stems exclusively from a legitimate regulatory distinction."[242] The AB applied this standard once more in *US—Tuna II* and *US—COOL*.[243] The AB has regard to the circumstances of the case, the design and application of the regulation *inter alia*, as well as "whether that technical regulation is even-handed", in order to determine whether a measure is discriminatory.[244] This concept of even-handedness has proved to be critical in some decisions. In *US—Tuna II*, the AB found that the differences in labelling requirements for tuna caught in the Eastern Pacific Ocean and elsewhere were not

---

[241] Mitchell et al. claim that the tribunal in *Occidental (No 1)* refused to consider legitimate objectives at all. However it is unclear what legitimate regulatory objectives the tribunal could have considered. This case related to VAT refunds, including previously granted ones, which were now disputed. Ecuador argued these were based on a mistaken interpretation of its Tax Law and sought the return of previous refunds. Mitchell et al. (2016), p. 140.

[242] At the WTO, the TBT Agreement differs from the GATT in that it has no General Exceptions article, akin to GATT Article XX. This difference in the architecture of the Agreements has led to different tests being developed by the Appellate Body. Rather than deferring analysis of the purpose of the measure to an Exceptions Article (as above), the purpose of the measure is considered when determining whether TBT Article 2.1 has been breached.

[243] Appellate Body Report, *United States – Measures Concerning the Importation, Marketing and Sale of Tuna and Tuna Products*, WT/DS381/AB/R, adopted 13 June 2012, para 297; see also *Appellate Body Reports, United States – Certain Country of Origin Labelling (COOL) Requirements*, WT/DS384/AB/R, WT/DS386/AB/R, adopted 23 July 2012, para 340.

[244] Appellate Body Report, *United States – Measures Affecting the Production and Sale of Clove Cigarettes*, WT/DS406/AB/R, adopted 24 April 2012, para 182.

"even-handed in the relevant respects" or "calibrated" to the risks to dolphins arising from different fishing methods.[245]

The following year saw the re-emergence of this issue in *EC—Seal Products*. The EU described its interpretation of "even-handedness" in relation to TBT Article 2.1 as follows in its response to a question from the Panel in *EC—Seal Products*[246]:

"The assessment of a measure's "even-handedness" entails examining whether the measure is "fair", "non-discriminatory" and "calibrated" to the purpose its pursues...The concept of "even-handedness", like discrimination, refers to whether two similar factual situations are treated differently and whether the specific measure is "calibrated" (and does not go beyond what it is necessary) to achieve its purpose" (footnotes omitted).[247]

While the standard of proof for showing a measure stems *exclusively* from a legitimate regulatory purpose seems very high, it appears that consideration of whether a measure is designed and applied in an even-handed manner is a key component of this determination. This rather vague notion of even-handedness potentially brings the concept of necessity into Article 2.1, at least according to the EU's interpretation.[248] It may be difficult to design measures so they can be shown to stem exclusively from a legitimate purpose. Measures may unintentionally have a greater impact on another state's products or investments compared to domestic counterparts. As such, demonstrating this exclusive purpose may also prove difficult.

The Dominant Purpose Approach

This approach reflects the view that a measure should only be invalidated where there is clear and convincing proof that protectionism was the state's *dominant*

---

[245] Appellate Body Report, *United States – Measures Concerning the Importation, Marketing and Sale of Tuna and Tuna Products*, WT/DS381/AB/R, adopted 13 June 2012, para 297. This case concerned a 'dolphin-safe' labelling measure, which was found not to stem exclusively from a legitimate regulatory purpose, as it did not extend to other fishing methods that posed equivalent risks to dolphins. This measure was found not to stem exclusively from a legitimate regulatory distinction because it involved circling dolphin pods (groups) with nets as a way to catch tuna. This was not applied outside the ETP where the risk to dolphins was also high. This raises question of states applying different requirements or standards in different parts of its territory.

[246] The Appellate Body did not address even-handedness within the context of the TBT Agreement as it reversed the Panel's finding that the EU Seal Regime constituted a technical regulation.

[247] European Union's Responses to the First Set of Questions from the Panel, European Communities—Measures Prohibiting the Importation and Marketing of Seal Products (DS400, DS401) para 120.

[248] European Union's Responses to the First Set of Questions from the Panel, European Communities—Measures Prohibiting the Importation and Marketing of Seal Products (DS400, DS401) para 120.

purpose. Kurtz emphasises that the entirety of the evidence must be considered and that, for example, a speech of a single legislator would be no "smoking gun".[249]

An issue with the dominant purpose approach is that the bar for finding against host states may be set too high in requiring complainants to demonstrate that protectionist motives were 'dominant' in the design and application of a measure. The *de minimis* approach allows for some discriminatory regulatory purpose but would fall well below requiring a demonstration that protectionism was the state's dominant purpose.

Furthermore, there is the potential difficulty of the bar being set at different levels for different host states or WTO Members. Would it be easier for a Nordic country to claim environmentalism was the dominant purpose for a carbon emissions tax than a country with less environmental credentials? If a *significant* but not *dominant* discriminatory and protectionist purpose is permitted, how should this be applied to states with different track records?

The *de Minimis* Approach

Mitchell et al. refer to whether a measure has more than a *de minimis* differentiation of regulatory purpose between investors as "likely to be an important proxy" for whether it truly has a rational or reasonable connection to a legitimate object.[250] Another way of putting this is that if a measure has a "significant or important" discriminatory or protectionist regulatory purpose, it should be prohibited.[251] While the dominant purpose approach appears to give too much leeway to host states and to give rise to interpretative issues, the *de minimis* approach strikes a better balance between capturing discriminatory treatment and preserving the right to regulate.

If a measure is found to be necessary for public health or the conservation of natural resources, the inquiry should not end here. A measure should not be considered to be the LRM of achieving an objective if there is more than a *de minimis* level of differentiation in the design and application of the measure.[252] In conclusion, measures with a discriminatory effect should only be permitted where this is a result of a legitimate regulatory distinction, and this effect is of a *de minimis* nature.

---

[249] Kurtz (2014), p. 301.

[250] Mitchell et al. (2016), pp. 165–166.

[251] Mitchell et al. (2016), p. 167. This is somewhat undermined by their previous statement (p. 141) that "where a measure is appropriately connected to a legitimate objective, this justifies any differential treatment under the IIA".

[252] E.g. the health risks of tobacco may necessitate certain regulatory interventions, but any more than a *de minimis* differentiation between investors on the basis of nationality should be prohibited.

3.3.1.3 Consideration of Regulatory Purpose Under Treaty Exceptions

Consideration of the regulatory purpose of a measure is often provided for at the treaty exceptions stage. Pursuant to *EC—Seal Products*, interpretations of GATT Article III are primarily through an economic lens with the regulatory purpose of measures being examined at the treaty exceptions stage.[253]

This pathway is unlikely to be followed under IIAs, where quite a few treaties do not contain general exceptions provisions, particularly older IIAs such as NAFTA. According to UNCTAD's Investment Policy Hub, only 241 out of 2576 IIAs contained public health and environment exceptions (9.36%).[254] There is a divide in more recent agreements. Neither CPTPP nor USCMA contain general exceptions, while agreements concluded by the EU tend to include exceptions covering certain areas.

3.3.2 The Extent of Engagement

Nondiscrimination provisions are a shared norm of the trade and investment law regimes. Although national treatment and MFN provisions are common across trade and investment law, there are differences in how these provisions operate in the two regimes.[255] The national treatment standard is necessarily more abstract in trade law than in investment law and this is reflected in how the provisions have been interpreted. Investment law's focus is primarily on protecting investors whereas trade law focuses on trade liberalisation and market access. National treatment claims may be taken for a wider range of issues under the investment law regime as it "covers the entire lifecycle" of an investment.[256] Investment disputes involve specific investors claiming for breaches in relation to a specific investment. The type of review is also different, as damages should be specifically connected to measures of the host state for a remedy to be provided. This is why the criteria used in trade law cannot be directly imported into investment law and vice versa. Nonetheless,

---

[253] See Appellate Body Reports, *European Communities – Measures Prohibiting the Importation and Marketing of Seal Products*, WT/DS400/AB/R, WT/DS401/AB/R, adopted 18 June 2014, 5.88–5.130.

[254] UNCTAD's Investment Policy Hub website: https://investmentpolicy.unctad.org/international-investment-agreements/iia-mapping, last accessed 28 August 2020. This topic is explored in greater detail in Chap. 4.

[255] As per Section A, national treatment in trade focuses on competition, which requires a broad comparison of groups of like products or services. If there is competition, differential treatment is then assumed to be based on nationality. Investment law focuses on the individual foreign investor, rather than a group-based evaluation between classes of investors.

[256] Di Mascio and Pauwelyn (2008), p. 68.

there is a "convergence in functionality" in the role of national treatment across the systems.[257]

Likewise, MFN treatment differs at the WTO and under IIAs. Under the GATT, MFN treatment extends any advantage accorded to any product immediately and unconditionally to all like products or services of other Members. MFN treatment is broader under IIAs and concerns the treatment of investments as well as procedural provisions. They have been invoked to import more favourable substantive treatment from another treaty, to claim a general treatment not provided in the 'basic treaty', for disregarding limitations to treatment provided in the 'basic treaty', and for importing more favourable dispute settlement provisions.

Engagement may be impacted by the exclusion of legitimate regulatory purpose under GATT Article III in *EC—Seal Products*. This entails a divergence of outcomes for disputes under the GATT and TBT Agreements. It also limits engagement with nondiscrimination provisions in IIAs that explicitly require the consideration of the totality of the circumstances for findings of like circumstances.[258]

In line with *EC—Seal Products*, consideration of regulatory purpose has to be done under Article XX where the burden of proof lies with the defendant, there are limited grounds for justification, and these grounds were drawn up in 1947. Interpreting GATT Article III was complicated before *EC—Seal Products*, but its simplification risks coming at a high price.

3.3.3 Cross-Regime References

3.3.3.1 Why Make Cross-Regime References?

Nondiscrimination provisions are quasi-ubiquitous in the two regimes and there are significant commonalities between these provisions in trade and investment agreements. In line with Article 31(3)(c) of the VCLT, tribunals may consider in their interpretations "any relevant rules of international law applicable in the relations between the parties". Nondiscrimination provisions and norms common to the two regimes, such as likeness and less favourable treatment, form a part of this body of relevant rules and can thus be considered by tribunals in their interpretations.

---

[257] Kurtz (2016), p. 85.

[258] E.g. CPTPP's investment chapter contains a clarificatory footnote to the National Treatment provision, stating: "For greater certainty, whether treatment is accorded in "like circumstances" under Article 9.4 (National Treatment) or Article 9.5 (Most-Favoured-Nation Treatment) depends on the totality of the circumstances, including whether the relevant treatment distinguishes between investors or investments on the basis of legitimate public welfare objectives." This chapter contains no general exceptions provision and this clarification introduces an assessment as to the state's regulatory purpose to the test for likeness. The Drafters' Note from CPTPP has been replicated in PTIAs such as USMCA (2018) and RCEP (2020).

When interpreting these shared provisions, tribunals in the trade and investment regimes ask similar questions, and it may be useful for tribunals to consider how the norm in question has been interpreted in the other regime. The main (or at least typical) interpretative questions arising under national treatment and most-favoured nation provisions include: (i) identifying a comparator; (ii) demonstrating they are in like circumstances; and (iii) showing less favourable treatment has been accorded. Tribunals may refer to the other regime and take into consideration how they have dealt with these questions.

One of the major interpretative questions concerning national treatment at the WTO has centred on whether regulatory purpose should be considered under GATT Article III, or whether this should be reserved for when breach has been found, and a measure is being defended under GATT Article XX. In line with *EC- Seal Products*, consideration of regulatory purpose has to be done under GATT Article XX. This structure may not be replicated in PTIAs, even those directly incorporating general exceptions provisions.

The argument for cross-regime references would benefit from greater consistency in the trade law jurisprudence. The WTO jurisprudence on national treatment has seen at least six different phases of interpretation.[259] The reasoning has at times been artificial and very legalistic. This may have been simplified to some extent in *EC— Seal Products* but this comes at a price given the limitations of GATT Article XX.

Although WTO tribunals have not drawn upon investment law jurisprudence to date, such "reverse-crossfertilisation" is a lot easier to imagine in the case of IIAs such as CETA where: (1) the text of a WTO provision is directly incorporated into an investment agreement; (2) the structures of these agreements are similar; and (3) where an appellate organ may be interpreting these provisions. Other WTO Agreements such as the TBT Agreement and TRIPS do not contain General Exceptions and reverse-crossfertilisation is again easier to imagine in relation to Agreements with similar structures such as the USMCA and CPTPP, for example.

3.3.3.2 Have There Been Cross-Regime References?

When interpreting nondiscrimination provisions, cross-regime references have been unidirectional, with four investment tribunals referring to WTO jurisprudence. These four disputes all concerned investment tribunals considering the relevance of WTO law in relation to national treatment provisions. WTO tribunals have tended not to make external references when interpreting these provisions.

In *SD Myers v. Canada*, the tribunal made the first cross-regime reference when it endorsed a competition-based approach to likeness in its interpretation of NAFTA's

---

[259] See Pauwelyn 62–65 for periods one to five. A sixth period has undoubtedly commenced post EC-Seal Products.

national treatment provision. In doing so, the tribunal referred to WTO jurisprudence while taking into account contextual differences between the regimes.[260]

The tribunal in *Occidental v. Ecuador* rejected the relevance of trade law jurisprudence in its interpretation of the national treatment provision of the Ecuador—US BIT (1993) as being "not specifically pertinent".[261] The tribunal underlined the fact that disputes under investment treaties involve exporters and trade law involves imported products and based on this, it found that the purposes of national treatment in the two regimes are "opposite".[262]

In *Methanex v. United States* and *Merrill & Ring v. Canada,* the tribunals considered but ultimately rejected the relevance of trade law principles in relation to likeness. In *Methanex*, the tribunal found that it may "derive guidance" from legal reasoning developed in GATT and WTO jurisprudence on likeness.[263] Ultimately it was not persuaded as to the relevance of GATT jurisprudence and underlined the intent of the drafters to create "distinct regimes for trade and investment".[264] The tribunal noted that the drafting parties were fluent in GATT law and incorporated it "when they wished to do so" (i.e. in other chapters of NAFTA).[265] Kurtz has claimed that misuse of WTO law by the tribunals in *Occidental* and *Methanex* has been the controlling factor for critical inconsistency in investment law jurisprudence leading to "wildly inconsistent outcomes".[266]

In *Merrill & Ring v. Canada*, the tribunal followed a similar approach to *Methanex* and found that the investor must be compared to log producers subject to the same regime rather than producers in other provinces, this being the comparator in the most "like circumstances".[267] The tribunal did not exclude the possibility of a contextual interpretation of a treaty provision in the light of provisions of other treaties such as the GATT, *in appropriate cases.*[268]

However Canada "persuasively argued" that log exporters in British Columbia were the appropriate comparator. Canada argued that 'in like circumstances' should

---

[260] *SD Myers, Inc. v Government of Canada*, NAFTA/ UNCITRAL Tribunal, 1st Partial Award and Separate Opinion, IIC 249 (2000) para 243–251.

[261] *Occidental Petroleum Corp. v. The Republic of Ecuador*, Final Award, UNCITRAL Arbitration, London Court of International Arbitration Case No. UN 3467 (2004) paras. 175.

[262] *Occidental Petroleum Corp. v. The Republic of Ecuador*, Final Award, UNCITRAL Arbitration, London Court of International Arbitration Case No. UN 3467 (2004) paras. 174–175.

[263] *Methanex Corp. v U.S.A*, NAFTA/ UNCITRAL, Final Award of the Tribunal on Jurisdiction and Merits (2005) Part II Chapter B, para 6.

[264] *Methanex Corp. v U.S.A*, NAFTA/ UNCITRAL, Final Award of the Tribunal on Jurisdiction and Merits (2005) Part IV Chapter B, para 35.

[265] *Methanex Corp. v U.S.A*, NAFTA/ UNCITRAL, Final Award of the Tribunal on Jurisdiction and Merits (2005) Part IV Chapter B, para 30.

[266] Kurtz (2009), p. 6. Kurtz (2016), p. 18.

[267] *Merrill & Ring Forestry LP v. Canada*, ICSID Case No. UNCT/07/1, Award, 31 March 2010, para 71.

[268] *Merrill & Ring Forestry LP v. Canada*, ICSID Case No. UNCT/07/1, Award, 31 March 2010, para 84.

not be interpreted in the light of the GATT because Article 1102 reflects a specific understanding and intent of the parties and should be read on its own terms.[269]

3.3.3.3 Caveats When Making Cross-Regime References

When tribunals compare shared norms between the regimes, they must be mindful of certain differences between the regimes, including: (1) textual differences; (2) contextual differences; (3) the differing purposes of agreements; and (4) systemic differences.[270] These differences may justify tailored or nuanced approaches in the context of the particular regime where a norm is being applied.

Tribunals must be attentive to textual and contextual differences between agreements. The wording of agreements is a paramount consideration for tribunals when interpreting shared legal norms such as national treatment. While the wording may be fairly homogenous in some areas (e.g. the less favourable treatment standard), tribunals have to be particularly attentive to differences in wording concerning 'likeness' and wording that relates to regulatory purpose.[271] There are differences in the wording of provisions relating to likeness in trade and investment agreements. The WTO Agreements refer to 'like products' and 'like services' in the GATT and GATS. When incorporating the concept of likeness, drafters of IIAs typically refer to the need for investors to be 'in like situations'[272] or 'in like circumstances'[273] for investment and services chapters. For chapters concerning trade in goods, the drafters of IIAs have referred to 'any like, directly competitive or substitutable goods'[274] or just 'like, directly competitive or substitutable goods.'[275] Another

---

[269] *Merrill & Ring Forestry LP v. Canada*, ICSID Case No. UNCT/07/1, Award, 31 March 2010, para 91.

[270] Chapter 1.IV.4 outlines the primary considerations when comparing legal norms or concepts between the systems for the purposes of this book, including; (1) textual and contextual differences; (2) the differing purposes of agreements; and (3) systemic differences between the regimes.

[271] E.g. CPTPP's investment chapter contains a clarificatory footnote to the National Treatment provision, stating: "For greater certainty, whether treatment is accorded in "like circumstances" under Article 9.4 (National Treatment) or Article 9.5 (Most-Favoured-Nation Treatment) depends on the totality of the circumstances, including whether the relevant treatment distinguishes between investors or investments on the basis of legitimate public welfare objectives." This chapter contains no general exceptions provision and this clarification introduces an assessment as to the state's regulatory purpose to the test for likeness.

[272] See for example, CETA, Article 8.6: National treatment.

[273] See for example, KORUS, Article 11.3: National treatment.

[274] Chapter 3 NAFTA on national treatment and market access for goods, Article 301 states:

> 2. The provisions of paragraph 1 regarding national treatment shall mean, with respect to a state or province, treatment no less favorable than the most favorable treatment accorded by such state or province *to any like, directly competitive or substitutable goods*, as the case may be, of the Party of which it forms a part. (emphasis added)

[275] Chapter 2 CETA on national treatment and market access for goods, Article 2.3.

example of a textual difference between national treatment provisions is that of
GATT Article III:1, which unusually indicates the telos of the provision. No such
guidance is given in NAFTA Article 1102, CETA Article 8.6 etc.

To what extent should the different wordings of nondiscrimination provisions
facilitate or exclude the possibility of crossfertilisation? The tribunal in *Methanex
v. U.S.A* noted that while NAFTA referred to 'like circumstances', the GATT
referred to 'like products'.[276] It then constructed a hypothetical wording of Article
1102 referring to like goods concluding it would be "incongruous, indeed odd".[277]
The tribunal found that this showed the parties' intent to have distinct regimes for
trade and investment.[278] Kurtz disputes that the term 'like products' itself had played
a critical role in the jurisprudence of the GATT, finding that the likeness test
developed thereunder does not "flow from the use of the term 'like products'" but
rather from the overall context of GATT Article III.[279] The absence of a particular
wording, or the fact that it has not been incorporated directly need not preclude its
relevance and lessons being taken from other regimes. Minor differences in wording
need not be insurmountable in the making cross-regime references.

In terms of contextual differences, there is a difference between agreements that
contain a general exceptions provision, such as GATT Article XX, and those that do
not. Under NAFTA Article 1102, the purpose of a measure is considered when
examining whether there has been a breach of the article itself rather than doing so
under a treaty exception. While this was also the case under the GATT from 2001,
this position was reversed in *EC—Seal Products* (2014), where it was found that
there is no need to consider the regulatory purpose of the measure in Article III:1
separately, as the purpose of a measure is reserved exclusively for Article XX.[280]

---

[276] *Methanex Corp. v U.S.A*, NAFTA/ UNCITRAL, Final Award of the Tribunal on Jurisdiction and
Merits (2005): "It may also be assumed that if the drafters of NAFTA had wanted to incorporate
trade criteria in its investment chapter by engrafting a GATT-type formula, they could have
produced a version of Article 1102 stating "Each Party shall accord to investors [or investments]
of another Party treatment no less favorable than it accords its own investors, in like circumstances
with respect to any like, directly competitive or substitutable goods". It is clear from this construc-
tive exercise how incongruous, indeed odd, would be the juxtaposition in a single provision dealing
with investment of "like circumstances" and "any like, directly competitive or substitutable goods".

[277] Such a wording would have read: "Each Party shall accord to investors [or investments] of
another Party treatment no less favorable than that it accords its own investors, in like circumstances
with respect to any like, directly competitive or substitutable goods". *Methanex Corp. v U.S.A*,
NAFTA/ UNCITRAL, Final Award of the Tribunal on Jurisdiction and Merits (2005) Part IV
Chapter B, para 34.

[278] See also *Bayindir Insaat Turizm Ticaret Ve Sanayi A.S. v. Pakistan*, Award ICSID Case
No. ARB/03/29 (2009) para 389.

[279] Kurtz (2009), p. 767.

[280] Appellate Body Report, *European Communities – Measures Prohibiting the Importation and
Marketing of Seal Products*, WT/DS400/AB/R and WT/DS401/AB/R, adopted on 18 June 2014. Di
Mascio and Pauwelyn (2008), p. 72. The trade and investment regimes jointly look to likeness (via a
test for competition), less favourable treatment (via a test for disparate impact) and to other reasons
that may justify a measure. In trade law, differential treatment (less favourable treatment) of

The Appellate Body had previously found in *EC-Asbestos* that GATT Articles III and XX "are distinct and independent provisions" and so a measure may be deemed unjustifiable for public health reasons under both.[281]

Tests at the WTO in relation to national treatment have been developed within a different context to that that facing an investment tribunal. This is easiest to see in relation to GATT Article III, which has a complicated textual set up. Notwithstanding its textual set up, many tribunals at the WTO and in investment law still look to jurisprudence under the GATT because of its status as the grandmother provision of national treatment provisions at the WTO and the number of disputes that have been taken under it. Any attempt to draw upon GATT jurisprudence must be mindful of contextual differences which GATT Article III:1 and XX likely represent. A major difference between GATT Article III and Article 1102 of NAFTA is that there is no guide in the latter which tells us what type of discrimination tribunals should be looking for.

GATT Article III:1 explicitly tells us that the purpose of the national treatment provision is so that taxes and regulations "should not be applied to imported or domestic products so as to afford protection to domestic production." NAFTA's much-litigated national treatment provision can be a useful comparator to the trade law approach. There is no such guide, or limitations, on the purpose of Article 1102. A significant difference between considering regulatory purposes as justification rather than as a substantive element of nondiscrimination is in the burden of proof.[282] GATT Article XX also provides a list of General Exceptions that is not present in IIAs such as NAFTA.

The *SD Myers* tribunal carefully considered the contextual difference between national treatment under the WTO Agreements and under the NAFTA, with regard to the fact that there are no general exceptions under Article XX in NAFTA. The tribunal then found that SD Myers was in like circumstances with Canadian operators based on the competitive relationship between them. SD Myers were "in a position to attract customers that might otherwise have gone to the Canadian operators".[283] Thus the tribunal endorsed a competition-based approach to likeness.

Even where wordings are very similar, context may lead to diverging interpretations. This is the case in relation to 'less favourable treatment', where the assessment under the TBT is different to that under the GATT and the GATS, which are impacted by the presence of GATT Article XX and GATS Article XIV respectively. Likeness has however been interpreted differently under the GATS compared to the

---

competing products is enough to find a prima facie violation of the GATT or the GATS. Under PTIAs such as NAFTA, this is not enough as other policy justifications can be referred to.

[281] Appellate Body Report, *European Communities – Measures Affecting Asbestos and Asbestos-Containing Products*, WT/DS/135/AB/R, adopted on 5 April 2001, para 115.

[282] Diebold (2010), p. 87.

[283] *SD Myers, Inc. v Government of Canada*, NAFTA/ UNCITRAL Tribunal, 1st Partial Award and Separate Opinion, IIC 249 (2000) para 251. Wu categorises regard to these differences as a "rejection of the WTO approach" in emphasising the contextual differences between the regimes. Wu (2014), p. 64/82.

GATT and the TBT Agreement given the textual differences between the Agreements.[284]

Tribunals must also consider the different purposes of the agreements when interpreting nondiscrimination provisions. Deciding on, for example, whether competition plays a role in establishing likeness comes down to how the purpose of national treatment in investment law is understood. For Kurtz, the telos of such provisions is to "prevent discrimination based upon nationality"[285] as opposed to discrimination for other reasons, much like under the WTO regime.

For example, the object and purpose of an investment agreement could feed into a tribunal's analysis of the regulatory purpose of a measure in its likeness analysis. A strong reference in the preamble to the right to regulate could affect a tribunal's interpretation of what constitutes a legitimate regulatory purpose and how broadly it could distinguish between investors.

A treaty is to be interpreted in light of "its object and purpose" which is to be found in the treaty's preamble. This could affect an interpretation of a national treatment provision in a couple of key ways. Preambles can facilitate crossfertilisation based on: (1) a reference to WTO law in the preamble; and (2) the strength of any reference to the host state's right to regulate within the preamble. In the absence of any such provisions in the preamble, tribunals have to be careful, particularly in relation to older style BITs, that they strike an appropriate balance in their interpretations between the protection of investment and that the host state's right to regulate.

Finally, tribunals must consider systemic differences and differences in the remedy structures between the two regimes when interpreting nondiscrimination provisions under PTIAs and BITs. These differences mean that there are potentially severe consequences if a tribunal gives an overly broad or narrow reading of a provision, particularly if it gives rise to monetary damages. Findings of breach under IIAs are not confined to the removal of measures or the authorisation of counter-measures, as is the case in the trade law regime. For Kurtz, the inter-state character of the WTO acts as a "filter against improper or incautious invocation of rights", while such a filter does not exist in investor-state arbitration.[286] A further difference is the lack of a possibility of appeal in the investment regime except for a very limited number of grounds in all but the most recent IIAs, e.g. CETA. Tribunals have to be mindful of these factors in their awards and in striking a balance that is appropriate for the investment regime, rather than following a test that may have been designed and calibrated to the systemic features of the WTO.

---

[284]To summarise: In terms of likeness, interpretations under the GATT have been similar to those under the TBT and unlike those under GATS. Interpretations under the GATT are similar to those under the TBT but have been different to those under the GATS (GATT $\equiv$ TBT $\neq$ GATS). In terms of less favourable treatment, interpretations under the GATT have been similar to those under the GATS and unlike those under TBT (GATT $\equiv$ GATS $\neq$ TBT).

[285]Di Mascio and Pauwelyn (2008), p. 72.

[286]Kurtz (2016), p. 92.

3.3.4   The Role of PTIAs

This section considers whether nondiscrimination provisions in PTIAs result in increased levels of engagement between the trade and investment law regimes compared to their counterparts in BITs.[287] In terms of parallels in content, the four norms and standards considered in this chapter were all highly prevalent throughout the 120 PTIAs and BITs contained in this study. National treatment, MFN treatment and LFT were close to ubiquitous throughout the agreements. Likeness on the other hand featured in 59/60 PTIAs and 31/60 BITs (52%) in this study's sample. Likeness is thus considerably more prevalent in the sample of PTIAs compared to the BITs. For the other three provisions, there is a negligible increase in the parallels in the content of the PTIAs compared to the BITs at least from a quantitative perspective.[288] It is clear from the sample that nondiscrimination provisions are highly prevalent and potentially a catalyst for inter-regime engagement.

The second measure for increased engagement concerns cross-regime references and whether they are more likely to occur because of the nondiscrimination provisions in PTIAs compared to their counterparts in BITs. Such references are more likely to occur in relation to a standard such as 'likeness', which was found to be more prevalent in PTIAs than in BITs.[289] Tribunals are more likely to draw upon these PTIA provisions.

The role of PTIAs in relation to nondiscrimination provisions and the scope for crossfertilisation depends on several factors. One of the most important of these is the stage, or stages, at which the regulatory purpose of a measure is considered. Under the GATT, following *EC—Seals*, the regulatory purpose of a measure is considered exclusively under GATT Article XX. It appears that this is also the case under the GATS.[290] Under the TBT Agreement, which does not contain general exceptions, regulatory purpose has formed part of the LFT analysis in line with

---

[287] Engagement was defined in Chap. 1: Engagement between trade and investment occurs wherever the content of an investment agreement has a parallel in the trade regime or vice versa. The term 'content' can cover an agreement's preamble, definitions, substantive provisions, exceptions etc. Engagement also occurs in dispute settlement whenever there are cross-regime references by the parties or the tribunal or parallels in the practices or features of dispute settlement. Engagement does not imply convergence and may fall short of this in a given area between the two regimes.

[288] A national treatment provision featured in all of the PTIAs and 58/60 BITs (96.66%). The MFN standard featured in 55/60 PTIAs (91.66%) and 58/60 BITs (96.66) surveyed as part of this study. The concept of less favourable treatment featured in 60/60 PTIAs and 59/60 BITs (98.33%) surveyed as part of this study.

[289] National treatment, MFN treatment and LFT were as prevalent in PTIAs as they were in BITs for the sample taken in this study. It is thus inconclusive whether tribunals would be more likely to draw upon these PTIA provisions on this basis alone.

[290] See Appellate Body Report, *Argentina – Measures Relating To Trade In Goods And Services*, WT/DS453/AB/R, adopted 9 May 2016, para 6.31. The Appellate Body endorsed employing the same criteria to determine likeness when assessing the competitive relationship of services and service suppliers "provided that they are adapted as appropriate to account for the specific characteristics of trade in services".

approach formerly adopted under the GATT following *EC—Asbestos*. Thus, the regulatory purpose of a measure may be considered (1) at the stage of the comparator; (2) when determining less favourable treatment; and/or (3) based on treaty exceptions. The stage at which investment tribunals consider the regulatory purpose of a measure impacts crossfertilisation and the WTO agreement that might be have the most useful approach for the purposes of making a cross-regime reference. E.g. If an IIA incorporates GATT Article XX *mutatis mutandis*, it could be implied that GATT jurisprudence (e.g. the *EC—Seal Products* approach) would be most relevant for the purposes of making a cross-regime reference.

There are additional considerations for tribunals when interpreting provisions and comparing shared norms of the systems between the regimes that may impact upon the frequency of cross-regime references. Tribunals must consider the textual differences between the nondiscrimination provisions of PTIA and BITs. The wording of national treatment or MFN provisions can either facilitate or minimise the potential for crossfertilisation. The potential for cross-regime references is influenced by the text and any indications whether, for example, the regulatory purpose of a measure is a factor in determining likeness.[291]

Such references have appeared in the preambles of PTIAs such as CPTPP and USMCA, but tend not to appear in the preambles of BITs.[292] Exceptions to this include the Australia—Uruguay BIT (2019)[293] and Myanmar—Singapore BIT (2019).[294] Tribunals interpreting IIAs containing such references may be less likely to make a cross-regime reference in the post *EC—Seals* era where the regulatory purpose of a measure is not considered under GATT Article III. If it does become a trend that references to the regulatory purpose of a measure as a factor in determining likeness are more common in PTIAs than in BITs, cross-regime references may be more likely under BITs.

---

[291] E.g. CPTPP's investment chapter contains a clarificatory footnote to the National Treatment provision, stating: "For greater certainty, whether treatment is accorded in "like circumstances" under Article 9.4 (National Treatment) or Article 9.5 (Most-Favoured-Nation Treatment) depends on the totality of the circumstances, including whether the relevant treatment distinguishes between investors or investments on the basis of legitimate public welfare objectives." This chapter contains no general exceptions provision and this clarification introduces an assessment as to the state's regulatory purpose to the test for likeness.

[292] E.g. the most recent BITs of CPTPP Members concluded post CPTPP, such as Georgia – Japan BIT (2021), Mexico – Hong Kong, China SAR BIT (2020), and Canada – Moldova, Republic of BIT (2018) as of April 2021.

[293] The reference to 'in like circumstances' in the MFN provision (Article 5) contains a footnote: "For greater certainty, whether treatment is accorded in "like circumstances" under Article 5 depends on the totality of the circumstances, including whether the relevant treatment distinguishes between investors or investments on the basis of legitimate public welfare objectives."

[294] The General Exceptions provision's title (Article 29) contains a footnote: "For greater certainty, the application of the general exceptions to these provisions shall not be interpreted so as to diminish the ability of governments to take measures where investors are not in like circumstances due to the existence of' legitimate regulatory objectives."

Tribunals must be attentive to differences in the purposes of the regimes when interpreting nondiscrimination provisions. PTIA preambles also tend to refer to a broader treaty purpose, including references to 'building on' the WTO Agreements. How does this impact upon the interpretation of nondiscrimination provisions? Tribunals could take their general omission from BITs as evidence they are included in PTIAs because of their trade chapters. However, a fundamental rule of preambles is that they have a single object and purpose and that this applies to the entirety of an agreement. As such, where such references are included, regard must be had to the fact that the parties are "building on" or "reaffirming"[295] their rights and obligations under the WTO Agreement. This applies to the entirety of the agreement including the investment chapter and this alters the purpose of the agreement in a way that encourages cross-regime references.

Tribunals must consider the contextual differences relating to national treatment provisions in PTIAs and BITs. The context of nondiscrimination provisions is different among IIAs just as it is different between the trade and investment law regimes. The context of the national treatment provision in the US- Ecuador BIT is different to that of USMCA Article 14.4, or CETA Article 8.6.[296] PTIAs tend to be larger agreements that often contain more expansive preambles than their BIT counterparts. The context of the national treatment provision of USMCA is also different to that of CETA. Inquiries into the purpose of a measure are carried out exclusively under the national treatment provision in Article 14.4 of the USMCA.

CETA directly incorporates WTO exceptions that are applicable to the national treatment provision of its investment chapter and this facilitates cross-regime references, even in the post *EC—Seals* era. In terms of context, this question of whether the purpose of a measure is considered as part of the national treatment provision or as part of a general exceptions provision may be the most important.

The Drafters' Note from CPTPP has been replicated in PTIAs such as USMCA and RCEP (2020).[297] However, it has also been replicated in the recent BITs of

---

[295] Japan- Malaysia EPA (2005) (Agreement Between The Government Of Japan And The Government Of Malaysia For An Economic Partnership).

[296] It is noted that the text of USMCA Article 14.4 is very similar to that of NAFTA Article 1102. Both contain four paragraphs, with the major difference being between Article 1102.4 and Article 14.4.4. Article 14.4.4 replicates part of the Drafters' Note on Interpretation of "In Like Circumstances" from CPTPP: "For greater certainty, whether treatment is accorded in "like circumstances" under this Article depends on the totality of the circumstances, including whether the relevant treatment distinguishes between investors or investments on the basis of legitimate public welfare objectives."
NAFTA Article 1102.4: 4. For greater certainty, no Party may: (a) impose on an investor of another Party a requirement that a minimum level of equity in an enterprise in the territory of the Party be held by its nationals, other than nominal qualifying shares for directors or incorporators of corporations; or (b) require an investor of another Party, by reason of its nationality, to sell or otherwise dispose of an investment in the territory of the Party."

[297] RCEP, Article 10.3, National Treatment, FN17, "For greater certainty, whether the treatment is accorded in "like circumstances" under this Article depends on the totality of the circumstances,

certain CPTPP Members including the Australia- Uruguay BIT (2019) and Chile - Hong Kong, China SAR BIT (2016).

Tribunals must also consider systemic differences and differences in the remedy structures between the two regimes when interpreting the nondiscrimination provisions of PTIAs and BITs.[298] Findings of breach under IIAs give rise to monetary damages and are not confined to the withdrawal of inconsistent measures as is the case in the trade law regime.[299] A key systemic difference between the regimes is the lack of the possibility of appeal in the investment regime except on a very limited number of grounds in all but a few recent IIAs.[300] These differences mean that there are potentially severe consequences if an MFN provision is used to import standards the parties have not agreed to. Interpretations of the provisions such as in *Bayindir v. Pakistan* may no longer be possible under recent IIAs where this is expressly prohibited.[301] Such interpretations could lead to treaty exit and have the long-term effect of undermining the intensification of the parties' economic relations.

A further consideration in this area in relation to PTIAs, is the reluctance some parties may have to exit a treaty, where the overall package is beneficial to them, but they would terminate the investment agreement if it were a standalone agreement. Tribunals have to be mindful of these factors in their awards and in striking a balance that is appropriate for the investment regime, rather than following a test developed in line with a different set of considerations in the trade regime.

References

Arato J, Claussen K, Benton Heath J (2020) The perils of pandemic exceptionalism. Am J Int Law 114(3):8
Di Mascio N, Pauwelyn J (2008) Nondiscrimination in trade and investment treaties: worlds apart or two sides of the same coin? Am J Int Law 102:68
Diebold N (2010) Non-discrimination in international trade in services: 'likeness' in WTO/GATS. Cambridge University Press, pp 15–17
Iacovides M (2016) A 'more economic approach' to WTO law's relevant market definition, trade harm, and quantification of trade effects and countermeasures. Uppsala University, p 125
Kurtz J (2009) The use and abuse of WTO law in investor–state arbitration: competition and its discontents. Eur J Int Law 20:752

---

including whether the relevant treatment distinguishes between investors or investments on the basis of legitimate public welfare objectives."

[298] Chapter 1.IV.4 discusses factors tribunals should consider when making cross-regime references, including (c) systemic differences.

[299] Temporary remedies can be applied pending withdrawal or modification of the measure, including compensation and the suspension of concessions or other obligations. See Van den Bossche and Zdouc (2017), p. 458.

[300] This more comprehensive right of appeal is included in recent IIAs of the EU such as CETA.

[301] *Bayindir v. Pakistan* is a well-known example of this occurring, where the FET provisions of the Turkey- Switzerland BIT was imported on the basis of a MFN provision. *Bayindir Insaat Turizm Ticaret Ve Sanayi A.S. v. Pakistan*, Award ICSID Case No. ARB/03/29 (2009).

Kurtz J (2014) Balancing investor protection and regulatory freedom in international investment law: the necessary, complex and vital search for state purpose. In: Bjorklund A (ed) Yearbook on international investment law & policy 2013-14. Oxford University Press, pp 276–277

Kurtz J (2016) The WTO and international investment law: converging systems. Cambridge University Press, 179.

Matsushita M (2015) The World Trade Organization: law, practice, and policy, 3rd edn. Oxford University Press, p 158.

Mitchell A, Munro J, Voon T (2018) Importing WTO general exceptions into international investment agreements: proportionality, myths and risks. In: Yearbook on International Investment Law & Policy 2016–2017. Oxford University Press, 116

Mitchell AD, Heaton D, Henckels C (2016) Non-discrimination and the role of regulatory purpose in international trade. Edward Elgar Publishing, p 36

Moran N (2017) The first twenty cases under GATT Article XX; tuna or shrimp dear? In: Adinolfi G, Baetens F, Caiado JLA, Micara AG (eds) International economic law- contemporary issues. Springer, Cham, pp 3–21

Newcombe A, Paradell L (2009) Law and practice of investment treaties: standards of treatment. Kluwer Law International

Sacerdoti G (2000) The admission and treatment of foreign investment under recent bilateral and regional treaties. J World Investment 1:109

Sacerdoti G, Moran N (2022) Non-discrimination clauses: an analysis of major decisions in international investment law. In: Ruiz Fabri H, Stoppioni E (eds) International investment law: an analysis of major decisions. Hart Publishing (forthcoming)

Schebesta H, Sinopoli DA (2018) The potency of the SPS agreement's excessivity test the impact of Article 5.6 on trade liberalization and the regulatory power of WTO members to take sanitary and phytosanitary measures. J Int Econ Law 21:125–126

Schill S (2009) The multilateralisation of international investment law. Cambridge University Press, p 78

Stone Sweet A, Della Cananea G (2014) Proportionality, general principles of law, and investor-state arbitration: a response to Jose Alvarez. NYU J Int Law:4–5

Stone Sweet A, Mathews J (2008) Proportionality balancing and global constitutionalism. Columbia J Transnatl Law 47:76

Van den Bossche P (2008) The law and policy of the World Trade Organisation, text cases and materials, 2nd edn. Cambridge University Press

Van den Bossche P, Zdouc W (2017) The law and policy of the World Trade Organisation, text cases and materials, 4th edn. Cambridge University Press, p 715

Wagner M (2014) Regulatory space in international trade law and international investment law. Univ Pa J Int Law 36(1):68

Wu M (2014) The scope and limits of trade's influence in shaping the evolving international investment regime. In: Douglas Z, Pauwelyn J, Vinuales JE (eds) The foundations of international investment law. Oxford University Press, p 64/82

Part III
Host State Flexibilities

Chapter 4
Treaty Exceptions

4.1 Introduction

Where a state is *prima facie* in breach of its treaty obligations, it may defend a measure using treaty exceptions.[1] Treaty exceptions provisions allow for derogations from treaty obligations where there is some legitimate purpose manifested in the measure.[2] Reasons why a rule should not be applied in a given case, include: when a rule's application would not serve its proper purpose; when its application would conflict with another rule from the system; and when its application would conflict with a value within the same legal system.[3]

The spirit of the WTO is infused with the principle of 'embedded liberalism', where the GATT's contracting parties envisaged "targeted, if conditional, departures" from obligations.[4] General exceptions have not been as central to the investment regime, particularly in older styles IIAs, which often placed the emphasis on investment protection without expressly balancing this against the state's inherent right to regulate. There is an increasing tendency to include general exceptions modelled on WTO exceptions in IIAs.

---

[1] This is how general exceptions provisions have typically been understood to operate in the trade regime, for example. Henckels, however, considers that exceptions provisions in IIAs should be characterized as scope limitations on substantive obligations rather than defences once breach has been established. See Henckels (2018), p. 2829. This is discussed in Sect. 4.2.1.

[2] The WTO's Appellate Body considers that "[A] measure's purposes, objectively manifested in the design, architecture and structure of the measure, are intensely pertinent to the task of evaluating whether or not that measure is applied so as to afford protection to domestic production." Report of the Appellate Body, *Chile – Taxes on Alcoholic Beverages*, WT/DS110/AB/R, adopted 12 January 2000, para 71.

[3] Bartels and Paddeu (2020), p. 2.

[4] Kurtz (2016), p. 83.

General exceptions provisions apply to the entirety of a treaty and may cover measures relating to legitimate regulatory purposes[5] or essential security interests.[6]

Specific exceptions only apply to certain parts of a treaty.[7] Where a chapter contains both types of exceptions, specific exceptions should generally prevail where they are applicable.[8] In addition to exceptions provisions expressly included within treaties, there are a number of circumstances that preclude a state's actions from being wrongful under customary international law. These include self-defence, *force majeure* and necessity, *inter alia*.[9]

Exceptions provisions come in a myriad of forms in international economic law and can be distinguished from treaty carve-outs, which exclude entire subject matters from the scope of a treaty. Carve-outs may cover sensitive areas such as taxation, public procurement or tobacco control measures.[10] Exceptions can also be distinguished from reservations, which are akin to unilateral carve-outs, and usually only apply to one of the parties.[11]

---

[5] Mitchell et al. define regulatory purpose as "the actual effects and the intended effects that are objectively ascertainable and rational". Mitchell et al. (2016), p. 17.

[6] An example of a general exceptions provision that also incorporates essential security interests can be found in Canada-Moldova BIT (2018), Article 17.

[7] Article 10.9(c) of the US-Colombia FTA (2006) is an example of a specific exception as it only applies to the treaty's article on performance requirements:

> Provided that such measures are not applied in an arbitrary or unjustifiable manner, and provided that such measures do not constitute a disguised restriction on international trade or investment, paragraphs 1(b), (c), and (f), and 2(a) and (b), shall not be construed to prevent a Party from adopting or maintaining measures, including environmental measures:
>
> (i) necessary to secure compliance with laws and regulations that are not inconsistent with this Agreement,
> (ii) necessary to protect human, animal, or plant life or health, or
> (iii) related to the conservation of living or non-living exhaustible natural resources.

[8] E.g. Clarificatory annexes in provisions such as expropriation.

[9] See Chapter V 'Circumstances Precluding Wrongfulness' of the Draft Articles on the Responsibility of States for Internationally Wrongful Acts (2001), which includes the listed defences at Articles 21, 23 and 25 respectively.

[10] See the Agreement to Amend the Singapore-Australia Free Trade Agreement (2016), Article 22: Tobacco Control Measures: "No claim may be brought under this Section in respect of a tobacco control measure[19] of a Party."

---

[19] "Tobacco control measure" means a measure of a Party related to tobacco products (including products made or derived from tobacco), such as for their production, consumption, distribution, labelling, packaging, advertising, marketing, promotion, sale, purchase, or use, as well as fiscal measures such as internal taxes and excise taxes, and enforcement measures, such as inspection, recordkeeping, and reporting requirements. "Tobacco products" means products under Chapter 24 of the Harmonised System, including processed tobacco, or any product that contains tobacco, that is manufactured to be used for smoking, sucking, chewing or snuffing.

[11] See for example the Iceland-Lebanon BIT (2004), Article 3.5 on National and Most-Favoured-Nation Treatment: "The provisions of paragraphs 1 and 2 of this Article shall not be construed so as

Treaty exceptions are a shared norm in trade and investment law and this chapter looks at how they have been formulated and interpreted in the two regimes (Sect. 4.2). In terms of the trade regime, Sect. 4.2 examines the evolution of interpretations of exceptions articles across the WTO Agreements and the low success rate for defences under general exceptions provisions. For the investment regime, the methodologies employed when interpreting whether a measure is 'necessary' within the context of investment agreements are examined. This chapter then considers (Sect. 4.3) the extent to which engagement[12] already exists between the regimes, whether this should influence tribunals, and whether PTIAs have any kind of an impact on this engagement.

4.2 Treaty Exceptions in the Trade and Investment Law Regimes

This section first considers how treaty exceptions provisions have been drafted in the trade and investment law regimes. It then focuses on a specific element of how these provisions have been interpreted: necessity analysis. Interpreting general exceptions provisions often involves a two-tier test, e.g. under GATT Article XX. Firstly, a measure must be capable of being provisionally justified under one of the policy objectives contained in subparagraphs (a)–(j) of Article XX. Secondly, a measure must comply with Article XX's chapeau, or introductory clauses. The chapeau's primary purpose is prevention of abuse of the exceptions listed in the subparagraphs.[13]

Subparagraphs (a), (b) and (d) all contain the nexus requirement that a measure be "necessary to" achieve a certain goal. Necessity analysis has also been an important interpretative question in the investment regime, which is why it is considered in depth in this chapter.

---

to oblige Lebanon to extend to the investors and investments of the other Contracting Party the treatment granted to its own investors regarding ownership of real estate and other real rights."

[12] Engagement between trade and investment law was described in Chap. 1 as occurring wherever the content of one of the regimes has a parallel in the other or wherever there are cross-regime references in dispute settlement or parallels in the practices of tribunals.

[13] Appellate Body Report, *European Communities – Measures Prohibiting the Importation and Marketing of Seal Products*, WT/DS401/AB/R, adopted 18 June 2014, para 5.327.

4.2.1 Treaty Exceptions Provisions

4.2.1.1 Treaty Exceptions in the Trade Regime

(a) Treaty exceptions at the WTO

General exceptions provisions address the conflict between trade and other legitimate policy objectives of WTO Members. GATT Article XX contains ten such objectives while GATS Article XIV includes five. Both exceptions provisions provide for the protection of public morals, as well as human, animal or plant life or health. These two provisions are the core general exceptions provisions of the WTO Agreements.[14] As GATT Article XX is the most frequently invoked exceptions article before the WTO's Dispute Settlement Body, it is the central focus of this chapter.[15]

(b) Treaty exceptions elsewhere in the trade regime

General exceptions provisions in the trade chapters of PTAs and PTIAs tend to refer to the WTO Agreements.[16] Disputes under the trade chapters of these agreements have been rare, with only two cases being completed under PTAs or the non-investment chapters of PTIAs between 2007 and 2016.[17] A recent dispute was however taken under Title IV (Trade And Trade-Related Matters) of the EU-Ukraine Association Agreement. *Ukraine-Wood Products*[18] concerned an export ban on wood and this Panel Report was issued in December 2020. The export ban was challenged under Article 35 of the Association Agreement.[19] Article 35 incorporates GATT Article XI and makes it "an integral part" of the Agreement. The Panel found

---

[14] Underlining this, Article 3 of the Agreement on Trade-Related Investment Measures (TRIMS) expressly incorporates "All exceptions under GATT 1994...as appropriate".

[15] Viñuales gives GATT Article XX as an example of 'exceptions stricto sensu', one of seven categories of exceptions to general rules he identifies. Viñuales (2020), p. 73. It is noted that there are no general exceptions under the TRIPS Agreement or the TBT Agreement.

[16] E.g. for the chapters of the EU-UK Trade and Cooperation Agreement (TCA) concerning National Treatment and market access for goods inter alia, Title XII on Exceptions provides that, "Nothing... shall be construed as preventing a Party from adopting or maintaining measures compatible with Article XX of GATT 1994. To that end, Article XX of GATT 1994, including its Notes and Supplementary Provisions, is incorporated into and made part of this Agreement, *mutatis mutandis*."

[17] See Vidigal (2017), p. 928; See also Foreign Trade Information System (SICE), Trade Policy Developments, Central America-Dominican Republic-United States (CAFTA), Documents relating to the CAFTA-DR Dispute Settlement. WTO Members have tended to litigate at the WTO rather than under the Dispute Settlement Mechanisms (DSMs) of PTAs for various reasons including the levels of trust in the system, its relative predictability, the enforceability of its awards, and the reputational damage for offending an Member if it is seen to be violating its WTO commitments.

[18] Final Report, *Restrictions applied by Ukraine on exports of certain wood products to the European Union*, 11 December 2020.

[19] Article 35 (Import and Export Restrictions) of the Agreement, along with Article 34 (National Treatment), make up Section 3 of the Agreement on Non-Tariff Measures. The two Articles

that the two Articles "impose identical obligations".[20] Article 36 of the Agreement incorporates Articles XX and XXI of GATT 1994 and its interpretative notes, which are also an integral part of the Agreement.[21]

4.2.1.2   Treaty Exceptions in IIAs

General exceptions provisions commonly feature in modern, balanced IIAs and clarify the regulatory space enjoyed by host states.[22] These provisions tend to increase the regulatory autonomy of host states, at least compared to agreements that do not feature such exceptions.[23] The inclusion of general exceptions in IIAs also counteracts any claim from investors of a legitimate expectation that certain regulation would not occur.[24] Treaty drafters should carefully consider omitting general exceptions from investment chapters, where similar provisions feature in other chapters of PTIAs.[25] This absence of exceptions may affect the interpretation of obligations in the investment chapter and diminish the flexibility of the host state. Although not considered in detail here, it is noted that certain provisions on the right to regulate, such as Article 9 of the recent Rwanda-UAE BIT (2017), have begun to approximate to treaty exceptions provisions.[26]

Treaty exceptions provisions commonly feature in IIAs and featured in 28/60 BITs and the investment chapters of 59/60 PTIAs surveyed in Chap. 2. While exceptions provisions are quite common, not all of them directly incorporate general exceptions from the trade regime and in fact many contain a much lower level of interaction with the trade regime.

---

incorporate GATT Article XI and III respectively and make them "an integral part of the Agreement".

[20] Final Report, *Restrictions applied by Ukraine on exports of certain wood products to the European Union*, 11 December 2020, para 204.

[21] *Ukraine-Wood Products* is covered in greater detail in Sect. 1.5.2.

[22] Titi reminds us that regulatory space would ultimately be increased in the absence of an IIA. Titi (2014), p. 119.

[23] Kurtz has described the recalibration of treaties as reflecting an attempt to "delineate the outer limits of the constraint on state autonomy" imposed by investment norms. Kurtz (2014), p. 302. Mitchell et al. warn that the inclusion of general exceptions in IIAs "risks undermining" policy objectives in unintended ways. Mitchell et al. (2018), p. 1. When incorporated 'correctly', general exceptions clarify the regulatory autonomy of the host state. Titi (2014), p. 119.

[24] Mitchell et al. (2018), p. 15.

[25] Mitchell et al. (2018), p. 36. See also Alvarez and Brink (2012), pp. 319–362.

[26] Article 9 Rwanda-UAE BIT (2017), provides: "Right to Regulate

   1. Nothing in this Agreement shall be construed to prevent a Contracting Party from adopting, maintaining, or enforcing any measure that it considers appropriate to ensure that an investment activity in its territory is undertaken in accordance with the applicable public health, security, environmental and labour law of the Contracting Party, such measures should not be applied in a manner that would constitute arbitrary or unjustifiable discrimination between investments and investors."

Four categories of 'treaty exceptions' were categorised in Chap. 2, which were given different weightings based on their potential to impact engagement between the regimes. These categories include exceptions explicitly modelled on WTO law (weighting = 1), exceptions implicitly modelled on WTO law (1), exceptions thinly connected to WTO law (0.66), and exceptions within articles on performance requirements (0.25).

i. Exceptions Explicitly Modelled on WTO Law

In Chap. 2, treaty exceptions *explicitly* modelled on WTO law were found in 25/60 PTIAs (43%) and none of the BITs. A typical example of the phrasing of an exception explicitly modelled on WTO law is found in Chapter 16.1.2 of the Korea-Vietnam FTA (2015), which reads: "2. For the purposes of Chapters 8 (Trade in Services) and 9 (Investment), Article XIV of GATS (including its footnotes) is incorporated into and made part of this Agreement, mutatis mutandis."[27] Not only does the direct incorporation of exceptions modelled on WTO law facilitate engagement between the regimes, it may require it.[28]

ii. Exceptions Implicitly Modelled on WTO Law

Treaty exceptions implicitly modelled on WTO law were found in 26/60 PTIAs and in 23/60 BITs (38%).[29] A variation of the implicit form of incorporation can be seen in the Canada-Panama FTA (2010). This Agreement replaces the 'relating to' test under GATT Article XX(g), with a necessity test. Measures must be necessary "for the conservation of living or non-living exhaustible natural resources".[30] The investment chapter of the Korea-EFTA FTA contains exceptions implicitly based on

---

[27] Chapter 16.1.2 of the Korea-Vietnam FTA (2015), available at: investmentpolicy.unctad.org/international-investment-agreements/treaty-files/3582/download (last accessed 23 March 2021).

[28] See Kurtz (2016), p. 198.

[29] A typical example of the phrasing of an implicit exception is found in Article 9.8 (General Exceptions) of the Australia-China FTA (2015), which reads as follows:

1. For the purposes of this Chapter and subject to the requirement that such measures are not applied in a manner which would constitute arbitrary or unjustifiable discrimination between investments or between investors, or a disguised restriction on international trade or investment, nothing in this Agreement shall be construed to prevent a Party from adopting or enforcing measures:
    (a) necessary to protect human, animal or plant life or health; (b) necessary to ensure compliance with laws and regulations that are not inconsistent with this Agreement; (c) imposed for the protection of national treasures of artistic, historic or archaeological value; or (d) relating to the conservation of living or non-living exhaustible natural resources.
2. The Parties understand that the measures referred to in subparagraph 1(a) include environmental measures to protect human, animal or plant life or health, and that the measures referred to in subparagraph 1(d) include environmental measures relating to the conservation of living or non-living exhaustible natural resources.

[30] Canada-Panama FTA (2010), Article 23.02.3.

GATT XX(a), (b) and (d) but excludes any reference to a GATT XX(g) equivalent.[31] Exceptions implicitly modelled on WTO law facilitate a high level of engagement between the two regimes.

iii. Exceptions Thinly Connected to WTO Law

Exceptions 'thinly connected' to WTO law were found in none of the PTIAs in this study and 4/60 BITs (7%).[32] These provisions typically cover subject matters such as national security or the preservation of public order. Such provisions may provide that any action by a host state that breaches a treaty obligation but which is necessary to preserve public order does not constitute derogations from the treaty.[33] Exceptions thinly connected to WTO law facilitate engagement between the regimes albeit to a lesser extent than exceptions modelled on WTO law. This has been borne out in the jurisprudence on exceptions to date.[34]

Henckels makes the case that exceptions provisions in IIAs should (subject to the language of the provision) be characterized as scope limitations rather than as affirmative defences.[35] This would have practical implications for the burden of proof and for the coherence of the trade and investment law regimes.[36] It is easier to make this case in relation to provisions thinly connected to WTO law than in those where the connection to WTO law is more explicit.

---

[31] Article 20, Agreement on Investment Between the Republic of Korea and the Republic of Iceland, the Principality of Liechtenstein and the Swiss Confederation.

[32] An example of the phrasing of an exception 'thinly connected' to WTO law is found in Article 14 (General Derogations) of the Kenya-Slovakia BIT (2011), which reads as follows: "Nothing in this Agreement shall be construed as preventing a Contracting Party from taking any action that it considers necessary for the protection of its essential security interests in time of war or armed conflict, financial, economic, social crisis or other emergency in international relations, provided that such measures are not applied in a manner that would constitute a means of arbitrary or unjustifiable discrimination by a contracting party, or a disguised investment restriction, nothing in this agreement shall be construed as preventing the contracting parties from taking any measure necessary for the maintenance of public order."

[33] An example of a thin exception is found in Article 13 (General Exceptions) of the BIT between the Republics of Kazakhstan and Macedonia (2012), which reads as follows:

> 1. Nothing in this Agreement shall be interpreted as interfering to commit by the Parties of the actions necessary for protection of national security or measures necessary for maintenance of a public order, or measures in line with their obligations under the United Nations Charter for maintenance of international peace and security, provided that application of such measures would not mean unconditioned or unreasonable discrimination by the Party, or the latent restriction of investments.

[34] See Sect. 4.2.3.2 of this chapter on *Continental Casualty Company v. The Argentine Republic*, Award ICSID Case No. ARB/03/9, IIC 511 (2008).

[35] Henckels (2020), p. 374.

[36] Henckels (2020), p. 364.

iv. Exceptions Within Articles on Performance Requirements

Performance requirements are conditions imposed upon foreign investors that are often explicitly trade distorting (such as domestic content requirements). The WTO Agreement on Trade-Related Investment Measures (TRIMs) disciplines the use of performance requirements and many IIAs do likewise. Performance requirements provisions containing exceptions provisions that are modelled on or closely resemble those found in WTO law were found in 18/60 PTIAs (30%) and none of the BITs in this study.[37] The incorporation of these exceptions facilitates engagement between the regimes albeit within the limited context of performance requirements. While exceptions relating to performance requirements have been the subject of an investment dispute, it was not an exceptions provision resembling those found in WTO law.[38]

Treaty exceptions provisions vary significantly among IIAs. This is now illustrated in relation to three EU PTIAs and CPTPP, which contain significant differences.[39] The differences between these exceptions provisions are considered in relation to how they apply to the national treatment provisions of these agreements. Significant differences between these provisions may hamper the development of a coherent body of investment jurisprudence under the EU's recently launched Investment Court System.

CETA includes two General Exceptions provisions, both of which apply to Section C (Non-discrimination) of its Investment Chapter inter alia.[40] Article 28.3.1 of CETA's Exceptions chapter directly incorporates GATT Article XX into the Agreement. Article 28.3.2 implicitly incorporates GATS Article XIV.[41] Article 28.3.2 is more relevant for investment tribunals as it covers services. Furthermore it

---

[37] A typical example of exceptions within articles on performance requirements is found in Article 10.9(c) of the US-Colombia FTA (2006), which reads as follows:

> Provided that such measures are not applied in an arbitrary or unjustifiable manner, and provided that such measures do not constitute a disguised restriction on international trade or investment, paragraphs 1(b), (c), and (f), and 2(a) and (b), shall not be construed to prevent a Party from adopting or maintaining measures, including environmental measures: (i) necessary to secure compliance with laws and regulations that are not inconsistent with this Agreement, (ii) necessary to protect human, animal, or plant life or health, or (iii) related to the conservation of living or non-living exhaustible natural resources.

[38] See *Mobil Investments Canada Inc. and Murphy Oil Corporation v. Canada*, ICSID Case No. ARB(AF)/07/4, Decision on Liability and on Principles of Quantum, 22 May 2012. The exception in question NAFTA Article 1108(1) on "any existing non-conforming measure" and whether it applied to performance requirements caught by NAFTA Article 1106(1).

[39] These include CETA, the EU-Vietnam FTA, the EU-Singapore FTA/ IPA and the updated EU-Mexico FTA.

[40] Chapter 8 on Investment and Chapter 28 on Exceptions are the relevant Chapters of CETA for this analysis.

[41] It has been noted by Mitchell that the language of 28.3.1 fails to adapt the trade specific language of GATT to the investment context by not including the words *mutatis mutandis*. This issue is resolved however if note is taken of the contents of Article 28.3.2.

is incorporated *mutatis* mutandis, unlike Article 28.3.1.[42] The subparagraphs of Article 28.3.2 do not contain nexus requirements as it is stated in the chapeau of the Article that measures must be 'necessary' for the policy objectives contained in the subparagraphs.

The EU-Singapore Investment Protection Agreement unusually contains a list of specific exceptions in the national treatment article of the investment chapter itself (Article 2.3.3). These are modelled on WTO law, although the language in the chapeau is adapted and refers to 'covered investments'.[43]

The EU-Vietnam IPA contains General Exceptions to the Agreement in Article 4.6. Subparagraphs (a)–(e) in this Article are similar, but not identical, to those in Article 2.3.3 of the EU-Singapore IPA.[44] The chapeau of Article 4.6 is similar to that of GATS Article XIV but is adjusted to reflect the context of this investment agreement.[45]

As a final example, CPTPP contains General Exceptions, but these do not apply to its investment chapter.[46] It does however provide a series of specific exceptions and clarifications in relation to its provisions on fair and equitable treatment,

---

[42] Henckels suggests that rather than incorporating WTO provisions by reference, governments negotiating IIAs "would be wise to adapt treaty language to the investment context". Henckels (2020), p. 374.

[43] EUSIPA Article 2.3.3. "Notwithstanding paragraphs 1 and 2, a Party may adopt or enforce measures that accord to covered investors and investments of the other Party less favourable treatment than that accorded to its own investors and their investments, in like situations, subject to the requirement that such measures are not applied in a manner which would constitute a means of arbitrary or unjustifiable discrimination against the covered investors or investments of the other Party in the territory of a Party, or is a disguised restriction on covered investments, where the measures are: (a) necessary to protect public security, public morals or to maintain public order; (b) necessary to protect human, animal or plant life or health; (c) relating to the conservation of exhaustible natural resources if such measures are applied in conjunction with restrictions on domestic investors or investments; (d) necessary for the protection of national treasures of artistic, historic or archaeological value; (e) necessary to secure compliance with laws or regulations which are not inconsistent with the provisions of this Chapter including those relating to: (i) the prevention of deceptive or fraudulent practices or to deal with the effects of a default on a contract; (ii) the protection of the privacy of individuals in relation to the processing and dissemination of personal data and the protection of confidential of individual records and accounts; (iii) safety; (f) aimed at ensuring the effective or equitable imposition or collection of direct taxes in respect of investors or investments of the other Party."

[44] Subparagraph (f): "inconsistent with paragraph 1 of Article 2.3 (National Treatment) provided that the difference in treatment is aimed at ensuring the effective or equitable imposition or collection of direct taxes in respect of economic activities or investors of the other Party¹."

[45] The chapeau to Article 4.6 states: Subject to the requirement that such measures are not applied in a manner which would constitute a means of arbitrary or unjustifiable discrimination between countries where like conditions prevail, or a disguised restriction on covered investment, nothing in Articles 2.3 (National Treatment) and 2.4 (Most-Favoured-Nation Treatment) shall be construed as preventing the adoption or enforcement by any Party of measures:". The underlined sections respectively replace the words "trade in services" and "this Agreement" from the chapeau of GATS Article XIV.

[46] CPTPP Article 29.1 'General Exceptions'.

expropriation and non-discrimination.[47] CPTPP also contains Security Exceptions.[48]

4.2.2 Interpreting 'Necessity' at the WTO

When a government measure is found to restrict trade, the general exceptions of GATT Article XX may be invoked as a defence. A measure is analysed in two stages under Article XX in assessing whether it qualifies for protection. Firstly, it must be capable of being provisionally justified under one of the ten policy objectives contained in subparagraphs (a)–(j) of Article XX. Of these ten policy objectives, only those in subparagraphs (a), (b) and (d) require that a measure be 'necessary'.[49]

Secondly, a measure must comply with Article XX's chapeau, or introductory clauses. The chapeau's primary purpose is prevention of abuse of the exceptions listed in the subparagraphs.[50] It has been the traditional view in WTO dispute settlement, that before turning to the chapeau, the Panel or Appellate Body must consider whether a measure is: (a) necessary to protect public morals; (b) necessary to protect human, animal or plant life or health; or justified under another one of the subparagraphs. Article XX(a) and (b) are the primary focus of this section.[51] In determining whether a measure is "necessary" under Article XX(a) and (b), the Appellate Body has balanced factors including the contribution of a policy to its objective, the importance of the objective, and its impact on international trade.[52] If a

---

[47] E.g. A footnote to the National Treatment and MFN provisions of the Agreement's Investment Chapter, states:

"For greater certainty, whether treatment is accorded in "like circumstances" under Article 9.4 (National Treatment) or Article 9.5 (Most-Favoured-Nation Treatment) depends on the totality of the circumstances, including whether the relevant treatment distinguishes between investors or investments on the basis of legitimate public welfare objectives." This clarification introduces an assessment as to the state's regulatory purpose to the test for likeness.

[48] Article 29.2: Security Exceptions

Nothing in this Agreement shall be construed to: (. . .)(b) preclude a Party from applying measures that it considers necessary for the fulfilment of its obligations with respect to the maintenance or restoration of international peace or security, or the protection of its own essential security interests.

[49] Article XX (a), (b), (d), (g) and (j) are the only subparagraphs that have formed the basis of disputes that have come before the Appellate Body.

[50] See Appellate Body Report, *European Communities – Measures Prohibiting the Importation and Marketing of Seal Products*, WTO doc. WT/DS401/AB/R, adopted 18 June 2014, para 5.327.

[51] While Article XX (a), (b) and (d) require that a measure be 'necessary', Article XX(d) is thematically different from the others. It concerns measures necessary for compliance with laws in areas such as customs enforcement. Article XX(j) concerns measures essential to the acquisition or distribution of products in general or local short supply. For this reason the content of disputes under these subparagraphs is not analysed here.

[52] See Appellate Body Report, *Korea – Measures Affecting Imports of Fresh, Chilled and Frozen Beef*, WT/DS161/AB/R, 11 December 2000, para 164.

measure is confirmed as being necessary preliminarily, the measure may then be compared to less restrictive alternative measures.

To comply with the chapeau, inter alia, a measure must not be applied in a manner that constitutes "arbitrary or unjustifiable discrimination" or "a disguised restriction on international trade". It is a flexible tool provided by the Agreements to provide for the balancing of rights based on the facts of the case. Given that it is a tool for balancing, the Appellate Body has a degree of freedom in attributing weight to the various concerns of the parties. Factors considered by the Appellate Body in its balancing have included a measure's design, flexibility, rationale and whether it has been exercised in good faith. Article XX functions as a two-tier test, a sequence that has been deemed by the Appellate Body to be logical and fundamental to the Article.[53] Interpreting the chapeau without this sequence of investigation has been deemed by the Appellate Body to be difficult "if...possible at all".[54] The idea is that the specific exception outlined in the subparagraph should be examined first to set the context before turning to the delicate balancing that is to be undertaken under the chapeau.[55] Given the two-tier nature of this test, interpretations of the chapeau are also considered in this section.

Davies has questioned whether an examination of the application of a measure under the chapeau is needed at all: "the nexus requirements in the heads of provisional justification provide ample protection" against the abuse of Article XX.[56] However, along this line of thinking, if something is "necessary" to protect life or "related to" the conservation of exhaustible natural resources" it should automatically qualify for an Article XX exemption. The impact of removing the chapeau from Article XX's two-tier structure would be to restrict tribunals to solely looking at the nature of a measure without regard to discriminatory treatment in place resulting from the measure.

---

[53] Appellate Body Report, *US – Import Prohibition of Certain Shrimp and Shrimp Products*, WTO doc. WT/DS58/AB/R, 12 October 1998, para 119.

[54] Appellate Body Report, *US – Import Prohibition of Certain Shrimp and Shrimp Products*, WTO doc. WT/DS58/AB/R, 12 October 1998, para 120.

[55] This logic of interpreting the provisions before the chapeau has been disputed and labelled as "arbitrary" by Bartels though he cedes that a two-tier test is appropriate on the grounds of judicial economy. Bartels (2014), p. 7. In *Indonesia – Import Licensing Regimes* (2017) the Panel only assessed the measures in question under the chapeau and did not examine whether these measures were provisionally justified under the relevant paragraphs of Article XX. Panel Report, *Indonesia – Importation Of Horticultural Products, Animals And Animal Products*, WT/DS477/R, adopted 22 November 2017, paras. 7.829–7.830. As Indonesia failed to demonstrate that its import licensing regimes were applied in a manner consistent with the chapeau of Article XX, the measure was not examined under Article XX(b). The Appellate Body accepted that a panel that deviates from the sequence of analysis might not, for that reason alone, commit a legal error. Appellate Body Report, *Indonesia – Importation Of Horticultural Products, Animals And Animal Products*, para 5.101).

[56] Davies (2009), p. 32.

4.2.2.1 Why Defences Under Article XX(a) and (b) Have Failed

In August 2014, the Appellate Body issued its twentieth report concerning General Exceptions in the *China-Rare Earths* case.[57] When the general exceptions under GATT Article XX have been invoked, they have only been deemed a legitimate defence in two cases since the inception of the WTO and its Dispute Settlement Body (DSB) in 1995.[58] Of these twenty disputes, the *Shrimp/Turtle* case in 2001 was the last where a measure defended under Article XX was deemed compliant with the WTO Agreements. This section looks at the reasons why measures have failed the necessity test for Article XX(a) and (b) or failed to comply with Article XX's chapeau. The success rate for these first twenty Article XX claims was 2/20.

a. Article XX(a) defences

Under WTO dispute settlement, an Article XX(a) defence has failed on each of the four occasions it has been invoked. While the measures in *China-Audiovisual*[59]

---

[57] Appellate Body Report, *China – Measures Related to the Exportation of Rare Earths, Tungsten and Molybdenum*, WTO doc. WT/DS431/AB/R, 7 August 2014.

Since August 2014, the Appellate Body has concluded five other Reports concerning GATT Article XX (*US – Tuna II (Mexico) (Article 21.5-Mexico)* (2015), *US – COOL Art. 21.5* (2015), *Colombia – Textiles* (2016), *India – Solar Cells* (2016), and *Indonesia – Import Licensing Regimes* (2017). The first of these two cases were taken under the TBT Agreement and there is little analysis of GATT Article XX(a) or (b), the primary focus of this section. *Colombia – Textiles* (2016) concerned a measure "designed" to protect public morals. The Appellate Body found, however, that Colombia failed to demonstrate that the compound tariff was **"necessary"** for the protection of public morals within the meaning of Art. XX(a). Analysis of this dispute is considered in Section 2.

India – Solar Cells (2016) considered GATT Article XX(d), but primarily concerned GATT Article XX(j), which has the nexus requirement 'essential' rather than 'necessary'. The Appellate Body upheld the Panel's finding that solar cells and modules were not "products in general or local short supply" within the meaning of Art. XX(j), and that the DCR measures were not justified under this provision. According to the Appellate Body, an assessment of whether products are in short supply should give consideration to all relevant factors.

In *Indonesia – Import Licensing Regimes* (2017), the Panel only assessed the measures in question under the chapeau and did not examine whether these measures were provisionally justified under the relevant subparagraphs of Article XX (Panel Report, paras. 7.829–7.830). As the measures were not applied in a manner consistent with the chapeau, the measure was not examined under Article XX(b). The Appellate Body accepted that a panel that deviates from the sequence of analysis might not, for that reason alone, commit a legal error.

[58] See Annex. The general exception clause is also found under Article XIV of GATS, which has an identical wording to the GATT in the parts considered here. As the vast majority of cases in this area have been taken under the GATT, for the sake of simplicity the general exceptions clauses are referred to as being under GATT Article XX in this section. See Moran (2017), pp. 3–21.

[59] *China – Audiovisual Services* (2009) concerned a Chinese measure seeking to reserve the importation of various forms of media solely for certain Chinese State-owned enterprises was contested in this case. The ban was defended under Article XX(a). The panel and AB determined that because there was at least one other reasonably available alternative, China's measures were not "necessary" to protect public morals. The AB did not complete an analysis of the chapeau.

and *Colombia – Textiles*[60] failed the necessity test, those in *US-Gambling*[61] and *EC-Seals*[62] failed to satisfy the chapeau.

The necessity test was failed because of the availability of alternatives (*China-Audiovisual*) and the failure to demonstrate the tariff was designed to combat money laundering and protect public morals (*Colombia – Textiles*[63]).

Reasons why measures have been deemed not to comply with Article XX's chapeau have included the application of a prohibition to foreign, but not domestic, service suppliers (*US-Gambling*) and the lack "comparable efforts" in enabling one group to qualify for an exception to a ban (*EC-Seals*).

---

[60] In *Colombia – Textiles* (2016), the AB reversed the Panel's finding and found that the measure was designed to protect public morals. However, it found that Colombia had failed to demonstrate that the compound tariff was "necessary" for the protection of public morals within the meaning of Art. XX(a).

Likewise it was found to be the case for the claim under Article XX(d) that Colombia had failed to demonstrate that the compound tariff was "necessary" to secure compliance with Article 323, within the meaning of Article XX(d). As the measure could not be provisionally justified, there was no need to examine the Panel's findings in relation to the chapeau.

[61] *US – Gambling* (2005) concerned a US measure affecting the cross-border supply of gambling and betting services was contested in this case. The ban was defended under GATS Article XIV (a) and was found to be designed to protect public morals by both the panel and Appellate Body. Unlike the panel, the AB considered the measure was "necessary" as the US had made a prima facie case of necessity and Antigua had failed to give a reasonably available alternative measure. The fact that the US had not entered into consultations did not render the measure invalid. On appeal, it was found that the US prohibition was only applied to foreign and not to domestic service suppliers and so it fell foul of Article XIV's chapeau.

[62] *EC – Seals* (2014) concerned the EU seal regime (under Regulation 1007/2009 of 16 September 2009 on trade in seal products, OJ 2009 L 286/36), which sought to ban the importation of seal products into the EU, was contested in this case. Norway alleged certain exceptions to the ban were discriminatory and favoured products from the EU certain third countries.

The EU defended the ban under Article XX(a) and as expected, a ban on seal products came under the traditionally broad scope of moral questions. Proving it to be "necessary" to protect public morals was more difficult but the EU succeeded before the panel and at appeal.

The AB corrected the panel's finding that applying the same legal test as was applied to Article 2.1 of TBT Agreement was appropriate in analysing Article XX's chapeau. Ultimately however it found that the EU had not demonstrated that the EU seal regime complied with the chapeau and thus could not be justified under Article XX. The EU had not made "comparable efforts" to allow Canadian Inuits to qualify for the IC exception compared to the efforts it had made in relation to Greenlandic Inuits. Furthermore, to comply with the Regulation, a certificate from a recognised body is necessary. Such a body had been approved in Greenland but not in Canada. The AB deemed this burdensome.

It has been noted (Catti de Gasperi 2015, p. 17) that the EU can comply by removing the Inuit exception, which would be more trade restrictive and would not necessarily benefit Canada or its Inuit population. See Appellate Body Report, *European Communities – Measures Prohibiting the Importation and Marketing of Seal Products*, WT/DS401/AB/R, adopted 18 June 2014.

[63] Appellate Body Report, *Colombia – Measures Relating to the Importation of Textiles, Apparel and Footwear,* WT/DS461/AB/R and Add.1, adopted 22 June 2016, para 5.92.

b. Article XX(b) defences

In relation to Article XX(b), since 1995 two defences have failed the necessity test (*China-Rare Earths, EC-Tariff Preferences*), four have failed to comply with the chapeau (*EC-Tariff Preferences, Brazil-Retreaded Tyres, US-Shrimp (1998 & 2008)*), while one has succeeded (*EC-Asbestos*).

The necessity test was failed because of the "piece-meal"[64] manner of its application (*China-Rare Earths*) and the fact that there was no relationship between the objectives stated and the measures put in place (*EC-Tariff Preferences*).

Reasons why measures have failed to comply with Article XX's chapeau have included the existence of an exception to a ban for neighbouring countries, which ran contrary to the objective invoked for provisionally justifying the measure (*Brazil-Retreaded Tyres*).

EC– Asbestos is the only successful claim that has been taken under GATT Article XX(b).[65] The EU successfully defended its ban on asbestos under Article XX(b) and both the Panel and Appellate Body upheld its claim that no reasonable "alternative measure" could be adopted. This shows that WTO rules can be used to challenge domestic measures protecting citizens against the most dangerous of materials. The Appellate Body found that Articles III and XX "are distinct and independent provisions" and so a measure may be deemed unjustifiable for public health reasons under both.[66] Considerations of health reasons under Article III do not deprive Article XX(b) of its *effet utile* as different inquiries are made under the different Articles.

---

[64] Appellate Body Reports, *China – Measures Related to the Exportation of Rare Earths, Tungsten, and Molybdenum*, WT/DS431/AB/R, WT/DS432/AB/R, WT/DS433/AB/R, adopted 29 August 2014, para 5.116.

[65] France placed a ban on both imported and domestically produced asbestos and so the measure complied with Article XX's chapeau. Canada claimed that the measures used by France were more trade-restrictive than necessary and that if used in a safe manner, chrysotile (the type of asbestos it produces) does not pose health risks. Thus chrysotile was "like" other construction products and should be protected under the national treatment clause. Chrysotile is considered a human carcinogen by the WHO's cancer agency (IARC), as per its 1998 Monograph: 'WHO IARC Monographs on the Evaluation of Carcinogenic Risks to Humans Overall: Evaluations of Carcinogenicity: an Updating of IARC Monographs,' Volumes 1 to 42, Supplement 7 (1998).

[66] Appellate Body Report, *European Communities – Measures Affecting Asbestos and Asbestos – Containing Products*, WT/DS135/AB/R, 12 March 2001, para 115. The Panel had concluded that France had violated Article III.4 of the GATT and that chrysotile and non-asbestos based construction products were like products. In their view, to consider health risks under Article III.4 was "not appropriate" and would be to "nullify" the effect of Article XX(b). This approach would guarantee market access subject to the defendant being able to find a non-protectionist justification under Article XX. Panel Report, *European Communities – Measures Affecting Asbestos and Asbestos-Containing Products*, WT/DS135/R and Add.1, adopted 5 April 2001, paras 3.450 and 3.512 for the respective quotations.

4.2.2.2 Has the Right Balance Been Struck?

Despite the low success rate of Article XX defences, many measures designed to protect the environment and public morals have been deemed provisionally justifiable, satisfying the first part of the two-tier test. For nine of the first 20 disputes under Article XX, the measures in question were deemed to be provisionally justifiable (45%). Taking Article XX(d) out of an analysis of provisional justification, nine out of twelve of the measures defended under XX(a), (b) and (g) were found to be provisionally justifiable (75%).[67]

Does this represent a silver lining public policy makers and that the right balance has been struck in Article XX's first twenty cases? Or is a revised Article XX, or way of interpreting Article XX, needed given the low success rate for defences? The *US–Tuna* case (1991) challenged the view that an appropriate balance had been struck between trade and public policy considerations under free trade agreements when an ostensibly environmental measure taken by the US was deemed to be inconsistent with the GATT. Following the inception of the WTO in 1995, greater weight appeared to be given to environmental concerns in *US– Shrimp I* (2001), where it was found that to ensure a measure is compliant with the chapeau, a Member must make efforts to find a cooperative solution to the problem.[68] Secondly, a Member needs to consider the conditions in other territories when designing measures. However this did not herald in a new era and there has not been a successful Article XX defence since this dispute.

On the face of it, the low success rate of Article XX defences may indicate a priority being given by tribunals to market access over concerns such as environmental protection. Other reasons that are systemic to the functioning of the DSB may be put forward in explanation. One reason may be that the environmental measures may be permissible under GATT Article XX by themselves, but their discriminatory application of measures under the chapeau may not be. Other reasons may be that disputes involving discriminatory measures are more likely to be resolved at the consultation stage or may not be appealed to the Appellate Body. Members also tend to take cases they believe they have a good chance of winning.

While successful defences before the Appellate Body have been uncommon, the two-tier test has been passed in *EC – Asbestos* and *US – Shrimp I*. These represent two of the twenty disputes where an Article XX exception was invoked before the Appellate Body. In *US-Shrimp I* discrimination was not found once "similar opportunities" were provided to all exporters. This was the case regardless of the outcome

---

[67] This paper has excluded Article XX(d) from its analysis for thematic reasons. All eight defences under XX(d) have failed the necessity test and in the only case where an analysis of the chapeau was carried out, it was also deemed non-compliant (*US-Thai Cigarettes*). If Article XX(g) is removed from the analysis, 6/10 of the measures defended under XX(a) and (b) were found to be provisionally justifiable. This analysis includes *Colombia – Textiles* (2016), which was not one of the first twenty cases considered under these General Exceptions provisions.

[68] This was largely viewed as a positive development but was criticised by Bhagwati claiming the Appellate Body bowed to international environmental pressure. Bhagwati (2001), pp. 15–29.

of these negotiating opportunities. In *EC-Asbestos,* this decision affirmed the large degree of discretion Members have when regulating public health issues.

The 75% success rate for measures under Article XX(a), (b) and (g) in terms of being found to be preliminarily justifiable reflects the fact that the Panels and Appellate Body are often willing to deem measures to be 'necessary' when the aim is to protect life, the environment and public morals. As the Appellate Body stated in *Korea-Beef*: "The more vital or important the common interests or values pursued, the easier it would be to accept as 'necessary' the measures designed to achieve those ends."[69]

Brazil– Retreaded Tyres shows the Appellate Body's willingness to accept environmental and health risks as legitimate and complex concerns that can be tackled by a wide range of measures. Although this measure was found to infringe Article XX's chapeau, this was on the basis of discriminatory treatment, which is primarily a question of fairness in the accordance of rights equally to all WTO Members.

Seven of the twelve cases brought under Article XX(a), (b) and (g) failed to comply with the chapeau. Given the difficulty Article XX defences have had in complying with the chapeau, the suitability of its current formulation may be questioned.

Compliance with Article XX's chapeau has proved a sticking point in some cases, but to discard the chapeau would be to deprive the Appellate Body of its ability to balance competing rights and to look at the discriminatory effects of measures.[70] The chapeau remains integral in obliging Members to show that environmental or moral measures do not discriminate between Members in an unjustified way.

A more plausible proposition would be to relax the requirements of the chapeau and what constitutes arbitrary or unjustifiable discrimination. One way of doing this is to delink the objective for a trade restriction and the reason behind discriminatory treatment under the chapeau. Another way would be for the Appellate Body to look at other "additional factors" that may be considered which would allow it more room in its considerations under the chapeau. This was done in *EC– Seals* where for the first time the design, architecture and revealing structure of a measure was "relevant to consider". In terms of other additional factors that may be considered in future Appellate Body reports, guidance could be drawn from disputes under the TBT Agreement. In *US – COOL,*[71] the even-handedness of measures was determined based on whether or not they were applied in a manner that "constitutes a means of arbitrary or unjustifiable discrimination". This wording largely resembles the

---

[69] Appellate Body Report, *Korea – Measures Affecting Imports of Fresh, Chilled and Frozen Beef,* WT/ DS161/AB/R, WT/DS169/AB/R, adopted 10 January 2001, para 162.

[70] This is not to mention the uncertainty that would surround measures previously found incompatible with the chapeau.

[71] Appellate Body Reports, *United States – Certain Country of Origin Labelling (COOL) Requirements,* WT/DS384/AB/R, WT/DS386/AB/R, adopted 23 July 2012.

chapeau test and future interpretations of GATT Article XX may make reference to the jurisprudence developed under the TBT Agreement and vice versa.[72]

4.2.3 Interpreting 'Necessity' in IIAs

This section considers how tribunals have interpreted the concept of necessity under treaty exceptions provisions in disputes taken under IIAs such as the US-Argentina BIT (1994). A series of disputes were initiated under this BIT in the aftermath of the Argentinian economic crisis in 2001–02.[73] This section considers the merits and demerits of two of the methodologies employed by tribunals when interpreting Article XI of this BIT, as well as proposals for further interpretative methodologies from commentators. These methodologies were employed to give a framework for interpreting whether a measure is 'necessary' within the context of a particular investment agreement. The methodologies employed by tribunals and proposed by commentators have ranged from decisions entirely removed from the influence of WTO law to a decision that borrows heavily from it. This has led to much discussion on the subject of fragmentation within international economic law and the desirability of crossfertilisation of jurisprudence. This section examines this question of the appropriateness of investment tribunals taking into account principles developed under WTO law in interpreting exceptions provisions found in investment law.

The two approaches seen in the disputes under the US-Argentina BIT include what are called here the Orrega Vicuña approach and the Common Derivation approach. The former looks to customary international law in interpreting the concept of necessity in Article XI of the US-Argentina BIT.[74] The state of necessity in customary international law was codified by the International Law Commission in its Draft Articles on the Responsibility of States for Internationally Wrongful Acts (ARSIWA) (2001). ARSIWA Article 25 reads:

> 1. Necessity may not be invoked by a State as a ground for precluding the wrongfulness of an act not in conformity with an international obligation of that State unless the act: (*a*) is

---

[72] Asmelash (2013), p. 36.

[73] For an account of this crisis, see Alvarez and Brink (2012), pp. 321–322. This BIT is selected as tribunals have employed differing methodologies when interpreting necessity under the treaty.

[74] US-Argentina BIT, Article XI: "This Treaty shall not preclude the application by either Party of measures necessary for the maintenance of public order, the fulfillment of its obligations with respect to the maintenance or restoration of international peace or security, or the Protection of its own essential security interests."

This article provides for three exceptions to the Agreement. These are exceptions to the Agreement that function in a manner similar to the policy objectives set out in subparagraphs (a)–(j) of GATT Article XX. This article also contains a necessity test which is found in subparagraphs (a), (b) and (d) of the GATT. These elements represent commonalities between the GATT and US-Argentina BIT, albeit thin commonalities. The degree of engagement present in the treaty text affects the legitimacy afforded to cross-regime borrowing is explored in Sect. 4.3 of this chapter.

the only way for the State to safeguard an essential interest against a grave and imminent peril; and (*b*) does not seriously impair an essential interest of the State or States towards which the obligation exists, or of the international community as a whole.

2. In any case, necessity may not be invoked by a State as a ground for precluding wrongfulness if: (*a*) the international obligation in question excludes the possibility of invoking necessity; or (*b*) the State has contributed to the situation of necessity.

The latter approach was taken by the tribunal in *Continental Casualty v. Argentina*, which drew upon WTO case law in its interpretation of necessity. The tribunal in this case found that as Article XI is derived from non-precluded measures articles found in US FCN Treaties,[75] which themselves reflect the formulation of the GATT, it would be more appropriate to draw upon jurisprudence under the GATT than the customary international law.

These two approaches have attracted considerable praise and criticism. The next section attempts to outline the main points for and against each approach. Two other methodologies, proposed by Stone Sweet and Kurtz, are then examined. The first of these methodologies is based on general principles of law and this can either be viewed as a supplement to the second method, or else as a stand-alone methodology. The second methodology proposed involves separating primary and secondary applications.[76]

4.2.3.1   The Orrega Vicuña Approach

(a) The approach

The Orrega Vicuña approach involves interpreting the customary international law defence of necessity as being "synonymous" with exceptions enunciated in provisions such as Article XI of the US-Argentina BIT.[77] The tribunals in *CMS, Enron* and *Sempra* all conducted a necessity analysis under the US-Argentina BIT. The tribunals, which were all chaired by Professor Orrega Vicuña, placed the customary international law defence of necessity at the heart of their interpretations of the concept of necessity.[78] In interpreting the customary international law defence of necessity, all three tribunals determined that: (1) an essential interest was not

---

[75] The US-Nicaragua FCN treaty (1956) is an example of a non-precluded measures article. It states:

1. The present treaty shall not preclude the application of measures:. . .(d) necessary to fulfil the obligations of a party for the maintenance or restoration of international peace and security, or necessary to protect its essential security interests.

[76] Kurtz (2010), p. 35.

[77] Alvarez and Brink (2012), p. 333.

[78] For an account of the early cases under Article XI US-Argentina BIT and the diffusion of proportionality analysis, see Stone Sweet and della Canacea (2014), pp. 924–940.

threatened; (2) this was not the "only means" at Argentina's disposal; and (3) that Argentina had contributed to the state of necessity.[79]

The CMS tribunal found that ARSIWA Article 25 "adequately reflect (sic) the state of customary international law on the question of necessity."[80] The litigation strategy of Argentina may have been a contributory factor leading to what Annulment Committees have described as a conflation between Article XI of the BIT and Article 25 of the ILC's Draft Articles. The respondent claimed that the right to invoke Article XI was self-judging despite the lack of words such as "it considers" as found in other agreements.[81]

This conflation of the Articles was not necessary however as the textual set up of Article 25 is different to Article XI, making it more difficult to satisfy in four key ways.[82] The first difference between Article 25 and Article XI is that the former applies to wrongful acts of states, which makes it contextually different. Secondly, a state claiming necessity under customary international law must demonstrate that it is protecting an "essential interest against a grave and imminent peril". Thirdly the response of the State must be the "only way" to protect its interest. Lastly the defence is precluded if the State has contributed to the situation of necessity.

José Alvarez has endorsed this customary international law approach in articles and opinions as the claimant's expert in *CMS* (not public) and *Sempra* (public).[83] Alvarez suggests that the tribunals should have looked to the ordinary meaning under Article 31 VCLT in light of the object and purpose of the treaty. Alvarez deems the "only means test" to be the most appropriate and has objected where tribunals have adopted another methodology.[84] Alvarez describes the tribunal in *Continental Casualty* as having avoided the "only way" test laid down under customary international law.[85]

---

[79] See *CMS Gas Transmission Company v. Argentine Republic*, Award, 12 May 2005, ICSID Case No. ARB/01/08, IIC 303, paragraph 315–331; *Enron Corporation and Ponderosa Assets, L.P. v. Argentine Republic*, Award, 22 May 2007, ICSID Case No. ARB/01/3, para 294–313; and *Sempra Energy International v. The Argentine Republic*, Award, 28 September 2007, ICSID Case No. ARB/02/16, para 325–354.

[80] *CMS Gas Transmission Company v. Argentine Republic*, Award, 12 May 2005, ICSID Case No. ARB/01/08, IIC 303, paragraph 315.

[81] See for example, *Sempra Energy International v. The Argentine Republic*, Award, 28 September 2007, ICSID Case No. ARB/02/16 (2007) para 368.

[82] A comparison of the texts of the US-Argentina BIT Article XI and ARSIWA Article 25 can be made by reference to the previous section.

[83] See Alvarez and Brink (2012), pp. 319–362; Alvarez (2014); *Sempra Energy International v. The Argentine Republic*, Opinion of José E. Alvarez, 12 September 2005, ICSID Case No. ARB/02/16.

[84] Alvarez and Brink (2012), p. 328.

[85] Alvarez and Brink (2012), p. 328.

(b) Criticism of the approach

The Annulment Committees in *CMS, Enron* and *Sempra* were unanimously critical of the Orrega Vicuña approach.[86] The Committees in *Enron* and *Sempra* annulled the awards, though the Committee in *CMS* could not. The CMS Annulment Committee was composed of two members of the ICJ, as well as Professor James Crawford, who drafted the ARSIWA in his capacity as Special Rapporteur on State Responsibility at the ILC from 1997 to 2001.[87] The Committee reminded the parties that an *"ad hoc* committee is not a court of appeal" and that annulment could only be granted in line with Article 52 of the ICSID Convention.[88] The Committee stated that it had no jurisdiction to consider whether the Tribunal had "made any error of

---

[86] The Committee found that the failure to separately analyse and apply Article XI BIT constituted a "total" failure to apply the law and thus a "manifest excess of powers".

It is further noted that Orrega Vicuña was disqualified from serving as an arbitrator in *CC/Devas (Mauritius) Ltd, Devas Employees, Mauritius Private Limited & Telcom Mauritius Limited v Republic of India, PCA Case No. 2013-09*. This decision was taken by Judge Peter Tomka President, International Court of Justice. The case involved interpretation of "essential security interests" under Article 11.3 of the Mauritius India BIT (2000), which reads as follows: *"The provisions of this Agreement shall not in any way limit the right of either Contracting Party to apply prohibitions or restrictions of any kind or take any other action which is directed to the protection of its essential security interests, or to the protection of public health or the prevention of diseases in pests and animals or plants."*

This provision is markedly different to Article XI of the US-Argentina BIT (1994). Nonetheless, Orrega Vicuña was precluded from serving in the proceedings. This decision was largely based on an academic article written by Orrega Vicuña, which was the fourth time he had expressed himself on the subject of "essential security interests" and where he defended his approach to interpreting it. This was despite three separate annulment committees criticising and overturning his approach as it had failed to separately analyse and apply Article XI of the US-Argentina BIT. In the article, Orrega Vicuña wrote:

> While the interlinking of treaty and customary law requirements in respect of necessity has been held to be a manifest error of law in the context of a particular case [referring to the decision of the CMS annulment committee], one may respectfully wonder whether the error of law might not lie with the approach suggesting that a rather vague clause of a treaty might be able to simply do away with the obligations established under the same treaty.[. . .] In this light the discussion about whether the availability of the defense should first be examined under the treaty and, only if unsuccessful, examined next under customary international law, *appears to be somewhat circular.* If the treaty precludes the defense there is no second shot at it under customary law. If it provides for an exception and this is not defined, its examination under customary international law will be the first and only shot supplementing the treaty vacuum. It is the two shots that would appear to run counter to the strictness of the requirements of international law. (emphasis added)

[87] His views on this can also be found in: Crawford (2002).

[88] Article 52 (1) provides for annulment on five grounds: (a) that the Tribunal was not properly constituted; (b) that the Tribunal has manifestly exceeded its powers; (c) that there was corruption on the part of a member of the Tribunal; (d) that there has been a serious departure from a fundamental rule of procedure; or (e) that the award has failed to state the reasons on which it is based.

fact or law."[89] Nonetheless the CMS Committee gave its view on "certain points of substance" where the Tribunal had made errors as multiple claims had been made which covered similar subject matter. The Committee found that the Tribunal made two manifest errors of law that had a decisive impact on the award. The first involved conflating Article 25 of the ILC's Draft Articles and Article XI of the US-Argentina BIT. The second involved not taking a position on the relationship between the two texts and assuming they were "on the same footing".[90] The Committee stated that if it was "acting as a court of appeal, it would have to reconsider the Award on this ground."[91] Although these errors were not sufficient for annulment, the findings offer a "cogent taxonomy" for understanding the relationship between treaty and customary norms.[92] Thus all three Annulment Committees found this conflation highly problematic.[93]

Where such a conflation occurs, it is particularly onerous for respondents in investment claims to satisfy the test for necessity under Article 25 of the ILC's Draft Articles. A State claiming necessity under customary international law must demonstrate that it is protecting an "essential interest against a grave and imminent peril". The plea is thus reserved for "rare emergencies" as opposed to how necessity analysis typically operates under exceptions articles in trade and investment law where no such imminent threat needs to be demonstrated.

Secondly where a state acts through necessity, it must be the "only way" to protect its interest. This is an exceedingly stringent test, which was conceived in relation to the use of force.[94] In the context of a financial crisis, there are inevitably many ways for the state to respond and it may be difficult to prove that any action is the only way to respond.[95]

Furthermore, the defence is precluded if the State has contributed to the situation of necessity. In the aftermath of an economic crisis, some degree of contribution would usually be attributable to a government. On this question, the Enron Annulment Committee found that the tribunal had not applied Article 25(2)(b) ARSIWA but has instead applied an expert opinion on an economic issue.[96] The Committee

---

[89] *CMS Gas Transmission Company v. Argentine Republic*, Annulment Decision, 25 September 2007, ICSID Case No. ARB/01/08, IIC 303, para 121.

[90] *CMS Gas Transmission Company v. Argentine Republic,* Annulment Decision, 25 September 2007, ICSID Case No. ARB/01/08, IIC 303, para 131.

[91] *CMS Gas Transmission Company v. Argentine Republic*, Annulment Decision, 25 September 2007, ICSID Case No. ARB/01/08, IIC 303, para 135.

[92] Kurtz (2016), p. 268.

[93] Stone Sweet & Cananea describe these findings as having "destroyed the Orrega Vicuña approach". Stone Sweet and della Canacea (2014), p. 932.

[94] Kurtz (2010), p. 17.

[95] The LG&E tribunal found that Argentina took "the only means to respond to the crisis" in its Report. See *LG&E Energy Corp., LG&E Capital Corp., and LG&E International, Inc .v. Argentine Republic*, Award, 25 July 2007, ICSID Case No. ARB/02/1, para 257.

[96] *Enron Corporation and Ponderosa Assets, L.P. v. Argentine Republic,* Decision on the Application for Annulment of the Argentine Republic, 30 July 2010, para 377, 393.

found that while an economist may regard policies as misguided, this does not mean that as a matter of law that the state has contributed to its state of necessity.[97]

For Alvarez, tribunals need to consider how the structures of institutions influence the principles they adopt and apply and how institutional factors make certain interpretative techniques more acceptable.[98] However, narrow interpretations of necessity such as Alvarez advocates under Article 25 ARSIWA may be even more likely to lead to treaty exit by countries like Argentina.[99]

4.2.3.2 The Common Derivation Approach

(a) The approach

The *Continental Casualty v. Argentina* Award came in the aftermath of the CMS Annulment Proceeding.[100] In this context, it is understandable that the tribunal was looking for a different approach to the question of necessity analysis. In interpreting Article XI, the tribunal in *Continental Casualty* drew on WTO case law and how it has dealt with necessity. The tribunal adopted what is called here the 'Common Derivation Approach' explaining that WTO jurisprudence was taken into account as Article XI of the US-Argentina BIT was derived from US FCN treaties, which reflect the formulation of GATT 1947's Article XX.[101] The tribunal found that although the US-Argentina BIT is structurally very different to Article XX of GATT 1947, the BIT's non-precluded measures article was derived from similar articles in US FCN

---

[97] *Enron Corporation and Ponderosa Assets, L.P. v. Argentine Republic,* Decision on the Application for Annulment of the Argentine Republic, 30 July 2010, para 393. The Annulment Committee stated that the Tribunal's process of reasoning should have been as follows: "First, the Tribunal should have found the relevant facts based on all of the evidence before it, including the Edwards Report. Secondly, the Tribunal should have applied the legal elements of the Article 25(2)(b) to the facts as found (having if necessary made legal findings as to what those legal elements are). Thirdly, in the light of the first two steps, the Tribunal should have concluded whether or not Argentina had "contributed to the situation of necessity" within the meaning of Article 25(2)(b). For the Tribunal to leap from the first step to the third without undertaking the second amounts in the Committee's view to a failure to apply the applicable law. This constitutes a ground of annulment under Article 52(1)(b) of the ICSID Convention."

[98] Alvarez and Brink (2012), p. 352.

[99] See the end of the next section, 2.b) for more on how this could lead to treaty exit.

[100] As referred to in the last section, the CMS Annulment Committee characterised the conflation of Art XI and Article 25 ARSIWA as a "manifest error in law". *CMS Gas Transmission Company v. Argentine Republic,* Decision of the *ad hoc* Committee on the Application for Annulment of the Argentine Republic, paras 45 & 130.

[101] *Continental Casualty Company v. The Argentine Republic,* Award, 5 September 2008, ICSID Case No. ARB/03/9, IIC 511 (2008) para 192: "Since the text of Art. XI derives from the parallel model clause of the U.S. Friendship, Commerce, and Navigation treaties and these treaties in turn reflect the formulation of Art. XX of GATT 1947, the Tribunal finds it more appropriate to refer to the GATT and WTO case law which has extensively dealt with the concept and requirements of necessity in the context of economic measures derogating to the obligations contained in GATT, rather than to refer to the requirement of necessity under customary international law."

Treaties, which were inspired by GATT Article XX. Article XI was derived from provisions that reflected the formulation of the GATT, such Article XX of the US-Ireland FCN treaty (1950).[102]Article XX of the US-Ireland FCN treaty (1950) reflects Article XX of GATT 1947.[103] Both articles contain a list of non-precluded measures with nexus requirements including "relating to" and "necessary to". This link between the FCN treaty and the GATT was found to be sufficient to consider the jurisprudence developed under the GATT as a source of guidance when interpreting a norm common to all three of the treaties.

The tribunal in *Continental Casualty* referred to GATT jurisprudence in developing its necessity analysis and was "guided by the principles" enunciated in *Korea—Beef*.[104] The tribunal considered the "process of weighing and balancing of factors" in determining whether a measure that is not indispensable may be deemed necessary.[105]

The tribunal elicited one positive principle regarding necessity, which was that the necessity of a measure should be determined by the weighing and balancing of "usually" three factors including the importance of the measure, its contribution to the ends pursued and the restrictiveness imposed by the measure.[106] The tribunal further elicited one negative principle regarding necessity, which was that a measure would not be deemed necessary if a "less inconsistent alternative measure, which the member State concerned could reasonably be expected to employ is available".[107]

---

[102] According to the 'Treaties in Force' section of the US Department of State website, the US only concluded one Friendship, Commerce and Navigation treaty in the twentieth century prior to the signing of the GATT in 1947. This is in line with the idea that Article XI of the US-Argentina BIT (1994) was derived from US FCN treaties, which reflect the formulation of GATT 1947's Article XX. There is no non-precluded measures clause in the US-Liberia FCN Treaty (1939) unlike FCN treaties such as the US-Ireland FCN Treaty (1950) and the US-Nicaragua FCN Treaty (1956) concluded after the conclusion of the GATT 1947. See Article XX (d) of US-Ireland FCN Treaty and Article XXI (d) of the US-Nicaragua FCN Treaty. US-Liberia FCN Treaty available at: tcc. export.gov/Trade_Agreements/All_Trade_Agreements/exp_005851.asp,   last   accessed 1 April 2021.

[103] US-Ireland FCN treaty Article XX (d): "1. The present treaty shall not preclude the application of measures:. . .(d) necessary to fulfil the obligations of a party for the maintenance or restoration of international peace and security, or necessary to protect its essential security interests;". Available at: 'tcc.export.gov/trade_agreements/all_trade_agreements/exp_005438.asp',   last   accessed 1 April 2021.

[104] *Continental Casualty Company v. The Argentine Republic*, Award, 5 September 2008, ICSID Case No. ARB/03/9, IIC 511, para 198.

[105] The tribunal cited various WTO Reports in FN294, including: Panel Report, EC-Tyres, para. 7.104, summing up the Appellate Body case law in Korea-Beef; EC-Asbestos, para. 172; US-Gambling, para. 306; Dominican Republic-Cigarettes, para. 70, also stating: "Within this weighing and balancing of those various factors, the WTO case law stresses the assessment of the importance of the interests or values furthered by the challenged measure."

[106] *Continental Casualty Company v. The Argentine Republic*, Award ICSID Case No. ARB/03/9, IIC 511 (2008) para 194. The tribunal cited Panel Report, *EC-Tyres*, WT/DS332/R, para. 7.104, summing up the Appellate Body case law.

[107] *Continental Casualty Company v. The Argentine Republic*, Award ICSID Case No. ARB/03/9, IIC 511 (2008) para 195. In this regard, the tribunal cited Appellate Body Report, *US-Gambling*, WT/DS285/AB/R, para 308, as well as Panel Report *EC-Tyres*, WT/DS332/R, 7.211.

The tribunal was guided by these principles in assessing the contribution of the measure and whether there was a reasonably available alternative measure or measures available to the government.

The Continental Annulment Committee emphasised that the tribunal is "clearly not purporting to apply" WTO law but merely taking it into account as relevant to interpreting Article XI.[108] The tribunal deemed this to be a more appropriate approach than drawing on customary international law, the latter approach having been described as a manifest error of law by the CMS Annulment Committee.[109]

(b) Criticism of the approach

Alvarez, one of the key proponents of the customary international law methodology, has been critical of the common derivation approach.[110] Alvarez has claimed that the tribunal in *Continental Casualty* "simply reached for an off-the-shelf model of balancing"[111] and in doing so "appeared to ignore text, context, object and purpose, *and* relevant negotiating history".[112] Rather, the tribunal in *Continental Casualty* should have looked to the ordinary meaning of Article XI in light of the object and purpose of the treaty in line with Article 31 VCLT.[113] Alvarez contends that this approach would have led the tribunal to the customary international law methodology. Art. 31(3)(c) of the VCLT provides that "any relevant rules of international law applicable in the relations between the parties" may be looked to as a source for interpreting treaties.

---

[108] *Continental Casualty Company v. The Argentine Republic,* Decision on the Application for Partial Annulment of Continental Casualty Company, and the Application for Partial Annulment, 16 September 2011, para 133.

[109] *CMS Gas Transmission Company v. Argentine Republic*, Decision of the Ad Hoc Committee on the Application for Annulment of the Argentine Republic Annulment Committee, 25 September 2007, para 130.

[110] See Alvarez (2014) and 'Revisiting the Necessity Defense' (2011).

[111] Alvarez describes the reasoning behind this as being "presumably because it was familiar- at least to the president of that tribunal." This is a reference to the fact the President of the Tribunal, Professor Giorgio Sacerdoti, was previously Chairperson of the WTO's Appellate Body.

[112] Alvarez and Brink (2012), pp. 355–356.

[113] Alvarez and Brink (2012), p. 337.

Article 31 VCLT concerns the 'General rule of interpretation' and states: "1. A treaty shall be interpreted in good faith in accordance with the ordinary meaning to be given to the terms of the treaty in their context and in the light of its object and purpose. 2. The context for the purpose of the interpretation of a treaty shall comprise, in addition to the text, including its preamble and annexes: a. Any agreement relating to the treaty which was made between all the parties in connexion with the conclusion of the treaty; b. Any instrument which was made by one or more parties in connexion with the conclusion of the treaty and accepted by the other parties as an instrument related to the treaty. 3. There shall be taken into account, together with the context: a. Any subsequent agreement between the parties regarding the interpretation of the treaty or the application of its provisions; b. Any subsequent practice in the application of the treaty which establishes the agreement of the parties regarding its interpretation; c. Any relevant rules of international law applicable in the relations between the parties. 4. A special meaning shall be given to a term if it is established that the parties so intended."

Alvarez & Brink disagree with the "application" of GATT Article XX in *Continental Casualty*.[114] They offer five reasons for their disagreement with the tribunal's "inadequate and flawed reasoning", which are now examined as concisely as can be managed.[115] The authors' main critique is the 'mistake' to import GATT Article XX jurisprudence.[116] Alvarez deems it to be a major weakness in the tribunal's methodology that there is no consideration of why the GATT Article XX approach should be 'applied' to interpret Article XI. This premise is questionable as the *Continental* tribunal did not purport to apply GATT jurisprudence. Although it was guided by the approach of WTO tribunals, the LRM test employed was not a WTO test per se, as confirmed by the Continental Casualty Annulment Committee.[117]

GATT Article XX was not applied but rather that the tribunal drew upon a principle elucidated in WTO jurisprudence.[118]

Alvarez and Brink claim that the interpretative steps set out in Article 31 and 32 of the VCLT are entirely absent.[119] In particular, the authors lament the lack of emphasis on the ordinary meaning in the light of the treaty's object and purpose as well as the *travaux préparatoires*, a method that would have led the tribunal to the customary international law approach to necessity. At no point do they address the CMS Annulment Committee's findings that their suggested approach involved conflating Article 25 of the ILC's Draft Articles and Article XI of the US-Argentina BIT.[120]

---

[114] As confirmed by the Annulment Committee, "[T]he Tribunal was clearly not purporting to apply that body of law, but merely took it into account as relevant to determining the correct interpretation and application of Article XI of the BIT". *Continental Casualty Company v. The Argentine Republic*, Decision on the Application for Partial Annulment, ICSID Case No. ARB/03/9, IIC 511 (2011) para 133.

[115] Alvarez and Brink (2012), p. 362.

[116] Alvarez and Brink (2012), p. 335.

[117] As confirmed by the Annulment Committee, "the Tribunal was clearly not purporting to apply that body of law, but merely took it into account as relevant to determining the correct interpretation and application of Article XI of the BIT". *Continental Casualty Company v. The Argentine Republic*, Decision on the Application for Partial Annulment, ICSID Case No. ARB/03/9, IIC 511 (2011) para 133. Alvarez does not say that there is no place for balancing rights and is less critical of the approach of the tribunal in National Grid that "balanced implicitly". Alvarez and Brink (2012), p. 354. For Alvarez & Brink, balancing should be confined to weighing up interests rather than the multi-step process advocated by Stone Sweet & Canacea.

[118] *Continental Casualty Company v. The Argentine Republic*, Decision on the Application for Partial Annulment, ICSID Case No. ARB/03/9, 16 September 2011, para 133. "[T]he Tribunal was clearly not purporting to apply that body of law, but merely took it into account as relevant to determining the correct interpretation and application of Article XI of the BIT."

[119] Alvarez and Brink (2012), p. 337.

[120] *CMS Gas Transmission Company v. Argentine Republic*, Annulment Decision ICSID Case No. ARB/01/08, IIC 303 (2005).

(1) Failure to state reasons

Alvarez & Brink claim that the members of the tribunal "scarcely address" why the trade rule was relevant to an investment treaty dispute.[121] The tribunal did however justify its reference to WTO case law by stating that it sees it as "more appropriate. . .than to refer to necessity under customary international law".[122] This was due to the fact that Article XI is derived from the model clause for US FCN treaties which reflects the formulation of Article XX of GATT 1947.[123] Although the authors may not agree with the reasons given, this is a different matter to a tribunal failing to give reasons.

Alvarez & Brink then invoke the separate matter of the partial annulment of the *CMS* decision (for a failure to state its reasons) stating "a similar criticism can be made here".[124] However, there was no partial annulment of the Continental award, and it can be further distinguished from the CMS decision on two grounds. Firstly, the *CMS* Annulment Committee was addressing the application of an umbrella clause rather than a non-precluded measures clause. Secondly, the authors may have preferred if there had been discussion of the *travaux* in *Continental*, but the fact that the tribunal did not discuss this does not lead to a conclusion that the tribunal failed to state its reasons.[125] Furthermore, the tribunal in *Continental* did in fact consider the negotiating history of the BIT in its Award.[126]

(2) Erroneous reading of history

The authors critique the tribunal's interpretation of 'public order' as well as its justification for 'applying' GATT Article XX. Alvarez & Brink strongly disagree with the finding that the term "maintenance of public order" embraces the French

---

[121] Alvarez and Brink (2012), p. 335.

[122] *Continental Casualty Company v. The Argentine Republic*, Award, 5 September 2008, ICSID Case No. ARB/03/9, IIC 511 (2008) para 192. The tribunal referred to trade jurisprudence, which is a relevant rule under VCLT 31.3(c): "There shall be taken into account, together with the context: (. . .) c. Any relevant rules of international law applicable in the relations between the parties."

[123] *Continental Casualty Company v. The Argentine Republic*, Award, 5 September 2008, ICSID Case No. ARB/03/9, IIC 511, para 192.

[124] In *CMS v. Argentina*, damages were awarded based on independent findings of breach of Article II(2)(a) and (c) of the BIT and so the Committee's finding "does not entail the annulment of the Award as a whole" but rather the annulment of certain provisions of the operative part of the Award. When discussing the umbrella clause under Article II(2)(c) of the Treaty, the Tribunal stated that it "will not discuss the jurisdictional aspects involved in the Respondent's argument, as these were dealt with in the decision on jurisdiction." (para 86). CMS had argued that Article II(2)(c) of the BIT allowed it to invoke certain obligations under Argentine law. The Committee accepted that this may have been implicit within its reasoning "But the Tribunal nowhere addressed this point expressly." (para 94) The Annulment Committee later states *obiter* that "There is no discussion in the award of the *travaux* of the BIT on this point, or of the prior understandings of the proponents of the umbrella clause as to its function."

[125] See Alvarez and Brink (2012), pp. 337–338.

[126] *Continental Casualty Company v. The Argentine Republic*, Award, 5 September 2008, ICSID Case No. ARB/03/9, IIC 511 (2008) para 176.

legal concept of *ordre public,* which the tribunal found to be a "broad synonym" for public peace.[127] If the US drafters had wanted to exempt a raft of government measures, they had tools at their disposal to do so which wouldn't include "resort to a foreign civil law concept".[128] The context in which the term *ordre public* is raised is in the following paragraph of the *Continental* award:

> This is the ordinary and principal meaning of "orden publico" in the Spanish text of the BIT, corresponding to the same meaning in the French legal concept of "ordre public" in public and criminal law.[129]

Alvarez & Brink only address the French concept of *ordre public* but the award first refers to the Spanish language concept of *orden publico.* The treaty was concluded in English and Spanish and the Spanish version is equally authentic as per Article XIV.4 of the BIT.[130] Concerning the 'application' of GATT Article XX, the authors find that the tribunal in *Continental* ignored fundamental differences between the three provisions in question.[131] They find that Article XI is based on part of the FCN derogation clause and bears "no resemblance" to GATT Article XX, which covers "entirely different subject matter".[132]

Alvarez & Brink recall that the US continues to resist the inclusion of a GATT Article XX like article in its IIAs and questions why the drafters did not include a broad list of exceptions such as those found in the GATT or the FCN treaties.[133] The drafters saw a distinction between relative and absolute guarantees under BITs and deliberately excluded the application of a host of public policy exceptions as they were "not regarded as appropriate".[134]

The authors note that in the 2004 US Model BIT, a provision that mirrors GATT Article XX is included as part of Article 8, which deals with performance requirements.[135] They argue that the US includes them where it sees appropriate and that consequently their absence in Article XI denotes their intentional absence. A list of

---

[127] Decision on the Application for Partial Annulment of Continental Casualty Company, and the Application for Partial Annulment, 16 September 2011, para 174.

[128] Alvarez and Brink (2012), p. 340.

[129] Decision on the Application for Partial Annulment of Continental Casualty Company, and the Application for Partial Annulment, 16 September 2011, para 174.

[130] Article XIV.4: "...DONE in duplicate at Washington on the fourteenth day of November, 1991, in the English and Spanish languages, both texts being equally authentic."

[131] Again, the tribunal was not *applying* GATT Article XX (see the Decision of the Annulment Committee), but rather drew upon a principle elucidated in WTO jurisprudence.

[132] Alvarez and Brink (2012), p. 338.

[133] For Alvarez & Brink, FCN treaties only contain a necessity test with respect to the obligation of international peace and security and essential security. E.g. the necessity test contained in Article XXI (d) of the US-Nicaragua FCN Treaty. Article XI most closely resembles this clause, which has little to do with the right to regulate and everything to do with preserving States' customary law defences.

[134] Alvarez and Brink (2012), p. 342.

[135] Alvarez and Brink (2012), p. 344.

exceptions is included under Article 8 but this not a general exception to all
obligations under the treaty.

Furthermore, the authors point out that necessity has not been interpreted under
the GATT in relation to essential security interests but rather under Article XX (a),
(b) and (d), subjects which are "nowhere to be found" under Article XI.[136] While
there are fundamental differences between the three articles considered under the
Common Derivation approach, there are also significant similarities. The main area
of similarity is between Article XI of the US-Argentina BIT and FCN exceptions
clauses, rather than between the GATT and Article XI.[137] Article XI and the FCN
derogation clause also have a common genesis or derivation (GATT 1947). Article
XI of the US-Argentina BIT is derived from trade and investment agreements
(US FCN treaties), which is derived from a trade agreement (GATT 1947).

This common derivation is deemed to override the dissimilarities between the
provisions. Furthermore, the agreements all deal with the concept of necessity within
two branches of international economic law that are interrelated and often negotiated
as part of one agreement, such as FCN treaties. This was also an area where the
GATT had built a rich jurisprudence (in contrast to the investment law regime) and
this was deemed to be a sufficient reason to *draw upon* a principle elucidated in
WTO jurisprudence.

(3) Failure to consider Article XX text and jurisprudence

Alvarez & Brink argue that any reference to GATT Article XX jurisprudence
must consider the Article's chapeau.[138] They claim that the tribunal in *Continental*
ignored the chapeau and its impact on the necessity test when interpreting Article
XX's subparagraphs. Although they acknowledge the nature of the two-tier test, they
claim exceptions are grounded in a balancing test (the chapeau), which is absent
from the US-Argentina BIT. Alvarez reminds us that in *US-Shrimp I* the Appellate
Body found Article XX's general exceptions to be "limited and conditional,"[139] but
this merely means that they are "subject to the compliance by the invoking Member
with the requirements of the chapeau."[140]

At the WTO, necessity tests are not carried out with reference to the chapeau. The
implication of it being a two-tiered test is that the analyses are conducted separately

[136] Alvarez and Brink (2012), p. 340.

[137] It is noted that only specific sectoral exemptions were included in US BITs, which was an
alternative solution to the list of policy exemptions such as those pursued in GATT Article XX.

[138] Alvarez and Brink (2012), pp. 345–347.

[139] *Continental Casualty Company v. The Argentine Republic,* Decision on the Application for
Partial Annulment of Continental Casualty Company, and the Application for Partial Annulment,
16 September 2011, para 157.

[140] Decision on the Application for Partial Annulment of Continental Casualty Company, and the
Application for Partial Annulment, 16 September 2011, para 157.

and independently. This is why the Appellate Body may refrain from completing its analysis under the chapeau where the necessity test is failed.[141]

The Appellate Body has deemed this two-tier sequence to be both logical and fundamental to the operation of the Article.[142] It has found interpreting the chapeau without this sequence of analysis to be difficult "if. . .possible at all".[143] Giorgio Sacerdoti, president of the tribunal in *Continental*, has noted that, "the definition of 'necessity' in WTO case law is not affected by the presence of the chapeau."[144] Sacerdoti cites *US-Shrimp I*,[145] which discusses the sequence of steps to be taken which are not "random choice, but rather the fundamental structure and logic of Article XX".[146]Alvarez & Brink maintain that the chapeau has "subtly affected" how the subparagraphs have been interpreted.[147] As measures still have to be compliant with the chapeau, tribunals may give more leeway, as it provides a second level to combat for discriminatory or protectionist intent.

However, this is not the view taken at the WTO, as cases taken under the TBT and SPS Agreements (which do not contain chapeaux) have drawn upon jurisprudence under other WTO Agreements such as GATT and GATS.[148] While the GATT Article XX chapeau may have influenced the development of the jurisprudence under the GATT and the GATS, the test is "wholly capable of standing on its own", and its presence does not preclude the WTO necessity test informing the approach of investment tribunals.[149] Finally, where a test fails the chapeau and the discriminatory element of the measure is removed, the measure may then be permissible.

---

[141] This was the case in *China—Audiovisual Services* (2009), where the Appellate Body found that China's measures were not necessary to protect public morals due to the existence of at least one other reasonably available alternative. WT/DS363/AB/R, Appellate Body Report, *China — Measures Affecting Trading Rights and Distribution Services for Certain Publications and Audiovisual Entertainment Products*, 21 December 2009.

[142] Appellate Body Report, *US – Import Prohibition of Certain Shrimp and Shrimp Products*, WT/DS58/AB/R, adopted on 6 November 1998, para 119.

[143] Appellate Body Report, *US – Import Prohibition of Certain Shrimp and Shrimp Products*, WT/DS58/AB/R, adopted on 6 November 1998, para 120.

[144] Sacerdoti (2013), p. 32, FN120.

[145] Appellate Body Report, *US – Import Prohibition of Certain Shrimp and Shrimp Products*, WT/DS58/AB/R, adopted on 6 November 1998, Para 115ff.

[146] Appellate Body Report, *US – Import Prohibition of Certain Shrimp and Shrimp Products*, WT/DS58/AB/R, adopted on 6 November 1998, Para 119.

[147] Wagner views the argument that the two-tiered analysis affects the interpretation of necessity as "valid". See Wagner (2014), p. 73.

[148] Alvarez & Brink continue that to apply a GATT Article XX necessity analysis without consideration of the chapeau "suggests that what *Continental* applied as "WTO law" does not even accurately reflect trade law much less investment law." As the Annulment Committee tell us, the tribunal did not apply WTO law in *Continental*.

[149] Mitchell and Henckels (2013), p. 137.

(4) Differing purposes

Alvarez & Brink emphasise that necessity analysis should be carried out in the light of the object and purpose of the treaty in question. They distinguish the fundamental purposes of the regimes.[150] The authors note that the purpose of the GATT is reflected in its preamble but they do not mention the preamble to the US-Argentina BIT. The latter preamble focuses on economic cooperation and the encouragement and protection of investment, without mention of state behaviour in times of crisis.[151]

The authors lament the fact that the tribunal in *Continental* did not further examine the nature of the exception and whether it operates as a "blanket excuse from liability" no matter what the action is so long as it is for actions taken during a period of economic crisis.[152] Presumably it is for individual tribunals to determine whether a measure taken by a state is "necessary for the maintenance of public order" and this does not operate as a blanket excuse. For example, the tribunal in *Continental* found that a measure is not deemed necessary where a reasonably available alternative measure exists and cited *US-Gambling*.[153]

What constitutes a "reasonably available alternative measure" is further disputed.

The Continental tribunal cited the AB Report in *US-Gambling,* which found that an alternative measure must be a measure that would preserve for the state its right to achieve its "desired level of protection with respect to the objective pursued".[154] Alvarez & Brink contend that the term "desired level of protection" is ill-fitted to the investment law context. The GATT is categorised as a negative integration agreement (based on combatting protectionism etc.) while the purpose of investment treaties is to provide actionable rights to private actors. However, in *US-Gambling*

---

[150] Alvarez and Brink (2012), p. 347. While the GATT seeks to reduce tariffs, barriers to trade and discriminatory treatment, the US-Argentina BIT provides a recourse for individuals to seek remedies while disciplining "the behaviour of States during periods of alleged economic crisis" *inter alia.*

[151] Preamble to US-Argentina BIT (1994): "The United States of America and the Argentine Republic, hereinafter referred to as the Parties; Desiring to promote greater economic cooperation between them, with respect to investment by nationals and companies of one Party in the territory of the other Party; Recognizing that agreement upon the treatment to be accorded such investment will stimulate the flow of private capital and the economic development of the Parties; Agreeing that fair and equitable treatment of investment is desirable in order to maintain a stable framework for investment and maximum effective use of economic resources; Recognizing that the development of economic and business ties can contribute to the well-being of workers in both Parties and promote respect for internationally recognized worker rights; and having resolved to conclude a Treaty concerning the encouragement and reciprocal protection of investment; Have agreed as follows:"

[152] Alvarez and Brink (2012), p. 348.

[153] The Continental tribunal cited Appellate Body Report, *United States – Measures Affecting the Cross-Border Supply of Gambling and Betting Services*, WT/DS285/AB/R, adopted 20 April 2005, para 308. *Continental Casualty Company v. The Argentine Republic*, Award ICSID Case No. ARB/03/9, IIC 511 (2008) para 195.

[154] Ibid.

where the term "desired level of protection" is used, it refers to the state's right to "achieve objectives relating to public morals or public order", rather than protectionism.[155] The objective in *US-Gambling* is also not dissimilar to the one found in Article XI of the US-Argentina BIT ("the maintenance of public order").

(5) Structural differences

For Alvarez & Brink, it is not clear why treaty exceptions involving different obligations, for different reasons, with different remedies "should be viewed as comparable".[156] The structural differences identified include the fact that IIAs give rights to third parties with the prospect of damages and in the absence of an appellate mechanism or legal secretariat.[157] These differences and the fact that the WTO is interstate may lead to WTO tribunals having a more "deferential view of what constitutes a legitimate government measure".[158] Investment tribunals are more "intent on protecting the rights of their third party beneficiaries" and might not be as deferential.[159] However it could also be argued that because of the political sensitivity surrounding large settlements against host states under BITs, that tribunals might be more inclined to show deference to the state in this context.

The potential for exit from ICSID and BITs is another structural difference between the two regimes. Alvarez & Brink urge caution against "facile conclusions from regimes where the possibility of exit/ voice is far more constrained."[160] However, if non-precluded measures clauses are interpreted in an overly restrictive manner, this could lead to treaty exit. States may anticipate the difficulty of meeting the stringent standard of Article 25 ARSIWA. This would particularly be the case where states have no option to appeal and are required to make significant settlements on the basis of such an interpretation.[161] States seeking greater investment protection are not the ones exiting BITs and leaving an investment treaty because investment protection is not sufficiently high under it would seem counterproductive. This is particularly the case where there is the possibility of amending the treaty or issuing a joint interpretation as an alternative to exit.

---

[155] Appellate Body Report, *United States – Measures Affecting the Cross-Border Supply of Gambling and Betting Services*, WT/DS285/AB/R, adopted 20 April 2005, para 309.

[156] Alvarez and Brink (2012), p. 350.

[157] Alvarez and Brink (2012), pp. 349–350.

[158] Alvarez and Brink (2012), p. 350.

[159] Alvarez and Brink (2012), p. 350.

[160] Alvarez and Brink (2012), p. 351.

[161] E.g. *CMS Gas Transmission Company v. Argentine Republic*, Award, 12 May 2005, ICSID Case No. ARB/01/08, IIC 303; *Enron Corporation and Ponderosa Assets, L.P. v. Argentine Republic*, Award, 22 May 2007, ICSID Case No. ARB/01/3; and *Sempra Energy International v. The Argentine Republic*, Award, 28 September 2007, ICSID Case No. ARB/02/16.

4.2.3.3 Other Approaches

Sections (a) and (b) considered two approaches taken by tribunals when interpreting necessity in IIAs. This section considers two methodologies proposed by commentators as means of supplementing or replacing the Common Derivation Approach when interpreting necessity under IIAs. While the common derivation approach was preferred to the Orrega Vicuña approach in the last section, some of the reasons for this were specific to the context of the US-Argentina BIT and may not be relevant when considering other treaties.[162] The common derivation approach can however serve as a starting point for interpreting exceptions in IIAs.

(a) Proportionality Analysis as a general principle of law

The tribunal in *Continental Casualty* made no reference to proportionality analysis or to general principles of law. It did however refer to the concept of necessity as it has been interpreted in WTO case law.[163] The version of necessity analysis laid down in *Korea-Beef* was determined through "a process of weighing and balancing of factors" in determining whether a measure that is not indispensable may be deemed necessary.[164] This version of necessity analysis closely resembles proportionality analysis as described by Stone Sweet.[165] Proportionality Analysis (PA) is

---

[162] The Common Derivation approach takes account of WTO jurisprudence as Article XI of the US-Argentina BIT was derived from the FCN treaties which reflect the formulation of GATT Article XX. This common derivation is not common under other IIAs.

[163] The tribunal found it more appropriate to do so based on the common derivation method: "Since the text of Art. XI derives from the parallel model clause of the U.S. FCN treaties and these treaties in turn reflect the formulation of Art. XX of GATT 1947," *Continental Casualty Company v. The Argentine Republic*, Award, 5 September 2008, ICSID Case No. ARB/03/9, IIC 511, para 192.

[164] The tribunal cited various WTO Reports in FN294, including: Panel Report, EC-Tyres, para. 7.104, summing up the Appellate Body case law in Korea-Beef; EC-Asbestos, para. 172; US-Gambling, para. 306; Dominican Republic-Cigarettes, para. 70, also stating: "Within this weighing and balancing of those various factors, the WTO case law stresses the assessment of the importance of the interests or values furthered by the challenged measure." Appellate Body Report, *Korea – Measures Affecting Imports of Fresh, Chilled and Frozen Beef*, WT/ DS161/AB/R, WT/DS169/AB/R, adopted 10 January 2001, para 164.

[165] In its fully developed form, proportionality analysis contains four steps; the first concerns whether the government has the legitimacy to take such a measure; the second considers the suitability of the means in attaining the ends; the third step looks at the necessity of the measure where the "core" is an LRM test; if the first three criteria are fulfilled, the last step involves balancing by the judge where she weighs the benefits of the act against the cost of the infringement. This is a condensed description of Stone Sweet's description of Proportionality Analysis in 'Proportionality Balancing and Global Constitutionalism,' Stone Sweet (2008), p. 76.
See also Stone Sweet and della Canacea (2014), pp. 917–918, where PA is described as a multi-stage analytical procedure for resolving legal conflicts involving three main steps: (1) inquiry into the "suitability" of the measure under review. The government must demonstrate that the relationship between the means chosen and the ends pursued is rational and appropriate; (2) "necessity analysis" involving a least-restrictive-means (LRM) test, through which the judge ensures that the measure under review does not curtail the right at stake more than is necessary for the government to achieve its declared purposes; and (3) balancing *stricto sensu*—is also known as "proportionality

an adjudicative process used by tribunals to settle competing rights claims. Proportionality analysis is used in assessing the balance between the restrictiveness of a measure and the severity of the nature of the prohibited act. Alvarez agrees that such "weighing and balancing" has a place under BITs, but questions the rationale of its application under the US-Argentina BIT.[166]

PA is a means of balancing competing rights and its use when interpreting treaty exceptions has proved controversial. Mitchell et al describe proportionality tests as involving a question of value judgement "that gives an undesirable degree of discretion to adjudicators" and "requires a tribunal to second-guess the level of protection" a state has chosen.[167] Kurtz is sceptical of balancing that involves "complex value-laden and empirical judgments." In his view, the lack of an appellate mechanism in investment law also makes the LRM test a "better institutional fit".[168]

Schill finds that investment tribunals in recent years have shown "increasing sensitivity" to the principle of proportionality and that they may be more likely to turn to PA to balance interests in the future.[169] Necessity analysis has however been incorporated into the structure of many recent IIAs, including in provisions that incorporate references to WTO law.

Stone Sweet & Canacea are of the view that proportionality analysis is a general principle of law and that the *Continental* tribunal could have strengthened its position by appealing to general principles of law: "General principles are a recognized source of international law (Article 38 of the Statute of the ICJ); second, under the Vienna Convention on the Law of Treaties (Art. 31(3)(c)), judges are to take into account the 'relevant rules of international law applicable in the relations between the parties' when they interpret treaties, and proportionality may well be a 'relevant rule.'"[170]

For Stone Sweet & Canacea, proportionality is a "widely-recognized general principle of law that judges in the most powerful international courts use to adjudicate derogation clauses."[171] The appeal to general principles of law is based on the idea that states have traditionally concluded IIAs as incomplete contracts. They leave

---

in the narrow sense." In this phase, the judge weighs, in light of the facts, the benefits of the act (already found to have been narrowly tailored) against the costs incurred by infringement of the right, in order to decide which side shall prevail.

[166] Alvarez and Brink (2012), p. 352.

[167] Mitchell et al. (2016), pp. 165, 150.

[168] Kurtz (2016), pp. 201–202. Voon et al. describe the use of PA as "significantly restrict[ing] host States' ability to determine and prioritise their own policy objectives and implementation." Mitchell et al. (2018), p. 48. They do acknowledge that the flexibility provided by PA has been described as greater "than may be suggested" by the low success rate at the WTO (page 49). PA has also been described as entailing an "inherent power shift" towards tribunals. Wagner (2014), p. 68. Finally, Alvarez & Brink are of the view that PA is unlikely to oust the customary international law approach to necessity, as few BITs will trigger it. Alvarez and Brink (2012), p. 357.

[169] Schill and Djanic (2016), p. 18.

[170] Stone Sweet and della Canacea (2014), p. 938.

[171] Stone Sweet and della Canacea (2014), p. 938.

terms such as fair and equitable treatment undefined and in order to resolve disputes, judges are "all but required" to turn to general principles of law.[172] The argument for proportionality analysis being a general principle of law is grounded in the idea that it has been used by tribunals around the world and has diffused across a variety of jurisdictions from national courts, to the ECJ, ECtHR and WTO Appellate Body.[173]

Alvarez contests the idea that proportionality is a general principle of law.[174] The "least restrictive alternative" balancing test which *Continental* imports from the WTO is neither a rule of customary law, or, "absent considerable broadening of the concept…a genuinely general principle of law".[175] Alvarez views this as a case of regime-borrowing or boundary crossing that cannot be justified by the traditional gap-filling interpretative rules in the VCLT or by the gap-filling interpretative canons outlined by the ILC.[176]

(b) Separating Primary and Secondary Applications

This approach, proposed by Jürgen Kurtz, involves looking for breach under the treaty *before* having recourse to a defence of necessity under customary international law.[177] In some ways, this approach merges the customary international law and *lex specialis* approaches Kurtz initially considers and rejects. This approach could also be a possible addendum to the Common Derivation Approach and/ or the General

---

There is no prescribed method for identifying and applying (general principles)…The ECJ, the ECtHR, and the WTO AB use PA—in particular, LRM testing—to adjudicate provisions that allow states to claim derogations from their obligations under the treaty's law, for measures that are "necessary" to achieve public policy purposes.…states have proved unwilling or unable to produce treaties that are relatively "complete" contracts that could potentially constrain judicial lawmaking. Instead, states routinely leave crucial terms undefined, an example being the FET standard in BITs, or the necessity clause in Article XI of the U.S.-Argentina BIT. Judges are thus all but required to develop general principles in order to resolve disputes effectively.

[172] Stone Sweet and della Canacea (2014), p. 942.

[173] See Stone Sweet and della Canacea (2014), pp. 918–924.

[174] Stone Sweet & Canacea are of the view that proportionality is a widely-recognised general principle of law and that Alvarez and Khamsi were wrong when they found: "the 'least restrictive alternative' rule is not connected to any principle of international law that is relevant to interpreting the U.S.-Argentina BIT." See Stone Sweet and della Canacea (2014), p. 938; Alvarez and Khamsi (2008), p. 54.

[175] Alvarez (2014), p. 28.

[176] 'Fragmentation Of International Law: Difficulties Arising From The Diversification And Expansion Of International Law,' A/CN.4/L.682 (2006). Alvarez does not consider the WTO's balancing test to be a relevant rule under Art. 31(3)(c). Alvarez ultimately fears that leaps to the trade regime may inspire an all-purpose necessity defence where arbitrators address the most critical questions at the heart of State sovereignty where such decisions are not necessary.

[177] Kurtz (2010), pp. 325–371. Kurtz examines three interpretative methods in the jurisprudence. He views the customary international law/ Orrega Vicuña approach to necessity as a mistake. He then examines treating exceptions articles such as Article XI US-Argentina BIT as *lex specialis*, but concludes that Methodology III (Separating Primary and Secondary Applications) is the most "convincing and coherent". (page 371)

Principles of Law Approach. Kurtz generally agrees with the common derivation approach describing the Continental award as being characterised by "careful and sophisticated use of WTO exceptions jurisprudence."[178]

Under this primary and secondary applications approach, breach under the treaty in question is first considered. Where breach is found, the state may then be able to fall back on a customary international law defence. Kurtz suggests that this approach "overcomes the deficiencies" of the other approaches.[179]

The customary international law approach is however constructed to provide relief in a very narrow set of circumstances. This is certainly the case in relation to the exceptions provisions typically found in modern IIAs, and so this recourse to the customary international law defence of necessity after necessity has been considered under an IIA provision may give rise to limited success.

Kurtz pre-empts the criticism that going to the treaty first will render the customary law defence redundant. If the scope of the treaty provision is broader than the customary international law provision, then invocation of the clause will "always" preclude custom.[180] Philippe Sands, in his Dissenting Opinion in *Bear Creek v. Peru*, found that whatever the requirements of the FTA, recourse to Article 25 ARSIWA "is not excluded by the FTA".[181]

4.3 Treaty Exceptions and Engagement

The degree of separateness, overlap and convergence between the two regimes is now considered as well as the role of PTIAs, and the appropriateness of drawing on WTO law for guidance in investment law disputes and vice versa.

4.3.1 The Extent of Engagement

General exceptions provisions are a shared norm of the trade and investment law regimes that limit the scope of treaty obligations and safeguard the state's right to regulate. There is great potential for engagement in the area of treaty exceptions

---

[178] Kurtz (2009), p. 771.

[179] Kurtz refers to the other approaches as the 'confluence' and '*lex specialis*' approaches. *CMS, Enron* and *Sempra* fall into the confluence category. *LG&E* is the best candidate for the *lex specialis* approach "although there are intriguing hints in this direction in the Continental award as well". Kurtz (2010), pp. 355–356.

[180] Kurtz (2010), p. 358. Kurtz reminds us that it is not a flaw of the methodology if in certain circumstances the customary approach in rendered inutile as it is designed to apply across the entirety of international law.

[181] *Bear Creek Mining Corporation v. Republic of Peru*, ICSID Case No. ARB/14/21, Partial Dissenting Opinion of Professor Philippe Sands, 30 November 2017, para 41.

given how common these provisions are and how closely the treaty texts can mirror each other. This overlap extends to the questions faced by tribunals when interpreting these provisions. While these general exceptions provisions may apply in different contexts, tribunals may be required to interpret shared or similar concepts such as when a measure is necessary, or when its application would constitute arbitrary or unjustifiable discrimination. The more similar the content of these provisions, the more likely tribunals are to draw upon the jurisprudence of the other regime. Parties can adapt the content of agreements to encourage or discourage such practices as appropriate.

Four categories of 'treaty exceptions' are outlined in this study including those explicitly modelled on WTO law, implicitly modelled on WTO law, those within articles on performance requirements, and those thinly connected to WTO law. The first three of these are closely modelled on WTO law and facilitate a high level of engagement between the regimes. These provisions have the clearest potential for facilitating engagement between the regimes, as tribunals may be required to turn to WTO law in their interpretations.

Provisions thinly connected to WTO law also facilitate engagement between the regimes albeit to a lesser extent. Article XI of the US-Argentina BIT is an example of such a provision. When interpreting Article XI, the tribunal in *Continental Casualty v. Argentina* referred to WTO jurisprudence. This is the sole reference to WTO jurisprudence that has been made by an investment tribunal when interpreting exceptions to IIAs to date. The tribunal drew upon the experience of the trade regime in dealing with treaty exceptions when interpreting the concept of 'necessity' in Article XI of the US-Argentina BIT.[182] This 'common derivation approach' was based on the fact that the US-Argentina BIT's non-precluded measures article was derived from similar articles in US FCN treaties, which in turn were inspired by GATT Article 1947. This common heritage was deemed to be sufficient for the tribunal to consider the jurisprudence developed under the GATT as a source of guidance when interpreting a norm common to all three of the treaties.

The extent of inter-regime engagement is impacted by other considerations, such as whether exceptions provisions are characterized as scope limitations on substantive obligations or as defences once breach has been established.[183] Henckels considers that exceptions provisions in IIAs should be characterized as scope limitations.[184] Henckels acknowledges that this is "inconsistent" with the WTO approach to general exceptions whereby they have long been classified as affirmative defences.[185] Where a provision is thinly modelled on WTO law (such as Article XI of the US-Argentina BIT), it is easier to make the case that it should function in a manner similar to a carve out or 'permission', falling outside the scope of the BIT.

---

[182] *Continental Casualty Company v. The Argentine Republic*, Award, 5 September 2008, ICSID Case No. ARB/03/9, IIC 511, para 189–195.

[183] See Henckels (2018), p. 2829.

[184] See Henckels (2018), p. 2829.

[185] Henckels (2020), p. 373.

Where provisions are explicitly or implicitly modelled on GATT Article XX, this it is much harder to make this case.

Modern IIAs contain balance between investment protection and the right to regulate and exceptions are an essential part of this balance. Treaty exceptions facilitate inter-regime engagement and it is for the parties negotiating IIAs to decide how the relationship between trade and investment should develop under these provisions. The greater the similarity between the norms of the regimes, the more likely tribunals will be to make cross-regime references.

4.3.2   Cross-Regime References

4.3.2.1   Why Make Cross-Regime References?

Treaty exceptions provisions are commonly found in WTO and investment treaties and they represent one of the clearest areas for potential interaction between the regimes. In line with Article 31.3(c) of the Vienna Convention, tribunals may consider in their interpretations "any relevant rules of international law applicable in the relations between the parties". Treaty exceptions of the other regime form a part of this body of relevant rules and can thus be considered by tribunals.

Investment treaties have incorporated WTO-based exceptions in a number of ways. Consideration of WTO law may be required when interpreting IIAs that incorporate WTO exceptions provisions *mutatis mutandis*.[186] The context for considering these exceptions is also similar; e.g. when breach of a nondiscrimination provision, which is also a shared norm, has been found. If a party is found to breach CETA's nondiscrimination provisions aimed at protecting investors,[187] and invokes an exception under CETA Article 28.3, the tribunal will likely have to consider the relevant WTO jurisprudence. Tribunals could also consider other similarities between CETA and the trade regime including the structure of the rule-exception dyad and the presence of an appellate mechanism interpreting these provisions.

Other WTO Agreements such as the TBT Agreement and TRIPS Agreement do not contain general exceptions provisions and where IIAs have similar structures, this could also facilitate cross-regime references. There are many IIAs for which the regulatory purpose of a measure is examined when considering the substantive provision itself rather than under a general exceptions provision. The findings of tribunals under provisions with these shared structures may be at least as relevant as those under agreements in the same regime, but with dissimilar structures. Where

---

[186]E.g. Article 16.1 Vietnam-Korea FTA: "2. For the purposes of Chapters 8 (Trade in Services) and 9 (Investment), Article XIV of GATS (including its footnotes) is incorporated into and made part of this Agreement, *mutatis mutandis*."

[187]Article 8.6 National treatment, Article 8.7 Most-favoured-nation treatment, or Article 8.8 Senior management and boards of directors.

investment tribunals have considered WTO provisions that have been directly incorporated into IIAs, their findings may also be relevant to WTO tribunals.

The potential for cross-regime references extends to exceptions in IIAs that are thinly connected to WTO law. These include treaty exceptions in BITs with similar features to the WTO Agreements such as necessity tests. For such provisions, tribunals must examine the potential for crossfertilisation based on the provision at hand.

4.3.2.2 Have There Been Cross-Regime References?

For treaty exceptions, there has been one major investment dispute where a tribunal has referred to WTO jurisprudence.[188] As discussed in Sect. 4.2, the tribunal in *Continental Casualty v. Argentina* employed the Common Derivation Approach, as Article XI of the US-Argentina BIT was derived from US FCN treaties, which reflect the formulation of GATT Article XX.[189]

4.3.2.3 Making Cross-Regime References

Investment tribunals have not yet interpreted an exceptions provision directly incorporating WTO exceptions into an IIA.[190] The Panel in *Ukraine-Wood Products* recently interpreted provisions directly incorporating WTO provisions into the trade

---

[188] For a general discussion of cross-regime references, see Sect. 1.5.

[189] This approach has received criticism (as well as praise) as outlined in Sect. 4.2. Alvarez has claimed that the tribunal in *Continental Casualty* ignored "stark differences" between the regimes. Tribunals must, of course, take into consideration the fact that the WTO is inter-state in nature. For Alvarez & Brink, tribunals need to consider how the structures of institutions influence the principles they adopt and apply and how institutional factors make certain interpretative techniques more acceptable. Alvarez (2014), p. 27. These include the fact that the investment regime involves "private complaints against states" for property rights violations, whereas the trade regime provides an "interstate remedy intended to prod a state into removing protectionist measures". Alvarez and Brink (2012), p. 352. Alvarez advocates an interpretation of Article XI of the US-Argentina BIT under Article 25 ARSIWA. See Sect. 4.2.3.1.

[190] The tribunal in *Copper Mesa Mining v. Ecuador* decided a claim for expropriation and FET with reference to a general exceptions provision, found in Article XVII of the Canada-Ecuador BIT (1996), that implicitly incorporated GATT Article XX(b), (d) and (g). It found that a finding of expropriation required inter alia, the non-application of the exception provision. *Copper Mesa Mining Corporation v. Republic of Ecuador*, PCA No. 2012-2, Award, 15 March 2016, para 6.58. The Respondent sought to justify its measure as a legitimate response to a social and political problem. The tribunal found that the justification of the exercise of the regulatory powers and the applicability of the exceptions "turn on the same factors" and did not go into a detailed consideration of the exceptions provision. The tribunal found that there was a "substantial deprivation" amounting to indirect expropriation.

provisions of the EU-Ukraine Association Agreement.[191] When investment tribunals do interpret such a provision, their analysis may resemble parts of the analysis undertaken here. This dispute concerned two export bans and whether they breached Article 35 of the Association Agreement (directly incorporating GATT Article XI). The Panel then considered their compliance with Article 36, which directly incorporated GATT Article XX into the Agreement.[192]

In its Report, the Panel considered both export bans and whether they were export restrictions within the meaning of Article 35 of the Agreement. The Panel found that the export bans were incompatible with Article 35 of the Agreement, without prejudice to the defences available under Article 36.[193] The Panel then considered whether the bans could be justified under Article 36 of the Agreement, conducting separate analyses for the 2005 and 2015 bans under GATT Article XX(b) and (g) respectively.

In relation to the 2005 ban, the Panel's sequence of analysis in relation to the GATT Article XX(b) defence was as follows: (i) the Panel found there was a risk to plant life or health;[194] (ii) the Panel found that the design of the measure was capable of protecting plant life or health;[195] (iii) the Panel found that the measure was 'necessary' to protect plant life or health;[196] (iv) the Panel then considered the requirements of Article XX's chapeau and the 2005 export ban was found to be compliant.[197]

---

[191] Final Report, *Restrictions applied by Ukraine on exports of certain wood products to the European Union*, 11 December 2020.

[192] Article 36, General exceptions "Nothing in this Agreement shall be construed in such a way as to prevent the adoption or enforcement by any Party of measures in accordance with Articles XX and XXI of GATT 1994 and its interpretative notes, which are hereby incorporated into and made an integral part of this Agreement.

[193] Final Report, *Restrictions applied by Ukraine on exports of certain wood products to the European Union*, 11 December 2020, para 218.

[194] Final Report, *Restrictions applied by Ukraine on exports of certain wood products to the European Union*, 11 December 2020, para 288.

[195] Final Report, *Restrictions applied by Ukraine on exports of certain wood products to the European Union*, 11 December 2020, para 297. The Panel referred to the Appellate Body in *Colombia – Textiles*, where it was found that this is "not a particularly demanding step" in contrast to the assessment of the necessity of a measure. Para 5.70.

[196] Final Report, *Restrictions applied by Ukraine on exports of certain wood products to the European Union*, 11 December 2020, para 303 & 344. This involved consideration of four factors, which were assessed holistically. These factors included: the importance of the interests or values at stake, the existence of a material contribution, the trade restrictiveness of the measure, and the existence of alternative measures.

[197] Final Report, *Restrictions applied by Ukraine on exports of certain wood products to the European Union*, 11 December 2020. The Panel looked at whether the export ban was applied in a manner that would constitute "arbitrary or unjustifiable discrimination", noting that this clause imposed three conditions: (1) there must be discrimination; (2) the discrimination must be arbitrary or unjustifiable; and (3) it must occur in countries where the same conditions prevail. The Panel found that the ban does not create discrimination (para 365). It noted that the ban was focused specifically on endangered species, that it also applied to sawn wood of these species, and that there

Concerning the 2015 ban, the Panel's analysis focused on the requirements of GATT Article XX(g), which the ban did not fulfil. The Panel referred to the rational connection test and that there must be a "close and genuine relationship of ends and means" established case-by-case.[198] To establish such a relationship, it found that the measure must "bring about" a material contribution to the objective of conservation, for which there was no clear evidence.[199] It had not been demonstrated that the measure was applied to contribute to this policy.[200] The Panel found that the absence of domestic restrictions until 2018 reinforced the hypothesis that did not principally pursue a conservation objective.[201]

Article XX(g)'s second prong requires that measures are taken "in conjunction with restrictions on domestic production or consumption". The Panel noted that this embodies the notion of even-handedness and requires real restrictions to be imposed domestically.[202] The Panel found that the limit of 25 million cubic metres was not an effective domestic consumption cap and so the trees were not protected.[203] The Panel therefore found that the 2015 export ban did not meet the requirements of Article XX(g).

The above analyses under the EU-Ukraine Association Agreement are very similar to those conducted at the WTO. To what extent would this be replicated in an investment dispute taken as a result of an export ban where the IIA directly incorporated WTO provisions? In relation to the 2005 ban, the Panel asked four

---

were restrictions on the domestic market, preventing the commercial exploitation of these species (para 366). The Panel found it to be irrelevant whether the "same conditions prevail" as there was no discrimination (para 367). The Panel noted however that there was no evidence suggesting different conditions between the forests or their markets (para 368). A fourth requirement was that the measure must not constitute a "disguised restriction on international trade". The Panel noted that the text is public and found that the considerations on whether the ban was arbitrary were relevant to this and that the measure did not restrict trade under a false environmental pretence (para 372).

[198] Final Report, *Restrictions applied by Ukraine on exports of certain wood products to the European Union*, 11 December 2020, para 424. GATT Article XX(g) requires that a measure "relates" to the "conservation" of an exhaustible natural resource. The Panel began by emphasising the different subject matter of the two bans, with the 2015 ban concerning pine trees and other commercially exploited trees (para 393).

[199] Final Report, *Restrictions applied by Ukraine on exports of certain wood products to the European Union*, 11 December 2020, para 430.

[200] Final Report, *Restrictions applied by Ukraine on exports of certain wood products to the European Union*, 11 December 2020, para 434.

[201] Final Report, *Restrictions applied by Ukraine on exports of certain wood products to the European Union*, 11 December 2020, para 435. The Panel was not convinced that the ban met the test of Article XX(g)'s first prong but postponed its final finding until it had examined the second prong. Final Report, *Restrictions applied by Ukraine on exports of certain wood products to the European Union*, 11 December 2020, para 439.

[202] Final Report, *Restrictions applied by Ukraine on exports of certain wood products to the European Union*, 11 December 2020, para 455. Priority is given to the design and structure of domestic restrictions, while market effects may also be considered.

[203] Final Report, *Restrictions applied by Ukraine on exports of certain wood products to the European Union*, 11 December 2020, para 461, 463.

interpretative questions before finding the ban to be compliant with GATT Article XX(b). These questions of whether there is a genuine risk to plant life or health (or whatever concern is cited), whether the measure is designed to address this concern, whether the measure is necessary, and whether it is applied in a way unjustifiable discrimination, would likely be replicated in an investment dispute taken under an IIA directly incorporating WTO provisions. However, some of the questions asked by the tribunal when interpreting the chapeau are an uneasy fit in the investment context. GATT Article XX refers to countries "where the same conditions prevail", and measures which are a "disguised restriction on international trade", language ill-adapted to the investment context.[204] Nonetheless, there may be some instances where investment tribunals can consider this latter question.[205] Generally speaking, the language should be adapted to the investment context or the words *mutatis mutandis* should be included. Recent IIAs tend to adapt their language to make them specific to the investment context.[206]

It remains an open question whether and to what the extent investment tribunals would follow a sequence of analysis similar to WTO tribunals and the Panel in *Ukraine-Wood Products*. However certain caveats can be observed for tribunals comparing shared norms between the regimes. If an investment tribunal were to follow a sequence of analysis similar to WTO tribunal, in respect of any of the above questions, they should state their reasons and be mindful of certain differences between the regimes, including textual differences, contextual differences, the differing purposes of agreements, and systemic differences between the regimes.

In relation to textual differences, exceptions provisions may be close to identical, but may require completely different tests because they include different nexus requirements.[207] For exceptions provisions that incorporate WTO law, tribunals must take into account how the treaty drafters have deviated from the text the provision is based on (if they do so). For example, Article 22.1.3 of the Canada-Korea FTA (2014) incorporates General Exceptions that are implicitly based on GATT Article XX. A key difference in this provision compared to the wording of Article XX is that the nexus requirement is contained in the Article's chapeau.[208] This Article is clearly inspired by the language of GATT Article XX. While the word

---

[204] Where the language is not adapted, the words *mutatis mutandis* should be included. This raises questions for general exceptions provisions that directly incorporate GATT Article XX, such as CETA Article 28.3.1, without the words *mutatis mutandis*.

[205] E.g. The question of whether a measure constituted a "disguised restriction on trade" was considered in the Separate Opinion of Dr. Bryan Schwartz (on the Partial Award) in *SD Myers v. Canada*. Dr. Schwartz found that the export ban did in fact amount to "arbitrary or unjustifiable discrimination" and to a "disguised restriction on trade" (para 174).

[206] CETA Article 28.3.2 adapts the language of its chapeau to reflect the investment context when incorporating exceptions akin to GATS Article XIV. Another example of this is Article 29 'General Exceptions' of the Myanmar-Singapore BIT (2019).

[207] For discussion of nexus requirements, and the appropriate standard of review for legitimate regulatory purposes, see Sect. 3.2.4.2(b).

[208] Article 22.1.3 of the Canada-Korea FTA (2014):

of Article 3(c) is similar to GATT Article XX(g), the fact that the nexus requirement is "necessary" rather than "relating to" impacts the ability of a tribunal to draw upon the jurisprudence developed under Article XX(g).

Tribunals must also be wary of contextual differences when drawing on the jurisprudence of the other regime. Tests at the WTO in relation to treaty exceptions were developed in relation to the specific context of the WTO Agreements. Any attempt to draw upon the treaty exceptions contained in GATT Article XX or GATS Article XIV must be done with these contextual differences in mind. The EU-Singapore IPA contains a list of specific exceptions that are modelled on GATT Article XX and contained within the national treatment provision in the investment chapter. These are modelled on WTO law, although the language in the chapeau is adapted and refers to 'covered investments.'[209] This contextual difference of having exceptions contained within the article itself could affect its interpretation, including but not limited to, the burden of proof. One way of minimising potential contextual issues is to incorporate the WTO Agreements directly into the agreement *mutatis mutandis*. This gives some latitude to tribunals where certain concepts from the GATT need to be adapted to the investment context.[210]

While the examples above consider provisions directly incorporating WTO provisions, tribunals should be particularly mindful of these textual and contextual differences for IIA exceptions that are thinly connected with provisions in the trade regime. These include treaty exceptions in BITs with similar features to the WTO Agreements such as a necessity test. The tribunal in *Continental* drew upon WTO jurisprudence when interpreting Article XI of the US-Argentina BIT as this article was derived from the FCN treaties which reflect the formulation of GATT Article XX.[211] This common derivation of the texts makes up part of the 'context' of Article XI, although typically in this section context refers to the structure of agreements.

For the purposes of Chapter Eight (Investment), subject to the requirement that those measures are not applied in a manner that would constitute arbitrary or unjustifiable discrimination between investments or between investors, or a disguised restriction on international trade or investment, this Agreement is not to be construed to prevent a Party from adopting or enforcing measures necessary: (a) to protect human, animal or plant life or health; (b) to ensure compliance with laws and regulations that are not inconsistent with this Agreement; or (c) for the conservation of living or non-living exhaustible natural resources.

[209] See EU-Singapore trade and investment agreements (authentic texts as of April 2018), Brussels, 18 April 2018. Available at: http://trade.ec.europa.eu/doclib/press/index.cfm?id=961 (last accessed 1 May 2021).

[210] E.g. Article 16.1 Vietnam-Korea FTA: "2. For the purposes of Chapters 8 (Trade in Services) and 9 (Investment), Article XIV of GATS (including its footnotes) is incorporated into and made part of this Agreement, *mutatis mutandis*."

[211] The tribunal was guided by principles drawn from the GATT in analysing Article XI of the BIT. This is because Article XI was derived from provisions which reflect the formulation of the GATT, such as those found in FCN treaties like the US-Nicaragua FCN treaty (1956).

Even where provisions are phrased identically, as has been the case where PTIA provisions directly incorporate GATT Article XX or XXI, converging outcomes should not be presumed. Alvarez reminds us that this is because the structure of dispute settlement matters.[212] The fact that GATT Article XXI jurisprudence relates to an inter-state system of dispute resolution would be a key factor for tribunals considering how similarly worded provisions under IIAs should be interpreted in a distinct manner.

In *Russia-Transit*, the Panel relied upon the negotiating history of GATT Article XXI to confirm that compliance with the subparagraphs of Article XXI be made objectively, rather than in a self-judging way.[213] When interpreting non-precluded measures clauses under IIAs, Alvarez notes that examinations of the history of trade law negotiations are "not likely to produce harmonious interpretations" between the regimes.[214] While the preparatory work of the treaty is a supplementary means of interpretation, different negotiating histories of IIAs may lead to different outcomes.

Tribunals must consider the different purposes of agreements when interpreting treaty exceptions. Necessity analysis is a feature of the majority of exceptions provisions featured in this study and for Alvarez, this should be carried out in light of the object and purpose of the treaty in question.[215] It seems correct that the more similar the purposes of agreements, the easier it would be for tribunals to make reference to the other agreement and how its provisions have been interpreted. The preambles of some BITs in particular reflect the narrow purposes of "intensifying economic cooperation" and "creating favourable conditions for investment" without acknowledging the right to regulate. Such agreements are clearly emphasising the economic purpose of these agreements, without calling into question the state's inherent right to regulate. Even in relation to such agreements, tribunals should not be precluded from drawing on the experience of other investment agreements where

---

[212] See Alvarez (2020), p. 311. In *Russia-Transit*, the WTO Panel did not consider whether a state that invokes an emergency caused it and "faithfulness to precedent" in the investment regime would make this approach unlikely (ibid page 311). This interpretation is based upon Article 25 ARSIWA, under which necessity may not be invoked where "the State has contributed to the situation of necessity". However, other tribunals have not taken this approach to necessity and the CMS Annulment Committee found that this approach of conflating Article 25 ARSIWA and Article XI of the US-Argentina BIT was a manifest error of law. *CMS v. Argentina*, Decision of the Ad Hoc Committee on the Application for Annulment of the Argentine Republic Annulment Committee, 25 September 2007, para 130.

[213] Panel Report, *Russia-Traffic in Transit*, WT/DS512/R, adopted on 26 April 2019, para 7.100.

[214] See Alvarez (2020), p. 308.

[215] Alvarez and Brink (2012), pp. 347–348. Alvarez gives a very narrow reading of the purpose of the US-Argentina BIT as being to "discipline the behaviour of States during periods of alleged economic crisis". Alvarez further states that the purpose of the GATT, as reflected in its preamble and in the chapeau of Article XX, is sufficiently different to that of the US-Argentina BIT to prevent any cross-regime borrowing. The purpose of the BIT in question as per its preamble is to encourage economic cooperation and protection of investment, which is closer to that of the trade regime than in Alvarez's characterisation.

Table 4.1 Categories and values of engagement for treaty exceptions

	Explicit	Implicit	Thin	Performance requirements	Total
Weighting	**1**	**1**	**0.66**	**0.25**	
PTIAs	25	26	–	8 (2)	53
BITs	–	24	4 (2.66)	–	26.66

the object and purpose of the treaty is expressed in a more balanced manner.[216] Likewise, where such treaties contain provisions with analogues in the trade regime, and these provisions require the answering of similar questions, a narrow preamble should not preclude drawing upon the experience of the other regime.

There are also structural differences between the WTO Agreements and IIAs. Tribunals must be cautious when drawing lessons from a regime in which exit is constrained (at the WTO) for the benefit of a regime in which exit is significantly easier. This is particularly the case where the investment regime traditionally has limited grounds for appeal and where disputes frequently result in significant monetary damages.

4.3.3   The Role of PTIAs

This section considers whether treaty exceptions in PTIAs result in increased levels of engagement between the trade and investment law regimes compared to those in BITs.[217] In terms of parallels in content, treaty exceptions featured in 59/60 PTIAs and in 28/60 BITs (47%) contained in this study. For the sample, there were significantly more parallels between the content of the investment chapters of PTIAs and the trade regime than there were between BITs and the trade regime. Not only were treaty exceptions more prevalent in PTIAs, but the references to them tended to be significantly stronger than those found in the BITs in this study.

Treaty exceptions were found more than twice as often for the sample of PTIAs, but the weighted score for provisions across the 120 Agreements was significantly higher too. Chapter 2 attributed weights to the four types of treaty exceptions found in the IIAs in this study. These provisions were given a score from 0 to 1 based on the strength of these references and the findings are contained in Table 4.1.

---

[216] See *Philip Morris Brands Sàrl, Philip Morris Products S.A. and Abal Hermanos S.A. v. Oriental Republic of Uruguay*, Award, 8 July 2016, ICSID Case No. ARB/10/7, para 300–301, where the tribunal referred to recent trade and investment treaties such as CETA and EU-Singapore FTA.

[217] Engagement was defined in Chap. 1: Engagement between trade and investment occurs wherever the content of an investment agreement has a parallel in the trade regime or vice versa. The term 'content' can cover an agreement's preamble, definitions, substantive provisions, exceptions etc. Engagement also occurs in dispute settlement whenever there are cross-regime references by the parties or the tribunal or parallels in the practices or features of dispute settlement. Engagement does not imply convergence and may fall short of this in a given area between the two regimes.

By this weighted measure also, the conclusion of PTIAs has resulted in treaty exceptions connected to WTO law being included at approximately twice the rate of their inclusion in BITs.

The second measure for increased engagement concerns cross-regime references and whether they are more likely to occur because of treaty exceptions in PTIAs compared to BITs. Treaty exceptions were shown to be considerably more common and stronger in PTIAs than in BITs for the treaties in this study. This is the main reason cross-regime references are more likely to occur under these PTIAs than under the BITs.

However, there are additional considerations for tribunals when comparing legal norms between the systems that may impact upon the frequency of cross-regime references. Tribunals must be attentive to the wordings of treaty exceptions in PTIAs and BITs. Minor textual differences may impact upon the interpretation of agreements based on the wording of the provision at hand. One observation that can be made about Table 4.1 is the seeming preference for the implicit incorporation of WTO exceptions provisions in BITs.

In the Japan-Jordan BIT (2018), the parties implicitly incorporate WTO exceptions, but a tribunal would have to be attentive to the subtle differences in the languages of the subparagraphs and the chapeau.[218] Such differences in the wordings of provisions are more common in provisions that implicitly incorporate WTO exceptions provisions than in those that incorporate them by reference *mutatis mutandis*. These differences in the wordings may reduce the likelihood of a tribunal making cross-regime references.

Tribunals must consider the contextual differences relating to treaty exceptions in PTIAs and BITs. The EU-Singapore IPA contains a list of specific exceptions that are modelled on GATT Article XX and contained within the national treatment provision in the investment chapter.[219] This contextual difference of having exceptions contained within the article itself could affect its interpretation, including but not limited to, the burden of proof. This provision was negotiated as part of a PTIA but there does not appear to be an emerging trend of including exceptions within the substantive provisions in PTIAs. One way of minimising potential contextual issues is to incorporate the WTO Agreements directly into the agreement *mutatis mutandis*. This gives some latitude to tribunals where certain concepts from the GATT need to

---

[218] Japan-Jordan BIT (2018), Article 15 General and Security Exceptions, "1. Subject to the requirement that such measures are not applied by a Contracting Party in a manner which would constitute a means of arbitrary or unjustifiable discrimination against, or a disguised restriction on investors of the other Contracting Party and their investments in the Area of the former Contracting Party, nothing in this Agreement shall be construed so as to prevent the former Contracting Party from adopting or enforcing measures: (a) necessary to protect human, animal or plant life or health;. . . .".

[219] See EU-Singapore trade and investment agreements (authentic texts as of April 2018), Brussels, 18 April 2018. Available at: http://trade.ec.europa.eu/doclib/press/index.cfm?id=961 (last accessed 1 May 2021). These exceptions are modelled on WTO law, although the language in the chapeau is adapted and refers to 'covered investments.'

be adapted to the investment context.[220] Such explicit incorporation appears to be more characteristic of PTIAs than BITs, as per Table 4.1 and this encourages cross-regime references. Tribunals should be particularly mindful of textual and contextual differences for IIA exceptions that are thinly connected with provisions in the trade regime. These include treaty exceptions in BITs with similar features to the WTO Agreements such as a necessity test.

Tribunals must also consider the different purposes of the agreements when interpreting treaty exceptions under PTIAs and BITs. A treaty is to be interpreted in light of "its object and purpose" which is to be found in the treaty's preamble.

PTIA preambles tend to refer to a broader treaty purpose, including references to 'building on' the WTO Agreements and strong references to the right to regulate. How does this impact upon the interpretation of exceptions provisions? Stronger references in these areas facilitate crossfertilisation. In the absence of any such provisions in the preamble, tribunals have to be careful, particularly in relation to older style BITs, that they strike an appropriate balance in their interpretations between the protection of investment and that the host state's right to regulate.

Tribunals could take their general omission from BITs as evidence they are included in PTIAs because of their trade chapters. However, a fundamental rule of preambles is that they have a single object and purpose and that this applies to the entirety of an agreement. As such, where such references are included, regard must be had to the fact that the parties are "building on" or "reaffirming"[221] their rights and obligations under the WTO Agreement. This applies to the entirety of the agreement including the investment chapter and this alters the purpose of the agreement in a way that encourages cross-regime references.

Finally, tribunals must consider systemic differences and differences in the remedy structures between the two regimes when interpreting treaty exceptions under PTIAs and BITs.[222] These differences mean that there are potentially severe consequences if a tribunal interprets treaty exceptions in an overly broad or narrow manner, particularly if it gives rise to monetary damages. Findings of breach under IIAs are not confined to the removal of measures or the authorisation of counter-measures, as is the case in the trade law regime. A key systemic difference between the regimes is the lack of the possibility of appeal in the investment regime except for a very limited number of grounds in all but the most recent IIAs such as CETA. Tribunals have to be mindful of these factors in their awards and in striking a balance that is appropriate for the investment regime, rather than following a test developed in line with a different set of considerations in the trade regime.

---

[220] See New EU-Mexico agreement: The Agreement in Principle and its texts, Brussels, 26 April 2018. Available at: http://trade.ec.europa.eu/doclib/press/index.cfm?id=1833 (last accessed 11 March 2021).

[221] Japan-Malaysia EPA (2005) (Agreement Between The Government Of Japan And The Government Of Malaysia For An Economic Partnership).

[222] Section 1.5.4 discusses factors tribunals should consider when making cross-regime references, including (c) systemic differences.

There are structural differences between the WTO Agreements and IIAs. IIAs frequently provide for the possibility of the parties exiting, renegotiating or issue binding interpretations of the agreement. Alvarez seems to suggest that the reaction of the parties may well be to exit the treaty but parties may also have recourse to the treaty's joint interpretation facility or to amend the treaty, depending on the treaty text. A further consideration in this area in relation to PTIAs, is the reluctance some parties may have to exit a treaty, where the overall package is beneficial to them, but they would terminate the investment agreement if it were a standalone agreement.

Annex: The Success Rate of General Exceptions Defences at the WTO

Cases where Article XX invoked by defendant	Article XX defence rejected by Appellate Body
US – Gasoline (1996)	X
Canada – Periodicals (1997)	X
US – Shrimp (1998)	X
Korea – Beef (2000)	X
EC – Asbestos (2001)	
US – Shrimp (Article 21.5 – Malaysia) (2001)	
EC – Tariff Preferences (2004)	X
Canada – Wheat Exports (2004)	X
Dominican Republic – Cigarettes (2005)	X
US – Gambling (2005)	X
Mexico – Soft Drinks (2006)	X
Brazil – Tyres (2007)	X
US – Custom Bond (2008)	X
US – Shrimp (Thailand) (2008)	X
China – Auto Parts (2008)	X
China – Audiovisual Services (2009)	X
Thailand – Cigarettes (2011)	X
China – Raw Materials (2011)	X
EC – Seals (2014)	X
China – Rare Earths (2014)	X

The twenty disputes considered here constitute a relatively small sample. If Panel reports which are not appealed to the Appellate Body are included, a similar trend of non-compliance can be observed. In *Tuna– Dolphin* (1991) the Article XX exception was of course rejected by the panel. The dispute in *Tuna– Dolphin II* (2012) was taken under the Technical Barriers to Trade Agreement.

References

Alvarez J (2014) Beware: boundary crossings. Public law & legal theory research paper series. New York University

Alvarez J (2020) Epilogue: 'convergence' is a many-splendored thing. In: Behn, Gáspár-Szilágyi, Langford (eds) Adjudicating trade and investment law: convergence or divergence? Cambridge University Press, p 311

Alvarez JE, Brink T (2012) Revisiting the necessity defense: Continental Casualty v. Argentina. In: Yearbook on international investment law & policy. Oxford University Press, pp 319–362

Alvarez J, Khamsi K (2008) The Argentina crisis and foreign investors: a glimpse into the heart of the international investment regime. Institute for International Law and Justice, Working Paper 2008/5, p 54

Asmelash HB (2013) WTO Case Law In 2012. It YIL 22:299–347

Bartels L (2014) The Chapeau of Article XX GATT: a new interpretation, paper no. 40/2014. University of Cambridge Faculty of Law Legal Studies Research Paper Series 7

Bartels L, Paddeu F (2020) Introduction. In: Bartels L, Paddeu F (eds) Exceptions in international law. Oxford University Press, p 2

Bhagwati J (2001) After Seattle: free trade and the WTO. In: Porter R, Sauvé P, Subramanian A, Beviglia Zampetti A (eds) Efficiency, equity, and legitimacy: the multilateral trading system at the millennium. Brookings Institution Press, Washington, DC

Catti de Gasperi G (2015) Case note and comment on European Communities – measures prohibiting the importation and marketing of seal products. WTO case law in 2014, It. YIL 24:395–430

Crawford J (2002) The international law commissions articles on state responsibility: introduction, text and commentaries. Cambridge University Press

Davies A (2009) Interpreting the Chapeau of GATT Article XX in light of the 'New' approach in Brazil–tyres. JWT 43:507–539

Henckels C (2018) Should investment treaties contain public policy exceptions? Boston Coll Law Rev 59(8):2825–2844

Henckels C (2020) Scope limitation of affirmative defence? The purpose and role of investment treaty exception clauses. In: Bartels L, Paddeu F (eds) Exceptions in international law. Oxford University Press, p 374

Kurtz J (2009) The use and abuse of WTO law in investor–state arbitration: competition and its discontents. Eur J Int Law 20(3):771

Kurtz J (2010) Adjudging the exceptional at international law: security, public order and financial crisis. Int Comp Law Q 59:35

Kurtz J (2014) Balancing investor protection and regulatory freedom in international investment law: the necessary, complex and vital search for state purpose. In: Bjorklund A (ed) Yearbook on international investment law & policy 2013-14. Oxford University Press, p 302

Kurtz J (2016) The WTO and international investment law: converging systems. Cambridge University Press, p 83

Mitchell AD, Henckels C (2013) Variations on a theme: comparing the concept of "necessity" in international investment law and WTO law. Chic J Int Law 14(1):137

Mitchell AD, Heaton D, Henckels C (2016) Non-discrimination and the role of regulatory purpose in international trade. Edward Elger Publishing, p 17

Mitchell AD, Munro J, Voon T (2018) Importing WTO general exceptions into international investment agreements: proportionality, myths and risks. In: Yearbook on international investment law & policy 2016–2017. Oxford University Press, p 1

Moran N (2017) The first twenty cases under GATT Article XX: Tuna or Shrimp Dear? In: Adinolfi G, Baetens F, Caiado J, Lupone A, Micara A (eds) International economic law-contemporary issues. Springer, Cham, pp 3–21

Sacerdoti G (2013) BIT protections and economic crises: limits to their coverage, the impact of multilateral financial regulation and the defence of necessity. ICSID Rev 32

Schill SW, Djanic V (2016) International investment law and community interests. Society of International Economic Law (SIEL), Fifth Biennial Global Conference, Online Proceedings, Working Paper No 2016/01, p 18

Stone Sweet A (2008) Proportionality balancing and global constitutionalism. Columbia J Transnatl Law 47:76

Stone Sweet A, della Canacea G (2014) Proportionality, general principles of law, and investor-state arbitration: a response to Jose Alvarez. NYU J Int Law Polit 46(3)

Titi A (2014) The right to regulate in international investment law. Hart Publishing, p 119

Vidigal G (2017) Why is there so little litigation under free trade agreements? Retaliation and adjudication in international dispute settlement. J Int Econ Law 20(4):927–950

Viñuales JE (2020) Seven ways of escaping a rule: of exceptions and their avatars in international law. In: Bartels L, Paddeu F (eds) Exceptions in international law. Oxford University Press, p 73

Wagner M (2014) Regulatory space in international trade law and international investment law. Univ Pa J Int Law 36(1):73

Chapter 5
Preambles and the Right to Regulate

5.1 Introduction

Preambles have an important role in either facilitating or excluding inter-regime
engagement. They set out the object and purpose of a treaty, one of the primary
considerations in treaty interpretation. Article 31(1) of the Vienna Convention on the
Law of Treaties (VCLT) tells us that a treaty is to be interpreted in terms of its
ordinary meaning in light of its object and purpose.[1] VCLT Article 31(2) tells us that
preambles make up part of the context for the purposes of treaty interpretation.[2]
Examples of these objects and purposes within the investment law context include
affirming the government's right to regulate, referring to the promotion of investment, sustainable development, building upon WTO commitments, and committing
not to relax standards.

Preambles regularly guide tribunals in interpreting treaty obligations under International Investment Agreements (IIAs) and the WTO Agreements.[3] However, there
is a general understanding that preambles do not create independent legal rights or
obligations in international investment agreements.[4] As preambles usually do not

---

[1] Vienna Convention on the Law of Treaties, General rule of interpretation, Article 31.1: "A treaty
shall be interpreted in good faith in accordance with the ordinary meaning to be given to the terms of
the treaty in their context and in the light of its object and purpose."

[2] Vienna Convention on the Law of Treaties, General rule of interpretation, Article 31.2: "The
context for the purpose of the interpretation of a treaty shall comprise, in addition to the text,
including its preamble and annexes (. . .)".

[3] For an account of this in investment law, see Newcombe and Paradell (2009), pp. 113–117.

[4] Preambles generally do not provide legally enforceable rights in and of themselves. See, for
example, Titi (2014), p. 115. See also Newcombe and Paradell (2009), p. 124.

  The tribunal in *Bayindir* described it as "doubtful" that, "in the absence of a specific provision in
the BIT itself, the sole text of the preamble constitutes a sufficient basis for a self-standing fair and
equitable treatment obligation under the BIT." *Bayindir Insaat Turizm Ticaret Ve Sanayi A.S. v.*

© The Author(s), under exclusive license to Springer Nature Switzerland AG 2021   203
N. Moran, *Engagement Between Trade and Investment*, EYIEL Monographs -
Studies in European and International Economic Law 18,
https://doi.org/10.1007/978-3-030-83259-9_5

provide legally enforceable rights in and of themselves, states should exercise caution in including rights they wish to be legally enforceable exclusively within the preamble.[5] If the parties wish to create a legally enforceable right, they can supplement a reference to a particular right in the preamble with a separate article covering the same right within the main body of the treaty text.[6] An example of this practice would be Agreements that refer to the right to regulate in the preamble as well as in a separate article elsewhere in the Agreement.[7]

PTIAs often contain many chapters and thus a wider range of areas than BITs. This is reflected in their preambles, which tend to be longer and broader than those found in BITs. This could affect how a tribunal interprets the object and purpose of the agreement. For example, references to the obligations of the parties under the WTO Agreements may facilitate inter-regime engagement and these are far more frequent in PTIAs than in BITs.[8]

Pakistan, Award ICSID Case No. ARB/03/29 (2009) para 230. The relevant section of the Turkey-Pakistan BIT's preamble reads as follows: "The Islamic Republic of Pakistan acting through its President and the Republic of Turkey (...) Agreeing that fair and equitable treatment of investment is desirable in order to maintain a stable framework for investment and maximum effective utilization of economic resources".

It has similarly been confirmed by a GATT Panel that objectives contained in the preamble generally do not generate substantive legal commitments. See *US- Norwegian Salmon: United States- Imposition of Anti-Dumping Duties on Imports of Fresh and Chilled Atlantic Salmon from Norway*, Panel Report, 30 November 1992, ADP/87 (adopted by the Committee on Anti-Dumping Practices on 27 April 1994) para 369.

[5]Nonetheless, treaty makers are sovereign and in some exceptional instances a preamble can have legally binding clauses. See Orgad, Liav on the French *Conseil Constitutionnel* recognising the preamble of the French constitution's binding force in: (2010), p. 727. The legal status of such clauses "depends on various criteria" among which is the content of the preamble". Orgad further states: "Preambles are more likely to grant substantive rights when they establish "concrete norms rather than abstract ideas...". (730).

[6]Article 12 of Norway Model BIT (2007) on the Right to Regulate contains such a provision: "Nothing in this Agreement shall be construed to prevent a Party from adopting, maintaining or enforcing any measure otherwise consistent with this Agreement that it considers appropriate to ensure that investment activity is undertaken in a manner sensitive to health, safety or environmental concerns."

[7]Titi (2014).

Van Damme (2009). See Titi for discussion of the mixed results of this practice. Titi concludes that the inclusion of these provisions in their current formulations may have the reverse effect of narrowing host state policy space if due care is not taken. Titi notes that such provisions "fall short of their ambition to introduce this right" (page 115). Provisions such as Article 12 of Norway Model BIT (2007) include the wording that nothing shall prevent a party from adopting any measure "Otherwise consistent with" this agreement and that the result of this may be to "narrow policy space rather than the opposite." Investment treaties are neutral objects. Their contents reflect the choices of their drafters. While traditionally it may have been the case that investment treaties have overly focused on protecting the rights of investors, it can equally be the case that their design may be overly focused on protecting host states' right to regulate in any circumstance it deems appropriate. See Titi (2014), p. 112.

[8]See Annex 1, which shows that such a reference appeared in 59/60 PTIAs, while only featuring in the Chile-Hong Kong BIT (2016).

The content of a preamble applies to the entirety of a treaty and this fundamental notion has implications for inter-regime engagement. The contents of PTIA preambles inform not only the trade chapters but also the investment chapter of the agreement. Elements of the preamble, which may be primarily designed to inform the object and purpose of the trade chapter, may also inform interpretations of the object and purpose of the investment chapter. In the case of a BIT, the content of the preamble is likely to be more specific to investment concerns than in a PTIA given the more restricted subject matter of BITs.

The Appellate Body in *EC—Chicken Cuts* stated that the starting point for ascertaining the object and purpose of a treaty is "the treaty itself, in its entirety".[9] This does not mean that individual provisions do not have an object and purpose but rather that when interpreting them they will be "informed by, and in consonance with, the object and purpose of the entire treaty of which it is but a component".[10]

Differences in the wording of preambles are ultimately indicators of the objectives of the parties in concluding a given treaty. Different treaty contexts require different preambles.[11] The careful selection of the wording of a preamble is key to striking a balance between the interests of the investor and the host state.

This chapter examines the role of preambles within the trade and investment law regimes. It considers the extent to which engagement[12] already exists between the two regimes, whether this should influence tribunals, and whether PTIAs have any kind of an impact on engagement.

5.2   A. Preambles in the Trade and Investment Law Regimes

This section looks at how preambles are structured in the WTO Agreements and across a series of investment agreements. BITs and PTIAs have a single preamble covering the entire treaty, whereas many of the WTO Agreements contain chapter specific preambles, individual provisions with wording that indicates their purpose, as well as the introductory preamble to the Marrakesh Agreement (the WTO

---

[9]Appellate Body Report, *European Communities — Customs Classification of Frozen Boneless Chicken Cuts*, WT/DS269/AB/R, adopted 27 September 2005, para 238.

[10]Appellate Body Report, *European Communities — Customs Classification of Frozen Boneless Chicken Cuts*, WT/DS269/AB/R, adopted 27 September 2005, para 238.

[11]The parties may be concluding a treaty that aims to offer certain guarantees to investors in a volatile, but potentially lucrative host state. The parties may alternatively be concluding a treaty with the simple aim of encouraging investment between the parties, guaranteeing certain minimum protections both parties can commit to upholding, with a series of exceptions for areas of crucial importance to the public good.

[12]Engagement between trade and investment law was described in Chap. 1.I as occurring wherever the content of one of the regimes has a parallel in the other or wherever there are cross-regime references in dispute settlement by the parties or the tribunal or parallels in the practices of tribunals.

Agreement) that applies not just to the Agreement itself, but to all of the WTO Agreements.

5.2.1 The WTO Agreements

The preamble to the Marrakesh Agreement sets out the objects and purposes of the WTO. These key objects include the "elimination of discriminatory treatment" as well as; "Recognizing that their relations in the field of trade and economic endeavour should be conducted with a view to *raising standards of living, ensuring full employment* and a large and steadily *growing volume of real income* and effective demand, and *expanding the production of and trade in goods and services*, while allowing for the optimal use of the world's resources in accordance with the objective of *sustainable development*" (emphasis added).

The WTO legal texts are the result of the Uruguay Round of negotiations and are made up of close to twenty individual Agreements. Some of these Agreements have their own preambles that contain more specific language in terms of the aims of that particular agreement.

One example of a WTO Agreement that does not contain its own preamble is the Agreement on Subsidies and Countervailing Measures. This is the only Agreement in Annex 1 to the Marrakesh Agreement without its own preamble. This was noted by the Panel in *Canada- Aircraft* which deemed it "unwise to attach undue importance" to arguments concerning the object and purpose of the Agreement as a result.[13] This did not stop the panel from going on to give what it considers to be an appropriate summary of the object and purpose of the Agreement.[14] A preamble features in each of the 120 PTIAs or BITs analysed in Chap. 2. None of the PTIAs analysed contained chapter specific preambles for investment.

The inclusion of the general preamble to the Marrakesh Agreement and chapter specific preambles raises the question of how tribunals should interpret the object and purpose of an Agreement where both are present. Tribunals may be guided by both of these preambles in their interpretation of a provision. Indeed, some provisions within agreements, notably GATT Article III:1, also have sections that indicate the purpose of a specific provision. Where such guidance is provided,

---

[13]Panel Report, *Canada — Measures Affecting the Export of Civilian Aircraft*, WT/DS70/R, adopted on 20 August 1999, para 9.119.

[14]Panel Report, *Canada — Measures Affecting the Export of Civilian Aircraft*, WT/DS70/R, adopted on 20 August 1999, para 9.119: "[W]e consider that the object and purpose of the SCM Agreement could more appropriately be summarised as the establishment of multilateral disciplines "on the premise that some forms of government intervention distort international trade, [or] have the potential to distort [international trade]".

tribunals must also take this into account when interpreting the object and purpose of the provision.[15]

Both trade and investment law cover the provision of services and this gives rise to a significant overlap in terms of treaty coverage. The preamble to the GATS is closer to that of many IIAs than the WTO Agreement's preamble as it explicitly recognises "the right of Members to regulate, and to introduce new regulations on, the supply of services within their territories in order to meet national policy objectives." Interpretations of the preamble to the GATS could play an important role in terms of engagement between the two regimes. In *Argentina- Financial Services*, the Appellate Body recognised that national policy objectives "may cover a wide array of objectives"[16] and "is broader than the objectives listed in the exceptions."[17]

5.2.2   *Investment Law*

The general aim of IIAs is to promote and protect foreign investment in host states. The emphasis on promotion and protection differs among treaties, particularly in relation to whether or not pre or post-establishment rights are granted to investors. As this is a key object and purpose of investment treaties, it is noted that it has been contested that IIAs actually attract foreign investment.[18]

The landscape of investment agreements is characterised by heterogeneity and this characteristic holds true for the preambles of IIAs, the form of which varies significantly across treaties and the content of which has changed significantly over time. An additional element that adds to the diversity of the landscape of IIA preambles is the variations between the styles of preamble that appear in PTIAs compared to BITs. The next section compiles a brief survey of some of the most

---

[15] GATT Article III: 1 on 'National Treatment on Internal Taxation and Regulation' states: "The contracting parties recognize that internal taxes and other internal charges, and laws, regulations and requirements affecting the internal sale, offering for sale, purchase, transportation, distribution or use of products, and internal quantitative regulations requiring the mixture, processing or use of products in specified amounts or proportions, should not be applied to imported or domestic products so as to afford protection to domestic production".

[16] Appellate Body Report, *Argentina — Measures Relating to Trade in Goods and Services*, WT/DS453/AB/R, adopted 9 May 2016, para 6.114.

[17] Appellate Body Report, *Argentina — Measures Relating to Trade in Goods and Services*, WT/DS453/AB/R, adopted 9 May 2016, para 6.117.

[18] See e.g. Mary Hallward-Driemeier, 'Do Bilateral Investment Treaties attract foreign direct investment? Only a bit - and they could bite,' *World Bank Policy Research Working Paper WPS3121* (2003) 22, which finds "little evidence" that BITs have stimulated additional investment. In Chap. 1, it was noted that Bonnitcha et al cover 35 studies in their book and a majority find "a positive and statistically significant impact on inward FDI". They found that "studies examining signalling effects seem more likely to find that IIAs have a positive impact". Bonnitcha et al. (2017), p. 159.

prominent types of preambles of the old and new styles, drawing from PTIAs and BITs, and featuring some of the most important preambular elements in IIAs that have been significant in litigation or are likely to be in the future.

5.2.2.1 Older Style Agreements

An example of an old style preamble is that of the US- Ecuador BIT (1997),[19] which reads: "The Preamble states the goals of the Treaty. The Treaty is premised on the view that an open investment policy leads to economic growth. These goals include *economic cooperation*, increased flow of capital, *a stable framework for investment*, development of respect for internationally-recognized worker rights, and maximum efficiency in the use of economic resources. While the Preamble does not impose binding obligations, its statement of goals may serve to *assist in the interpretation of the Treaty*." (emphasis added).

Preambles such as this one are notable in that they focus exclusively on investment promotion and protection and don't attempt to balance this with recognition of the host state's right to regulate. Preambles that do not make any explicit reference to preserving the host state's right to regulate were common in BITs in the 1990s.[20]

This style of BIT preamble is markedly different to that of some of the older style PTIAs some of which featured more balanced preambles that included a reference to the right to regulate etc. The preamble to the NAFTA (1994) refers to the parties who have resolved to: "Preserve their flexibility to safeguard the public welfare; Promote sustainable development; (. . .) Build on their respective rights and obligations under the General Agreement on Tariffs and Trade and other multilateral and bilateral instruments of cooperation;".[21]

5.2.2.2 More Recent Agreements

Preambles in more modern IIAs often balance the protection of investment with some reference to the right to regulate of the host state. This contrast is now

---

[19] The Treaty Between The United States of America and the Republic of Ecuador concerning the encouragement and Reciprocal Protection of Investment, with Protocol and a related Exchange of Letters, signed at Washington on August 27, 1993.

[20] Other examples of such a preamble include the heavily litigated US-Argentina BIT (1994), as well as the UK-Azerbaijan BIT (1996). The main body of the preamble of the UK-Azerbaijan BIT states: "Desiring to create favourable conditions for greater investment by nationals and companies of one State in the territory of the other State; Recognising that the encouragement and reciprocal protection under international agreement of such investments will be conducive to the stimulation of individual business initiative and will increase prosperity in both States;".

[21] NAFTA entered into force on 1 January 1994, 1 year prior to the establishment of the WTO, which explains why the parties refer to the GATT rather than the WTO.

examined with reference to the preambles of four IIAs, which were all concluded in 2015.

The Australia-China FTA contains strong, seemingly binding language uphold-ing the right to regulate and "to preserve their flexibility to safeguard public welfare".[22]

The parties to the China- Korea FTA state that they are "mindful" of the role that environmental protection etc. can play in promoting sustainable development.

While some preambles state that the parties are "mindful of" the principle of sustainable development, others state that the parties: "Recognizing the need to promote investment based on the principles of sustainable development". It is a stronger statement to *recognise* a principle than it is to be *mindful of* it, and naturally the stronger the language is, the more likely the tribunal will be to uphold the host state's right to regulate. Whether these different nexus requirements affect interpre-tations of a host state's obligations depends on other factors such as the text of the substantive provision. The preamble to the Marrakesh Agreement recognises that relations should be conducted "in accordance with the objective of sustainable development" and this has helped ground defences of measures before the Appellate Body.[23]

The Canada- Burkina Faso BIT (i) recognises the role of protecting investors and investments in promoting sustainable development; and (ii) recognises the right to adopt measures consistent with the Agreement, but gives priority to the agreement.[24]

The Japan-Oman BIT recognises that "these objectives can be achieved without relaxing health, safety and environmental measures of general application". This recognition is not as far reaching as a commitment to uphold measures currently in place.[25]

---

[22] "Upholding the rights of their governments to regulate in order to meet national policy objectives, and to preserve their flexibility to safeguard public welfare;".

[23] Appellate Body Report, *United States - Import Prohibition Of Certain Shrimp And Shrimp Products*, WT/ DS58/AB/R, adopted 6 November 1998, at para 12: "An environmental purpose is fundamental to the application of Article XX, and such a purpose cannot be ignored, especially since the preamble to the *Marrakesh Agreement Establishing the World Trade Organization*33 (the "*WTO Agreement*") acknowledges that the rules of trade should be "in accordance with the objective of sustainable development", and should seek to "protect and preserve the environment"."

[24] "Recognizing that the promotion and the protection of investments of investors of one Party in the territory of the other Party help (. . .) promote sustainable development, RECOGNIZING the right of each Party to adopt or maintain any measures that are consistent with this Agreement and that relate to health, safety, the environment, or public welfare, as well as the difference in the Parties' respective economies;".

[25] The Kenya- Slovakia BIT (2011) and Switzerland- Trinidad & Tobago BIT (2010) contain a similar section to the Japan-Oman BIT, with the exact same wording except for the nexus requirements. The Kenya-Slovakia BIT states that the parties "Agreeing that these objectives can be achieved", while the Switzerland- Trinidad & Tobago BIT states that the parties are "convinced that" these measures can be achieved. Of the three, "Agreeing" that these objectives can be achieved as per the Kenya- Slovakia BIT represents the strongest and most binding wording and tribunals should have regard to the nuanced wordings of these nexus requirements.

5.2.3 Interpreting the Object and Purpose of Trade and Investment Agreements

5.2.3.1 Preambles at the WTO-Checks on the Textual and Holistic Approaches

Todd Weiler has characterised the hallmark of the WTO interpretative approach as a "preference for literalism, supported by the teleology of economic liberalism, along with some additional references to the preambular language of the WTO Agreements".[26] This section considers how preambles have been interpreted at the WTO and whether these 'additional references' embody more of a textual or a holistic approach to treaty interpretation.

The Appellate Body has described treaty interpretation as an integrated operation, where interpretative rules and principles must be understood and applied as "connected and mutually reinforcing components of a holistic exercise".[27]

One of the benefits of the holistic approach is that it allows greater flexibility than the textual approach. This flexibility allows tribunals to recognise the "hermeneutic value to each individual dimension" of Article 31(1) of the Vienna Convention and to "accommodate broader policy considerations" in their interpretations.[28]

Tribunals and various commentators have underlined the importance of the holistic nature of treaty interpretation at the WTO. This recognition of its importance can be traced to *US—Shrimp I*, where it was found that the object and purpose of the treaty may be looked to for guidance where there is ambiguity as to the meaning of a provision.[29] The Appellate Body then stated that preambular language reflects the intentions of the negotiators of the WTO Agreement, and "must add colour, texture and shading to our interpretation."[30]

Nonetheless, the Appellate Body has found that the starting point for determining this 'object and purpose' is the treaty itself *in its entirety* rather than the preamble.[31]

---

[26] Weiler (2003), p. 28.

[27] Appellate Body Report, *China – Measures Affecting Trading Rights and Distribution Services for Certain Publications and Audiovisual Entertainment Products*, WT/DS363/AB/R, adopted 19 January 2010, para 399. The Appellate Body then stated that it is the role of the treaty interpreter to elucidate the relevant meaning of terms by having "recourse to context and object and purpose" in finding their ordinary meaning.

[28] Federico Ortino (2006), p. 148.

[29] Appellate Body Report, *United States - Import Prohibition Of Certain Shrimp And Shrimp Products*, WT/ DS58/AB/R, adopted 6 November 1998, para. 114: "It is in the words constituting that provision, read in their context, that the object and purpose of the states parties to the treaty must first be sought. Where the meaning imparted by the text itself is equivocal or inconclusive, or where confirmation of the correctness of the reading of the text itself is desired, light from the object and purpose of the treaty as a whole may usefully be sought."

[30] Appellate Body Report, *United States - Import Prohibition Of Certain Shrimp And Shrimp Products*, WT/ DS58/AB/R, adopted 6 November 1998, para 153.

[31] Appellate Body Report, *European Communities — Customs Classification of Frozen Boneless Chicken Cuts*, WT/DS269/AB/R, adopted on 27 September 2005, para 47. The Appellate Body

In *US—Shrimp I*, the Appellate Body referred to the preamble to the WTO Agreement as evidencing the commitment of the signatories to environmental protection as it explicitly acknowledges "the objective of sustainable development". It was claimed in this case that the exhaustible natural resources protected by GATT Article XX(g) referred to "finite resources such as minerals rather than biological or renewable resources."[32] The Appellate Body found that while GATT Article XX was not modified in the Uruguay Round, the treaty must be interpreted in light of contemporary concerns as reflected in the preamble to the WTO Agreement "which informs not only the GATT 1994 but also the other covered agreements".[33]

The holistic approach to treaty interpretation at the WTO is not without checks. No interpretation of the object and purpose of the treaty can run contrary to the express terms of the text. This serves as a check on the holistic approach and mitigates the risk that holistic interpretation will give tribunals too much flexibility when interpreting the Agreements.[34]

The Appellate Body's finding that a treaty term cannot be interpreted in a way that runs contrary to the purpose of the WTO Agreements also serves as a check on the textual approach.[35] The Appellate Body's finding in *Japan—Taxes on Alcoholic Beverages II* serves as a further check on overly emphasising the importance of the preamble where it was found that the preamble is to be referred to in determining the meaning of the terms of the treaty "and not as an independent basis for interpretation".[36] Ortino describes the Appellate Body as "trying to emancipate itself" from a rigorous textualist approach and he emphasises that this approach must be qualified by VCLT Article 31(1).[37] The textual approach has contributed to the consistency and coherence of Appellate Body reports though it places less of an emphasis on the object and purpose of the treaty.

---

went on to say that it did not believe Article 31(3) of the VCLT "excludes taking into account the object and purpose of particular treaty terms, if doing so assists the interpreter in determining the treaty's object and purpose on the whole." See Federico Ortino (2006), p. 148.

[32] Panel Report, *US – Import Prohibition of Certain Shrimp and Shrimp Products*, WT/DS58/R, adopted on 6 November 1998, para. 3.237.

[33] Appellate Body Report, *US – Import Prohibition of Certain Shrimp and Shrimp Products*, WT/DS58/AB/R, adopted on 6 November 1998, para 129.

[34] See Federico Ortino (2006), p. 147, see also, as noted by Ortino, *US—Corrosion-Resistant Steel Sunset Review*, at paras 7.43–7.44, where the Panel noted that 'Article 31 of the Vienna Convention requires that the text of the treaty be read in light of the object and purpose of the treaty, not that object and purpose alone override the text.'

[35] Appellate Body Report, *European Communities — Customs Classification of Frozen Boneless Chicken Cuts*, WT/DS269/AB/R, adopted on 27 September 2005, para. 238: The object and purpose of a treaty provision is "informed by, and will be in consonance with, the object and purpose of the entire treaty of which it is but a component."

[36] See Appellate Body Report, *Japan—Taxes on Alcoholic Beverages II*, WT/DS10/AB/R, WT/DS11/AB/R, WT/DS8/AB/R, adopted on 1 November 1996, page 12, including FN20.

[37] See Federico Ortino (2006), p. 117. VCLT Article 31.1. A treaty shall be interpreted in good faith in accordance with the ordinary meaning to be given to the terms of the treaty in their context and in the light of its object and purpose.

Mitchell et al. have questioned whether the Appellate Body has sufficiently engaged with the object and purpose of the WTO Agreements when interpreting the concept of likeness.[38] This failure is described as the "fundamental difficulty" of the Appellate Body Reports from *Japan—Alcoholic Beverages II* through to *EC—Seals*.[39] The fundamental purposes of the WTO Agreement, as expressed in its preamble, "require recourse to differences between products" beyond those that affect competition.[40]

5.2.3.2 Interpreting IIA Preambles

The international investment regime has been described as being, at its heart, about the promotion and vindication of the rights of non-state actors via an expedited legal outlet.[41] However this is not its sole purpose; Van Aaken illustrates the broader goals of investment policy noting that the ICSID Convention was developed under the auspices of the World Bank whose primary aim is to foster sustainable development rather than the protection of private property.[42] The ultimate goal of the two regimes remains "the facilitation of economic efficiency through international economic activity".[43] Recent EU FTAs contain sustainable development chapters and a commitment to this principle in their preambles.[44] EU trade and investment strategy supports this push for sustainable development via high standards in the areas of labour, environment, climate protection and responsible sourcing.[45]

Tribunals must bear these purposes in mind when interpreting the object and purpose of IIAs and this role can be a delicate one. Older BITs in particular can be succinct documents with titles and preambles that refer solely to the aim of promoting and protecting investment without balancing this against the right to regulate. This can make it difficult for tribunals to discern what kind of balancing of rights the parties had in mind when concluding the treaty. Although the pendulum seems to be

---

[38] Mitchell (2016), p. 174 & 56.

[39] Mitchell (2016), p. 174 & 56–57. Mitchell et al state that: "The fundamental difficulty with these decisions was the failure to engage with the meaning of the treaty provision in light of its context and the treaty's object and purpose, and thereby to state a normative understanding of discrimination…Making the purpose of the enquiry explicit and relying on it in treaty interpretation strengthens the institutional legitimacy of [tribunals]." 174–175.

[40] Mitchell (2016), p. 57.

[41] Wu (2014). Wu makes the point that these are the fundamental purposes of the IIAs at 66 & 79. See also Chap. 1.II.3 on 'the Impact of PT(I)As, IIAs and investment chapters' on the purpose of IIAs.

[42] Anne van Aaken (2008), p. 8.

[43] Broude (2011), p. 5.

[44] E.g. the EU- Canada Comprehensive Economic and Trade Agreement (CETA) and the EU-Singapore FTA.

[45] DG Trade, Strategic Plan 2020-24, 9. Available at: https://trade.ec.europa.eu/doclib/docs/2020/november/tradoc_159104.pdf (last accessed 15 February 2021).

swinging back to recognition of the right to regulate in recent cases, the style of preamble found in older BITs led to favourable outcomes for investors in cases such as *Siemens AG v. Argentina*,[46] *SGS v. Philippines*,[47] and *Enron v. Argentina*.[48]

In *Siemens AG v. Argentina,* the preamble recognised the desire to promote "greater economic cooperation" and the titles recognise the reciprocal encouragement and protection of investment.[49] The tribunal stated that it would not interpret the Treaty restrictively or broadly but would adhere to the rules of the VCLT and "be guided by the purpose of the Treaty as expressed in its title and preamble."[50] It found that creating favourable conditions for investments was the clear intention of the parties.[51]

In their interpretations, tribunals should give some recognition of the state's inherent right to regulate. Where a preamble aims to promote investment and this is found to indicate "the intention of the parties to adhere to conduct in accordance with such purposes", there is a risk of overly broad interpretations of the substantive provisions of IIAs.[52] This could lead to breaches from a wide range of measures and findings unanticipated by the parties when concluding the treaty. This purposive

---

[46] *Siemens A.G. v. The Argentine Republic*, Award, ICSID Case No. ARB/02/8, 17 January 2007.

Técnicas Medioambientales Tecmed, S.A. v. The United Mexican States, Award ICSID Case No. ARB (AF)/00/2, 29 May 2003.

[47] *SGS (Société Générale de Surveillance) S.A. v. Republic of the Philippines*, Decision of the Tribunal on Objections to Jurisdiction ICSID Case No. ARB/02/6, 29 January 2004.

[48] *Enron Corporation and Ponderosa Assets, L.P. v. Argentine Republic*, Award ICSID Case No. ARB/01/3 22 May 2007. Article XI of the US-Argentina BIT has been interpreted as an exception to the host state's obligations under the treaty. The tribunal in *Enron* interpreted the Article XI exception to the US-Argentina BIT narrowly based on the object and purpose of the treaty, in relation to its application in situations of economic difficulty. The tribunals stated that: "[A]ny interpretation, resulting in an escape route from the obligations defined cannot be easily reconciled with that object and purpose. Accordingly, a restrictive interpretation of any such alternative is mandatory" (para 331).

[49] The tribunal in *Siemens* found that breach of FET necessitated bad faith would be "inconsistent with such commitments and purpose and the expectations created by such a document". Such a finding had been made by the tribunal in *Alex Genin, Eastern Credit Limited, Inc. and A.S. Baltoil v. The Republic of Estonia, ICSID Case No. ARB/99/2. Siemens* was taken under the Treaty Between The Federal Republic Of Germany and the Argentine Republic on the Encouragement and Reciprocal Protection Of Investments (1994). The wording of the full title and preamble of the Argentina- Germany BIT (1994) is similar to the Argentina- US BIT (1994), under which the *Enron* case was taken.

[50] *Siemens v. Argentina*, Decision on Jurisdiction, 3 August 2004, paragraphs 80 & 81.

[51] *Siemens v. Argentina*, Decision on Jurisdiction, 3 August 2004, para 81. In a further reading into the objective of the parties in the Award, the tribunal referred to the nexus requirements of the preamble, which stated the parties desire to "promote" and recognition that investment protection "stimulate" flows of capital and economic development. This was found to indicate that it is "the intention of the parties to adhere to conduct in accordance with such purposes". *Siemens v. Argentina*, Award at para. 290.

[52] *Siemens A.G. v. The Argentine Republic*, Award, ICSID Case No. ARB/02/8, 17 January 2007, para. 290. The tribunal found that it was bound to interpret fair and equitable treatment "bearing in mind their ordinary meaning, the evolution of international law and the specific context in which

approach where the object and purpose of the treaty as derived from the title and preamble play a significant role in the treaty's interpretation can lack balance and nuance. This reading by the tribunal is on the most restrictive end of the scale in terms of the scope of the host state's right to regulate.[53]

Investment treaties aim to promote and protect investment but there should be no general preference to investors over host states in interpreting these treaties. Nonetheless, the tribunal in *SGS v. Philippines* followed this line of reasoning when it found for the Swiss investor.[54] The title of the Philippines-Switzerland BIT[55] describes it as a treaty "on the promotion and reciprocal protection of investments", but this does not absolve the tribunal of its task of balancing the rights of the investor and the host state. Similarly in *Occidental v. Ecuador*, the preamble to the US-Ecuador BIT expressly refers to the importance of creating "a stable framework for investment".[56] The tribunal cited this as constituting an "essential element of fair and equitable treatment".[57] The tribunal in *Occidental* did not consider legitimate objectives at all as part of discrimination analysis or as a separate justification.

It is the role of tribunals to interpret the text of the treaty and undue weight should not be placed on a treaty title that states its aim as being the promotion and protection of investment. Any such teleological reading of a treaty's title must be balanced against the host state's inherent right to regulate, and consider the level of generality at which the preamble is framed.

The primary source for tribunals in their interpretation of a treaty is the text of the treaty itself. The object and purpose of a treaty is "realized by its provisions"[58] and there are limitations to finding a treaty's purpose as being solely expressed in its title

---

they are used". The tribunal derived the objective of the treaty from the title and preamble and presumably this is part of the "specific context" referred to. *Siemens v. Argentina,* Award, para 291.

[53] Such purposive interpretations where the object and purpose of IIAs plays a determinative role and is cast in such a pro-investment manner have been deemed "untenable". Mitchell (2016), p. 140.

[54] "The object and purpose of the BIT supports an effective interpretation of Article X(2). The BIT is a treaty for the promotion and reciprocal protection of investments. According to the preamble it is intended 'to create and maintain favourable conditions for investments by investors of one Contracting Party in the territory of the other'. *It is legitimate to resolve uncertainties in its interpretation so as to favour the protection of covered investments.*" (emphasis added) *SGS (Société Générale de Surveillance) S.A. v. Republic of the Philippines*, Decision of the Tribunal on Objections to Jurisdiction ICSID Case No. ARB/02/6 (2004) at para. 116.

[55] Agreement Between the Republic of the Philippines and the Swiss Confederation on the Promotion and Reciprocal Protection of Investments (1999).

[56] *Occidental Exploration and Production Company v. The Republic of Ecuador,* Final Award, 1 July 2004, LCIA Case No. UN3467, para 183. In their decision, the Occidental tribunal referred to a similar finding in para 292 of *Ronald S. Lauder v. Czech Republic* (Final Award, 3 September 2001). This line of reasoning has been followed by subsequent tribunals as noted by Newcombe & Paradell.

[57] *Occidental Exploration and Production Company v. The Republic of Ecuador,* Final Award, 1 July 2004, LCIA Case No. UN3467, para 183.

[58] Newcombe and Paradell (2009), p. 115.

and preamble. If a treaty contains an exception for necessary actions to be taken by the host state in emergency circumstances, the title of the treaty should be secondary to the language of the exception provision itself.

In *Saluka v. Czech Republic*, the tribunal deemed the desire to extend and intensify relations as extending the aim of the Treaty beyond mere investment protection.

The tribunal placed a greater emphasis on the need to balance the rights of the investor with those of the host state in its assessment of the Agreement's object and purpose.[59] Such a finding acknowledges the larger context within which the undermining of a host state's ability to take regulatory measures in the public interest will ultimately undermine the "overall aim" of intensifying economic relations.[60]

The Netherlands-Slovakia BIT expressly mentions the desirability of fair and equitable treatment and extending and intensifying economic relations as one of the objectives in the main body of the preamble.[61] The treaties that formed the basis of the *Occidental* and *SGS v. Philippines* cases contained similar wordings in their preambles,[62] underlining how tribunals can interpret similarly worded preambles differently.

Philip Morris v. Uruguay concerned tobacco plain packaging measures and was a major test of the conflict between investor protection and the state's right to regulate in the area of public health. This dispute was taken under the Switzerland-Uruguay BIT (1988), which did not contain any explicit reference to the right to regulate. Concerning indirect expropriation under Article 5(1) of the BIT, the Tribunal found the challenged measures were "a valid exercise of the State's police powers".[63] Although not explicitly mentioned in the treaty, the tribunal found that the doctrine has found confirmation in recent trade and investment treaties such as CETA and

---

[59]The tribunal noted: "[A]n interpretation which exaggerates the protection to be accorded to foreign investments may serve to dissuade host States from admitting foreign investments and so undermine the overall aim of extending and intensifying the parties' mutual economic relations". *Saluka Investments B.V. v. The Czech Republic*, UNCITRAL, Partial Award (2006) para 300. This dispute was taken under the Agreement on encouragement and reciprocal protection of investments between the Kingdom of the Netherlands and the Czech and Slovak Federal Republic (1992).

[60] *Saluka Investments B.V. v. The Czech Republic*, UNCITRAL, Partial Award, 17 March 2006, para 300.

[61] Main body of the Netherlands- Slovakia BIT (1992): "Desiring to extend and intensify the economic relations between them particularly with respect to investments by the investors of one Contracting Party in the territory of the other Contracting Party, Recognizing that agreement upon the treatment to be accorded to such investments will stimulate the flow of capital and technology and the economic development of the Contracting Parties and that fair and equitable treatment is desirable, Taking note of the Final Act of the Conference on Security and Cooperation in Europe signed on August, 1st 1975 in Helsinki".

[62] The cases were taken under the US- Ecuador BIT (1992) which states: "Desiring to extend and intensify the economic relations between them", and the Philippines- Swiss BIT (1999) which states: "Desiring to promote greater economic cooperation between them".

[63] *Philip Morris Brands Sàrl, Philip Morris Products S.A. and Abal Hermanos S.A. v. Oriental Republic of Uruguay*, Award ICSID Case No. ARB/10/7, 8 July 2016, para 287.

EU- Singapore FTA.[64] The tribunal found that these provisions, whether or not introduced *ex abundanti cautela*, reflect the position under general international law.[65]

The *Philip Morris v. Uruguay* and *Saluka* approaches of emphasising the right to regulate based on general international law, or a reference to the desire to "intensify economic relations" in the preamble, were both the correct approach in this author's view. Any other approach would prove unsustainable and pro-investment interpretations could lead to treaty exit and have the long-term effect of undermining the intensification of the parties' economic relations. Tribunals must recognise that there is some balance between investment protection and host state's right to regulate. It is for the parties to decide the level of protection they wish to accord to investors and if they disagree with the interpretations of the tribunals in *Occidental* (or *Saluka*), they can re-examine and amend the wordings of the preambles that grounded these interpretations. In particular, careful preamble drafting is required to prevent arbitrators from focusing solely on investment protection.

When defending a measure under a BIT or PTIA, a host state is likely to refer to the object and purpose of the treaty as set out in the preamble, especially if the preamble contains some acknowledgement of the right to regulate (and this should be a pre-requisite for every IIA). This would give tribunals an explicit basis for balanced readings of the rights and obligations under the treaty.

Recent preambles such as that of the Australia-China FTA (2015) refer to the right to regulate in a direct and clear manner: "Upholding the rights of their governments to regulate in order to meet national policy objectives, and to preserve their flexibility to safeguard public welfare". Narrow interpretations of the purpose of investment treaties such as in *SGS v. Philippines* would be difficult to sustain under these IIAs.

A final question concerns supplementary means of interpretation for tribunals via the preparatory work of the treaty, as provided for by VCLT Article 32.[66] Alvarez has argued that the *raison d'être* of the US-Argentina BIT was to protect investments during volatile economic times in a context where such crises had been invoked as an excuse by Argentina "to escape its obligations to foreign investors".[67] The specific

---

[64] *Philip Morris Brands Sàrl, Philip Morris Products S.A. and Abal Hermanos S.A. v. Oriental Republic of Uruguay*, Award ICSID Case No. ARB/10/7, 8 July 2016, para 300.

[65] *Philip Morris Brands Sàrl, Philip Morris Products S.A. and Abal Hermanos S.A. v. Oriental Republic of Uruguay*, Award ICSID Case No. ARB/10/7, 8 July 2016, para 301.

[66] Article 32, VCLT: "Supplementary Means Of Interpretation: Recourse may be had to supplementary means of interpretation, including the preparatory work of the treaty and the circumstances of its conclusion, in order to confirm the meaning resulting from the application of article 31, or to determine the meaning when the interpretation according to article 31: (a) Leaves the meaning ambiguous or obscure; or (b) Leads to a result which is manifestly absurd or unreasonable." The use of *travaux préparatoires* by tribunals has been scarce to date. One reason for this has been the lack of documentary evidence surrounding BIT negotiations. See Newcombe & Paradell (2009) Chapter 2.28.

[67] See Alvarez and Brink (2011), p. 343.

purpose of the US-Argentina BIT was "to provide a credible commitment" that this wouldn't occur again and the BIT should be read in the light of the context and in particular the negotiating history of the treaty in question.[68]

Tribunals may only factor into their interpretations such background and the negotiating history of a treaty in line with Article 32 VCLT, which states that this should be where an interpretation according to Article 31 leads to ambiguity or a manifestly absurd or unreasonable result.[69] In line with Article 31, tribunals interpret treaties in accordance with their ordinary meaning in their context and in light of their object and purpose, and this is where drafters must ensure the *raison d'être* for a treaty sure is primarily reflected. The preparatory work of the treaty remains a supplementary means of interpretation and it is for the parties to ensure that the treaty text strikes the right balance in terms of substantive protection, exceptions, and the surrounding context for these protections.

Investment protection is the primary purpose of investment agreements[70] but even where this is the fundamental intention behind concluding the treaty, it does not fatally undermine treaty exceptions such as Article XI of the US Argentina BIT. A balance must be found in the interpretation of investment treaties as to do otherwise would undermine the overall aim of intensifying economic relations as was found by the tribunal in *Saluka v. Czech Republic*.[71]

5.3 Engagement and Object and Purpose

This section looks at similarities between the content of preambles in the trade and investment law regimes, whether tribunals in one regime should have regard to the interpretation of preambles in the other regime, and the role of PTIAs.

---

[68] A fuller discussion of this can be found in Chap. 4 on treaty exceptions and the necessity defence; see Alvarez and Brink (2011), pp. 351–352.

[69] See FN68. Article 32, VCLT: "Supplementary Means Of Interpretation: Recourse may be had to supplementary means of interpretation, including the preparatory work of the treaty and the circumstances of its conclusion, in order to confirm the meaning resulting from the application of article 31, or to determine the meaning when the interpretation according to article 31: (a) Leaves the meaning ambiguous or obscure; or (b) Leads to a result which is manifestly absurd or unreasonable."

[70] See Titi (2014), p. 119.

[71] *Saluka Investments B.V. v. The Czech Republic*, UNCITRAL, Partial Award, 17 March 2006, para 300.

5.3.1 Comparing the Content of Preambles Across the Regimes

Preambles setting out the object and purpose of agreements are a shared norm of the trade and investment law regimes. As outlined in Section A, the preamble to the WTO Agreement has more in common with the preambles of PTIAs than those of BITs, particularly older ones. This is because the preambles of these agreements such as the US-Ecuador BIT focus exclusively on the promotion and protection of investment, a concept that does not feature in the preamble to the WTO Agreements. On the other hand, the preambles of PTIAs (e.g. NAFTA and the Australia-China FTA) often refer to objectives such as the right to regulate and promoting sustainable development. These IIAs also frequently attempt to balance investment protection and the host state's right to regulate or recognising the importance of other societal interests. The wording of the preambles of more modern BITs, such as the Canada-Burkina Faso BIT, are closer in style to those of PTIAs and the preamble of the WTO Agreement.

It can be argued that the differences between the objects and purposes of trade and investment agreements are insignificant given the overlap in their objects and purposes, such as raising living standards, economic development, and sustainable development. While these instances of overlap can certainly be pointed to, this is not to say that the preambles of the WTO Agreements, PTIAs, and BITs are indistinguishable and generally ought to have a negligible influence on treaty interpretation. The preambles of both regimes often attempt to strike a balance between competing objectives, however the emphasis placed on the right to regulate versus the commitment to liberalise trade or protect investment can have subtle variations.[72] Each IIA has a specific purpose and background that led to its conclusion. Tribunals must give due consideration to this and caution should be exercised before concluding that trade and investment agreements have the same general objects and purposes or that any two investment agreements have the same objects and purposes.

Where IIAs contain a reference to the right to regulate and to the WTO Agreement in their preambles, this facilitates cross-regime references.[73] Chapters 3 and 4 considered how these references and the different purposes of agreements affect interpretations of nondiscrimination provisions and treaty exceptions. In the absence of any such references in an agreement's preamble, the tribunal must ensure that it

---

[72] Consider the preambles of the US Model BIT and the WTO Agreement, both of which balance the competing objectives of economic gains and protecting the right to regulate, but whose objects and purposes remain largely distinct.

[73] Although references to WTO law haven't traditionally featured in the preambles of BITs, tribunals cannot take their exclusion in all but a few recent BITs (e.g. Chile - Hong Kong, China SAR BIT (2016)) as evidence that it is only included in PTIAs because of the trade chapters therein. A fundamental rule concerning preambles is that they have a single object and purpose and that they apply to the entirety of an agreement. As such, where such references are included, regard must be had to the fact that the parties are building on or reaffirming their "rights and obligations under the WTO Agreement".

strikes an appropriate balance in its interpretation between the protection of invest-ment and that the host state's right to regulate.

5.3.2 Cross-Regime References

5.3.2.1 Why Make Cross-Regime References?

There are significant commonalities between the preambles of the WTO Agree-ments, those of BITs, and those of PTIAs. In line with the Vienna Convention, the preambles of these trade and investment agreements may influence the interpretation of other similar agreements in three ways:

(a) A treaty and its terms are to be interpreted "in their context and in the light of its object and purpose" in accordance with VCLT Article 31(1). The preamble is the primary source where the parties set out statements of object and purpose.
(b) The preamble forms part of the text of a treaty and thus part of a holistic treaty analysis, in line with VCLT Article 31(2).[74] These first points apply to the preambles of both the trade and investment law regimes. Preambles influence the interpretation of the agreements they form a part of, but tribunals may also wish to consider how similar preambular provisions have been interpreted in other agreements.
(c) In line with Article 31(3)(c) of the Vienna Convention, tribunals may consider in their interpretations "any relevant rules of international law applicable in the relations between the parties". The agreements of the other regime *and their preambles* form a part of this body of these relevant rules and can thus be considered by tribunals in their interpretations.

Although the preambles of the other regime, and how they have been interpreted, *can* be drawn upon when interpreting trade and investment agreements, it is noted that tribunals tend not to make external references. The tribunals in the trade and investment regimes do however ask similar questions, and so it may be useful to consider how they have been interpreted in the other regime. Tribunals may refer to the other regime and take into consideration their approach to certain interpretative questions.

There are parallels between the objectives stated in the preamble to the Marrakesh Agreement and those stated in IIAs. Like the preamble to the Marrakesh Agreement,

---

[74] "Vienna Convention on the Law of Treaties, General rule of interpretation, Article 31.1: A treaty shall be interpreted in good faith in accordance with the ordinary meaning to be given to the terms of the treaty in their context and in the light of its object and purpose. 31.2: The context for the purpose of the interpretation of a treaty shall comprise, in addition to the text, including its preamble and annexes (...)"

the preambles of many modern IIAs refer to raising living standards,[75] sustainable development, economic development, and the need to balance this with other societal interests. The empirical study in Chap. 2 focused on two aspects of preambles that facilitate inter-regime engagement, including references to: (1) the right to regulate; and (2) building on the parties' rights and obligations under the WTO Agreement. The right to regulate is commonly included in modern IIAs and thus shared ground between the two regimes. References in IIAs to the rights and obligations under the WTO Agreement clearly facilitate engagement and were included in the vast majority of PTIAs contained surveyed in Chap. 2. Such a reference was contained in only one of the BITs in this study.

5.3.2.2 Have Tribunal Made Cross-Regime References?

When interpreting the object and purpose of agreements in the two regimes, tribunals tend not to make external references and there have been no cross-regime references to date. As outlined in Section A, some investment tribunals have given very narrow interpretations of the object and purpose of IIAs, while others have placed a greater emphasis on the need to balance the rights of the investor with those of the host state.

Investment tribunals tend not to refer to interpretations of object and purpose made in other investment cases, with just one of the awards discussed in Section A making such a reference. In *SGS v. Philippines*, the tribunal referred to the ICSID Tribunal in *Salini v. Morocco*, but only to note that the two tribunals had reached the same conclusion.[76]

Tribunals at the WTO have placed an emphasis on the holistic nature of treaty interpretation at the WTO. The Appellate Body has found that "light from the object and purpose" of the treaty may be looked to for guidance where there is ambiguity as

---

[75] On raising living standards, see for example the 2012 US Model BIT. The latter three objectives are more common across modern IIAs.

[76] *SGS (Société Générale de Surveillance) S.A. v. Republic of the Philippines*, Decision of the Tribunal on Objections to Jurisdiction ICSID Case No. ARB/02/6, 29 January 2004, paras 116–118, 135. In FN67, the tribunal referred to *Salini Construttori SpA v. Kingdom of Morocco* (2001) 6 ICSID Reports 398, 415, para. 61; Other investment disputes discussed in Section A included *Siemens AG v. Argentina*, where the tribunal only referred to the text of the BIT itself and the Oxford English Dictionary. The *Enron. v. Argentina* tribunal only referred to the legal opinion of José E. Alvarez (paras 330–332), while in *Philip Morris v. Uruguay* and *Saluka v. Czech Republic,* no reference to an external source was made.

to the meaning of a provision.[77] The starting point for determining object and purpose is the treaty in its entirety rather than the preamble.[78]

Despite the emphasis on the holistic approach, no interpretation of the object and purpose of the treaty can run contrary to the express terms of the text. For the trade disputes considered in Section A, tribunals referred to interpretations of object and purpose in other trade disputes more often than their investment law counterparts referred to other investment disputes. However, in these trade disputes, the tribunals did not refer to external sources, either in investment law or from the wider field of public international law. In *EC—Chicken Cuts,* the Appellate Body made extensive references when interpreting the object and purpose of the GATT. It referred to the Appellate Body Reports in *EC—Computer Equipment, Argentina–Textiles and Apparel, US–Line Pipe,* and *Chile–Price Band System.*[79] The tribunal also referred to Sir Ian Sinclair's book 'The Vienna Convention and the Law of Treaties,'[80] as well as evidence of the object and purpose provided by heading 02.10 of the EC Schedule.[81] The tribunal in *US—Shrimp I* referred to the preamble of the WTO Agreement and to how object and purpose was determined in *US—Gasoline.*[82]

5.3.2.3 Making Cross-Regime References

The above analysis indicates reluctance on the part of trade and investment tribunals to consider interpretations given in other regimes when interpreting the object and purpose of the agreement before them. Tribunals do however seem to be quite willing to consider interpretations of preambles given in other disputes under the same regime. There may be reasons to consider interpretations of the preambles of the other regime and such references could take several forms. Cross-regime references in relation to preambles may not be as explicit as the references made in areas such as treaty exceptions or national treatment provisions. They would not

---

[77] Appellate Body Report, *US—Import Prohibition of Certain Shrimp and Shrimp Products,* WT/DS58/AB/R, adopted on 6 November 1998, para. 114: "It is in the words constituting that provision, read in their context, that the object and purpose of the states parties to the treaty must first be sought. Where the meaning imparted by the text itself is equivocal or inconclusive, or where confirmation of the correctness of the reading of the text itself is desired, light from the object and purpose of the treaty as a whole may usefully be sought."

[78] Appellate Body Report, *European Communities — Customs Classification of Frozen Boneless Chicken Cuts,* WT/DS269/AB/R, adopted on 27 September 2005, para 47.

[79] Appellate Body Report, *European Communities — Customs Classification of Frozen Boneless Chicken Cuts,* WT/DS269/AB/R, adopted on 27 September 2005, para 239, FN453, para 238 FN 450, and para 237, FN 445.

[80] Sir Ian Sinclair's book 'The Vienna Convention and the Law of Treaties,' *Manchester University Press* (2nd Edn.) (1984). The Appellate Body also referred to the *EC-Chicken Cuts* panel report.

[81] Appellate Body Report, *European Communities — Customs Classification of Frozen Boneless Chicken Cuts,* WT/DS269/AB/R, adopted on 27 September 2005, paras 236–240.

[82] Appellate Body Report, *US – Import Prohibition of Certain Shrimp and Shrimp Products,* WT/DS58/AB/R, adopted on 6 November 1998, paras 114–129.

necessarily involve the development of new legal tests or the transplanting of jurisprudence.

In relation to preambles, such references could be limited to interpretations in areas such as nexus requirements. These references may still be fundamental to the interpretation of the object and purpose of a treaty and investment tribunals can learn from trade tribunals' interpretative methods and vice versa. Conclusions as to the object and purpose based on the preamble may also affect the legal tests developed under other treaty provisions.

In *US—Clove Cigarettes*, the Appellate Body considered the balance set out in the preamble to the TBT Agreement in relation to trade liberalisation and the right to regulate.[83] Without discussing the differing implications of "recognizing" compared to "desiring", the Appellate Body discusses the relationship between Recitals 5 and 6 in the preambles in some detail: "The sixth recital 'recognizes' Members' right to regulate versus the 'desire' to avoid creating unnecessary obstacles to international trade expressed in the fifth recital".[84] The AB also noted that the balance set out in these recitals is not, in principle, different from the balance set out in the GATT 1994, where obligations such as national treatment in Article III are qualified by the general exceptions provision of Article XX.[85]

Investment tribunals may be required to make similar interpretations. For example, the Korea- US FTA (2019) contains the same nexus requirements as the TBT Agreement. The preamble states that the parties "recognise" the desire to strengthen their economic relations, but also their "desire" to strengthen labour and environmental laws and policies.[86] WTO tribunals have also gone into considerably more

---

[83] Recital 5 of the TBT Agreement's preamble emphasises trade liberalisation with the parties "desiring" that regulations "do not create unnecessary obstacles to trade". Recital 6 emphasises the right to regulate and "recognizes that no country should be prevented from taking measures to ensure...the protection of human, animal or plant life or health". Recital 5- "Desiring however to ensure that technical regulations and standards, including packaging, marking and labelling requirements, and procedures for assessment of conformity with technical regulations and standards do not create unnecessary obstacles to international trade;". Recital 6- "Recognized that no country should be prevented from taking measures to ensure the quality of its exports, or for the protection of human, animal or plant life or health, of the environment, or for the prevention of deceptive practices, at the levels it considers appropriate, subject to the requirement that they are not applied in a manner which would constitute a means of arbitrary or unjustifiable discrimination between countries where the same conditions prevail or a disguised restriction on international trade [...]."

[84] Appellate Body Report, *United States — Measures Affecting the Production and Sale of Clove Cigarettes*, WT/DS406/AB/R, adopted on 24 April 2012, paras. 95.

[85] Appellate Body Report, *United States — Measures Affecting the Production and Sale of Clove Cigarettes*, WT/DS406/AB/R, adopted on 24 April 2012, paras. 96.

[86] "Recognizing their longstanding and strong partnership, and desiring to strengthen their close economic relations; (...) Desiring to strengthen the development and enforcement of labor and environmental laws and policies, promote basic workers' rights and sustainable development, and implement this Agreement in a manner consistent with environmental protection and conservation;".

detail in relation to the interpretation of nexus requirements elsewhere in the WTO Agreements.[87]

The Appellate Body has made extensive references when interpreting the object and purpose of provisions in some recent disputes. For example, in *EC—Chicken Cuts*, the AB referred to five other WTO reports, evidence furnished by the EC, as well as an academic work on the VCLT.[88] If such comprehensive analysis becomes the standard for tribunals interpreting the object and purpose of trade and investment provisions, cross-regime references may feature before long. What constitutes an appropriate cross-regime reference and the extent to which it is appropriate to draw upon the experience of the other regime when interpreting the object and purpose of trade and investment agreements remains to be seen.

5.3.3   Preambles and the Role of PTIAs

This section considers whether PTIA preambles result in increased levels of engagement between the trade and investment law regimes compared to BIT preambles. In terms of parallels in content, two provisions relating to preambles were included in this study of inter-regime engagement.[89] These provisions included preambles referring to the WTO and preambles referring to the right to regulate. There was greater evidence of engagement in PTIAs, compared to BITs, for both provisions. Preambles referring to the parties' WTO obligations featured in 59/60 PTIAs and 1/60 BITs in this study's sample. Preambles referring to the right to regulate were also more common in PTIAs than in BITs, featuring in 48/60 PTIAs (80%) and 30/60 BITs contained in this study. As references to the right to regulate were significantly more common for the PTIAs featured in this study, they clearly contain greater parallels of content compared to the BITs.

---

[87] Under GATT Article XX for example, the requirement that a measure is "necessary" to fulfil a certain goal under Article XX(b) is more onerous than the requirement that a measure is "relating to" the conservation of exhaustible natural resources under Article XX(g). The Appellate Body in *Korea- Beef* found that the factors to be taken into account by tribunals in establishing necessity included: (1) the importance of the objective; (2) the contribution of the measure to the objective; and (3) the impact of the law or regulation on imports or exports. See Appellate Body Report, *Korea – Measures Affecting Imports Of Fresh, Chilled And Frozen Beef*, WT/DS161/AB/R, WT/DS169/AB/R, para. 164.

[88] Appellate Body Report, *European Communities — Customs Classification of Frozen Boneless Chicken Cuts*, WT/DS269/AB/R, adopted on 27 September 2005, para 239, FN453, para 238 FN 450, and para 237, FN 445.

[89] Engagement was defined in Chap. 1: Engagement between trade and investment occurs wherever the content of an investment agreement has a parallel in the trade regime or vice versa. The term 'content' can cover an agreement's preamble, definitions, substantive provisions, exceptions etc. Engagement also occurs in dispute settlement whenever there are cross-regime references by the parties or the tribunal or parallels in the practices or features of dispute settlement. Engagement does not imply convergence and may fall short of this in a given area between the two regimes.

Not only were preambles referring to the right to regulate more prevalent in PTIAs, but the references to this right tended to be stronger than those found in BITs in this study.[90] This may be for many reasons such as the fact that PTIAs apply to a wider range of subject matters. The reasons for their inclusion are not considered in depth here.

Cross-regime references were also a component of the definition of engagement. Such references are the second measure of engagement and whether the potential for them increases based on the preambles of PTIAs compared to those of BITs. Preambles referring to the WTO and the right to regulate were shown to be more common and stronger in PTIAs than in BITs for the sample in this study. For these reasons tribunals are more likely to draw upon these PTIA provisions. However, there are additional considerations for tribunals when interpreting provisions and comparing shared norms of the systems that may impact upon the frequency of cross-regime references.

Tribunals must consider the contextual differences relating to PTIA and BIT preambles. BIT preambles refer to investment concerns alone whereas PTIA preambles set out the purpose of broader agreements that often feature chapters in a wide range of areas.[91] This broader context seems to be a factor in PTIA preambles referring to WTO law and such references were found in 59/60 PTIAs compared to just 1/60 BITs. Although references to the WTO Agreement have not traditionally featured in standalone investment agreements, this may change in the future.[92]

---

[90] E.g. for the first year of this study (2005), on a scale of 0-5 the PTIAs had an average score of 3 for the strength of the references to the right to regulate in their preambles. The BITs had an average score of 0.25.

The PTIAs included: New Zealand–Thailand EPA (5), the India–Singapore Comprehensive Economic Cooperation Agreement (5), Guatemala–Taiwan FTA (5), Korea–EFTA FTA (3), the Korea–Singapore FTA (0), and the Japan–Malaysia EPA (0). The BITs included: Jordan–Thailand BIT (0), Guyana–Switzerland BIT (0), China–Portugal BIT (0), and the Serbia–Switzerland BIT (1).

[91] E.g. CPTPP contains a preamble and 30 chapters, including: 1. Initial Provisions and General definitions; 2. National Treatment and Market Access; 3. Rules of Origin and Origin Procedures; 4. Textiles and Apparel; 5. Customs Administration and Trade Facilitation; 6. Trade Remedies; 7. Sanitary and Phytosanitary Measures; 8. Technical Barriers to Trade; 9. Investment; 10. Cross Border Trade in Services; 11. Financial Services; 12. Temporary Entry for Business Persons; 13. Telecommunications; 14. Electronic Commerce; 15. Government Procurement; 16. Competition; 17. State-Owned Enterprises; 18. Intellectual Property; 19. Labour; 20. Environment; 21. Cooperation and Capacity Building; 22. Competitiveness and Business Facilitation; 23. Development; 24. Small and Medium-Sized Enterprises; 25. Regulatory Coherence; 26. Transparency and Anti-Corruption; 27. Administrative and Institutional Provisions; 28. Dispute Settlement; 29. Exceptions; and 30. Final Provisions.

[92] The preamble of the EU-Singapore IPA refers to the parties respective rights and obligations under the WTO Agreement, as does the Chile—Hong Kong BIT. EUSIPA: "(...) BUILDING on their respective rights and obligations under the WTO Agreement and other multilateral, regional and bilateral agreements and arrangements to which they are party, in particular, the EUSFTA (...) Have Agreed as follows:" The Chile—Hong Kong, China SAR BIT is one of the 120 IIAs featured in Chapter 2's empirical study.

How does this dichotomy between the two systems impact upon the interpretation of agreements? Tribunals could take the exclusion of such a provision in all but the most recent BITs as evidence that it is only included in PTIAs because of the trade chapters therein. At the same time, where a preamble acknowledges that the parties are building on their WTO obligations, this may have implications in the investment context and such provisions have been included in BITs.

Tribunals must be attentive to differences in the purposes of the regimes when interpreting the preambles of IIAs. The PTIAs and BITs that featured in this study tended to have different types of preambles. Many of the PTIAs had lengthier preambles taking into account a wider range of concerns largely because of the broader scope of these Agreements. This raises the question of how tribunals should interpret the object and purpose of an Agreement where there is a preambular reference that typically has more of a trade orientation (i.e. it would be unlikely to feature in a BIT between the parties) but it applies to the whole agreement.

De Brabandere does not believe that investment tribunals should interpret the investment provisions of a PTIA differently to those of a BIT: "[I]t does not seem reasonable to conclude that international investment tribunals, confronted with investment protection provisions in a PTIA would interpret these provisions differently than in the case of a BIT. One cannot infer from the, compared to BITs, broader context and object and purpose of PTIAs that the intent of the parties in respect of the protection of foreign investment, and thus the intended meaning of the substantive standards of protection contained in PTIAs, would be any different than in the case of BITs."[93]

However, each treaty has only one object and purpose, or at least one predominant object and purpose, as expressed in its preamble. It is a fundamental rule of preambles that they have a single object and purpose and that this applies to the entirety of an agreement. The VCLT's use of the singular is important where it states that the content of a preamble is to be interpreted in light of "its object and purpose". The implication of the word "its" is that there is a main or predominant object and purpose and that the treaty must be interpreted in such a way as to advance this main or predominant purpose. This main object and purpose applies to the entirety of an agreement, including the investment chapter, regardless of whether a preambular reference was included primarily, or exclusively, with another chapter of the agreement in mind.

As such, regard must be had to the fact that the parties are "building on" or "reaffirming"[94] their rights and obligations under the WTO Agreement where such references are included. These references apply to the entirety of the agreement including the investment chapter and this alters the purpose of the agreement and

---

[93] De Brabandere (2013), p. 66. In the same collection, Jacob finds that investment provisions in PTIAs can be construed differently even if their wording is (virtually) identical to provisions in BITS "on account of the typically broader coverage". Jacob (2013), p. 88.

[94] Japan-Malaysia EPA (2005) (Agreement Between The Government Of Japan And The Government Of Malaysia For An Economic Partnership).

how it should be interpreted. The extent to which the inclusion of references to the WTO Agreement should affect the interpretation of IIAs will have to be approached on a case-by-case basis.

Tribunals must further consider differences in the wording of the agreements when interpreting the preambles of PTIAs and BITs. Even slight differences in the wording of preambles are ultimately clues for tribunals as to the objectives of the parties in concluding a given treaty. Different treaty contexts require different preambles and careful selection of the wording of a preamble is the key to striking a balance between the interests of the investor and the host state.

The wordings of PTIA preambles for this sample contained stronger (on average) and more common references to the right to regulate and this was shown to be facilitative of engagement between the regimes. Even where recitals are very similar, there may be differences in 'recognising' a principle compared to being 'mindful' or 'aware' of it, and this may have implications when determining the purpose of the agreement. The closer the content of recitals in preambles, the easier it is for tribunals to consider the experience of the other regime and to make cross-regime references.

Tribunals must also consider systemic differences and differences in the remedy structures between the two regimes when interpreting the preambles of PTIAs and BITs.[95] Findings of breach under IIAs give rise to monetary damages and are not confined to the withdrawal of inconsistent measures as is the case in the trade law regime.[96] A key systemic difference between the regimes is the lack of the possibility of appeal in the investment regime except on a very limited number of grounds in all but a few recent IIAs.[97] These differences mean that there are potentially severe consequences if a tribunal reads the preamble of an older style BIT and takes the view that the treaty's purpose is focused primarily on the protection of investment and that the host state's right to regulate is an ancillary concern. Narrow interpretations of the purpose of investment treaties such as in *SGS v. Philippines* would be difficult to sustain under recent IIAs where the right to regulate is clearly stated, e.g. Australia- China FTA (2015).[98] Such interpretations could lead to treaty exit and have the long-term effect of undermining the intensification of the parties' economic relations.

---

[95] Chapter 1.IV.4 discusses factors tribunals should consider when making cross-regime references, including (c) systemic differences.

[96] Temporary remedies can be applied pending withdrawal or modification of the measure, including compensation and the suspension of concessions or other obligations. See Van den Bossche and Zdouc (2017), p. 458.

[97] This more comprehensive right of appeal is included in recent IIAs of the EU such as CETA.

[98] See also *Siemens v. Argentina*, Award, para. 290. When interpreting the objectives of the parties, the tribunal referred to the nexus requirements of the preamble, which stated the parties desire to "promote" and recognition that investment protection "stimulate" flows of capital and economic development. This was found to indicate that it is "the intention of the parties to adhere to conduct in accordance with such purposes". This reading by the tribunal is on the most restrictive end of the scale in terms of the scope of the host state's right to regulate.

A further consideration in this area in relation to PTIAs, is the reluctance some parties may have to exit a treaty, where the overall package is beneficial to them, but they would terminate the investment agreement if it were a standalone agreement.

Tribunals have to be mindful of these factors in their awards and in striking a balance that is appropriate for the investment regime, rather than following a test developed in line with a different set of considerations in the trade regime.

Preambles can either facilitate or exclude the possibility of inter-regime engagement. Balanced preambles facilitate inter-regime engagement and it is for the parties to choose how they balance investment protection with the right to regulate. References to the right to regulate facilitate inter-regime engagement by diminishing the PTIAs play a clear role in facilitating engagement between the regimes as they contain references to the WTO and the right to regulate that tend to be stronger and more common than BITs. These references should inform the interpretation of the treaty's object and purpose.

5.3.4 Why Balanced Preambles Are a Good Thing

Preambles guide tribunals in interpreting treaty obligations under IIAs and the WTO Agreements. The objects and purposes in trade and investment agreements are similar but distinct, and, as a starting point, it is important to acknowledge that preambles *can* guide a tribunal in developing a legal test. The extent to which different objects and purposes can lead to the development of different legal tests remains to be seen. While there is a general approximation between the wordings of preambles in the two regimes, this is often less important than fundamental differences between the objects and purposes of the two regimes.[99] Each IIA has a specific purpose and background that led to its conclusion. Tribunals must give due consideration to this and caution should be exercised before concluding that: (1) any two international investment agreements have the same objects and purposes; and (2) that trade and investment agreements have the same general objects and purposes.

Preambles can facilitate inter-regime engagement, particularly in relation to the two types of preambular provisions included in Chap. 2. Compared to the trade regime, IIAs have tended to place less of an emphasis on balancing the state's right to regulate with the substantive rights accorded, particularly in older style BITs. Tribunals and commentators who have rejected looking to the trade regime in particular instances have emphasised the differing purposes of IIAs and the WTO Agreements. IIAs are about protecting investments and individual property rights, but this must be done in a way that is in accordance with other legitimate policy objectives of the state. The panel in *Lemire v. Ukraine* found *obiter dicta* that some

---

[99] See Alvarez and Brink (2011), p. 343.

kind of balance had to be found as the state had an "inherent right to regulate its affairs and adopt laws in order to protect the common good of its people".[100]

Other examples of differences in the objects and purposes of IIAs include the emphasis that is placed on: the government's right to regulate; investment promotion and protection; sustainable development; building upon WTO commitments; and not relaxing standards. Drafters must then consider which of these, *if any*, they wish to include in an agreement or whether other objects and purposes may be more appropriate.

The degree of balance between the right to regulate and investment protection has been drafted in many ways with various degrees of strength in the wordings of IIA preambles. The Philip Morris cases taken under the Hong Kong- Australia BIT[101] and Switzerland-Uruguay BIT[102] have led to significant criticism of the investment law regime. The problem with the preambles in some older style BITs such as the Hong Kong-Australia BIT is the lack of any balance between investment protection and the right to regulate. As well as this, there is a lack of any exceptions for measures necessary for the protection of public health.

Section A outlined restrictive readings as well as a more balanced reading of the host state's right to regulate in the investment jurisprudence. Earlier readings such as *SGS v. Philippines* lacked balance and nuance and it is questionable whether such readings are sustainable, or indeed permissible under newer IIAs. While traditionally it has been the case that investment treaties have focused too narrowly on protecting the rights of investors, attempts to correct this can result in provisions that overly focus on protecting the host states' right to regulate in any circumstance it deems appropriate. Provisions concerning the right to regulate also inform the object and purpose of treaties and supplement preambular provisions.[103] The parties should keep in mind that the main purpose of investment treaties is the promotion and protection of investment between the parties rather than the preservation of policy space.[104]

---

[100] *Lemire v. Ukraine*, Decision On Jurisdiction And Liability, ICSID Case No. ARB/06/18, 14 January 2010, para 505-07. This was stated in relation to Article II.6 of the US- Ukraine BIT (1996) which prohibits "performance requirements . . . which specify that goods or services must be purchased locally".

[101] *Philip Morris Asia Limited v. The Commonwealth of Australia*, Award on Jurisdiction and Admissibility, UNCITRAL, PCA Case No. 2012-12, 17 December 2015.

[102] *Philip Morris Brands Sàrl, Philip Morris Products S.A. and Abal Hermanos S.A. v. Oriental Republic of Uruguay*, ICSID Case No. ARB/10/7, Award, 8 July 2016.

[103] It should also be noted that provisions such as Article 12 of Norway Model BIT (2007) include the wording that nothing shall prevent a party from adopting any measure "Otherwise consistent with" this agreement and that the result of this may be to "narrow policy space rather than the opposite." Investment treaties are neutral objects. Their contents reflect the choices of their drafters. Titi (2014), p. 112. The focus of this chapter is preambles but the object and purpose these can be clarified and the right to regulate can be reinforced by a separate provision in this area.

[104] Titi reminds us that regulatory space would ultimately be increased in the absence of an IIA. See Titi (2014), p. 119.

Parties should therefore consider what level of protection they wish to accord to investment and what kind of balance they wish to strike between this and the right to regulate. It is for the drafters to ensure that the preambles to IIAs reflect the parties' purposes in concluding an agreement. This study has considered the texts of many preambles and finds that in order to do this, parties should be careful to ensure that there is some balance expressed in treaty preambles between investment protection and the right to regulate to aid tribunals in their interpretations. This has been the case in many modern IIAs and at the WTO.

References

Alvarez JE, Brink T (2011) Revisiting the necessity defense: continental casualty v. Argentina. Yearb Int Invest Law Policy, p 343

Bonnitcha J, Poulsen LS, Waibel M (2017) The political economy of the investment regime. Oxford University Press, p 159

Broude T (2011) Investment and trade: the "Lottie And Lisa" of international economic law? Int Law Forum Hebrew Univ Jerusalem Law, p 5

De Brabandere E (2013) Co-existence, complementarity or conflict? Interaction between preferential trade and investment agreements and bilateral investment treaties. In: Hofmann CJT, Schill SW (eds) Preferential trade and investment agreements: from recalibration to reintegration. Nomos, Baden, p 66

Federico Ortino (2006) Treaty interpretation and the WTO- Appellate Body Report in US – gambling: a critique. J Int Econ Law 9(1):148

Jacob M (2013) Technique and contents of international investment treaties: can the form affect the substance? In: Hofmann CJT, Schill SW (eds) Preferential trade and investment agreements: from recalibration to reintegration. Nomos, Baden, p 88

Mitchell A, Heaton D, Henckels C (2016) Non-discrimination and the role of regulatory purpose in international trade. Edward Elgar, p 174 & 56

Newcombe A, Paradell L (2009) Law and practice of investment treaties: standards of treatment. Kluwer Law Int 124–126:113–117

Orgad L (2010) The preamble in constitutional interpretation. Int J Const Law 8(4):727

Titi A (2014) The right to regulate in international investment law. Hart 115

van Aaken A (2008) Perils of success? The case of international investment protection. Eur Bus Organ Law Rev (EBOR) 9(1):1–27

Van Damme I (2009) Treaty interpretation by the WTO appellate body. Oxford University Press

Van den Bossche P, Zdouc W (2017) The law and policy of the World Trade Organisation, text cases and materials, 4th edn. Cambridge University Press, p 458

Weiler T (2003) 2002 in review: from expropriation to non-discrimination. Yearbook of international environmental law, vol 12. Clarendon, Oxford, p 28

Wu M (2014) The scope and limits of trade's influence in shaping the evolving international investment regime. In: Douglas Z, Pauwelyn J, Vinuales J (eds) The foundations of international investment law. Oxford University Press

Part IV
Procedural Provisions

Chapter 6
Appellate Mechanisms

6.1 Introduction

Part IV looks at procedural rules in the area of dispute settlement. It considers the rules and procedures of the appellate mechanisms of the two regimes as well as the operation of *amicus curiae* submissions.

While dispute settlement under PTIAs tends to be siloed into state-to-state dispute settlement for trade disputes, and ISDS for investment disputes, this does not preclude engagement between the procedural rules of the two regimes.[1] Despite the fundamental differences between the two regimes in terms of dispute settlement, there have been high levels of engagement between the procedural rules in some PTIAs, notably in agreements such as those containing ICS, where appeal mechanisms have been introduced.

6.2 Appellate Mechanisms

6.2.1 Appeal in the Trade Regime

Despite the abundance of trade law texts outside of the WTO Agreements, dispute resolution in international trade law has been dominated by the WTO since its establishment in 1995. Six-hundred cases had been initiated under the WTO's

---

[1] Gáspár-Szilágyi and Usynin note that "[O]ne would have expected that any disputes...would be handled by the same, state-to-state dispute settlement mechanism," but that this is not the case. Gáspár-Szilágyi and Usynin (2020), p. 42.

dispute settlement system by May 2021.[2] From 1995 to 2019, 178 notices of appeal were filed at the WTO.[3] The WTO's Appellate Body (AB) was established in line with the rules and procedures laid out in Article 17 of the Dispute Settlement Understanding (DSU).[4] The AB was referred to as the 'jewel in the crown of the WTO' by Directors-General of the WTO as early as 1996 and as recently as 2013.[5] However, it is now a jewel in need of polishing as a result of the US blocking the (re-)appointment of Appellate Body Members since 2016.[6] This culminated in the system's paralysis on 10 December 2019 with the expiry of the terms of office of two of the three remaining AB Members.[7]

This section considers the rules and procedures governing the WTO's appellate system as they functioned before the current impasse. Part B considers the lessons a potential investment law appellate mechanism can take from the WTO system. Any comparison with investment law and any lessons it could take would have to take the current institutional dysfunction at the WTO into account.

6.2.1.1   Rules and Procedures of the Appellate Body

The most pertinent features of the AB relevant for a comparison with appellate mechanisms of the investment regime, both current and prospective, are now briefly recalled. Article 17.1 of the DSU sets out the composition of the AB and that its

---

[2] See the WTO's Chronological list of disputes at: www.wto.org/english/tratop_e/dispu_e/dispu_ status_e.htm.

[3] The Appellate Body has been defunct since 11 December 2019. Of these 178 notices of appeal, 147 related to original proceedings rather than compliance proceedings. 32 notices of appeal were brought in Article 21.5 proceedings, where there is the possibility of second level appeals. See Appellate Body Annual Report For 2019-2020, July 2020, Annex 6, 175. As of February 2021, there are 17 'current notified appeals' that have been filed. 7 of these were filed after 11 December 2019 by Members including Saudi Arabia, the US (x3), EU, Indonesia, Korea. See WTO website, Dispute Settlement, Appellate Body, available at: https://www.wto.org/english/tratop_e/dispu_e/ appellate_body_e.htm#fnt-1. The EU claims that it did not appeal 'into the void' in DS494 but rather stands ready to move "to final resolution of the dispute in appeal proceedings pursuant to Article 25 of the DSU, on a reciprocal basis" based on the MPIA. See EU Notification of Appeal, *EU — Cost Adjustment Methodologies II (Russia)*, WT/DS494/7, 1 September 2020.

[4] Annex 2 of the WTO Agreement.

[5] This description is attributed to DG Renato Ruggiero (1996), p. 574. See also speech of DG Pascal Lamy, 'Receiving honorary doctorate in Turkey, Lamy warns against remote global governance,' 15 March 2013. Available at: https://www.wto.org/english/news_e/sppl_e/sppl272_e.htm.

[6] See Inside US Trade, 'U.S. Slammed At DSB For Blocking Korean Appellate Body Reappointment,' May 23, 2016.

[7] See 'Members urge continued engagement on resolving Appellate Body issues,' 18 December 2019, available at: https://www.wto.org/english/news_e/news19_e/dsb_18dec19_e.htm. This summary from the WTO website reports that "On 10 December the Appellate Body was reduced to one member after the second terms for two of the remaining three members expired. Normally composed of seven members, the Appellate Body no longer has the minimum three members needed to hear new appeals." See also Statements by the United States at the Meeting of the WTO Dispute Settlement Body Geneva, August 31, 2017: https://geneva.usmission.gov/wp-content/ uploads/2017/08/Aug31.DSB_.Stmt_.as-delivered.fin_.public.pdf. The two former ABMs referred to include Ujal Singh Bhatia of India and Thomas R. Graham of the United States.

Members shall serve in rotation.[8] Members shall serve a 4-year term, renewable once (DSU Article 17.2). Appellate Body Members (ABMs) comprise persons of recognised authority, who are unaffiliated with any government and are broadly representative of the WTO membership (17.3). AB proceedings shall in no case exceed 90 days (17.5). Appeals are limited to issues of law covered in the panel report (17.6) and appropriate administrative and legal support is provided as required (17.7).

The AB draws up its own working procedures in consultation with the Chairman of the DSB and the Director-General (17.9). Its proceedings are confidential and opinions expressed by individual ABMs are anonymous (17.10 & 17.11). The Members must address each issue raised on appeal that falls within the terms of reference (17.12). The AB may uphold, modify, or reverse the legal findings and conclusions of the panel (17.13).[9]

Beyond the DSU, the Appellate Body has developed its procedural law in areas where the WTO Agreement is silent such as burden of proof, standing, representation before Panels, the retroactive application of treaties or error in treaty formation.[10] In doing so, it has frequently referred to the practices of other international tribunals.[11] In relation to the burden of proof, the AB has referred to the practices of various international tribunals, including the ICJ, which have accepted and applied the rule that the party asserting a fact is responsible for providing proof thereof.[12] The alleged shortcomings of the Appellate Body in terms of respect for the procedural limitations of the DSU are explored in Section B.I.

6.2.1.2   Rules and Procedures of DSMs Elsewhere in the Trade Regime

An appellate mechanism has not been replicated elsewhere in the trade regime. Part of the reason for this may be the dominance of the WTO in terms of dispute settlement from 1995 to 2019. WTO Members have tended to litigate at the WTO rather than under the Dispute Settlement Mechanisms (DSMs) of PTAs for various reasons. These include the high levels of trust in the WTO dispute settlement system, the relative predictability of the system, the enforceability of WTO awards, and the reputational damage the offending Member may suffer if it is seen to be violating its WTO commitments.

---

[8] It shall be composed of seven persons, three of whom shall serve on any one case.

[9] Article 18 provides that there shall be no *ex parte* communications between the panel and AB and written submissions shall be treated as confidential. In accordance with Article 19, adjudicators recommend that Members bring infringing measures into conformity with the WTO Agreement.

[10] See Pauwelyn (2003), pp. 997–998.

[11] See e.g. Cook (2015), pp. 121–152, on the influence of the practice of international tribunals concerning the role of evidence, including the burden and standard of proof.

[12] Appellate Body Report, *United States - Measures Affecting Imports of Woven Wool Shirts and Blouses from India*, WT/DS33/AB/R, adopted 23 May 1997, page 14.

In contrast to this dynamism, there was a general paucity of litigation of trade matters under PTAs or the trade chapters of PTIAs during these years. Between 2007-16, only two cases were successfully completed under PTAs.[13] *Costa Rica v. El Salvador*[14] and *Guatemala—Issues Relating to the Obligations Under Article 16.2.1(a) of the CAFTA-DR* were both taken under CAFTA-DR (Dominican Republic-Central America FTA).[15] The former concerned non-compliance with import obligations and the latter a labour dispute.[16]

The purpose of concluding a PTA or PTIA is to go beyond what has been agreed among all 164 WTO Members either in terms of subject matter, depth, or both. When litigating a WTO-plus or WTO-extra matter, the regional dispute settlement mechanism (DSM) including these provisions may be more appropriate. The adjudicatory functions of regional agreements are likely to be of increasing importance in light of the recent cessation of the functioning of the WTO's Appellate Body. Such mechanisms may become desirable where there is a fear that the other party will appeal a WTO panel report 'into the void'.[17] In December 2020, the first Report for a trade dispute under an FTA involving the EU was issued in *Ukraine- Wood Products.*[18]

For WTO Members wishing to retain the right to appeal, the EU led multi-party interim appeal arrangement (MPIA) shows that at least 25 WTO Members wish to keep a two-tier WTO-centric model of dispute settlement.[19] For those not looking to sign up to the MPIA, two-tier systems of dispute settlement could emerge under the trade chapters of regional agreements to fill the void left by the Appellate Body.

---

[13] See Vidigal (2017), p. 928; See also Foreign Trade Information System (SICE), Trade Policy Developments, Central America—Dominican Republic—United States (CAFTA), Documents relating to the CAFTA-DR Dispute Settlement.

[14] Informe Final del Grupo Arbitral, *Costa Rica v. El Salvador – Tratamiento Arancelario a Bienes Originarios de Costa Rica*, 18 November 2014 (CAFTA-DR/ARB/2014/CR-ES/17).

[15] Final Report of the Panel, *Guatemala – Issues Relating to the Obligations Under Article 16.2.1 (a) of the CAFTA-DR* (2017).

[16] See *Costa Rica v. El Salvador* para 4.1.(iii).

[17] Of the 5 panel reports on the DSB agenda in 2020, all 5 were appealed into the void. Joost Pauwelyn, (@JoostPauwelyn 31 December 2020) https://twitter.com/JoostPauwelyn/status/1344681024509325320, last accessed 16 February 2021.

[18] Final Report, *Restrictions applied by Ukraine on exports of certain wood products to the European Union*, 11 December 2020.

[19] The MPIA has been notified to the WTO. This arrangement provides for a formal two-step dispute settlement system for the 25 WTO Members that have signed on to date, counting the European Union as a single Member. See WTO website, 'Statement on a mechanism for developing, documenting and sharing practices and procedures in the conduct of WTO disputes,' 30 April 2020, JOB/DSB/1/Add.12. The 20 initial signatories included: Australia; Brazil; Canada; China; Chile; Colombia; Costa Rica; the European Union; Guatemala; Hong Kong, China; Iceland; Mexico; New Zealand; Norway; Pakistan; Singapore; Switzerland; Ukraine and Uruguay. Benin, Ecuador, Nicaragua, Macao and Peru have subsequently joined.

6.2.2 Appeal in Investment Law

Appeal has traditionally been limited to the five grounds provided for under Article 52 of the ICSID Convention including where a tribunal has manifestly exceeded its powers or failed to state the reasons for its award.[20] This section looks at the main rules and procedures of appeal mechanisms in the investment regime, both current and prospective, and how they meet the aims set out by parties pursuing them.

6.2.2.1 Rules and Procedures for Appeal Under the EU's Investment Court System

From 2004, US IIAs began to feature provisions contemplating the establishment of appellate mechanisms. This was in the aftermath of the publication of its 2004 Model BIT.[21] As seen in Chap. 2, provisions contemplating such mechanisms became quite common in PTIAs around this period, but not in BITs, outside of ones concluded by the US.[22]

The first instances of trade and investment agreements providing for the establishment of bilateral appellate mechanisms took place between the EU and its partners following the 2009 ratification of the Lisbon Treaty.[23] The European

---

[20] Article 52.1: (1) Either party may request annulment of the award by an application in writing addressed to the Secretary-General on one or more of the following grounds: (a) that the Tribunal was not properly constituted; (b) that the Tribunal has manifestly exceeded its powers; (c) that there was corruption on the part of a member of the Tribunal; (d) that there has been a serious departure from a fundamental rule of procedure; or (e) that the award has failed to state the reasons on which it is based.

[21] 2004 Model BIT Article 28.10. "If a separate, multilateral agreement enters into force between the Parties that establishes an appellate body for purposes of reviewing awards rendered by tribunals constituted pursuant to international trade or investment arrangements to hear investment disputes, the Parties shall strive to reach an agreement that would have such appellate body review awards rendered under Article 34 in arbitrations commenced after the multilateral agreement enters into force between the Parties."

[22] See e.g. Taiwan- Nicaragua FTA (2006), Guatemala- Peru FTA (2011), Canada- Korea FTA (2014).

[23] The Lisbon Treaty entered into force in 2009 and it was generally understood that this conferred exclusive competence on the EU over foreign direct investment as part of its Common Commercial Policy. Up until this point, the EU had focused on Cooperation and Association Agreements, which aimed to promote investment, but did not provide for core investment protection provisions typical of BITs being concluded by Member States at the time *inter se* as well as with third parties. From 2009, the EU was responsible for investment treaty negotiations, which were carried out as part of larger trade agreements such as the EU-Singapore Free Trade Agreement. Questions over whether the EU had the competence to negotiate ISDS arrangements led to the Commission submitting a request for an opinion on this matter to the CJEU. The request asked whether the Union has the requisite competence to conclude the FTA with Singapore and which provisions fell under the Union's exclusive competence. Opinion 2/15 clarified that portfolio investment and ISDS procedures are a shared competence with the Member States.

Commission put forth its Investment Court System (ICS), partly as a response to criticism of ISDS and at the request of the European Parliament.[24] The right to appeal is a key component of ICS, which aims to replace ISDS thereby improving transparency, accountability, consistency and legitimacy in the system.[25]

The main elements of reform in ICS include the shift to a standing two-tier system with an appeal tribunal operating "on similar principles to the WTO Appellate Body", publicly appointed judges with "high qualifications", precisely defined grounds for investors taking cases, and reaffirming the right to regulate.[26] Versions of ICS to date include a permanent roster of tribunal members[27] who shall possess the necessary qualifications for appointment to judicial office or else be jurists of recognised competence with expertise in PIL.[28]

The EU included ICS in four of its trade and investment agreements signed between 2016 and 2018 including CETA,[29] the EU—Vietnam FTA,[30] the

---

[24] Puccio L. & Harte R, European Parliamentary Research Service, 'From arbitration to the investment court system (ICS) The evolution of CETA rules,' *PE 607.251,* June 2017, pages 1 & 13. The European Commission has proposed an Investment Court System to address "the inadequacies of ISDS including regarding human rights, the rule of law, democracy and national sovereignty." See Speech of Cecilia Malmstrom to Wojciech Sawicki, Secretary General of the Parliamentary Assembly of the Council of Europe (27 March 2017) https://ec.europa.eu/carol/index-iframe.cfm?fuseaction=download&documentId=090166e5b1460763&title=1348033_CM%20Letter%20COE.pdf.

[25] See 'Commission welcomes adoption of negotiating directives for a multilateral investment court,' 20 March 2018 http://trade.ec.europa.eu/doclib/press/index.cfm?id=1819. See also WTO Trade Policy Review of The European Union, 17 May 2017, WT/TPR/G/357/ page 49. ICS marks a move away from ISDS due to a "fundamental and widespread lack of trust" in the system. Blog of EU Commissioner for Trade Cecilia Malmström, 'Proposing an Investment Court System,' 16 September 2015. Available at: https://ec.europa.eu/commission/commissioners/2014-2019/malmstrom/blog/proposing-investment-court-system_en.

[26] See European Commission Press Release, 'Commission proposes new Investment Court System for TTIP and other EU trade and investment negotiations,' Brussels, 16 September 2015. ICS hopes to be a "clear break" from ISDS by processing investment claims in a court rather than through arbitration. European Commission Press release: 'CETA: EU and Canada agree on new approach on investment in trade agreement,' Brussels, 29 February 2016. Available at: http://europa.eu/rapid/press-release_IP-16-399_en.htm.

[27] The number of members of the tribunal of first instance is fixed under CETA, EUSIPA and EUVIPA. The number of members of the Appellate Tribunal is fixed under EUSIPA and EUVIPA, but to be determined under CETA.

[28] CETA Article 8.27.4, which provides that Members "shall have demonstrated expertise in public international law".

[29] See CETA, Section F on the Resolution of investment disputes between investors and states of Chapter 8, DG TRADE website: http://ec.europa.eu/trade/policy/in-focus/ceta/ceta-chapter-by-chapter/. It is noted that CETA was renegotiated in light of controversies surrounding ISDS and ICS was agreed to be incorporated into CETA instead.

[30] See EU-Vietnam Free Trade Agreement, Section 3 on the 'Resolution of Investment Disputes' of Chapter 8: Trade in Services, Investment and E-Commerce, DG TRADE website: http://trade.ec.europa.eu/doclib/press/index.cfm?id=1437.

EU-Singapore Agreement,[31] and the updated EU- Mexico FTA.[32] This section focuses on these appeal mechanisms as these have been concluded and texts for them are available.

Under these appellate mechanisms, the grounds for appeal have been widened to encompass errors in the interpretation or application of the law and manifest errors in the appreciation of facts.[33]

Appeal mechanisms under ICS are largely similar to the WTO's Appellate Body but do contain certain differences. These include the maximum duration of appeals,[34] the number of members of the appeal tribunal,[35] nationality requirements for adjudicators,[36] the appointment of adjudicators,[37] and the ability of the tribunal to complete the analysis rather than refer a matter back to the first instance tribunal.[38]

---

[31] See EU-Singapore Investment Protection Agreement, Article 3 of Chapter 3 on Dispute Settlement, DG TRADE website: http://trade.ec.europa.eu/doclib/press/index.cfm?id=961.

[32] The publicly available version of the Appeal Procedure under Article 30 MEUFTA represents the 'agreement in principle' as of 23 April 2018' See 'New EU-Mexico agreement, The agreement in principle,' DG TRADE website (23 April 2018). Available at: https://trade.ec.europa.eu/doclib/docs/2018/april/tradoc_156791.pdf (last accessed 8 August 2020).

[33] See EUSIPA Article 3.19.1 and EUVIPA Article 3.54.1.

[34] See EUSIPA Article 3.19.4 and EUVIPA Article 3.54.5, which provide that in no case should proceedings exceed 270 days. DSU Article 17.5: "As a general rule, the proceedings shall not exceed 60 days from the date a party to the dispute formally notifies its decision to appeal to the date the Appellate Body circulates its report. In fixing its timetable the Appellate Body shall take into account the provisions of paragraph 9 of Article 4, if relevant. When the Appellate Body considers that it cannot provide its report within 60 days, it shall inform the DSB in writing of the reasons for the delay together with an estimate of the period within which it will submit its report. In no case shall the proceedings exceed 90 days."

[35] The first instance tribunals of CETA, EUSIPA and EUVIPA respectively contain 15, 6 and 9 members. See CETA Article 8.27.2, EUSIPA Article 3.9.2, and EUVIPA Article 3.38.2. The appellate mechanism of CETA contain a yet to be defined number, while EUSIPA and EUVIPA both contain six members. See CETA Article 8.28.7(f), EUSIPA Article 3.10.2, and EUVIPA Article 3.39.2.

[36] The nationality requirements for adjudicators are as follows: under CETA Article 8.27.2, the fifteen tribunal members are made up of five nationals of EU MSs, five Canadian nationals, and five from third countries, while the appellate number and make up of appellate adjudicators is to be determined; under EUSIPA Article 3.9.2, both parties shall nominate two Members to the Tribunal of First Instance (with no reference to nationality), and two Members (who shall not be nationals of either) shall be jointly nominated. Under EUVIPA Article 3.10.2 this arrangement is replicated. Under EUVIPA Article 3.38.2, the nine tribunal members are made up of *up to* three nationals of EU MSs, three Viet Nam nationals, and three from third countries. Under Article 3.39.2 the six Appeal Tribunal members are evenly split among nationals of EU MSs, Viet Nam and third countries.

[37] Adjudicators are appointed as follows: Under CETA Article 8.27, the CETA Joint Committee appoints all fifteen Members of the Tribunal. Under EUSIPA Article 3.9.2 and 3.10.2, Members are directly nominated by the parties, and subsequently appointed by the Committee. Under EUVIPA Article 3.38.2 and 3.39.3, the Committee shall appoint all Members of the Tribunal and Appellate Mechanism.

[38] Under CETA Article 8.28.7(b) the CETA Joint Committee shall promptly take a decision in this regard. Under EUSIPA Article 3.19.3 the Appeal Tribunal shall modify or reverse the legal findings

Under each of the Agreements, the President of the Tribunal appoints three Members to hear each case, one from each party and one of a third country. These members are selected on a rotation basis, ensuring it is random and unpredictable.[39]

6.2.2.2 Rules and Procedures of a Multilateral Investment Court

The EU has been one of the chief proponents of a standing multilateral appellate mechanism.[40] To date, the EU has concluded trade and investment agreements that "anticipate the transition" from ICS to a permanent MIC with Canada, Singapore, Vietnam and Mexico.[41] According to the EU Commission, there is "broad agreement" among numerous governments that ISDS needs reform.[42]

UNCITRAL Working Group III (WGIII) is currently considering the reform of ISDS with a mandate to identify concerns with the current system, consider whether reform is desirable, and to develop solutions to be recommended.[43] The Working

---

and conclusions in the provisional award and refer it back to the Tribunal to revise accordingly. Under EUVIPA Article 3.54.4 "the Appeal Tribunal shall apply its own legal findings and conclusions to such facts and render a final decision. If that's not possible, it shall refer the matter back to the Tribunal." The lack of remand in WTO law has been described as a "design flaw" at the WTO, born of a mixture of civil and common law proposals. Civil law permits review of law and facts without remand, whereas common law permits only review of the law, with remand as a pivotal feature. See Joost Pauwelyn, 'Appeal Without Remand- A Design Flaw in WTO Dispute Settlement and How to Fix it,' ICTSD Dispute Settlement and Legal Aspects of International Trade Issue Paper No. 1 (2007) paras 25–27.

[39] See CETA Article 8.27.6 and 8.27.7; EUSIPA Article 3.9.7 and 3.9.8; and EUVIPA Article 3.38.6 and 3.38.7. Note: It shall be the President and Vice-President of the Tribunal under EUVIPA Article 3.38.8.

[40] See EU Submission to UNCITRAL Working Group III Section 3 and 3.3. 'Appellate Tribunal'. The European Commission received a mandate from the Council of the European Union to open negotiations towards the establishment of a Multilateral Investment Court (MIC) in March 2018. See Council of the European Union- Press Release: Multilateral investment court: Council gives mandate to the Commission to open negotiations, Brussels, 20 March 2018: http://www.consilium. europa.eu/en/press/press-releases/2018/03/20/multilateral-investment-court-council-gives-man date-to-the-commission-to-open-negotiations/.

[41] See DG TRADE website, 'The Multilateral Investment Court project,' last updated 20 March 2018 http://trade.ec.europa.eu/doclib/press/index.cfm?id=1608. The updated EU- Mexico FTA provides for example: "Multilateral Dispute Settlement Mechanisms 1. The Parties should cooperate for the establishment of a multilateral mechanism for the resolution of investment disputes. 2. Upon the entry into force between the Parties of an international agreement providing for such a multilateral mechanism applicable to disputes under this Agreement, the relevant parts of this Section shall be suspended and the Joint Council may adopt a decision specifying any transitional arrangements." Chapter 19, Article 14.

[42] EU Commission Factsheet on the Commission's proposal for a Multilateral Investment Court, available at: http://trade.ec.europa.eu/doclib/docs/2017/september/tradoc_156042.pdf (last accessed 16 February, 2021).

[43] Report of Working Group III. On the work of its thirty-fourth session, para 19, (Vienna, 27 November- 1 December 2017) A/CN.9/930/Rev.1.

Group's January 2020 meeting on ISDS reform was attended by 55 States with observers from 41 others, as well as observers from the European Union.[44] WGIII is the first multilateral discussion on ISDS reform since investor claims under modern Investment Agreements began in the 1990s.

Various models for appellate mechanisms are being discussed at Working Group III. These include: (1) appellate mechanisms that could be applied by treaty parties (similar to ICS), disputing parties on an ad hoc basis, or by an institution;[45] or (2) a permanent multilateral/plurilateral body. It remains unclear whether a MIC would resemble a multilateral version of ICS and whether it will gain significant traction at the multilateral level. Many of the proposals before WGIII replicate the key features of ICS, including commitment to values such as transparency, accountability,[46] consistency[47] and legitimacy in the system,[48] as well as institutional features such as a standing two-tier system, and publicly appointed judges.[49] WGIII has indicated that it aims to avoid the duplication of review proceedings and further fragmentation of investment law.[50]

---

[44] Report of Working Group III (Investor-State Dispute Settlement Reform) on the work of its resumed thirty-eighth session, (Vienna, 20–24 January 2020) A/CN.9/1004/Add.1. The Working Group's February 2021 meeting was attended by 52 States with observers from 33 others, as well as observers from the European Union.

[45] See 'Possible reform of investor-State dispute settlement (ISDS) Appellate mechanism and enforcement issues,', A/CN.9/WG.III/WP. III. 'Options for establishing an appellate mechanism'. To give a little more detail: (1) a treaty specific appellate mechanism as has been implemented in CETA; (2) an ad hoc appellate mechanism following the same pattern as the constitution of first instance tribunals currently; and (3) an institutional appellate mechanism for use by institutions handling ISDS cases, such as ICSID, which would approximate to a permanent mechanism.

[46] Report of Working Group III (Investor-State Dispute Settlement Reform) on the work of its thirty-sixth session (Vienna, 29 October–2 November 2018) A/CN.9/964, Section C.

[47] See Report of Working Group III (Investor-State Dispute Settlement Reform) on the work of its thirty-fifth session (New York, 23–27 April 2018), A/CN.9/935, Section B; Report of Working Group III (Investor-State Dispute Settlement Reform) on the work of its thirty-sixth session (Vienna, 29 October–2 November 2018)A/CN.9/964, Section B.

[48] Report of Working Group III (Investor-State Dispute Settlement Reform) on the work of its thirty-fifth session (New York, 23–27 April 2018) A/CN.9/935 Section D. Perceptions of States, investors and the public.

[49] Report of Working Group III (Investor-State Dispute Settlement Reform) on the work of its resumed thirty-eighth session, Vienna 20-24 January 2020 A/CN.9/1004/Add.1, Section D.

[50] 'Possible reform of investor-State dispute settlement (ISDS) Appellate mechanism and enforcement issues,', A/CN.9/WG.III/WP, para 3.

6.3 Appellate Mechanisms and Engagement

Engagement was defined as encompassing parallels in the practices and features of tribunals[51] and recent attempts at reforming the investment regime are pushing the regimes in this direction. Part B examines parallels in the institutional features of tribunals, which encompass the rules and procedures of the appellate mechanisms of the two regimes. It looks at the similarities between the appeal mechanisms of the trade and investment regimes, whether there is a case for greater similarities between these mechanisms, and the role of PTIAs in creating convergence between the systems.

6.3.1 The Extent and Desirability of Engagement

Appellate mechanisms such as ICS introduce some institutional and procedural features that increase the parallels between the regimes and some that entrench old differences. This section examines a series of convergence factors between the appellate mechanisms of the two regimes before looking at divergence factors.

It looks at these similarities and asks whether there should be convergence between the appellate mechanisms of the regimes. The cross-regime harmonisation of institutional features should only occur where appropriate and with due regard to systemic differences between the regimes.

6.3.1.1 Convergence Factors

The appellate mechanisms of systems such as ICS, or certain proposals relating to a MIC, facilitate engagement in areas including: (1) the creation of a permanent two-tier system; (2) the multilateralisation of proceedings; (3) the profile of adjudicators and their independence from governments; (4) greater predictability and consistency in the jurisprudence; and (5) procedural rules.

6.3.1.2 The Creation of a Permanent Two-Tier System

The EU has recently concluded agreements containing appellate mechanisms in its own trade and investment agreements. Appeal tribunals established under ICS are

---

[51] Engagement between trade and investment law was described in Chap. 1. I as occurring wherever the content of one of the regimes has a parallel in the other or wherever there are cross-regime references in dispute settlement or parallels in the practices and features of dispute settlement.

permanent and the EU has put forth a similar model in UNCITRAL Working Group III talks aimed at the establishment of a standing appellate mechanism.[52]

Various parties at WGIII have proposed a standing multilateral appellate mechanism.[53] Many of the participating states are open to the idea of reformed procedural rules in ISDS and the creation of a two-tier system.[54]

Standing two-tier systems of dispute settlement in the investment regime represent parallels with the institutional features of the trade regime. Despite the fact that the Appellate Body is not currently functioning, the right to appeal has been a longstanding feature of the trade regime and will persist in some form with the introduction of the MPIA.

ICS has been included in the EU's recent agreements with Canada, Vietnam, Singapore and Mexico, while 25 WTO Members are now parties to a multi-party interim appeal arrangement (MPIA), which provides for a formal two-step dispute settlement system. With the MPIA and the EU's Investment Court System, 'regional' appellate mechanisms are now common to the trade and investment regimes. The MPIA is open for other WTO Members to join. These bilateral or multi-party appeal systems as well as ongoing WGIII discussions increase the parallels between the institutional features of the regimes.

There is no systemic reason why appellate mechanisms ought not to be introduced to the investment regime, despite the concerns investors may have about their introduction.[55] The rationale for introducing appeal in the investment regime is the

---

[52] See EU Submission to UNCITRAL Working Group III Section 3 and 3.3. 'Appellate Tribunal'. See EUSIPA Article 3.10. DSU Article 17.1 provides that "A standing Appellate Body shall be established by the DSB".

[53] See A/CN.9/WG.III/WP.159/Add.1, Submission from the European Union and its Member States (Appellate body); A/CN.9/WG.III/WP.161, and A/CN.9/WG.III/WP.198, Submissions from the Government of Morocco (Prior scrutiny of the award and standing appellate mechanism); A/CN.9/WG.III/WP.163, Submission from the Governments of Chile, Israel and Japan (Treaty- specific appellate review mechanism); A/CN.9/WG.III/WP.175, Submission from the Government of Ecuador (Standing review and appellate mechanisms); A/CN.9/WG.III/WP.177, Submission from the Government of China (Stand-alone appellate mechanism); the reform option is also discussed in A/CN.9/WG.III/WP.176, Submission from the Government of South Africa and A/CN.9/WG.III/WP.180, Submission from the Government of Bahrain; A/CN.9/WG.III/WP.188.

[54] Potential models include: (1) a permanent multilateral/ plurilateral body; or (2) appellate mechanisms that could be applied by treaty parties (similar to ICS), disputing parties on an ad hoc basis, or by an institution; To give a little more detail: (1) a treaty specific appellate mechanism as has been implemented in CETA; (2) an ad hoc appellate mechanism following the same pattern as the constitution of first instance tribunals currently; and (3) an institutional appellate mechanism for use by institutions handling ISDS cases, such as ICSID, which would approximate to a permanent mechanism.

[55] The Corporate Counsel International Arbitration Group (CCIAG) finds that both a MIC and appellate mechanisms raise fundamental concerns that cannot be remedied with technical solutions. These include making erroneous decisions permanent and tilting the balance of dispute settlement against investors by eliminating party-appointment. Investor-State Dispute Settlement (ISDS) Reform Submission by the CCIAG to UNCITRAL Working Group III, December 18, 2019, paras 21–26 and 43–45.

need to ensure correctness, consistency and predictability of decisions.[56] Risks, including the making of erroneous decisions permanent, represent points of convergence with the trade regime.[57]

6.3.1.3 The Multilateralisation of Proceedings

One of the main impediments to procedural convergence between the trade and investment law regimes is the vast network of IIAs compared to the traditionally integrated appellate system at the WTO. There were 2654 IIAs in force at the start of 2020.[58] A high percentage of IIAs contain some form of ISDS and their own distinct dispute settlement mechanisms.[59] Despite the large number of IIAs, the content of dispute settlement systems often follows familiar themes. There may be distinctions but also significant similarities in areas such as the composition of tribunals, the following of UNCITRAL, ICSID or other rules, the relationship with other forums etc. A permanent multilateral appellate mechanism could bring dispute settlement to a common forum either as part of a two-tier MIC or at the level of appeal alone (i.e. with decentralised first instance tribunals).[60]

It has been claimed that the differences in ICS models seen to date makes the multilateralisation of ICS "entirely unrealistic".[61] Lenk is of the view that ICS is likely to entrench ISDS on an agreement-by-agreement basis that might impede a multilateral solution.[62] Nonetheless, the EU clearly believes that ICS paves the way for a multilateral investment court in the future and expressly provides for such a possibility in its recent agreements.[63] When the EU makes the case for an appellate mechanism, it may prove useful to be able to point to iterations that are already

---

[56] See Trade Policy Review of the European Union, Minutes Of The Meeting, 6 November 2017, WT/TPR/M/357/Add.1, 107. "The function of the Appeal Tribunal is to correct errors in the interpretation of the law or the appreciation of facts in the provisional decision and in the latter case the Appeal Tribunal may remand the case to the Tribunal of First Instance. The Appeal Tribunal is also designed to perform a consistency check to ensure predictability in the interpretation of the law, a key factor for both investors and states. In this sense an appeal mechanism is seen as enhancing public support for investor-state adjudication. The Investment Court System ensures that overall procedures do not become too lengthy as clear timelines are foreseen and the possibility to appeal is circumscribed to well-grounded cases."

[57] Further associated risks of appellate systems are discussed in points 4 and 5 of this section.

[58] 3,284 IIAs in total minus 349 terminated IIAs, UNCTAD, IIA Issues Note, July 2020, Issue 1, 1.

[59] According to UNCTAD's Investment Policy Hub, 2,441 out of 2575 IIAs contain ISDS (last checked 17 February 2021). See 'International Investment Agreements Navigator': https://investmentpolicy.unctad.org/international-investment-agreements/iia-mapping.

[60] UNCITRAL Working Group III, 'Possible reform of investor-State dispute settlement (ISDS) Appellate mechanism and enforcement issues,' Note by the Secretariat, A/CN.9/WG.III/WP. 18.

[61] Lenk (2020), p. 78.

[62] Ibid 78.

[63] See CETA Article 8.29, EUSIPA Article 3.12, and EUVIPA Article 3.41 on Multilateral Dispute Settlement Mechanisms.

functioning and can be learnt from. As ICS is explicitly based on the WTO's Appellate Body, significant engagement between the procedural principles of the trade and investment regimes would be expected.[64]

The appellate mechanisms that form part of the EU's ICS agreements have contained relatively minor differences to date, as outlined above. These differences tend not to present much of an obstacle to multilateralisation, e.g. variations in the number of adjudicators on rosters. Other areas, such as the manner of the appointment of adjudicators, may be more of an obstacle to multilateral agreement. Even if states were to decide that this or another feature of ICS was an impediment to multilateral agreement, there is nothing to stop the EU and its partners deviating from their previously agreed models.

This development of proceedings taking place in a single multilateral forum would be a parallel between the institutional features of the two regimes. The historically dispersed nature of the investment regime has been one of its defining characteristics and arguably there are few greater limitations on inter-regime engagement.

IIAs are concluded for different purposes and this is reflected in their content. These differences in the substantive content need not be reflected in IIAs' dispute settlement provisions, which makes a focus on procedural reforms a good starting point for WGIII. Should a multilateral appellate mechanism come into being, it would be a significant parallel between the institutional features of the two regimes.

6.3.1.4 The Profile of Adjudicators and Their Independence

The Members of ICS tribunals serve on a quasi-full-time basis.[65] The WTO's Appellate Body has worked on this basis in accordance with DSU Article 17.[66] This is a novel feature for the investment regime and is another parallel in the features of dispute settlement. The EU has replicated this model in its proposal at WGIII.[67] Other Members have raised concerns about the professionalism and

---

[64] See Trade Policy Review of the European Union, Minutes Of The Meeting, 6 November 2017 WT/TPR/M/357/Add.1, 124. DSU Article 17 on Appellate Review details the institutional features and working procedures of the WTO's Appellate Body.

[65] EUSIPA 3.9.15: "Upon a decision by the Committee, the retainer fee and other fees and expenses may be permanently transformed into a regular salary. In such an event, the Members shall serve on a full- time basis and the Committee shall fix their remuneration and related organisational matters. In that event, the Members shall not be permitted to engage in any occupation, whether gainful or not, unless exemption is exceptionally granted by the President of the Tribunal."

[66] DSU Article 17.3 provides that the Appellate Body membership "shall be available at all times and on short notice".

[67] E.g. See A/CN.9/WG.III/WP.159/Add.1, Submission from the European Union and its Member States to UNCITRAL Working Group III (Full-time adjudicators), 18 January 2019, 4.

independence of arbitrators[68] and a draft Code of Conduct for Adjudicators was published by the secretariats of UNCITRAL and ICSID on 1 May 2020.[69]

The independence and impartiality of adjudicators has been at the core of ethics provisions in trade and investment law.[70] Panellists at the WTO are "well-qualified" individuals, who are selected with a view to ensuring the independence of the members.[71] Appellate Body Members comprise persons of recognised authority who are "unaffiliated with any government."[72]

Tribunal members under ICS must be eligible for appointment to the "highest judicial offices".[73] They shall not be affiliated with any government or take instructions from any government with regard to matters related to the dispute.[74] The double-hatting of adjudicators also acting as counsel has raised concerns about their independence and as such has been prohibited under ICS and the draft Code of Conduct for Adjudicators released by the secretariats of UNCITRAL and ICSID.[75]

The traditional backgrounds of adjudicators and the manner of their selection are considered as divergence factors below. This section merely recognises that where

---

[68] E.g. A/CN.9/WG.III/WP.177, Submission from the Government of China (Arbitrators' professionalism and independence are questioned).

[69] See UNCITRAL, Working Documents, Working Groups, Working Group III: ISDS Reform, Code of Conduct. Available at: https://uncitral.un.org/en/codeofconduct (last accessed 17 February 2021).

[70] While this is certainly true at the appellate level (the focus of this section), there may be some divergences from at first instance. For example, WTO Members can object to certain panelists. The tribunal in *Suez et al. v Argentina* summarised the difference between these concepts: "Generally speaking, independence relates to the lack of relations with a party that might influence an arbitrator's decision. Impartiality, on the other hand, concerns the absence of a bias or predisposition toward one of the parties." *Decision on the proposal for the Disqualification of a member of the arbitral tribunal*, 22 Oct. 2007, Suez et al. v Argentina, ICSID Case No. ARB/03/17, para 28.

[71] DSU Article 8.1–8.4.

[72] DSU Article 17.3.

[73] See EUSIPA Article 3.10.4. CETA Article 8.27.4 and EUVIPA 3.38.3 do not contain the word "highest". The requirement that adjudicators are appointed on a full-time basis and are qualified for appointment to the highest judicial offices will lead to a shift in the profile of adjudicators. The CCIAG note that this would reduce the pool of qualified arbitrators. See Submission by the Corporate Counsel International Arbitration Group (CCIAG) to UNCITRAL Working Group III, 18 December 2019, para 31; It has also been noted that this could have implications for the diversity of adjudicators; Bjorklund et al. (2020), p. 440.

[74] See EUSIPA Article 3.11.

[75] For example, EUSIPA Article 3.11 provides: "In addition, [Members of the Tribunals] upon appointment, they shall refrain from acting as counsel, party-appointed expert or party-appointed witness in any pending or new investment protection dispute under this or any other agreement or domestic law." Article 6 of the draft Code of Conduct addresses limits on multiple roles and explains that an appellate mechanism "would probably not permit other simultaneous work but would assume that persons named to it will be full-time employees." Draft Code Of Conduct For Adjudicators in Investor-State Dispute Settlement, para 73.

adjudicators operate on a full-time basis with strong checks on independence and impartiality, this represents a parallel in the features of the regimes.

Investment tribunals composed of adjudicators independent of the parties would be a break from the ISDS system, but if a MIC comes to pass, this would likely be a feature. This would be a significant point of convergence between the procedural features of the regimes. Likewise, appellate mechanisms in investment law are harmonising the requirements for adjudicators in line with those of other international courts.

6.3.1.5 Greater Predictability and Consistency in the Jurisprudence

The institutionalisation of investment decision-making via appellate mechanisms would lead to advances in the predictability and coherence of the investment regime.[76]

The centralised nature of the WTO strengthens the case for "hard consistency" of jurisprudence.[77] In contrast, the decentralised model of decision makers at ICSID gives rise to inconsistency in the jurisprudence.[78] While there is still a case for consistency in investment law, it is "value neutral" without an appeal providing an independent check for legal correctness.[79]

Consistency is a fundamental feature of appellate mechanisms and it can almost be described as their *raison d'être*.[80] WGIII has recognised the legal and economic benefits of consistency in terms of enhancing legal certainty and the predictability of the system.[81] It has noted that consistency should not be to the detriment of the correctness of decisions, and that consistency is not a synonym for accuracy or correctness.[82] Consistency is elusive in the fragmented investment landscape, where different parties with different intentions negotiate treaty terms that are to be interpreted in line with VCLT Article 31.[83] Nonetheless, WGIII finds inconsistency to be a problem where "the same investment treaty standard or same rule of

---

[76]"Institutionalization would lead likely to advances in finality, predictability, and coherence in ISDS decision-making," but advances in correctness is less clear. Langford et al. (2020), p. 182.

[77]Kurtz (2016), p. 248.

[78]See Diel-Gligor (2017), p. 164. This is contrasted with "permanent judicial institutions such as the ICJ or the CJEU".

[79]Kurtz (2016), p. 248. For Kurtz, a limited case can still be made for some level of consistency in the investment regime but not to the extent of the "aggressive" findings of the tribunal in *Saipem v. Bangladesh*. Kurtz (2016), p. 248. In *Saipem*, the tribunal found that it had a duty to adopt solutions established "subject to compelling contrary grounds".*Saipem S.p.A. v. The People's Republic of Bangladesh*, ICSID Case No. ARB/05/7, Award (2009) para 90.

[80]Langford et al. (2020), p. 185.

[81]UNCITRAL, 'Report of Working Group III on the Work of Its Thirty-Fifth Session (New York, 23–27 April 2018) UN Doc A/CN.9/935, para. 24.

[82]Ibid para 22.

[83]Ibid para 27.

customary international law was interpreted differently in the absence of justifiable ground for the distinction."[84]

The EU believes that an appellate mechanism would develop consistency in terms of how investment law situates itself within the wider context of public international law.[85] The introduction of a MIC would be no guarantee of consistency in investment jurisprudence. A MIC would be expected to bring greater consistency to the jurisprudence and the case for consistency would increase with the multilateralisation of procedural rules. However, even at the WTO, there have been periods of flux in certain areas of its jurisprudence. E.g. there have been at least three distinct periods of national treatment jurisprudence at the WTO since 1995.[86] Despite these fluctuations in certain areas, the Appellate Body has brought consistency to a great many areas of WTO jurisprudence and this would likely be replicated in the investment law regime.[87]

6.3.1.6 Procedural Rules

Procedural rules such as those concerning *amicus curiae* submissions, transparency requirements, applicable rules of international law, and conflict of interest provisions for adjudicators all entail parallels in the practices of tribunals. These parallels affect inter-regime engagement. A multilateral appellate mechanism would likely bring a harmonised approach to many of these tribunal practices. Chapter 7 considers engagement in relation to *amicus* submission in terms of current levels and how procedural harmonisation could be between the regimes.

---

[84] Ibid, para 21.

[85] It submitted that an appellate mechanism would be better positioned "to gradually develop a more coherent approach" to the relationship between investment law and WTO law, as well as other domains of international law. "For instance, the WTO Appellate Body has made a number of pronouncements on the relationship of WTO law with other fields of international law, which have been helpful in elaborating the interactions between different fields of law." See Submission of the European Union and its Member States to UNCITRAL Working Group III, 18 January 2019, 10 & 11.

[86] The Appellate Body focused on a competition-based approach to likeness from 1995 to 2000. It then shifted to back to an aims-and-effects test from 2000 to 2009. A further shift came in the aftermath of *EC- Seals* in 2009, where the Appellate Body found that closeness of competition is the "only purpose" of the likeness comparison. The Appellate Body dismissed consideration of regulatory purpose as part of the analysis under GATT Article III.

[87] The level of consistency brought by an appellate mechanism can also be cast as a vice of the system rather than a virtue as explored in Sect. 3 below.

6.3.2 Divergence Factors

There have been significant parallels in the institutional features and procedural rules provided for in some PTIAs, notably those containing ICS. Nonetheless, appellate mechanisms may not overcome certain differences between the regimes, including: (1) fundamental divergences between the regimes in areas such as differences in the standing, remedies and the objectives of the regimes, governing rules, and the integrated nature of the trade regime compared to the dispersed nature of the investment regime; (2) the profile and backgrounds of adjudicators; (3) tribunal selection; and (4) the role of committees.

6.3.2.1 Fundamental Divergences

The addition of an appellate mechanism to dispute settlement under IIAs does not generally affect these overarching differences between the regimes. The exception here is the dispersed nature of the investment regime, and its procedural rules, compared to the integrated WTO system. The ICSID system operates with a large number of arbitrators on the same hierarchical level.[88] A multilateral appellate mechanism could tidy up the procedural divergences among IIAs, and introduce a roster system for adjudicators.

The objectives of the regimes remain the same and this may be seen in the different preambles of BITs compared to PTAs. It is further reflected in the differences in standing and remedies that persist even where trade and investment are brought together in a single agreement (i.e. a PTIA).[89] The differences in standing rights remain under ICS as well as all of the currently proposed appellate mechanisms at WGIII. That is to say that investors have standing under IIAs whereas standing is reserved for states in trade disputes.

In the investment regime, remedies take the form of retrospective damages. At the WTO, remedies take the form of recommendations that inconsistent measures be brought into conformity and temporary suspension of concessions or compensation while the implementation of recommendations is pending.[90]

There are also differences in the rules governing disputes. The rules and procedures of the DSU apply to WTO disputes. Investment disputes are decided under the rules of the ICSID Convention, UNCITRAL Arbitration Rules, or other arbitration institutions and their rules. This has been the case under BITs and it is no different under PTIAs.

---

[88] See Diel-Gligor (2017), p. 164.
[89] See Chap. 1.III.3.
[90] See DSU Article 19 'Panel and Appellate Body Recommendations,' and DSU Article 22 'Compensation and the Suspension of Concessions'. Compensation is also provided for under Article 22 but this is "voluntary" and the "full implementation of a recommendation to bring a measure into conformity with the covered agreements" is preferred.

6.3.2.2   The Profile and Backgrounds of Adjudicators

A significant difference between the regimes is the different backgrounds of adjudicators in the two regimes. Trade officials and lawyers, who often have backgrounds as government officials, have heavily influenced the trade regime, while the role of private parties and lawyers who come from a commercial arbitration background has been more pronounced in investment law.[91]

Although 40% of the Appellate Body Members appointed between 1995 and 2015 have served as ICSID arbitrators, there are only 13 overlaps in appointments of the 396 individuals who were ICSID arbitrators and 251 appointed as WTO panellists.[92]

While 88% of appointed panellists at the WTO had a "substantial government background", 76% had a private sector background at ICSID.[93]

This data represents all IIAs and does not distinguish between BITs and PTIAs. Cases taken under PTIAs make up a mere 10% of all ISDS cases and 6% of cases at ICSID.[94] Of the 674 concluded treaty-based ISDS cases, only 69 of them were taken under PTIAs (10.2%) and the vast majority of these cases were taken under two PTIAs.[95] Of the 69 cases taken under PTIAs, 64 were taken under NAFTA or the CAFTA-DR FTA.[96] These agreements were concluded in 1992 and 2004 respectively. That said, from the 14 cases that have been concluded under PTIAs signed during the 2000s, a total of 31/37 of the arbitrators had a private law background (83.7%).[97] While this difference in backgrounds has been borne out in recent cases

---

[91] See Pauwelyn 2015, p. 761.

[92] Pauwelyn (2015), p. 7.

[93] Pauwelyn (2015), p. 11. It is noted that the number of WTO panelists with a government background was found to be 74% in a concurrent study. See Johannesson and Mavroidis (2015), p. 688.

[94] Of the 514 concluded cases taken at ICSID, only 34 were taken under PTIAs (6.6%). 1 case was taken under both a BIT and PTIA, 34 under PTIAs, 356 under BITs, 88 under contracts, 19 under Treaties with Investment Provisions, and 16 under domestic investment laws. Note: cases taken under both a BIT and a local law were counted as having been taken under BITs. This was based on data available on 4 August 2020, available at https://icsid.worldbank.org/cases/case-database.

[95] Five-hundred and ninety one were taken under BITs or the ECT, and 14 other under instruments. This was compiled with reference to UNCTAD Investment Policy Hub database available at https://investmentpolicy.unctad.org/investment-dispute-settlement/.

[96] Of the remaining five cases, one was taken under the Central America- Panama FTA (2002), Peru- US FTA (2006), Oman- US FTA (2006), Korea- US FTA (2007) and Canada- Peru FTA (2008).

[97] These agreements include: Central America- Panama FTA (2002), CAFTA-DR FTA (2004) Peru- US FTA (2006), Oman- US FTA (2006), Korea- US FTA (2007) and Canada- Peru FTA (2008).While keeping in mind that one may have a background in more than one of the three categories, 14/37 had an academic background, 6/37 had a governmental background. Governmental, private sector and academic backgrounds were defined as follows: (1) Minimum 3 years in government as diplomat, negotiator, bureaucrat, minister etc.; (2) Minimum 3 years of experience with a law firm either before or after the WTO appointment; (3) Tenured or tenure-track academic appointment at a university, i.e. full-time academics.

under PTIAs, this may not be the case under PTIAs such as those based on ICS where the states draw up a permanent roster.

While the rosters for investment adjudicators of agreements such as USMCA, CPTPP and CETA are not yet public, the rosters for trade disputes that would be heard under the state-to-state dispute settlement chapters are available.[98] Based on these lists, the differences in epistemic communities do not seem to be vast. Of the CPTPP Roster, eleven of the fifteen arbitrators have experience in international commercial or investment arbitration.[99] From the CETA list, eight of the fifteen arbitrators have experience in international commercial or investment arbitration.[100] Under USMCA, the US list is "weighted towards people from the field of arbitration".[101]

At the WTO, prospective panellists who come from the parties to the dispute may not be selected. Under ICS, each party nominates one third of the roster members, who may have the nationality of the nominating party.[102] This difference in terms of the exclusion of nationals from panels has been described as an "irreconcilable" difference between the systems.[103] However, Appellate Body Members were selected on the basis of rotation "regardless of their national origin", so perhaps these differences merely reflect the bilateral nature of ICS agreements to date.[104] While the nomination of nationals has persisted under ICS, this likely would not be repeated under a MIC.

---

[98] See USMCA Chapter 31 Dispute Settlement Roster; the CPTPP Roster of Panel Chairs; and the CETA Joint Committee's List of Arbitrators under Chapter 29 (Dispute Settlement) based on Council Decision (EU) 2019/2246 of 19 December 2019 on the position to be taken on behalf of the European Union in the CETA Joint Committee as regards the adoption of the List of Arbitrators pursuant to Article 29.8 of the Agreement.

[99] Five were Members of Investment Tribunals or Annulment Committees: James Bacchus, Christopher Greenwood, Hugo Manuel Perezcano Díaz, and Noe Fernando Nicolás Pierola Castro. Two have served as Counsel in investment proceedings: Valerie Hughes and Joost Pauwelyn. Four have publications related to international commercial or investment arbitration: Hung Cuong Ha, Michael Johannes Hahn, Petros Mavroidis, and Penelope Jane Ridings. See for example Hung Cuong Ha, 'Le droit vietnamien sur l'arbitrage économique et sur la reconnaissance et l'exécution des sentences arbitrales étrangères au Vietnam,' Revue internationale de droit comparé (1997); Hahn (2015), pp. 653–670, and 671–684; Drabek and Mavroidis (2013); Investment Negotiations: Penelope Ridings (2015).

[100] These include Valarie Hughes, Matthew Kronby, Debra Steger, J. Christopher Thomas, Hélène Ruiz Fabri, Daniel Moulis, David Unterhalter, Seung Wha Chang. See Dana McGrath, 'CETA List of Arbitrators – Where are the Women?' Arbitral Women, 28 January 2020.

[101] Simon Lester, 'The USMCA Chapter 31 Dispute Settlement Roster Is Set,' IELP Blog, 3 July 2020.

[102] EUSIPA Article 3.9.2 (Tribunal of First Instance) or Article 3.10.2 (Appeal Tribunal).

[103] Lenk (2020), p. 90.

[104] Rule 6(2) of the Working procedures for appellate review, WT/AB/WP/6 (16 August 2010) (Working Procedures). Article 6 of the 'Multi-Party Interim Appeal Arbitration Arrangement Pursuant to Article 25 of the DSU' (27 March 2020) states that selection will also be done on the basis of Article 17.1 of the DSU and Rule 6(2) of the Working Procedures for Appellate Review, including the principle of rotation.

The EU Submission to WGIII sets out strict requirements for the avoidance of any conflict of interest. Adjudicators shall not have any outside activities and must ensure that there is no risk of conflict of interest that could affect their independence or impartiality.[105] Similar provisions feature in CETA,[106] EUSIPA,[107] as well as the draft Code of Conduct for arbitrators.[108] The conflict of interest provisions are less stringent at the WTO, reflecting the state-to-state nature of dispute settlement.[109]

6.3.2.3 Tribunal Selection

ISDS follows the model of commercial arbitration where tribunal members are selected directly by the parties. Under ICS, the manner of appointment for adjudicators has seen a shift away from this model of party autonomy model. ICS employs a fixed list of tribunal members. There is also a fixed list for WTO panellists, but in practice selections are often made from outside this set list.[110] While ICS replicates the WTO's two-tiered system of dispute settlement, it does not replicate the ad hoc nature of panel selection at the WTO.[111] The WTO Secretariat proposes

---

[105] EU Submission to UNCITRAL Working Group III, Section 3.4 on Full-time adjudicators & 3.5 on Ethical Requirements.

[106] CETA Article 8.30: The Members of the Tribunal shall be independent. They shall not be affiliated with any government. They shall not take instructions from any organisation, or government with regard to matters related to the dispute. They shall not participate in the consideration of any disputes that would create a direct or indirect conflict of interest.

[107] EUSIPA Article 3.11: 1. The Members of the Tribunal and of the Appeal Tribunal shall be chosen from amongst persons whose independence is beyond doubt. They shall not be affiliated with any government, and in particular, shall not take instructions from any government or organisation with regard to matters related to the dispute.

[108] This draft Code of Conduct is a collaboration between the Secretariats of ICSID and UNCITRAL for adjudicators in International Investment Disputes. Article 4 concerns 'Independence and Impartiality': "1. Adjudicators shall at all times be independent and impartial. 2. In particular, adjudicators shall not: (a) Be influenced by self-interest, outside pressure, political considerations, public clamour, loyalty to a party to the proceedings, or fear of criticism; (b) Allow any past or ongoing financial, business, professional, family or social relationships to influence their conduct or judgement; (c) Take action that creates the impression that others are in a position to influence their conduct or judgement; (d) Use their position to advance any personal or private interests; or (e) Directly or indirectly, incur an obligation or accept a benefit that would interfere, or appear to interfere, with the performance of their duties.

[109] DSU Article 8.8.

[110] DSU 8.4 provides for an "indicative list of governmental and non-governmental individuals possessing the qualifications outlined in paragraph 1, from which panelists may be drawn as appropriate". However, those actually selected frequently do not come from the indicative list. See Simon Lester 'The Roster of WTO Panelists vs. Actual WTO Panelists,' IELP Blog, 24 January 2016.

[111] EUSIPA Article 3.9 and 3.10 provide that the Committee shall appoint six Members to the tribunal of first instance and six Members to the Appeal Tribunal. CETA Article 8.27 provides for the appointment of fifteen Members of the Tribunal with the CETA Joint Committee do determine the number of Members of the Appellate Tribunal at a later date (Article 8.28.7).

nominations, which the parties shall not oppose "except for compelling reasons".[112] Under ICS, the parties cannot object to panellists.

At UNCITRAL's WGIII the idea that party autonomy was a fundamental characteristic of ISDS has been questioned.[113] There was consensus that reform of the party appointment system was needed, with some suggesting reform through appointment by an independent body.[114] It has also been suggested that appointments could involve consultations with representatives of investors.[115]

Paulsson views party-appointed arbitrators as being incompatible with impartial dispute resolution and resulting in 'moral hazard'.[116] Party-appointed arbitrators account for over 95% of dissenting opinions in both commercial arbitration and ISDS.[117] For Paulsson, this inevitability proves that unilateral appointments are incompatible with mutual confidence in arbitrators.[118]

Party appointment has its defenders. The CCIAG finds that any form of appellate mechanism that eliminates party autonomy in the selection of arbitrators tilts the balance of dispute settlement against investors.[119] For Brower & Rosenberg, critiques "assume a lack of good faith" from party-appointed arbitrators.[120] They point out that the right to appoint an arbitrator has existed for decades, even centuries and is critical to the investment law system.[121] Furthermore, appointment based on the belief that the arbitrator might share a party's interpretation of a case "neither implies nor necessitates" violation of the duty to remain independent and impartial.[122]

Rosters are not without their problems either. States have at times been "strikingly incapable" of agreeing on actual appointments to closed lists.[123] Kho et al state that

---

[112] DSU Article 8.6.

[113] Report of Working Group III (Investor-State Dispute Settlement Reform) on the work of its thirty-sixth session (Vienna, 29 October–2 November 2018) para 105. One reason for this is that parties have not been involved in the make up of annulment committees.

[114] Report of Working Group III (Investor-State Dispute Settlement Reform) on the work of its thirty-sixth session (Vienna, 29 October–2 November 2018) para 105–106. The key feature of reform was said to be effective dispute resolution through a fair and due process.

[115] Possible reform of investor-State dispute settlement (ISDS): comments by the Kingdom of Bahrain, 31 July 2019, para 42. "However, this begs two immediate questions; First, who would identify and appoint the business organizations? Second, unless there is an obligation on contracting States to follow the recommendations of such organizations, their degree of influence would be limited and of persuasive force only."

[116] Paulsson (2010).

[117] Redfern (2003), p. 223. The UNCTAD ISDS database showed that from 528 concluded cases, dissenting opinions appeared in 102 cases (19.31% of the total). Lazo and Desilvestro (2018), p. 26.

[118] Paulsson (2010), p. 349.

[119] Submission by the Corporate Counsel International Arbitration Group (CCIAG) to UNCITRAL Working Group III, 18 December 2019, 5.

[120] Brower and Rosenberg (2013), p. 1.

[121] Brower and Rosenberg (2013), p. 26.

[122] Ibid 18.

[123] Brower and Rosenberg cite NAFTA and the US- Iran States Claims Tribunal as examples of this in 'The Death of the Two-Headed Nightingale: Why the Paulsson and van den Berg Presumption

any impulse to select panel members "more sympathetic to the interests of the States" must be resisted and find that a roster system entails the risk that states may be defensive in their selection of panel members.[124] It is in the interest of the parties to select a list of arbitrators that reflects an appropriate balance between offensive and defensive interests.

If states wish to pursue a standing appellate mechanism, a fixed list system would likely be a necessary feature. While party appointments have persisted under ICS, this would not need to be replicated at the multilateral level. There may be little demand for reform of unilateral appointments in commercial arbitration,[125] but the sands appear to be shifting in international investment law.

6.3.2.4 The Role of Committees

The Appellate Body determines its own workings procedures in consultation with the Chairman of the DSB and the Director-General.[126] The influence of WTO Members is largely limited to the appointment and re-appointment of AB Members, which has proved to be problematic since 2016.[127] Under ICS, the parties have considerably more influence on tribunals via committees overseeing the implementation of these agreements. It is unclear whether the rules governing a potential MIC would be an adapted version of the WTO system or an enlarged version of the committee system operating under ICS. One such committee is established under Article 4.1 EUSIPA ('Committee'). It is co-chaired by the Singapore Minister for Trade and Industry and the Member of the EU Commission responsible for Trade. This Committee has a role in appointing and renewing Tribunal Members, similar to that of WTO Members in relation to AB Members. The EUSIPA Committee also has the power to increase or decrease the number of Members on the Tribunals.[128] It sets the retainer fee or salary of Members and can remove a Member from either of the Tribunals upon a reasonable recommendation from the Tribunal President.[129]

The Committee may adopt binding interpretations of provisions of the Agreement from a specific date.[130] Interpretations of the WTO Agreement can be made under

---

that Party-Appointed Arbitrators are Untrustworthy is Wrongheaded,' *Arbitration International*, Vol. 29, No. 1 LCIA (2013), p. 12.

[124] Kho et al. (2017), pp. 326–345, 344.

[125] Alexis Mourre, 'Are unilateral appointments defensible? On Jan Paulsson's Moral Hazard in International Arbitration,' Kluwer Arbitration Blog, 5 October 2010.

[126] DSU Article 17.9.

[127] See Financial Times 'WTO to suffer heavy blow as US stymies appeals body,' 8 December 2019. The Appellate Body has been defunct since 11 December 2019. See also, Inside US Trade, 'U.S. Slammed At DSB For Blocking Korean Appellate Body Reappointment,' May 23, 2016.

[128] EUSIPA Article 3.9.3 and Article 3.10.3.

[129] See EUSIPA Article 3.9.15 and Article 3.11.5.

[130] EUSIPA Article 3.13.3.

Article IX:2 of the Marrakesh Agreement on 'Decision-Making'.[131] Interpretations require a three-fourths majority and contain no specification that they their application can be 'from a specific date'. This apparent power of the Committee to issue an interpretation retrospectively is a significant divergence from practices at the WTO. Of course, in the context of a bilateral agreement, interpretations would have to be shared by both parties. There would be little incentive for the home state of an investor to agree to an interpretation that would be applied retrospectively to harm one of its investors.

6.3.2.5 Learning from the AB Experience

The tentative conclusions drawn in the last section are now examined in light of the recent Appellate Body experience. As ICS is based on the WTO's Appellate Body, the international community must take into account the current institutional dysfunction at the WTO and the features of the AB that have led to this situation.

Despite not tabling reform proposals, US blocking of the (re-)appointment of Appellate Body Members culminated in the system's paralysis in 2019.[132] The USTR's 2020 Report outlined detailed criticism of the AB's practices, claiming that the AB "chronically violates the rules imposed by WTO Members".[133] The allegation that the AB has caused the failure of the WTO's rule-making functions has been described as a "gross exaggeration."[134]

---

[131] Article IX: 2. The Ministerial Conference and the General Council shall have the exclusive authority to adopt interpretations of this Agreement and of the Multilateral Trade Agreements. In the case of an interpretation of a Multilateral Trade Agreement in Annex 1, they shall exercise their authority on the basis of a recommendation by the Council overseeing the functioning of that Agreement. The decision to adopt an interpretation shall be taken by a three-fourths majority of the Members. This paragraph shall not be used in a manner that would undermine the amendment provisions in Article X.

[132] On this lack of reform proposals, see Jennifer Hillman, 'Three Approaches to Fixing the World Trade Organization's Appellate Body: The Good, the Bad and the Ugly? Institute of International Economic Law, Georgetown University Law Center, p. 4. "The U.S. Ambassador to the WTO, Dennis Shea, recently stated that there is nothing to negotiate or change with respect to the WTO Appellate Body, since all the US wants is for the Appellate Body to apply the rules as they were written when the WTO was created in 1995. Alternatively, Ambassador Shea has said that the US concerns are those that have been articulated at recent meetings of the WTO's Dispute Settlement Body."

[133] United States Trade Representative, 'Report On The Appellate Body Of The World Trade Organization,' February 2020. Available at: https://ustr.gov/sites/default/files/Report_on_the_Appellate_Body_of_the_World_Trade_Organization.pdf.

[134] See Bronckers (2020), p. 232.

In its Report on the Appellate Body, the USTR outlines a number of criticisms of the AB that fall into two categories: (1) criticisms concerning violations of procedural rules; and (2) interpretative errors.[135]

In relation to interpretative errors, these include interpretations of the term 'public body', prohibition on the use of 'zeroing', tests to address subsidies by SOEs, and other interpretations that would not apply to investment appeal tribunals.[136] While an investment appeal tribunal would not face these questions, it would face other contentious issues with the potential to split members. If some form of multi-party appeal tribunal or MIC emerges, guidance would have to be given to adjudicators on the most contentious issues that would be sufficiently clear to avoid even one of its members becoming dissatisfied with the system, blocking appointments, and bringing about its paralysis.

The violations of procedural rules outlined by the USTR include issuing binding precedent, not respecting the mandatory 90-day deadline for issuing reports (Article 17.5 DSU), and AB Members finalising cases after their terms have ended (17.2), *inter alia*.[137]

Appeal mechanisms under ICS replicate some features of the WTO's Appellate Body[138] including the setting of a maximum duration of appeals, which in no case should exceed 270 days.[139] This is significantly longer than the 90-day limit set out in DSU Article 17.5 and may go a long way in addressing concerns about tribunals exceeding their deadlines.

Controversy surrounding the finalising of cases after an adjudicator's term has ended can be avoided by the parties agreeing this in advance. EUSIPA Article 3.5

---

[135] United States Trade Representative, 'Report On The Appellate Body Of The World Trade Organization,' February 2020. Available at: https://ustr.gov/sites/default/files/Report_on_the_Appellate_Body_of_the_World_Trade_Organization.pdf.

[136] United States Trade Representative, 'Report On The Appellate Body Of The World Trade Organization,' February 2020, Sections III.A, C and D.

[137] The other alleged violations include: reviewing Panel findings of fact (in violation of DSU Article 17.6); rendering advisory opinions (3.7); failing to make the necessary recommendations in certain instances; opining on matters within the authority of other WTO bodies; and deeming decisions not made under Article IX:2 of the WTO Agreement to be authoritative interpretations. United States Trade Representative, 'Report On The Appellate Body Of The World Trade Organization,' February 2020, Sections II.A, B and E.

[138] Other shared features are outlined in Section B.I. Many of the proposals before UNCITRAL's WGIII replicate the key features of ICS, including commitment to values such as transparency, accountability, consistency and legitimacy in the system, as well as institutional features such as a standing two-tier system, and publicly appointed judges.

[139] See EUSIPA Article 3.19.4 and EUVIPA Article 3.54.5, which provide that in no case should proceedings exceed 270 days. DSU Article 17.5: "As a general rule, the proceedings shall not exceed 60 days from the date a party to the dispute formally notifies its decision to appeal to the date the Appellate Body circulates its report. In fixing its timetable the Appellate Body shall take into account the provisions of paragraph 9 of Article 4, if relevant. When the Appellate Body considers that it cannot provide its report within 60 days, it shall inform the DSB in writing of the reasons for the delay together with an estimate of the period within which it will submit its report. In no case shall the proceedings exceed 90 days."

provides: "A person who is serving on a division of the Tribunal when his or her term expires may, with the authorisation of the President of the Tribunal, continue to serve on the division until the closure of the proceedings of that division and shall, for that purpose only, be deemed to continue to be a Member of the Tribunal."

The question of precedent is trickier; appellate mechanisms bring consistency but problems can arise where a stakeholder fundamentally disagrees with a line of jurisprudence that emerges.[140] In the investment context, the CCIAG believes that an appellate mechanism risks making erroneous decisions permanent and one bad decision could do "irreparable harm to the system".[141]

While predictability of the law is key for all parties, any plurilateral or multilateral appellate mechanism would have to be cautious in introducing consistency to the interpretation of similar concepts under different agreements. Given the fact that a multilateral appeal mechanism would likely be interpreting multiple IIAs, in such a scenario it would have to employ a soft doctrine of precedent rather than *stare decisis* or binding precedent.

The Appellate Body found in *US- Stainless Steel* that "absent cogent reasons, an adjudicatory body will resolve the same legal question in the same way".[142] The US objected to what it saw as the development of precedent rather than approaches based on persuasiveness and labelled the AB's approach "profoundly flawed".[143] Bacchus and Lester view the difference between these two approaches to be "one mainly of semantics".[144] They emphasise that this is a mere restatement of the previous view that it is 'appropriate and expected' to rely on rulings in previous disputes and that reasons would hardly suffice if they were *not* cogent.[145]

Despite some of the interpretative problems that have arisen at the WTO, appeals ensure the correctness, consistency and predictability of decisions. Risks, such as embedding erroneous decisions, represent a point of convergence between the regimes.[146]

While ICS operates "on similar principles to the WTO Appellate Body", designers of appellate mechanisms in the investment regime should be wary of the fundamental differences between the regimes.[147] Differences in standing, remedies and the objectives of the regimes do not stand in the way of appellate mechanisms

---

[140] "Institutionalization would lead likely to advances in finality, predictability, and coherence in ISDS decision-making," but advances in correctness is less clear. Langford et al. (2020), p. 182.

[141] Investor-State Dispute Settlement (ISDS) Reform Submission by the Corporate Counsel International Arbitration Group (CCIAG) to UNCITRAL Working Group III, December 18, 2019, paras 46-51.

[142] *US- Final Anti-Dumping Measures on Stainless Steel from Mexico*, WT/DS344/ AB/R, para. 160 (20 May 2008).

[143] Statements by the United States at the Meeting of the WTO Dispute Settlement Body, 21.

[144] Bacchus and Lester (2020), p. 194.

[145] Bacchus and Lester (2020), p. 192.

[146] Further associated risks of appellate systems are discussed in points 4 and 5 of this section.

[147] See e.g. European Commission Press Release, 'Commission proposes new Investment Court System for TTIP and other EU trade and investment negotiations,' Brussels, 16 September 2015.

being introduced in the investment regime, but they must inform the lessons that
should be taken from the trade regime.

6.3.3   The Role of PTIAs

6.3.3.1   How PTIAs Facilitate Engagement

The levels of convergence in the areas of dispute settlement between the trade and
investment chapters of PTIAs is lower than some would expect.[148] Of course an
integrated dispute settlement system under PTIAs would involve a fundamental
reimagining of ISDS, which Kurtz describes as facing "serious hurdles" in mustering
state support.[149] Under PTIAs, dispute settlement remains state-to-state for trade
disputes and ISDS is the norm for investment disputes. Although PTIAs have not
brought about a unified system of dispute settlement, this does not mean they do not
lead to increased engagement between dispute settlement in the two regimes.
Engagement in this area encompasses parallels in the practices and features of
dispute settlement and these may be significantly heightened even where the
DSMs remain separate. Appellate mechanisms that have been agreed as part of
PTIAs are a clear example of this.

This section examines four areas Gáspar-Szilágyi and Usynin identify where
convergence *could* occur in dispute settlement because of PTIAs. These include:
(1) structural convergence; (2) epistemic convergence; (3) convergence via borrowing; and (4) convergence in the interpretations of committees. Each of these four
factors is relevant in terms of the operation of the appellate mechanisms of the
regimes.

At the structural level, Gáspar-Szilágyi and Usynin emphasise that not all countries conclude PTIAs and so structural convergence because of PTIAs will happen
on a "region- or country-specific scale".[150] They note that dispute settlement under
PTIAs could be handled by the same, state-to-state dispute settlement mechanisms,
but that this has not been the case.[151]

---

[148] See Gáspar-Szilágyi and Usynin, "[O]ne would have expected that any disputes- be they trade or
investment related- arising under these 'hybrid' agreements would be handled by the same, state-to-
state dispute settlement mechanism." This has not been the case. Gáspar-Szilágyi and Usynin
(2020), p. 42.

[149] Kurtz envisages a new multinational architecture that could be designed to cover the entire
subject matter of a given FTA and finds that this could improve systemic coherence in IEL. The vast
majority of DSMs in FTAs do not include an appellate stage. Kurtz (2016), pp. 260–261.

[150] Gáspar-Szilágyi and Usynin (2020), p. 42. The authors further state that "One cannot talk about a
global pattern of including investment chapters into PTAs." (page 40).

[151] Ibid, 42. However, just because PTIAs have not led to complete convergence does not tell us
whether they increase engagement.

While appellate mechanisms bring about structural convergence between the regimes, it is difficult to say whether PTIAs lead to the inclusion of appellate mechanisms in agreements. Chapter 2 found that PTIAs tend to provide for, or at least contemplate, such mechanisms more frequently than BITs.[152] It may also be more likely that appellate mechanisms are included in the context of PTIA negotiations than in standalone investment agreements. E.g. if the wider context of the TTIP negotiations had been removed, it is unlikely that there would have been any EU-US negotiations on the establishment of an appellate mechanism for investment disputes.

Gáspar-Szilágyi and Usynin conclude that there are "striking differences" between the epistemic communities of the regimes, which explain impeded convergence and the lack of cross-fertilisation between the two fields.[153] They note the differences in requirements to be an arbitrator under the DSMs of the trade and investment chapters of the EU's recent PTIAs. While arbitrators of trade disputes merely require knowledge of trade law, it is specified that arbitrators of investment disputes shall have knowledge of public international law, trade law and investment law.[154] These requirements are not identical, but neither are they poles apart. As seen in Section B.2, the differences in epistemic communities do not seem to be vast based on the rosters for trade disputes of agreements such as CPTPP, USMCA and CETA.

Appellate mechanisms in investment law are harmonising the profile of adjudicators in a way that is consciously reminiscent of other international courts. ICS and a potential MIC aim to shift away from the party-appointment model towards full-time adjudicators via roster.[155] These shifts in the 'epistemic communities' have a significant harmonising effect between the regimes.

In terms of cross-regime borrowing, Gáspar-Szilágyi and Usynin emphasise the jurisdictional limitations of investment tribunals. They may only handle disputes arising under the investment chapter and will not interpret standards from the rest of

---

[152] 19/60 PTIAs provided for the establishment of appellate mechanisms compared to 0/60 BITs.

[153] Gáspar-Szilágyi and Usynin (2020), p. 47.

[154] Compare for example, EUSIPA Article 3.9.4 and EU- Singapore FTA Article 14.20.4: EUSIPA Article 3.9.4: "The Appeal Tribunal Members shall possess the qualifications required in their respective countries for appointment to the highest judicial offices, or be jurists of recognised competence. They shall have specialised knowledge of, or expertise in, public international law. It is desirable that they have expertise, in particular, in international investment law, international trade law, or the resolution of disputes arising under international investment or international trade agreements."

EU- Singapore FTA Article 14.20.4: "Arbitrators shall have specialised knowledge of or experience in law and international trade or in the settlement of disputes arising under international trade agreements. They shall be independent, shall serve in their individual capacities, shall not be affiliated with the government of either Party, and shall comply with Annex 14-B."

[155] The CCIAG note that this would reduce the pool of qualified arbitrators and it is also noted that this could have implications for the diversity of adjudicators. See Submission by the Corporate Counsel International Arbitration Group (CCIAG) to UNCITRAL Working Group III, 18 December 2019, para 31; Bjorklund et al. (2020), p. 440.

the agreement.[156] They acknowledge that tribunals may take the overall purpose of the treaty into account and may be influenced by the 'broader treaty context'.[157] In contrast, tribunals for trade disputes are often charged with interpreting the entire agreement. The authors point out that this could lead to a state initiating a claim including both trade and investment provisions.[158] While this may be a possibility, convergence in this area is likely to be hampered by the rare usage of state-to-state disputes under PTIAs and the jurisdictional limitations of investment tribunals.[159]

Concerning the last point on the interpretations of committees, (e.g. the power to issue binding interpretations) Gáspar-Szilágyi and Usynin see the role of committees as a potential source of convergence. While binding interpretations of committees are rare, they conclude that this may lead to some convergence between the regimes.[160] Where the same committee is responsible for investment, they argue that this "might lead to more coherence and convergence in the implementation and interpretation of these rules".[161]

PTIAs likely have others impacts upon the convergence and divergence factors outlined in Section B.I. PTIAs may lead to the creation of permanent two-tier systems at a greater rate than would occur in standalone investment agreements. This has a significant impact upon engagement and may in turn have a multilateralising effect. The impact of a recent CJEU Opinion on the conclusion of PTIAs is now examined.

6.3.3.2   Will Opinion 2/15 Weaken Inter-Regime Engagement?

On 16 May 2017, the CJEU found that provisions of the EU-Singapore Free Trade Agreement concerning investment protection and ISDS were shared competences between the European Union and its Member States.[162] In response to Opinion 2/15, the Agreement was split in two, separating trade and investment with the Investment Protection Agreement needing to be ratified by the Member States in line with their national procedures.In June 2017, the European Parliament adopted an amendment to the modernisation of the EU-Chile Association Agreement which proposed: "to

---

[156] Gáspar-Szilágyi and Usynin (2020), p. 49.

[157] Ibid, 53. This point is addressed in detail in Chap. 5.

[158] Ibid, 51. E.g. a home state could plead a breach of anti-discrimination provisions under both the trade and investment chapters of a PTIA.

[159] Ibid, 51.

[160] Ibid, 47.

[161] Ibid, 48.

[162] See Opinion Procedure 2/15, European Court of Justice (Full Court), 16 May 2017. Other areas found to be shared competences included: "the provisions of Chapters 1 (Objectives and General Definitions), 14 (Transparency), 15 (Dispute Settlement between the Parties), 16 (Mediation Mechanism) and 17 (Institutional, General and Final Provisions) of that agreement, in so far as those provisions relate to the provisions of Chapter 9 and to the extent that the latter fall within a competence shared between the European Union and the Member States."

negotiate with Chile two separate agreements clearly distinguishing between a trade and investment agreement only containing issues under EU exclusive competence and a second agreement including the subjects for which the competences are shared, as deducible from the opinion of the Court of Justice on the EU-Singapore FTA (. . .)".[163]

It was confirmed in the European Council's conclusions of May 2018 that the structure of EU Trade Agreements had been reconsidered and that trade and investment would henceforth be negotiated separately.[164] The EU Council also confirmed in its conclusions of May 2018 that it is for "the Council to decide, on a case-by-case basis, on the splitting of trade agreements".[165] Investment has been noticeably absent in more recent Agreements including the EU-Japan EPA. Investment is also absent from the scope of the negotiations launched with Australia and New Zealand. The Council has noted that this "should not set a precedent for the future".[166] While the EU has not launched negotiations for investment agreements in parallel to trade negotiations with these countries, it has been active at UNCITRAL WGIII.

Opinion 2/15 could thus lead to the negotiation of two separate agreements and so enable the Union to proceed with or without the agreement of national parliaments and others. Having a separate agreement that lies exclusively within EU competence would take the power out of the hands of national and regional parliaments to filibuster wider agreements. This could lead to the sidelining of investment in EU trade agreements. It could also potentially make it easier to ratify an investment chapter with ISDS provisions. If the power of the veto is diminished, assemblies may be less likely to use it, particularly where such provisions are included in a host of other agreements that have already been ratified.

Trade negotiations have proven to be lengthy and complicated for the EU in recent years.[167] While it may seem negotiating "several issues at once" would save

---

[163] European Parliament, Committee on International Trade, 2017/2057(INI) Amendment 33, Daniel Caspary, Gabriel Mato, 22 June, 2017.

[164] The Conclusions noted the Commission's intention to recommend negotiating directives for FTAs covering "exclusive EU competence on the one hand and separate mixed investment agreements on the other". See European Council Conclusions adopted on 22 May 2018 'New approach on negotiating and concluding EU trade agreements adopted by Council,' page 3, available on EU Council website, at: https://www.consilium.europa.eu/en/press/press-releases/2018/05/22/new-approach-on-negotiating-and-concluding-eu-trade-agreements-adopted-by-council/.
Mixed Agreements require the approval of the European Parliament, European Council, national parliaments as well as the approval of the regional parliaments of Belgium. Agreements that fall exclusively under EU competence merely require the approval of the European Parliament and the Council. See European Parliament Briefing, 'Ratification of international agreements by EU Member States,' November 2016. Available at: http://www.europarl.europa.eu/RegData/etudes/BRIE/2016/593513/EPRS_BRI(2016)593513_EN.pdf.

[165] Ibid footnote 13, European Council Conclusions adopted on 22 May 2018, page 3.

[166] Ibid, European Council Conclusions adopted on 22 May 2018, page 3.

[167] The Council agreed the mandate for negotiating CETA in 2009, a deal was agreed in principle in 2013, and the Agreement came into force provisionally in 2017. See Statement by the President of

time, this has not proved to be the case because of the backlash against some of the chapters of CETA, namely the investment chapter and ISDS.[168] Much of the delays in ratifying CETA have related to the investment chapter and EU trade policy could be made simpler and more efficient as a result of Opinion 2/15 separating the joint negotiation of trade and investment.[169] The removal of ICS from negotiations could affect the balance of future agreements. Removing a major element of any agreement affects bargaining dynamics and cross-issue linkages.[170] The separation of trade and investment in EU agreements could also make it more difficult to conclude standalone investment agreements because: (1) the wider context of a PTIA is removed; and (2) the ratification process.[171] The European Council noted in its Conclusions of 22 May 2018 that this separation "should not lead to a loss of negotiation leverage for. . .ambitious standalone investment agreements."[172] Despite the Council's optimism, ICS may be more difficult to pursue outside of the context of wider EU Trade Agreements.[173] The European Council found that EU investment agreements should "in principle be negotiated in parallel to FTAs" although this has not been the case for negotiations initiated with Australia and New Zealand.[174] Gáspar-Szilágyi notes that it is fairly likely a second agreement would be concluded

---

the European Commission, José Manuel Durão Barroso following his meeting with the Prime Minister of Canada, Stephen Harper, 18 October 2013. Available at: http://europa.eu/rapid/press-release_SPEECH-13-817_en.html.

[168] Szilárd Gáspár-Szilágyi, 'Opinion 2/15: Maybe It Is Time For The EU To Conclude Separate Trade And Investment Agreements,' European Law Blog, 20 June 2017. Available at: https://europeanlawblog.eu/2017/06/20/opinion-215-maybe-it-is-time-for-the-eu-to-conclude-separate-trade-and-investment-agreements/.

[169] Indeed, removing investment from the scope of the EU-Japan Economic Partnership Agreement led to a shorter delay between the conclusion of negotiations (8 December 2017) and the Agreement entering into force (1 February 2019). See European Commission website, 'EU-Japan Economic Partnership Agreement in focus'. Available at: http://ec.europa.eu/trade/policy/in-focus/eu-japan-economic-partnership-agreement/.

[170] Where dealing with a partner who is not receptive to ICS, its removal from negotiations will simplify proceedings for EU negotiators. It may also give EU negotiators more leverage in trade negotiations to push other potential offensive interests such as Geographical Indications, public procurement etc.

[171] Ratifying standalone investment agreements would be no easier than negotiating them. While the trade elements of these agreements are an exclusive EU competence, Opinion 2/15 found ISDS provisions (such as those found in ICS) to be a shared competence with the Member States. As such, ratifying standalone investment agreements would require the approval of the European Parliament, European Council, national parliaments, as well as the approval of the eight regional parliaments of Belgium including the Walloon parliament, which proved to be a sticking point in the final stages of approving CETA. As such, concluding these investment agreements could prove to be a lengthy and complicated process.

[172] Ibid, European Council Conclusions adopted on 22 May 2018, page 3.

[173] The example of the wider context of the TTIP negotiations seems informative once more; had this been removed, it is unlikely that there would have been any EU-US negotiations on the establishment of an appellate mechanism for investment disputes.

[174] Ibid, European Council Conclusions adopted on 22 May 2018, page 3.

given the EU's "negotiating power and clout".[175] It is hard to see this negotiating clout in bilateral talks being sufficient to convince a reluctant state to agree to ICS as a standalone agreement, short of it being linked to a larger (trade) agreement. The EU could link the conclusion of trade negotiations with investment negotiations taking place in parallel, accepting that the ratification of the agreements would then proceed differently. This option may become more appealing if standalone investment agreements prove difficult to conclude.

The separation of trade and investment could have a negative impact upon engagement in several ways. Firstly, this will likely be the case if it is accepted that PTIAs tend to accelerate engagement between the trade and investment law regimes. PTIAs were found to be vehicles for accelerated engagement between the trade and investment law regimes in Chap. 2. This was found to be the case in particular in relation to dispute settlement and provisions providing for host state flexibilities.[176] If this is the case, the new EU strategy of negotiating trade-only agreements such as the EU- Japan EPA may lessen engagement between the trade and investment law regimes. There is a significant possibility however that levels of engagement present in the investment chapters of EU Agreements would remain high for standalone EU investment agreements. It is likely that the provisions used in previous Agreements would be used again in an investment only agreement, even without the larger context of the negotiation of a PTIA. For example, it seems unlikely that provisions evidencing engagement such as those that refer to the applicability of rules of international economic law and the suitability of arbitrators with knowledge of international trade law will be revised to exclude these criteria in the future.[177] Similarly, it is unlikely that provisions that minimise conflict between the regimes or provisions that harmonise procedural rules between the regimes would be revised in a manner to diminish inter-regime engagement.

Even if this proves to be the case, the overall direction of EU economic policy may be to move in a direction that is less facilitative of engagement between the two regimes than it would have been without this separation. Opinion 2/15 may have a subtle impact on the other factors impacting upon engagement such as who will negotiate and adjudicate standalone investment agreements in the future. It remains

---

[175] Szilárd Gáspár-Szilágyi, 'Opinion 2/15: Maybe It Is Time For The EU To Conclude Separate Trade And Investment Agreements,' European Law Blog, 20 June 2017. Available at: https://europeanlawblog.eu/2017/06/20/opinion-215-maybe-it-is-time-for-the-eu-to-conclude-separate-trade-and-investment-agreements/.

[176] Chapter 2 coded for 24 provisions across 60 PTIAs and 60 BITs signed during the 2005–2019 period. These provisions were placed into the categories of: (1) Host State Flexibility; (2) Dispute Settlement; and (3) Substantive Provisions, which were found to increase engagement by 128%, 103% and 9% respectively for the period and agreements in question.

[177] See for example, CETA Article 8.27.4: 'The Members of the Tribunal shall possess the qualifications required in their respective countries for appointment to judicial office, or be jurists of recognised competence. They shall have demonstrated expertise in public international law. It is desirable that they have expertise in particular, in international investment law, in international trade law and the resolution of disputes arising under international investment or international trade agreements.'

to be seen whether the levels of engagement in the EU's standalone investment agreements will match those of the four PTIAs the EU concluded between 2016-18 and before Opinion 2/15.

Secondly, there will likely be a negative impact upon engagement if the EU's ICS fails to get significant traction at either the bilateral or multilateral level. The separation of ICS from the wider context of EU trade agreements could undermine the potential for inter-regime engagement represented by its previous PTIAs such as CETA, which included investment chapters with an appellate mechanism.

While there may be difficulties negotiating and ratifying standalone investment agreements, these potential negative effects upon engagement could be mitigated by a MIC, a successful multi-party appeal system, or the progress of ICS in bilateral agreements. It is possible that the separation of trade and investment in agreements could have a positive effect on engagement between the two regimes. This could happen if the separation accelerated the creation of a MIC or multi-party appeal system. If a critical mass of states were to buy in to the creation of a MIC, this would be very likely to increase engagement between the trade and investment law regimes.[178]

Opinion 2/15 appears to signal the end of the negotiation of PTIAs at the EU level. This represents a blow for those who view PTIAs as instruments for convergence. The impact of Opinion 2/15 will be felt in both regimes and will be determined by factors such as the EU's ability to conclude standalone investment agreements, the weight given to investment as part of its Common Commercial Policy, and a potential new preference for concluding trade agreements in a simpler, more efficient way.

The EU's proposed Investment Court System is a possible engine for driving engagement in the post-PTIA era. A recent EU report declared that ISDS is not acceptable and "For the EU, ISDS is dead".[179] These reports appear to be greatly exaggerated. Japan and Canada, the EU's partners in two of its recent flagship agreements, have signed up to CPTPP, which contains ISDS. It would seem that not everyone is converted to ICS and that agreements containing ISDS like CPTPP represent a counterforce to the emergence of ICS. CPTPP at least provides for a potential future appellate mechanism.[180] If states pursue a multilateral or multi-party

---

[178] A MIC would have a sizeable impact upon engagement in the area of dispute settlement. In relation to other areas, such as host state flexibilities and substantive provisions providing investment protection, the level of engagement would depend on the treaty provisions agreed by the parties in separate agreements that provide for the possibility of sending disputes to the MIC.

[179] EU Commission Factsheet on A new EU trade agreement with Japan, 1 July 2017: available at http://trade.ec.europa.eu/doclib/docs/2017/july/tradoc_155684.pdf   (last   accessed 17 November 2017)

[180] The US favours the traditional ISDS system, which was included in the Trans Pacific Partnership. CPTPP entered force on 30 December 2018 despite the Trump Administration withdrawing from the Agreement in 2017. Despite US withdrawal, the final TPP Agreement still included ISDS in the final Agreement, underlining the importance of being at the table when standards are being set among strategic partners. The inclusion of clauses such as this in agreements such as TPP demonstrates that US do not reject the central ideas underpinning the MIC.

appellate mechanism, this will likely share several features with ICS including two-tiers, full-time independent adjudicators with similar profiles, certain procedural rules, and the aspiration to be multilateral and to have consistency in their jurisprudence.

Where the dispute settlement mechanisms of the trade and investment law regimes share similar procedural and institutional features, this represents a harmonisation of the institutional features with the trade regime. Systemic differences between the features of the regimes would likely remain in the governing rules, remedies available, and rights of standing, inter alia, before these appellate mechanisms.

Broude asks whether the international community should "ambitiously reconceive (for lack of a better word) the two fields as one"? Engagement between the regimes has been piecemeal and unplanned, lacking a unifying logic"[181] and this may remain the case unless initiatives such as the Investment Court System can bring greater coherence and consistency to investment law jurisprudence. As appellate mechanisms emerge in the investment regime, the procedural features and requirements of the regimes approximate. The impact upon engagement of the reforms brought about in ICS and elsewhere should not be underestimated.

References

Bacchus J, Lester S (2020) The rule of precedent and the role of the appellate body. J World Trade 54(2):194

Bjorklund et al (eds) (2020) The diversity deficit in International Investment Arbitration. J World Invest Trade 21:440

Bronckers M (2020) Trade conflicts: whither the WTO? Legal Iss Econ Integr 47(3):232

Broude T (2011) Investment and trade: the "Lottie And Lis" of International Economic Law? Int Law Forum Hebrew Univ Jerusalem Law:12

Brower, Rosenberg (2013) The death of the two-headed nightingale: why the Paulsson—van den Berg presumption that party-appointed arbitrators are untrustworthy is wrongheaded. Arbitr Int 29(1):1. LCIA

Cook G (2015) A digest of WTO jurisprudence on public international law concepts and principles. Cambridge University Press, Cambridge, pp 121–152

Diel-Gligor K (2017) Towards consistency in international investment jurisprudence: a preliminary ruling system for ICSID arbitration. Brill Nijhoff, Leiden, p 164

Drabek, Mavroidis (eds) (2013) Regulation of foreign investment: challenges to international harmonization. World Scientific Publishing Co. Ltd, Singapore

---

CPTPP Article 9.23.11 "In the event that an appellate mechanism for reviewing awards rendered by investor-State dispute settlement tribunals is developed in the future under other institutional arrangements, the Parties shall consider whether awards rendered under Article 9.29 (Awards) should be subject to that appellate mechanism. The Parties shall strive to ensure that any such appellate mechanism they consider adopting provides for transparency of proceedings similar to the transparency provisions established in Article 9.24 (Transparency of Arbitral Proceedings).

[181] Broude (2011), p. 12.

Gáspar-Szilágyi S, Usynin M (2020) Investment chapters in PTAs and their impact on adjudicative convergence. In: Behn, Gáspár-Szilágyi, Langford (eds) Adjudicating trade and investment law: convergence or divergence? Cambridge University Press, Cambridge, p 42

Hahn M (2015) WTO rules and obligations related to investment, and EU rules and obligations related to investment. In: Bungenberg M, Griebel J, Hobe S, Reinisch A (eds) International investment law: a handbook. C.H. Beck, Munich, pp 653–670

Investment Negotiations: Penelope Ridings (2015) Walking the tightrope between offensive and defensive interests. New Zealand Bus Law Q 21(4)

Johannesson L, Mavroidis PC (2015) Black Cat, White Cat: the identity of WTO judges. J World Trade 49:685

Kho SS, Yanovich A, Casey BR, Strauss J (2017) The EU TTIP investment court proposal and the WTO dispute settlement system: comparing apples and oranges? ICSID Rev 32(2):326–345

Kurtz J (2016) The WTO and international investment law: converging systems, vol 248. Cambridge University Press, Cambridge

Langford et al (2020) Special issue: UNCITRAL and investment arbitration reform: matching concerns and solutions: an introduction. J World Invest Trade 21:182

Lazo RP, Desilvestro V (2018) Does an arbitrator's background influence the outcome of an investor-state arbitration? Law Practice Int Courts Trib 17:18–48, 26

Lenk H (2020) The EU investment court system and its resemblance to the WTO appellate body. In: Behn, Gáspár-Szilágyi, Langford (eds) Adjudicating trade and investment law: convergence or divergence? Cambridge University Press, Cambridge, p 78

Paulsson J (2010) Moral hazard in international dispute resolution, Inaugural lecture as holder of the Michael R. Klein distinguished scholar chair. University of Miami School of Law, Coral Gables

Pauwelyn J (2003) How to win a World Trade Organization dispute based on non-World Trade Organization Law? J World Trade 37(6):997–998

Pauwelyn J (2015) The rule of law without the rule of lawyers? Why investment arbitrators are from mars, trade panelists are from venus. *AJIL* 109:*761*

Redfern A (2003) Dissenting opinions in international commercial arbitration: the good, the bad and the ugly. Arb. Int'l 20:223. Freshfields Lecture. (2004)

Ruggiero DGR (1996) In: den Bossche V, Zdouc (eds) The law and policy of the World Trade Organisation, text cases and materials, 4th edn. 2017. Cambridge University Press, Cambridge, p 574

Vidigal G (2017) Why is there so little litigation under free trade agreements? Retaliation and adjudication in international dispute settlement. J Int Econ Law 20(4):927–950

Chapter 7
Amicus Curiae Briefs

7.1 *Amicus* Briefs in the Trade and Investment Law Regimes

This section looks at how *amicus curiae* briefs, which have typically been submitted by NGOs, international organisations and university professors have developed in the trade and investment law regimes. WTO tribunals may look for information from relevant sources in line with Article 13 of its Dispute Settlement Understanding (DSU).[1] Investment tribunals may accept *amicus* submissions in line with the ICSID and UNCITRAL Arbitration Rules inter alia. There is an emerging similarity of *amicus curiae* provisions in the trade and investment regimes. Such provisions harmonise the procedural rules between the regimes.

---

[1] Understanding on rules and procedures governing the settlement of disputes, Annex 2 of the WTO Agreement, Article 13 DSU: Right to Seek Information.

1. Each panel shall have the right to seek information and technical advice from any individual or body which it deems appropriate. However, before a panel seeks such information or advice from any individual or body within the jurisdiction of a Member it shall inform the authorities of that Member. A Member should respond promptly and fully to any request by a panel for such information as the panel considers necessary and appropriate. Confidential information which is provided shall not be revealed without formal authorization from the individual, body, or authorities of the Member providing the information.
2. Panels may seek information from any relevant source and may consult experts to obtain their opinion on certain aspects of the matter. With respect to a factual issue concerning a scientific or other technical matter raised by a party to a dispute, a panel may request an advisory report in writing from an expert review group. Rules for the establishment of such a group and its procedures are set forth in Annex 4.

© The Author(s), under exclusive license to Springer Nature Switzerland AG 2021   267
N. Moran, *Engagement Between Trade and Investment*, EYIEL Monographs -
Studies in European and International Economic Law 18,
https://doi.org/10.1007/978-3-030-83259-9_7

7.1.1 Amicus Curiae *Briefs in the Trade Regime*

The acceptance of *amicus curiae* briefs in WTO dispute settlement proceedings initially caused controversy between those advocating bringing the insights and perspectives of experts and civil society into the system and those who believed that such submissions could be prejudicial to the interests of Members with fewer resources.[2] DSU Article 13 provides that Panels may seek information from any relevant source and may consult experts concerning scientific or other technical matters.[3]

In 1996, the WTO's Appellate Body (AB) received its first *amicus curiae* submission in *EC—Hormones*. It did not find it necessary to rely on this brief in rendering its decision.[4] The landmark *Shrimp—Turtle* dispute followed, which had a strong public interest element.[5] *Shrimp—Turtle* was the third WTO dispute involving an *amicus curiae* submission from an NGO. In this case, the Appellate Body famously reversed the Panel's finding that such submissions were incompatible with the provisions of the DSU based on the right of panels to seek information found in DSU Article 13. The AB found that Panels have a discretionary authority to seek information "from any relevant source" and to determine the weight, if any, to be

---

[2] See Howse (2003), pp. 496–510.

[3] *Article 13 Right to Seek Information*

1. Each panel shall have the right to seek information and technical advice from any individual or body which it deems appropriate. However, before a panel seeks such information or advice from any individual or body within the jurisdiction of a Member it shall inform the authorities of that Member. A Member should respond promptly and fully to any request by a panel for such information as the panel considers necessary and appropriate. Confidential information which is provided shall not be revealed without formal authorization from the individual, body, or authorities of the Member providing the information.

2. Panels may seek information from any relevant source and may consult experts to obtain their opinion on certain aspects of the matter. With respect to a factual issue concerning a scientific or other technical matter raised by a party to a dispute, a panel may request an advisory report in writing from an expert review group. Rules for the establishment of such a group and its procedures are set forth in Appendix 4.

[4] Appellate Body Report, *EC Measures Concerning Meat and Meat Products (Hormones)*, WT/DS26/AB/R, WT/DS48/AB/R, adopted 13 February 1998. A 1996 Panel Report in US—Gasoline also received an amicus submission. There is a long record of disputes before the Appellate Body where similar findings have been made. E.g. Appellate Body Report, *United States—Measures Concerning the Importation, Marketing and Sale of Tuna and Tuna Products*, WT/DS381/AB/R, adopted 13 June 2012, para. I.8; Panel Reports, *European Communities—Measures Affecting the Approval and Marketing of Biotech Products*, adopted 21 November 2006 para. 7.11 (DS291, 292, 293); Appellate Body Report, *Brazil—Measures Affecting Imports of Retreaded Tyres*, WT/DS332/AB/R, adopted 17 December 2007, para. I.7.

[5] Appellate Body Report, *United States—Import Prohibition of Certain Shrimp and Shrimp Products*, WT/DS58/AB/R, adopted 6 November 1998.

ascribed to that information.[6] The AB further clarified that the Panel need not have requested such a submission.[7]

In *British Steel*, the European Communities questioned whether the AB could accept *amicus* submissions, as appeals are limited to issues of law. The EC argued that the basis for allowing such submissions at the Panel stage was Article 13 DSU, as per the *Shrimp—Turtle* decision, and this provision does not apply to the Appellate Body as it is limited to "factual information and technical advice, and would not include legal arguments or legal interpretations".[8]

The Appellate Body found that the DSU contains no explicit prohibition on the acceptance of such briefs and that they have broad authority to adopt their own procedural rules so long as they were consistent with the DSU and the covered agreements.[9]

The Panel Report in *US—Tuna II* provided a substantial account of where and how the Panel relied upon the single *amicus* submission it had received.[10] Its discussion of its treatment of this submission has been described as a "best-practice example".[11] The Panel informed the parties that in light of *US—Shrimp*, it was within its discretion to accept or reject the submission "as it deemed appropriate", and the parties were invited to provide their views on the submission.[12]

While this example may be considered 'best-practice', the Panel's analysis is focused on whether it has the authority to consider *amicus* submissions rather than scrutinising the relevance of the submission against a set of criteria. Panels may seek information from any relevant source but a set of criteria for the admission of *amicus* briefs is lacking. There is a need for such criteria to be developed and the Additional Procedure set down in *EC—Asbestos* could serve as a basis for further codification.[13]

---

[6] Panel Report, *US—Lead and Bismuth II*, WT/DS138/R 23 December 1999 para 104.

[7] Panel Report, *US—Lead and Bismuth II*, WT/DS138/R 23 December 1999 para 108.

[8] Appellate Body Report, *US—Lead and Bismuth II*, WT/DS138/AB/R, 10 May 2000, para 36.

[9] Appellate Body Report, *US—Lead and Bismuth II*, WT/DS138/AB/R, 10 May 2000, para 39.

[10] Panel Report, *United States—Measures Concerning the Importation, Marketing and Sale of Tuna and Tuna Products*, WT/DS381/R, adopted 13 June 2012, para 7.9. The submission was from the Humane Society International and the American University, Washington College of Law. The Panel report outlined the responses of the parties to questions put to them in relation to the submission and certain information contained therein. The Panel considered information in the brief to the extent that it was relevant to the claim, and sought the views of the parties in these areas in accordance with the requirements of due process.

[11] Marceau and Hurley (2012), p. 33.

[12] Panel Report, *United States—Measures Concerning the Importation, Marketing and Sale of Tuna and Tuna Products*, WT/DS381/R, adopted 13 June 2012, para 7.2.

[13] See Marceau and Hurley (2012), p. 43.

In *EC—Asbestos*, the Appellate Body invited submissions from third parties. 17 applications were received from NGOs such as Greenpeace and the World Wide Fund for Nature. Six were denied for late submission and the other eleven all failed to comply with the submission requirements. Submissions had to comply with the Additional Procedure, which was posted on the WTO website on 8 November 2000. Paragraph 3 of the Procedure stated that an application for leave to file such a written brief shall: (a) be made in writing, be dated and signed by the applicant, and

The Additional Procedure reflects commonalities with *amicus curiae* provisions in the investment law regime.[14]

Provisions for *amicus* submissions have long been a feature in the dispute settlement chapters of major agreements elsewhere in the trade regime. Under CAFTA—DR (2002), non-governmental entities may submit written views so long as the request identifies "the specific issues of fact or law directly relevant" and explains how the views "will contribute to resolving the dispute".[15]

CPTPP contains a nearly identical provision. The only differences include the fact that for the description of the entity, "sources of funding" is added as well as some other minor edits.[16] A similar nearly identical provision is found in Decision No. 6 of the Free Trade Commission of the US—Colombia Trade Promotion Agreement establishing rules of procedure.[17] The EU—UK Trade and Cooperation Agreement, EU—Vietnam FTA, EU—Singapore FTA and EU—Ukraine Association Agreement provide for *amicus* submissions provided they are directly relevant to the factual and/or legal issues under consideration and specify the nature of the interest of the person.[18]

---

include the address and other contact details of the applicant; (b) be in no case longer than three typed pages; (c) contain a description of the applicant, including a statement of the membership and legal status of the applicant, the general objectives pursued by the applicant, the nature of the activities of the applicant, and the sources of financing of the applicant; (d) specify the nature of the interest the applicant has in this appeal; (e) identify the specific issues of law covered in the Panel Report and legal interpretations developed by the Panel that are the subject of this appeal, as set forth in the Notice of Appeal (WT/DS135/8) dated 23 October 2000, which the applicant intends to address in its written brief; (f) state why it would be desirable, in the interests of achieving a satisfactory settlement of the matter at issue, in accordance with the rights and obligations of WTO Members under the DSU and the other covered agreements, for the Appellate Body to grant the applicant leave to file a written brief in this appeal; and indicate, in particular, in what way the applicant will make a contribution to the resolution of this dispute that is not likely to be repetitive of what has been already submitted by a party or third party to this dispute; and (g) contain a statement disclosing whether the applicant has any relationship, direct or indirect, with any party or any third party to this dispute, as well as whether it has, or will, receive any assistance, financial or otherwise, from a party or a third party to this dispute in the preparation of its application for leave or its written brief.

[14] See, *Methanex Corporation v. United States of America*, UNCITRAL/ NAFTA, Decision of the Tribunal on Petitions from Third Persons to Intervene as Amici Curiae, dated 15 January 2001.

[15] See CPTPP, Rules Of Procedure under Chapter 28 (Dispute Settlement) paras 62–69. Para 63: "(b) identify the specific issues of fact or law directly relevant to any factual or legal issue under consideration by the panel that the non-governmental entity intends to address in its written views; (c) explain how the non-governmental entity's written views will contribute to resolving the dispute and why its views would be unlikely to repeat factual or legal arguments that a participating Party has made or can be expected to make, or why it brings a perspective that is different from that of the participating Parties;".

[16] E.g. "The request shall: (b) identify the specific issues of fact and law" has been changed to "fact or law".

[17] Decision No. 6, Decision Establishing the Model Rules of Procedure (2018).

[18] See e.g. paragraphs 37–37 on 'Amicus Curiae Submissions' of Annex XXIV to Chapter 14 on Dispute Settlement of the EU—Ukraine Association Agreement (2014):

7.1.2 Amicus Curiae *Briefs and IIAs*

Three sets of rules of procedure are most influential in investment law in relation to *amicus curiae* submissions. These include those based on the Statement of the NAFTA Free Trade Commission (2003), ICSID Arbitration Rules (2006), and UNCITRAL's Transparency Rules (2014).

Prior to the adoption of these rules, an influential NAFTA decision in relation to *amicus* submissions came in *Methanex v. United States*. The tribunal found that allowing *amicus* submissions fell within its "broad procedural powers" to determine procedural issues stemming from Article 15(1) of the UNCITRAL Rules.[19] The tribunal found that it had no right to decide any substantive dispute determining the legal rights of third persons and its powers under 15(1) must be confined to procedural matters.[20] The tribunal clarified that the receipt of a written submission

---

37. Unless the Parties agree otherwise within three days of the date of the establishment of the arbitration panel, the arbitration panel may receive unsolicited written submissions from interested natural or legal persons established in the territories of the Parties, provided that they are made within 30 days of the date of the establishment of the arbitration panel, that they are concise, including any annexes, and that they are directly relevant to the factual and legal issues under consideration by the arbitration panel. The arbitration panel may decide to impose a page limit on such submissions.

38. The submission shall contain a description of the person making the submission, whether natural or legal, including its place of establishment, the nature of its activities and the source of its financing, and specify the nature of the interest that the person has in the arbitration proceeding.

Under the EU—UK TCA, the arbitration tribunal may receive submissions "directly relevant to a factual or a legal issue under consideration". Annex Inst: Rules of Procedure for Dispute Settlement, XII.

[19]Pursuant to Article 1120 NAFTA, UNCITRAL Arbitration Rules governed the arbitration. *Methanex Corp. v U.S.A, NAFTA/ UNCITRAL*, Decision of the Tribunal on Petitions from Third Persons to intervene as "Amici Curiae", para 25.

Article 15(1) of the UNCITRAL Rules:

1. 1. Subject to these Rules, the arbitral tribunal may conduct the arbitration in such manner as it considers appropriate, provided that the parties are treated with equality and that at any stage of the proceedings each party is given a full opportunity of presenting his case.
2. If either party so requests at any stage of the proceedings, the arbitral tribunal shall hold hearings for the presentation of evidence by witnesses, including expert witnesses, or for oral argument. In the absence of such a request, the arbitral tribunal shall decide whether to hold such hearings or whether the proceedings shall be conducted on the basis of documents and other materials.
3. All documents or information supplied to the arbitral tribunal by one party shall at the same time be communicated by that party to the other party.

[20]*Methanex Corp. v U.S.A, NAFTA/ UNCITRAL*, Decision of the Tribunal on Petitions from Third Persons to intervene as "Amici Curiae", para. 29.

is *not* equivalent to adding that person to the arbitration and their rights remain juridically unchanged.[21] The tribunal looked to the practices of the Iran-US Claims Tribunal and the WTO's Appellate Body before finding that it would accept the *amicus* submission.[22]

The distinction between parties to a dispute and third parties, in relation to the right to submit, had been made in paragraph 41 of the Appellate Body's Report in *British Steel*.[23] The Methanex tribunal further looked to the AB's finding that it had the power to accept *amicus* submissions under Article 17.9 DSU (working procedures). This power was deemed "significantly less broad" than those under Article 15(1).[24] The tribunal found that: "For present purposes, this WTO practice demonstrates that the scope of a procedural power can extend to the receipt of written submissions from non-party third persons, even in a juridical procedure affecting the rights and obligations of state parties".[25]

The tribunal set out a number of factors that influenced whether it would accept *amicus* submissions including public interest, cost and burden on the parties, utility, and precedent. Public interest was found to be relevant given the subject matter of the dispute and the tribunal noted the importance of being perceived as open and transparent to the arbitration process in general.[26] Concerning the burden to the parties, the tribunal said it "weighed heavily" on them that submissions were more likely to run counter to the claimant's position and that they should receive whatever procedural protections were necessary.[27] Finally, the tribunal acknowledged the petitioner's credentials and stated that although it did not know whether its

---

[21] Ibid, para. 30.

[22] Tribunal in *Iran v. United States*, Case A/15: see Award No 63-A115- IT.

[23] *United States—Imposition of Countervailing Duties on Certain Hot-Rolled Lead and Bismuth Carbon Steel Products Originating in the United Kingdom*, Appellate Body Report (adopted 10 May 2000) WT/DS138/AB/R para. 42. British Steel para. 41. Individuals and organizations, which are not Members of the WTO, have no legal *right* to make submissions to or to be heard by the Appellate Body. The Appellate Body has no legal *duty* to accept or consider unsolicited *amicus curiae* briefs submitted by individuals or organizations, not Members of the WTO. The Appellate Body has a legal *duty* to accept and consider *only* submissions from WTO Members which are parties or third parties in a particular dispute.[36]

36 Article 17.4 of the DSU and Rules 21 to 24 of the *Working Procedures*.

[24] *Methanex Corp. v U.S.A, NAFTA/ UNCITRAL*, Decision of the Tribunal on Petitions from Third Persons to intervene as "Amici Curiae", 15 January 2001, para. 33. UNCITRAL Arbitration Rules (1976) Article 15(1) states: "5. The arbitral tribunal may, having satisfied itself that the statement of one of the two Governments – or, under special circumstances, any other person -who is not an arbitrating party in a particular case is likely to assist the tribunal in carrying out its task, permit such Government or person to assist the tribunal by presenting oral or written statements." Available at: http://www.iusct.net/General%20Documents/5-TRIBUNAL%20RULES%20OF%20PROCE DURE.pdf (last accessed 8 March 2021).

[25] *Methanex Corp. v U.S.A, NAFTA/ UNCITRAL*, Decision of the Tribunal on Petitions from Third Persons to intervene as "Amici Curiae", 15 January 2001, para 33.

[26] Ibid, para 49.

[27] Ibid para 50.

submission would be of assistance, it *could* be of assistance.[28] It deemed the danger of setting a precedent as "less important" as arbitration tribunals cannot set a legal precedent.[29]

A second early decision on *amicus* submissions that referred to WTO practices came in *Suez/ Vivendi v. Argentina*. The submission in question concerned five NGOs that were denied access to hearings based on the refusal of the claimant for other persons to attend hearings. The tribunal found that this ICSID Arbitration Rule 32(2) required the consent of the parties.[30] The tribunal in *Suez/Vivendi* did however accept a single joint *amicus* submission in this case. It concluded that Article 15(1) of the UNCITRAL Rules was substantially similar to Article 44 of the ICSID Convention on procedural rules. The tribunal agreed with the *Methanex* tribunal that accepting *amicus* briefs was not the equivalent of adding a person to the arbitration and that it was a procedural question.[31] It further noted support for admission in the practices of the WTO.[32]

The tribunal then turned to the conditions for the admission of *amicus* briefs and found that their acceptance is based on criteria including (1) the appropriateness of the subject matter of the case; and (2) the suitability of a given non-party to act as an *amicus curiae*. Concerning the appropriateness of the subject matter, the tribunal found that there was a particular public interest in the case as it considered "the water distribution and sewage systems" of the city of Buenos Aires as well as the legality of the actions and measures taken by the government.[33] The tribunal acknowledged that certain non-parties may be able to provide "perspectives, arguments, and expertise" while having regard to the rights of the parties and the efficient conduct of the arbitration.[34] The tribunal viewed the acceptance of such submissions as increasing the transparency and legitimacy of international arbitration, noting that this has been the experience at the WTO.[35] In relation to the suitability of non-parties, the tribunal stated that it would only accept submissions from those with the "expertise, experience and independence" to be able to assist the tribunal.[36]

---

[28] Ibid para 48 (emphasis in original).

[29] Ibid para 51.

[30] *Suez, Sociedad General de Aguas de Barcelona S.A. and Vivendi Universal SA v Argentina*, Order in response to a petition for transparency and participation as amicus curiae, ICSID Case No. ARB/03/19, IIC 229 (2005), 19 May 2005, para. 5.

[31] *Ibid*, para 14.

[32] *Ibid*, para. 15. "The Tribunal in the present case finds further support for the admission of amicus submissions in international arbitral proceedings in the practices of NAFTA, the Iran-United States Claims Tribunal, and the World Trade Organization."

[33] *Ibid*, para 19.

[34] *Ibid*, para. 21.

[35] *Ibid*, para 22.

[36] *Ibid*, para 24. The tribunal specified that submissions should include: a. The identity and background of the petitioner, the nature of its membership if it is an organization, and the nature of its relationships, if any, to the parties in the dispute. b. The nature of the petitioner's interest in the case. c. Whether the petitioner has received financial or other material support from any of the

The NAFTA Free Trade Commission (FTC) issued a Statement on *amicus curiae* submissions in 2003.[37] Its formulation has been replicated in some subsequent agreements.[38] Section B.6 of the Statement set out four main factors for tribunals to consider in determining whether or not to accept *amicus* submissions: "[T]he Tribunal will consider, among other things, the extent to which: (a) the non-disputing party submission would assist the Tribunal in the determination of a factual or legal issue related to the arbitration by bringing a perspective, particular knowledge or insight that is different from that of the disputing parties; (b) the non-disputing party submission would address matters within the scope of the dispute; (c) the non-disputing party has a significant interest in the arbitration; and (d) there is a public interest in the subject-matter of the arbitration."

A first interpretation of the Statement of the FTC came in *Glamis Gold v. USA* where the tribunal found that the submission satisfied the principles of the Free Trade Commission's Statement, without much elaboration.[39] The submission came from the Quechan Indian Nation, which it is noted is an American Indian tribe rather than an NGO. The current ICSID Arbitration Rules came into force in April 2006 and brought in updated procedural rules in relation to non-party submissions, including Rule 37(2).[40] In considering whether to allow a written *amicus* submission, the Rule states that tribunals should have regard to: (1) the potential of the submission to

---

parties or from any person connected with the parties in this case. d. The reasons why the Tribunal should accept petitioner's *amicus curiae* brief.

[37] NAFTA Free Trade Commission's 2003 Statement on non-disputing party participation, available at: http://www.international.gc.ca/trade-agreements-accords-commerciaux/assets/pdfs/Nondisputing-en.pdf.

[38] See Article 39.4 of the Canada Model BIT or Article 836 of the Peru- Canada FTA (2009) on Submissions by Other Persons: "In determining whether to grant the leave the Tribunal shall consider, among other things, the extent to which: (a) the applicant's submission would assist the Tribunal in the determination of a factual or legal issue related to the arbitration by bringing a perspective, particular knowledge or insight that is different from that of the disputing parties; (b) the applicant's submission would address a matter within the scope of the dispute; (c) the applicant has a significant interest in the arbitration; and (d) there is a public interest in the subject-matter of the arbitration."

[39] *Glamis Gold v. USA*, Decision on Application and Submission by Quechan Indian Nation, 16 September 2005, para 10.

[40] ICSID Arbitration Rules, Rule 37(2):

After consulting both parties, the Tribunal may allow a person or entity that is not a party to the dispute (in this Rule called the "non-disputing party") to file a written submission with the Tribunal regarding a matter within the scope of the dispute. In determining whether to allow such a filing, the Tribunal shall consider, among other things, the extent to which: (a) the non-disputing party submission would assist the Tribunal in the determination of a factual or legal issue related to the proceeding by bringing a perspective, particular knowledge or insight that is different from that of the disputing parties; (b) the non-disputing party submission would address a matter within the scope of the dispute; (c) the non-disputing party has a *significant interest* in the proceeding.

The Tribunal shall ensure that the non-disputing party submission does not disrupt the proceeding or unduly burden or unfairly prejudice either party, and that both parties are

assist the tribunal; (2) whether the subject falls within the scope of proceedings; and (3) whether the petitioner has a "significant interest" in proceedings.

The main difference between this and the 2003 Statement of the NAFTA Free Trade Commission is the omission of subparagraph (d) on the need for a public interest in the subject matter of the arbitration. These three elements have been included in subsequent agreements such as CPTPP Article 9.23.3.[41]

The tribunal in *Biwater Gauff v. Tanzania* applied Rule 37(2) for the first time when it accepted an *amicus* brief filed by five NGOs. The tribunal found that the NGOs had approached the case with "interests, expertise and perspectives that have been demonstrated to materially differ from those of the two contending parties, and as such have provided a useful contribution to these proceedings."[42]

An *amicus* submission was also admitted in *Philip Morris v. Uruguay* pursuant to Rule 37(2).[43] The claimant argued the submission would unduly burden the parties and disputed the independence of the submission from the World Health Organization (WHO) and the WHO's Framework Convention on Tobacco Control (FCTC) as Uruguay was one of its active members. Uruguay argued they had a significant interest "in light of the far-reaching consequences for tobacco control that an outcome in this case may have on all WHO and FCTC Member States."[44] The tribunal stated that it would ensure that the submission did not unduly burden either party and found that the submission might be beneficial given the parties'

---

given an opportunity to present their observations on the non-disputing party submission. (emphasis added).

[41] TPP, Article 9.23 on the Conduct of the Arbitration:

3. After consultation with the disputing parties, the tribunal may accept and consider written amicus curiae submissions regarding a matter of fact or law within the scope of the dispute that may assist the tribunal in evaluating the submissions and arguments of the disputing parties from a person or entity that is not a disputing party but has a significant interest in the arbitral proceedings. Each submission shall identify the author; disclose any affiliation, direct or indirect, with any disputing party; and identify any person, government or other entity that has provided, or will provide, any financial or other assistance in preparing the submission. Each submission shall be in a language of the arbitration and comply with any page limits and deadlines set by the tribunal. The tribunal shall provide the disputing parties with an opportunity to respond to such submissions. The tribunal shall ensure that the submissions do not disrupt or unduly burden the arbitral proceedings, or unfairly prejudice any disputing party.

[42] *Biwater Gauff v Tanzania*, Award, ICSID Case No. ARB/05/22, 24 July 2008, para 359. In terms of the "significant interest" of the NGOs in the proceedings in line with the requirements of Rule 37 (2), they submitted that the arbitration had a: "[D]irect and indirect relevance to the Petitioners' mandates and activities at the local, national and international levels. The interest of the Petitioners in all of these public concerns is, without question, longstanding, genuine, and supported by their well- recognized expertise on these issues." (para 15).

[43] *Philip Morris Brand SARL and Others v Uruguay*, Procedural Order no 3, ICSID Case No. ARB/10/7, 17 February 2015, para 29.

[44] Ibid, para 19.

expertise.[45] It further noted the public interest element to the case and that granting the request would support transparency and acceptability.[46]

A final major development came in 2014, with the adoption of the UNCITRAL Transparency Rules, which entered into force on 18 October 2017.[47] These rules supplement pre-existing investment treaties in relation to transparency requirements and have been adopted in Agreements such as CETA and the EU—Vietnam FTA and IPA. Article 4 sets out the procedure for submissions by a third person.[48] Like the ICSID Arbitration Rules, it refers to three of the four factors set out in the 2003 Statement of the FTC, although it condenses them into two subparagraphs.[49] For Levine, once these central regimes begin adopting more comprehensive guidelines on *amicus* participation, there is a strong chance that a degree of "cross-fertilization" and harmonization between them will follow.[50]

In 2017, the tribunal in *Bear Creek v. Peru* gave a significant reading on the factors determining the admissibility of *amicus* submissions. This case was taken under the Peru—Canada FTA (2009), which, as noted, replicated the language of the 2003 FTC Statement on submissions. The tribunal placed the emphasis squarely on the first of the criteria from the FTC Statement, namely whether the *amicus* submission would assist the tribunal.[51] It found that the petitioners' knowledge and expertise "may add a new perspective that differs from that of the Parties". This element of adding a "new" perspective based on expertise was decisive.[52] The tribunal also downplayed the importance of a petitioner having a "significant interest" in the case, seemingly giving precedence to the fact that they offered a new perspective.

---

[45] Ibid, para 27–28.

[46] Ibid, para 28.

[47] UNCITRAL Rules on Transparency in Treaty-based Investor-State Arbitration (the "Mauritius Convention on Transparency") (New York, 2014).

[48] Article 4. Submission by a third person: "3. In determining whether to allow such a submission, the arbitral tribunal shall take into consideration, among other factors it determines to be relevant: (a) Whether the third person has a significant interest in the arbitral proceedings; and (b) The extent to which the submission would assist the arbitral tribunal in the determination of a factual or legal issue related to the arbitral proceedings by bringing a perspective, particular knowledge or insight that is different from that of the disputing parties."

[49] Section B6 of the NAFTA Free Trade Commission's 2003 Statement on non-disputing party participation set out four factors for a tribunal to consider in determining whether or not to accept amicus submissions: (1) the amicus submission would assist the tribunal; (2) the submission would be within the scope of the dispute; (3) the non-disputing party has a significant interest in the dispute; and (4) public interest in the subject matter of the arbitration. The first three questions of these questions are also the integral to Rule 37(2) of the ICSID Arbitration Rules and Article 4 of the UNCITRAL Transparency Rules.

[50] Levine (2011), p. 222.

[51] *Bear Creek Mining Corporation v. Republic of Peru*, Procedural Order No. 5, ICSID Case No. ARB/14/21, 21 July 2016, para 36.

[52] *Bear Creek Mining Corporation v. Republic of Peru*, Procedural Order No. 5, ICSID Case No. ARB/14/21, 21 July 2016 para 40.

When the tribunal was satisfied that the submission would assist the tribunal (in line with Art. 836.4(a)), it then commented on the other criteria in Art. 836, stating that they "need only be examined to establish whether the Tribunal considers them to be relevant, beyond the criteria of subsection (a)...[and they] do not provide a reason to depart from the Tribunal's conclusion based on subsection (a)."[53] It found that under Article 836.4, "it is made explicit that these are only 'criteria' and not conditions, and also that they are to be considered non-exhaustive."[54] It remains to be seen whether this approach will be followed under similarly worded provisions in agreements such as CPTPP.

7.2 *Amicus Curiae* Briefs and Engagement

Engagement was defined[55] as encompassing parallels in the practices and features of tribunals and recent attempts at reforming the investment regime are pushing the regimes in this direction. Parallels in the practices of tribunals encompass the admittance of *amicus curiae* briefs, which is the subject matter of this section.

7.2.1 How Similar Is the Content of Amicus Submissions in the Two Regimes?

The receipt of *amicus curiae* submissions is a key shared procedural standard of the trade and investment law regimes. As outlined in Sections A, the criteria for accepting *amicus* briefs have varied significantly within and between the regimes. Kurtz refers to a spectrum of treaty practice. On one end, Canadian IIAs admit *amicus* submissions with "extensive procedural checks" modelled on WTO law.[56]

---

[53] *Bear Creek Mining Corporation v. Republic of Peru*, Procedural Order No. 5, ICSID Case No. ARB/14/21, 21 July 2016, para 46. The tribunal accepted the two petitioners (a Legal Adviser and an Association of Human Rights) as *amici curiae*. In relation to the 'significant interest' of the parties, the tribunal found: "Dr. López's legal expertise and DHUMA's local knowledge of the facts may add a new perspective that differs from that of the Parties. This is so, irrespective of whether DHUMA speaks for the Aymara communities, or whether its interests may be synonymous with the communities' interests." (para 40). The claimant had contested the "mandate" of DHUMA in representing the Aymara communities and thus its significant interest in the case. (para 19).

[54] *Bear Creek Mining Corporation v. Republic of Peru*, Procedural Order No. 5, ICSID Case No. ARB/14/21, 21 July 2016, para 35.

[55] Engagement between trade and investment law was described in Chap. 1.I as occurring wherever the content of one of the regimes has a parallel in the other or wherever there are cross-regime references in dispute settlement or parallels in the practices and features of tribunals.

[56] Kurtz (2016), p. 273.

The US approach, on the other end, merely confers the authority on tribunals to admit *amicus* submissions.[57]

Investment tribunals have been accepting *amicus* briefs since 2001 with the first formalised rules for non-party submissions coming via the ICSID Arbitration Rules (2006). WTO tribunals have been accepting *amicus* briefs since 1996. DSU Article 13 merely stipulates that panels may seek information from any relevant source and so the criteria for their acceptance remain rather murky. When the WTO's Appellate Body laid down the 'Additional Procedure' for the submission of *amicus* briefs in *EC—Asbestos*, there was overlap with the three questions that are common to the most influential rules of procedure in relation to *amicus* submissions in investment law.[58] The Additional Procedure does not refer to 'public interest', but it does refer to the applicant making "a contribution to the resolution of this dispute" (paragraph (f)); identify the specific issues of law (. . .) which the applicant intends to address in its written brief (paragraph (e)); and the "nature of the interest" the applicant has in this appeal (paragraph (d)).

7.2.2   Cross-Regime References and the Harmonisation of Amicus Provisions

7.2.2.1   Why Make Cross-Regime References?

Concerning *amicus curiae* provisions, tribunals in the trade and investment law regimes interpret similar provisions and ask similar questions. Pauwelyn has described the filling of procedural gaps in areas where the WTO agreement is silent as one of the main roles of "non-WTO law" when interpreting the WTO Agreements.[59]

One reason for making cross-regime references is the significant commonalities between *amicus curiae* provisions across the two regimes. There are parallels in the questions asked by tribunals and it may be useful to consider how these questions have been interpreted in the other regime.

Ukraine—Wood Products was a rare trade case taken under the dispute settlement mechanism of a PTA outside of the WTO.[60] The provision for *amicus curiae*

---

[57] E.g. Article 28.3 of the US—Rwanda BIT (2008) provides: "The tribunal shall have the authority to accept and consider amicus curiae submissions from a person or entity that is not a disputing party."

[58] These include the UNCITRAL Rules, NAFTA FTC Statement and ICSID Rules and are outlined in section A.II.

[59] Pauwelyn (2003), pp. 997–998. Examples of where the WTO Agreement is silent are burden of proof, standing, representation before Panels, the retroactive application of treaties or error in treaty formation.

[60] Final Report of the Arbitration Panel, *Restrictions applied by Ukraine on exports of certain wood products to the European Union*, 11 December 2020.

submissions in the EU—Ukraine Association Agreement is nearly identical to those in the EUSIPA and EU—Singapore FTA.[61] The only differences between the texts concern timing and limits for submissions.[62] The *amicus* provisions of the EU—Singapore Agreement are nearly identical to the provisions concerning *amicus* submissions in the EU—Vietnam FTA and EUVIPA, which are identical *mutatis*

---

[61] EUSIPA is atypical for recent EU Agreements in that it does not incorporate the UNCITRAL Transparency Rules, unlike CETA, the EU-Vietnam Agreement, and the EU-Mexico Agreement.

[62] The texts of these two provisions are now compared, with these minor differences in timing and the limits for submissions italicized. Annex 9 EU- Singapore IPA (2015) on 'Amicus curiae submissions':

> 42. Unless the Parties agree otherwise within three days of the date of the establishment of the arbitration panel, the arbitration panel may receive unsolicited written submissions from interested natural or legal persons of the Parties, provided that they are made within *ten days* of the date of the establishment of the arbitration panel, that they are concise and in no case longer than *15 typed pages*, including any annexes, and that they are directly relevant to the factual issue under consideration by the arbitration panel.

> 43. The submission shall contain a description of the person making the submission, whether natural or legal, including *its nationality* or place of establishment the nature of *their* activities and the source of its financing, and specify the nature of the interest that the person has in the arbitration proceeding. *It shall be drafted in the languages chosen by the Parties in accordance with Rule 46 of this Annex.*

> 44. The arbitration panel shall list in its ruling all the submissions it has received that conform to Rules 42 and 43 of this Annex. The arbitration panel shall not be obliged to address in its ruling *the arguments made* in such submissions. Any submission obtained by the arbitration panel under this Annex shall be submitted to the Parties for their comments.

Annex XXIV to Chapter 14 on Dispute Settlement of the EU- Ukraine Association Agreement (2014), Amicus Curiae Submissions:

> 37. Unless the Parties agree otherwise within three days of the date of the establishment of the arbitration panel, the arbitration panel may receive unsolicited written submissions from interested natural or legal persons established in the territories of the Parties, provided that they are made within *30 days* of the date of the establishment of the arbitration panel, that they are concise, including any annexes, and that they are directly relevant to the factual and legal issues under consideration by the arbitration panel. *The arbitration panel may decide to impose a page limit on such submissions.*

> 38. The submission shall contain a description of the person making the submission, whether natural or legal, including its place of establishment, the nature of its activities and the source of its financing, and specify the nature of the interest that the person has in the arbitration proceeding.

> 39. The arbitration panel shall list in its ruling all the submissions it has received that conform to the above rules. The arbitration panel shall not be obliged to address in its ruling *the factual or legal arguments made* in such submissions. Any submission obtained by the arbitration panel under this rule shall be submitted to the Parties for their comments.

mutandis.[63] Based on these provisions, there appears to be an approximation between the *amicus* provisions in the trade and investment chapters of EU PTAs and PTIAs.

The tribunal in *Ukraine—Wood Products* received one *amicus* submission and its acceptance was not contentious.[64] If tribunals such as this one have to consider whether or not to accept *amicus* briefs, the questions asked would likely be similar to those asked under the investment chapters of EUSIPA and EUVIPA as outlined above. This is based on the quasi-identical nature of the text included in EU trade and investment agreements concerning the submissions of *amicus* briefs.

The questions raised under the *amicus* provisions of these Agreements[65] differ to those asked under the major sets of investment rules (ICSID, UNCITRAL, NAFTA) and the Additional Procedure set out in *EC—Asbestos*. These EU Agreements refer to the necessity that submissions be "directly relevant" to the issues under consideration and that the petitioner must specify "the nature of the interest" in proceedings. However, there is no reference to the assistance they would give to the tribunal,

---

[63] See EUVIPA Annex 7, and EU—Vietnam FTA Annex 15-A. The differences between the *amicus* provisions of EUSIPA and EU- Vietnam FTA/ IPA are minimal. Nonetheless, where the text deviates from EUSIPA, this is italicised below.

EU- Vietnam FTA Annex 15-A

40. Unless the Parties agree otherwise within three days of the date of the establishment of the arbitration panel, the arbitration panel may receive unsolicited written submissions *from natural or legal persons established in the territory of a Party who are independent from the governments of the Parties*, provided that they are made within 10 days of the date of the establishment of the arbitration panel, that they are concise and in no case longer than 15 pages typed at *double space*, and that they are directly relevant to a factual or a legal issue under consideration by the arbitration panel.

41. The submission shall contain a description of the person making the submission, whether natural or legal, including its nationality or place of establishment, the nature of *its* activities, its legal status, *general objectives and the source of its financing, and specify the nature of the interest that the person has in the arbitration proceedings*. It shall be drafted in the languages chosen by the Parties in accordance with Rules *44 and 45.*

42. The arbitration panel shall list in its ruling all the submissions it has received that conform to *Rules 40 and 41*. The arbitration panel shall not be obliged to address in its ruling the arguments made in those submissions. *Any such submission shall be submitted to the Parties for their comments. The comments of the Parties shall be submitted within 10 days and they shall be taken into consideration by the arbitration panel.*

[64] Neither of the parties referred to this *amicus* brief from the non-governmental organization "Ukrainian Association of the Club of Rome" in their submissions. The Arbitration Panel did not refer to this submission in its findings or comment further on its acceptance of this *amicus* brief. Final Report of the Arbitration Panel, *Restrictions applied by Ukraine on exports of certain wood products to the European Union*, 11 December 2020, para 10.

[65] E.g. Annex 9 of the EU—Singapore IPA and Annex XXIV to the EU- Ukraine Association Agreement.

which the tribunal in *Bear Creek v. Peru* found to be the most important criterion of the four outlined in Article 836.4 of the Canada– Peru FTA.[66]

7.2.2.2 Have There Been Cross-Regime References?

To date, tribunals in trade disputes before the WTO have made no external references when interpreting the right to make *amicus* submissions. A problem at the WTO is the lack of clear grounds on which submissions are accepted. There should be a "predictable and uniform" approach throughout WTO dispute settlement to *amicus* briefs.[67]

The murkiness of the criteria at the WTO has not prevented investment tribunals making cross-regime references. The cross-regime references made by the investment tribunals in *Methanex v. United States* and *Suez/ Vivendi v. Argentina* were of a limited nature. In *Methanex*, the tribunal referred to the Appellate Body Report in *British Steel* in interpreting the scope of its procedural powers. The tribunal noted the Appellate Body's acceptance of *amicus* submissions under powers "significantly less broad" than those under Article 15(1) of the UNCITRAL Rules.[68] The tribunal in *Suez/Vivendi v. Argentina* viewed the acceptance of such submissions as increasing the transparency and legitimacy of international arbitration, noting that this has been the experience of the WTO.[69]

7.2.2.3 Caveats When Making Cross-Regime References

There are three major criteria that are common to the ICSID, UNCITRAL and NAFTA rules for *amicus* submissions, as well as the WTO's Additional Procedure.[70] These include that a submission must be of assistance to the tribunal, be relevant to the dispute, and that the petitioner has a significant interest in the

---

[66] *Bear Creek Mining Corporation v. Republic of Peru*, Procedural Order No. 5, ICSID Case No. ARB/14/21, 21 July 2016, para 36. "In the view of the Tribunal, the most important criteria is the first mentioned and quoted above in subsection 4(a), namely whether the applicant's submission would assist the Tribunal. This is also inherent in the term "amicus curiae", used to describe such submissions and also used by the Parties in this case."

[67] Marceau and Hurley (2012), p. 43.

[68] *Methanex Corp. v U.S.A*, NAFTA/ UNCITRAL, Decision of the Tribunal on Petitions from Third Persons to intervene as "Amici Curiae", 15 January 2001, para. 33. UNCITRAL Arbitration Rules (1976) Article 15(1).

[69] *Suez, Sociedad General de Aguas de Barcelona S.A. and Vivendi Universal SA v Argentina*, Order in response to a petition for transparency and participation as amicus curiae, ICSID Case No. ARB/03/19, IIC 229 (2005), 19 May 2005, para. 22.

[70] For Levine, it is necessary to develop criteria allowing for mandatory rather than discretionary participation. Formalising the status of *amici curiae* is necessary from the perspective of legitimacy. See Levine (2011), p. 222.

dispute.[71] How should the acceptance of *amicus* briefs be regulated in trade and investment disputes with respect to these three criteria?

(i) The Assistance of Submissions to the Tribunal;

The investment tribunal in *Bear Creek v. Peru* emphasised the importance of the submission being of assistance to the tribunal.[72] It found that the petitioner added a "new" perspective, based on expertise, and that this was decisive. The tribunal in *Suez & Vivendi v. Argentina* would only accept submissions from those with the "expertise, experience and independence" to be able to assist the tribunal.[73] Gómez has found that the only *amicus* briefs that should be admitted are those with added value, that are "sufficiently novel", rather than containing overlapping arguments.[74]

(ii) Submissions and Relevance to the Dispute;

This criterion seems less controversial and would be for the tribunal to determine based on the facts and circumstances of the case and the profile of the petitioner.

Under EU Agreements, the notion of 'assisting the tribunal', which is not explicitly stated, could perhaps be imported into this requirement that submissions be "directly relevant" to proceedings.

(iii) The 'significant interest' of the petitioner in the dispute;

It is however far from clear what is meant by a "significant interest". It has been posited that it should be enough to show that the purpose for which an NGO is created is negatively affected and that pecuniary, intellectual or emotional elements could also be considered.[75] One of the problems with this idea of linking the interest with the "purpose" of an NGO is that it favours NGOs with broad objectives over those with specialised knowledge and more specific objectives.

Of the three criteria above, the requirement that *amicus* submissions would assist the tribunal seems to be the most important. The tribunal in *Bear Creek v. Peru* found that the other criteria "need only be examined to establish" that they do not provide a reason to depart from the conclusion that the submission would assist it.[76]

---

[71] It is noted that the first criterion is absent in EU Agreements. Criteria two and three are included in all five types of these sets of rules, i.e. The ICSID Arbitration Rules, the UNCITRAL Transparency Rules, the NAFTA Free Trade Commission's 2003 Statement on non-disputing party participation, those of the WTO's Additional Procedure, and those in recent EU Agreements.

[72] *Bear Creek Mining Corporation v. Republic of Peru*, Procedural Order No. 5, ICSID Case No. ARB/14/21, 21 July 2016, para 36.

[73] *Suez, Sociedad General de Aguas de Barcelona S.A. and Vivendi Universal SA v Argentina*, ICSID Case No. ARB/03/19, Order in response to a Petition for Transparency and Participation as Amicus Curiae, 19 May 2005, para 24.

[74] Gomez (2012), p. 559.

[75] See Gomez (2012), pp. 534, 558.

[76] *Bear Creek Mining Corporation v. Republic of Peru*, Procedural Order No. 5, ICSID Case No. ARB/14/21, 21 July 2016, para 46.

7.2.3 The Role of PTIAs

PTIAs may have a considerable role in bringing about increased engagement in this area. This is particularly the case where similar wordings, such as those outlined in the last section, are included in the *amicus curiae* provisions of the trade and investment chapters of PTIAs. The acceptance of unsolicited *amicus* briefs should be governed by a set of criteria.[77]

Three such criteria have emerged under the ICSID, UNCITRAL and NAFTA rules for *amicus* submissions. These criteria and their corresponding interpretative questions include that submissions assist the tribunal, are relevant to the dispute, and that the petitioner has a significant interest in the dispute. Only the latter two of these are made explicit in WTO law and jurisprudence. As guidelines become more comprehensive, there is a strong chance that a degree of "cross-fertilization" and harmonization between these investment rules will follow.[78]

The WTO's DSU is unlikely to be amended soon and change is unlikely to come from WTO Panels agreeing to new rules of procedure while the Appellate Body is in a state of paralysis. PTAs and PTIAs can bring some dynamism to the trade regime in this area. Where the provisions of these agreements have wordings for *amicus* submissions that approximate across their trade and investment chapters, this will facilitate cross-fertilisation between the regimes.

Investment tribunals have referred to the practices of adjudicators at the WTO in relation to *amicus* submissions. Where trade tribunals interpret provisions such as those pertaining to *amicus* submissions under the EU—Ukraine Association Agreement, it remains to be seen whether they will have regard to interpretations of similar provisions in the investment regime. In relation to the nearly identical provisions under the investment chapters of EU PTIAs, there have not yet been any disputes under these agreements. Where the wording of *amicus* provisions is identical *mutatis mutandis* under the trade and investment chapters of PTIAs, there should be an assumption that the main interpretative questions relating to them may be answered in a similar way. If a common or dominant practice emerges in the investment regime for interpreting the three criteria governing the admission of *amicus* submissions that are common to the ICSID, UNCITRAL and NAFTA rules, as well as the WTO's Additional Procedure, this will influence the interpretation of the investment chapters of PTIAs. When tribunals consider these same questions under the trade chapters of PTIAs, interpretations under the investment chapter may influence their interpretation of these criteria of assistance, relevance and significant interest. As the procedural rules approximate across the regimes, the barriers to tribunals and the parties to dispute making such cross-regime references decrease.

---

[77] Gomez (2012), p. 564.
[78] Levine (2011), p. 222.

References

Gomez KF (2012) Rethinking the role of Amicus Curiae in international investment arbitration: how to draw the line favorably for the public interest. Fordham Int Law J 35(1) Article 3, 559

Howse R (2003) Membership and its privileges: the WTO, civil society, and the amicus brief controversy. Eur Law J 9(4):496–510

Kurtz J (2016) The WTO and international investment law: converging systems. Cambridge University Press, p 273

Levine E (2011) Amicus Curiae in international investment arbitration: the implications of an increase in third-party participation. Berkeley J Int Law 29(1):222

Marceau G, Hurley M (2012) Transparency and public participation in the WTO: a report card on WTO transparency mechanisms 4(1). Trade Law Dev 19:33

Pauwelyn (2003) How to win a World Trade Organization dispute based on non-world Trade Organization Law? J World Trade 37(6):997–998

Chapter 8
Conclusion

This book examined the question of whether engagement between the trade and investment law regimes increases when parties conclude PTIAs rather than BITs. While the overall effect and underlying causes of negotiating investment protection as part of a larger overall agreement may be unclear, the empirical results in this study certainly indicate increased engagement.

Part I demonstrated that PTIAs play a role in facilitating engagement between the trade and investment law regimes. It charted areas of engagement between the two regimes empirically. For the 24 provisions measured, there was an average of 63% more provisions evidencing engagement in PTIAs compared to BITs across the 120 Agreements. Provisions indicating engagement were more frequent in PTIAs compared to BITs in the treaties examined for every year from 2005 to 2019. It was also shown that there is a general, but uneven, trend of increased engagement over time. Parts II–IV considered when engagement is appropriate and to what extent it is appropriate for certain key drivers of convergence across the three main areas of this study: host state flexibility, dispute settlement, and substantive provisions. These provisions included nondiscrimination provisions, treaty exceptions, preambles, appellate mechanisms, and *amicus curiae* briefs. Parts II–IV considered how these shared norms and features of the regimes have been included in treaties and how tribunals have interpreted them. For each of these norms and features, the following questions were considered: (1) the extent of inter-regime engagement; (2) the utility and practice of making references to the experience of the other regime; and (3) engagement and the role of PTIAs. While the findings for each of these provisions were highly nuanced, certain key themes emerged, including: the importance of balance in agreements, particularly in preambles and via the inclusion of exceptions adapted to the IIA context; the great potential for engagement in certain areas given how closely the trade and investment law texts mirror each other; and the increased possibility for cross-regime references that are attentive to the differences between the regimes, particularly where the structures of agreements are similar and certain features of the regimes are replicated (e.g. appellate mechanisms).

© The Author(s), under exclusive license to Springer Nature Switzerland AG 2021
N. Moran, *Engagement Between Trade and Investment*, EYIEL Monographs -
Studies in European and International Economic Law 18,
https://doi.org/10.1007/978-3-030-83259-9_8

A follow up question to the one asked in this book is whether states should focus on concluding these agreements if PTIAs increase inter-regime engagement compared to BITs. PTIAs have acted as catalysts for engagement between trade and investment law and could have substantial effects on the evolution of both regimes as well as international economic law in general. However, despite the higher levels of engagement in the sample of PTIAs compared to BITs in this study, this does not mean that PTIAs are necessary for high levels of inter-regime engagement. Rather than focusing on concluding PTIAs, it is recommended that the parties to IIAs should reflect upon certain matters when negotiating IIAs. These include:

(1) under which provisions engagement between the trade and investment law regimes is appropriate and to what extent it is appropriate;
(2) whether inter-regime engagement should influence the decision to conclude an agreements in the form of a BIT, PTA, or PTIA;
(3) the extent to which PTIAs facilitate engagement compared to BITs;
(4) how a standalone BIT should be drafted in light of the possibility that BITs may limit inter-regime engagement.

There are many factors influencing whether parties negotiate a BIT, PTA or PTIA. With certain partners the EU and US have concluded PTIAs, while with others, BITs have been viewed as a litmus test for the prospect of a larger FTA.[1] In the aftermath of Opinion 2/15, EU investment agreements should "in principle be negotiated in parallel to FTAs" but this will be decided on a case-by-case basis.[2] If the EU were to separate trade and investment negotiations, this may simplify certain negotiations, but may also affect the level of protection for EU investors if standalone BITs are more difficult to conclude.[3]

PTIAs may lead to higher levels of engagement than BITs, but ultimately these are "complementary instruments" when viewed through the lens of investment protection.[4] Whatever choice the parties make about the form of an IIA, they should be mindful of the impact this form has on inter-regime engagement. While provisions facilitating engagement can be contained in BITs, the trend has been for this to occur at a higher level when concluding PTIAs.[5] Parties negotiating IIAs should ask why this is, whether or not it represents a conscious choice, and whether it would be better to incorporate the type of investment provisions more frequently seen in PTIAs, even if the architecture of these agreements is different. The parties should

---

[1] See Chap. 1.II.

[2] European Council Conclusions adopted on 22 May 2018, page 3.

[3] See Chap. 6.B.II.2.

[4] De Brabandere (2013), p. 69.

[5] Generally speaking, while IIAs are characterised by a high degree of diversity, PTIAs seem to provide for greater levels of engagement, notwithstanding the fact that certain BITs provide for a very high level of engagement. The Chile-Hong Kong BIT (2016) contained 22/24 of the elements evidencing engagement, but on average, the number of provisions in BITs in a given year did not exceed their PTIA equivalents in this study.

consider which provisions (if any) should be isolated from interactions with trade law and for which provisions (if any) interactions should be encouraged.

Cross-regime references have been more common in the investment regime. Such references should continue where the structure and wording of provisions lend themselves to engagement in light of the purpose of the treaties at issue and the relevant institutional features.[6] Alvarez finds that the message in this area is not "no trespassing", but rather to proceed with caution.[7] Other questions remain such as what constitutes an appropriate cross-regime reference, as well as whether, and to what extent, tribunals will make such cross-regime references when interpreting trade and investment law agreements in the future. This remains to be seen, but where provisions in the trade and investment law regimes approximate, the argument to draw upon the experience of the other regime strengthens.

References

Alvarez J (2014) Beware: boundary crossings. Public law & legal theory research paper series. New York University, p 65

De Brabandere E (2013) Co-existence, complementarity or conflict? Interaction between preferential trade and investment agreements and bilateral investment treaties. In: Hofmann CJT, Schill SW (eds) Preferential trade and investment agreements: from recalibration to reintegration. Nomos, Baden, pp 37–70

---

[6] Although WTO tribunals have shown reluctance to make cross-regime references, this need not be the case. WTO tribunals are able to make such references in line with the VCLT and there are significant commonalities between many of the provisions considered here that are common to the trade and investment law regimes.

[7] Alvarez (2014), p. 65.

Annex

PTIAs 2005-19:	Preamble Reference to WTO law (1)/	Preamble to Agt/ Investment Chapter:/ 1. right	Treaty Exceptions- explicit 1,	Article on environmental/ health	Expropriation referring to TRIPS	Expropriation reference to public	Performance requirements reference to	Capital withdrawal safeguard within invst chapter
			Host State Flexibility					
Armenia- Singapore '19			2					
EU - Viet Nam IPA '19			2					
Australia - Hong Kong FTA '19			2					
Australia - Indonesia CEPA '19		2 & 4	17.2.3					
USMCA '18			4					
EU - Singapore IPA '18			2 (NT)					
CPTPP '18			4					
Central America - Korea FTA '18			4					
Australia - Peru FTA '18			2					
Singapore - Sri Lanka FTA '18			2					
Argentina - Chile FTA '17		8.19	2					
CETA '16			1					
Singapore - Turkey FTA '15		12.24	2					
Honduras - Peru FTA '15			4					
Korea- Vietnam FTA '15			1					
Australia- China FTA '15		5	2					
China- Korea FTA '15		1	1 GATT XXI mutatis					
Eurasia- Vietnam FTA '15			1					
Pacific Alliance '14 (Chile Col Mex Peru)		3	4					
Mexico- Panama FTA '14			4					
Canada- Korea FTA '14		5	2					
Singapore- Taiwan EPA '13			1					
Canada- Honduras FTA '13		5	2					
New Zealand- Taiwan ECA '13		5	1					
Israel- Colombia FTA '13			1					
Central America- Mexico '11		(0.25)	4					
Guatemala- Peru FTA '11		1 (0.25)	4					
India- Malaysia FTA '11			1					
India- Japan EPA '11			1					
Korea- Peru FTA '10		1	1+4					
Costa Rica- Singapore FTA '10		2	1+4					
Canada- Panama FTA '10		5	2					
New Zealand- Malaysia FTA '09		1	1					
China- Peru FTA '09		5	2 (XXI)					
AANZFTA '09		1						
Japan- Switzerland FTA '09		3	1 (XX + XXI mutandis) + 4					
Canada- Colombia FTA '08		5	2					
Australia- Chile FTA '08		1	2 (XXI)					
Peru- Singapore FTA '08		0	1					
China- New Zealand FTA '08		1	1					
Malaysia- Pakistan FTA '07		1	1					
Indonesia- Japan EPA '07		0	1 (XIV + XX + XXI mutandis)					
Korea- US FTA '07 (KORUS)		3	2 (XXI) + 4					
Panama- US FTA '07		5	2 (XXI) + 4					
Brunei- Japan EPA '07		2	1 (XIV + XX + XXI mutandis)					
Japan- Thailand EPA '07		0	1 (XIV + XX + XXI mutandis)					
Chile- Japan EPA '07		1	1 (XIV + XX + XXI mutandis)					
Colombia- US FTA '06		5	2 (XXI) + 4					
China- Pakistan FTA '06		1	0					
Chile- Peru FTA '06		2	2 (XXI) + 4					
Taiwan- Nicaragua FTA '06		5	1					
Peru- US FTA '06		5	2 (XXI) + 4					
Singapore- Panama FTA '06		0	1					
Oman- US FTA '06		2	2 (XXI) + 4					
Korea- EFTA FTA '05*		3	2					
Japan- Malaysia EPA '05		0	1 (XIV + XX + XXI mutandis)					
Guatemala- Taiwan FTA '05		5	1 (XX) + 4					
Korea- Singapore FTA '05		0	1 (XIV) + 4					
India- Singapore CECA '05		5	2 (GEs within Invst CH)					
New Zealand- Thailand EPA '05		5	2 (GE listed relating to INSVT)					
Number of provisions	59	48	59	45	48	40	40	34

BITS 2005-19:	Preamble Reference to WTO law (1)/	Right to regulate reference in Preamble to Agt/	General Exceptions- explicit 1,	Article on environmental/ health	Expropriation referring to TRIPS	Expropriation reference to public	Performance requirements reference to	Captial withdrawal safeguard within invst chapter / incl.
Iran- Nicaragua BIT (2019)								
Belarus - Uzbekistan BIT (2019)			2					
Hong Kong - UAE BIT (2019)		1						
Burkina Faso Turkey BIT (2019)		3 A.5	2					
Japan- Jordan BIT (2018)		3	2					
Kazakhstan - Singapore BIT (2018)			2					
UAE - Uruguay BIT (2018)		1	2					
Cambodia - Turkey BIT (2018)		3	2					
Ethiopia - Qatar BIT (2017)		1						
Turkey- Uzbekistan BIT (2017)		3	2					
Colombia - UAE BIT (2017)		1	2					
Singapore Qatar BIT (2017)								
Chile HK (2016)			2					
Morocco - Nigeria BIT (2016)								
State of Palestine - Russia BIT (2016)								
Argentina- Qatar BIT '16		1 2 (XXI)						
Japan- Oman BIT '15		2 2 (XXI)						
Denmark- Macedone FYR '15		0	0					
Canada- Burkina Faso BIT '15		3 2 (GEs) + 2 (XXI)						
Cambodia- Russia BIT '15		0	0					
Canada- Cote d'Ivoire BIT '14		3	2					
Japan- Kazakhstan BIT '14		2						
Colombia- Turkey BIT '14		1	2					
Russia- Azerbaijan BIT '14		0	0					
Japan- Myanmar BIT '13		2	2					
India- UAE BIT '13		0						
Guatemala- Russia BIT '13		0	0					
Colombia- Singapore BIT '13		0	2					
Bahrain- Mexico BIT '12		0	0					
Canada- China BIT '12		3	2					
Iraq- Japan BIT '12		2						
Kazakhstan- Macedonia FYR '12		0	3					
Canada- Kuwait BIT '11		3	2					
Colombia- Japan BIT '11		2 2 + 5						
Kenya- Slovakia BIT '11		2 3 (last part of A14)						
India- Nepal BIT '11		0						
Switzerland- Trinidad BIT '10		1						
Canada- Slovakia BIT '10		0 2 (GEs) + 2 (XXI)						
Austria- Tajikistan BIT '10		3	0					
Congo- Germany BIT '10		0						
Germany- Pakistan BIT '09		0						
St Vincent & the Grenadines- Taiwan BIT '09		0 2 (XXI) + 2 (GEs self judging)						
Ethiopia- UK BIT '09		0 3 (A7.1)						
Czech Republic- Saudi Arabia BIT '09		0 3 (A5.2)						
Congo- Spain BIT '08		2						
BLEU- Oman BIT '08		0	0					
Japan- Peru BIT '08		2	2					
China- Colombia BIT '08			2					
Libya- Spain BIT '07		2	arbitrary					
Djibouti- France BIT '07		0	0					
BLEU- Korea BIT '07		3						
Oman- Singapore BIT '07								
India- Jordan BIT '06		0 Security clause but neither modelled on WTO nor involving necessity test						
Canada- Peru BIT '06		3	2					
Switzerland- Kenya BIT '06		0						
India- China BIT '06								
Jordan- Thailand BIT '05		0						
Guyana- Switzerland BIT '05		0						
China- Portugal BIT '05		0						
Serbia- Switzerland BIT '05		1						
Number of provisions	1	30	28	20	16	21	8	24

* For the avoidance of doubt, the investment chapter is part of a wider FTA https://www.efta.int/free-trade/free-trade-agreements/korea#anchor-12

PTIAs 2005-19:	ISDS provisions							
	Amicus curiae submissions	Transparency of proceedings	Conflict of interest for arbitrators	Provision for review of DS (1) Agreement in	Provision contemplating appellate	Reference to 'applicable rules of	Reference to arbitrators knowledge of	Binding interpretatio
Armenia- Singapore '19				2			2	
EU - Viet Nam IPA '19							1 & 2	
Australia - Hong Kong FTA '19								
Australia - Indonesia CEPA '19							1 & 2	
USMCA '18								
EU - Singapore IPA '18							2	1
CPTPP '18								1
Central America - Korea FTA '18								
Australia - Peru FTA '18				2				1
Singapore - Sri Lanka FTA '18		Closed Session, Annex 16B, 35						
Argentina - Chile FTA '17							2	
CETA '16	CURIOUS, many p	8.36			8.28			1
Singapore - Turkey FTA '15								
Honduras - Peru FTA '15							2	
Korea- Vietnam FTA '15							1 & 2	
Australia- China FTA '15								
China- Korea FTA '15				2				
Eurasia- Vietnam FTA '15				2				
Pacific Alliance '14 (Chile Col Mex Peru)								
Mexico- Panama FTA '14							2	
Canada- Korea FTA '14								
Singapore- Taiwan EPA '13								
Canada- Honduras FTA '13				1 & 2				
New Zealand- Taiwan ECA '13								
Israel- Colombia FTA '13								
Central America - Mexico '11				2				
Guatemala- Peru FTA '11				2			2	
India- Malaysia FTA '11						16.2		
India- Japan EPA '11								
Korea- Peru FTA '10								
Costa Rica- Singapore FTA '10								
Canada- Panama FTA '10								
New Zealand- Malaysia FTA '09								
China- Peru FTA '09								
AANZFTA '09				1			1 & 2	
Japan- Switzerland FTA '09								
Canada- Colombia FTA '08				1				
Australia- Chile FTA '08								
Peru- Singapore FTA '08								
China- New Zealand FTA '08								
Malaysia- Pakistan FTA '07								
Indonesia- Japan EPA '07								
Korea- US FTA '07 (KORUS)								
Panama- US FTA '07								
Brunei- Japan EPA '07								
Japan- Thailand EPA '07								
Chile- Japan EPA '07								
Colombia- US FTA '06								
China- Pakistan FTA '06								
Chile- Peru FTA '06				2				
Taiwan- Nicaragua FTA '06				1&2				
Peru- US FTA '06								
Singapore- Panama FTA '06				2				
Oman- US FTA '06				2				
Korea- EFTA FTA '05				2				
Japan- Malaysia EPA '05				2				
Guatemala- Taiwan FTA '05				2				
Korea- Singapore FTA '05				2				
India- Singapore CECA '05				2				
New Zealand- Thailand EPA '05				2				
Number of provisions	28	31	28	60	19	37	19	40

BITS 2005-19:	Amicus curiae submissions	Transparency proceedings	Conflict of interest for arbitrators	Provision for review of DS (1) Agreement in	Provision contemplating appelate	Reference to 'applicable rules of	Reference to arbitrators knowledge of	Binding interpretations
Iran- Nicaragua BIT (2019)				■				
Belarus - Uzbekistan BIT (2019)				■				
Hong Kong - UAE BIT (2019)			■	■			1 & 2	■
Burkina Faso Turkey BIT (2019)				■				
Japan - Jordan BIT (2018)						■		
Kazakhstan - Singapore BIT (2018)				■				
UAE - Uruguay BIT (2018)			■			■	■	
Cambodia - Turkey BIT (2018)						■		
Ethiopia - Qatar BIT (2017)				■				
Turkey - Uzbekistan BIT (2017)				■		■		
Colombia - UAE BIT (2017)			■	■			2	
Singapore Qatar BIT (2017)						■	2	
Chile HK (2016)	■					■	2	■
Morocco - Nigeria BIT (2016)		■		■				
State of Palestine - Russia BIT (2016)				■				
Argentina- Qatar BIT '16		■		■				
Japan- Oman BIT '15				2		■		
Denmark- Macedone FYR '15				2		■		
Canada- Burkina Faso BIT '15	■					■		■
Cambodia- Russia BIT '15								
Canada- Cote d'Ivoire '14	■		1	2				■
Japan- Kazakhstan BIT '14						■		
Colombia- Turkey BIT '14			1	2			2	
Russia- Azerbaijan BIT '14				2				
Japan- Myanmar BIT '13				■		■		
India- UAE BIT '13				2		■		
Guatemala- Russia BIT '13				2				
Colombia- Singapore BIT '13				2		■	1	
Bahrain- Mexico BIT '12				2		■		
Canada- China BIT '12	■		1					
Iraq- Japan BIT '12				2				
Kazakhstan- Macedonia FYR '12	■					■		
Canada- Kuwait BIT '11	■		■			■		■
Colombia- Japan BIT '11				■			2	
Kenya- Slovakia BIT '11				2				
India- Nepal BIT '11				2				
Switzerland- Trinidad BIT '10								
Canada- Slovakia BIT '10								■
Austria- Tajikistan BIT '10						■		
Congo- Germany BIT '10								
Germany- Pakistan BIT '09								
St Vincent & the Grenadines- Taiwan BIT '09								
Ethiopia- UK BIT '09								
Czech Republic- Saudi Arabia BIT '09						■		
Congo- Spain BIT '08				2				
BLEU- Oman BIT '08								
Japan- Peru BIT '08			■	2		■		
China- Colombia BIT '08				■		■		
Libya- Spain BIT '07				2				
Djibouti- France BIT '07								
BLEU- Korea BIT '07								
Oman- Singapore BIT' 07						■		
India- Jordan BIT '06								
Canada- Peru BIT '06	■			1		■		■
Switzerland- Kenya BIT '06								
India- China BIT '06						■		
Jordan- Thailand BIT '05				2		■		
Guyana- Switzerland BIT '05								
China- Portugal BIT '05								
Serbia- Switzerland BIT '05								
Number of provisions	6	8	11	37	0	26	11	8

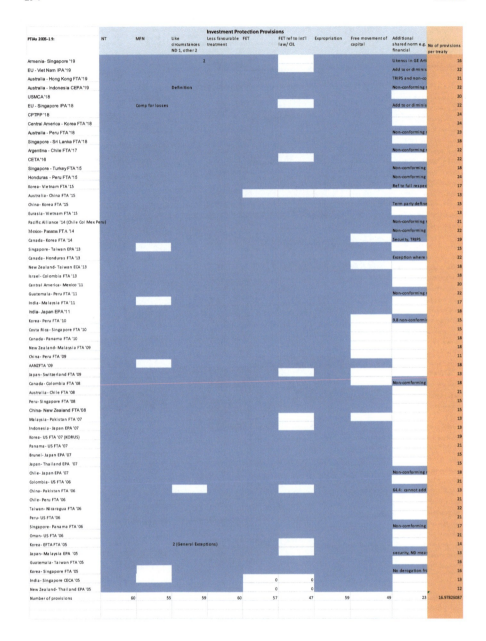

PTIAs 2005-19:	NT	MFN	Like circumstances ND 1, other 2	Less favourable treatment	FET	FET ref to int'l law/ CIL	Expropriation	Free movement of capital	Additional shared norm e.g- financial	No of provisions per treaty
Armenia- Singapore '19			2						Likens in GE Art	16
EU - Viet Nam IPA '19									Add to or diminis	22
Australia - Hong Kong FTA '19									TRIPS and non-co	21
Australia - Indonesia CEPA '19			Definition						Non-conforming	22
USMCA '18										20
EU - Singapore IPA '18		Comp for losses							Add to or diminis	22
CPTPP '18										24
Central America - Korea FTA '18										24
Australia - Peru FTA '18									Non-conforming	23
Singapore - Sri Lanka FTA '18										18
Argentina - Chile FTA '17									Non-conforming	22
CETA '16										22
Singapore - Turkey FTA '15									Non-conforming	18
Honduras - Peru FTA '15									Non-conforming	24
Korea- Vietnam FTA '15									Ref to full respec	17
Australia-China FTA '15										13
China- Korea FTA '15									Term party define	15
Eurasia- Vietnam FTA '15										13
Pacific Alliance '14 (Chile Col Mex Peru)									Non-conforming	21
Mexico- Panama FTA '14									Non-conforming	22
Canada- Korea FTA '14									Security, TRIPS	19
Singapore- Taiwan EPA '13										15
Canada- Honduras FTA '13									Exception where	22
New Zealand- Taiwan ECA '13										18
Israel- Colombia FTA '13										18
Central America- Mexico '11										20
Guatemala- Peru FTA '11									Non-conforming	22
India- Malaysia FTA '11										17
India- Japan EPA '11										18
Korea- Peru FTA '10									9.8 non-conformi	15
Costa Rica - Singapore FTA '10										15
Canada- Panama FTA '10										18
New Zealand- Malaysia FTA '09										18
China- Peru FTA '09										11
AANZFTA '09										18
Japan- Switzerland FTA '09										13
Canada- Colombia FTA '08									Non-conforming	18
Australia- Chile FTA '08										21
Peru- Singapore FTA '08										15
China- New Zealand FTA '08										15
Malaysia- Pakistan FTA '07										13
Indonesia- Japan EPA '07										13
Korea- US FTA '07 (KORUS)										19
Panama- US FTA '07										21
Brunei- Japan EPA '07										15
Japan- Thailand EPA '07										15
Chile- Japan EPA '07									Non-conforming	18
Colombia- US FTA '06										21
China- Pakistan FTA '06									64.4: cannot add	13
Chile- Peru FTA '06										21
Taiwan- Nicaragua FTA '06										22
Peru- US FTA '06										21
Singapore- Panama FTA '06									Non-conforming	17
Oman- US FTA '06										21
Korea- EFTA FTA '05				2 (General Exceptions)						14
Japan- Malaysia EPA '05									security, ND mea	13
Guatemala- Taiwan FTA '05										16
Korea- Singapore FTA '05									No derogation fr	16
India- Singapore CECA '05					0	0				13
New Zealand- Thailand EPA '05					0		0			12
Number of provisions	60	55	59	60	57	47	59	49	23	16.97825087

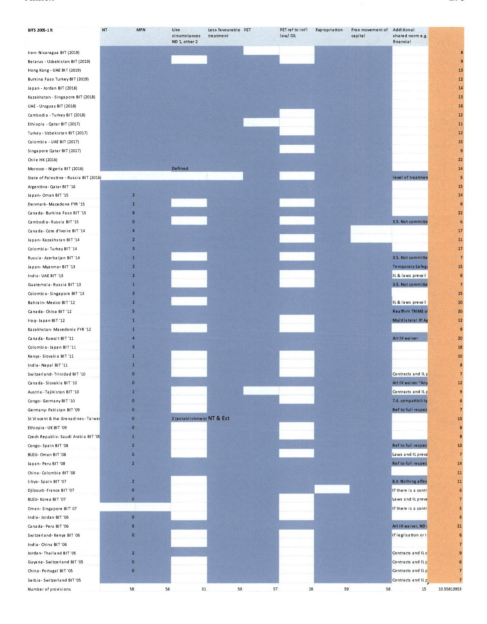

BITS 2005-19:	NT	MFN	Like circumstances ND 1, other 2	Less favourable treatment	FET	FET ref to int'l law/ CIL	Expropriation	Free movement of capital	Additional shared norm e.g. financial	
Iran- Nicaragua BIT (2019)										8
Belarus - Uzbekistan BIT (2019)										9
Hong Kong - UAE BIT (2019)										13
Burkina Faso Turkey BIT (2019)										12
Japan - Jordan BIT (2018)										14
Kazakhstan - Singapore BIT (2018)										13
UAE - Uruguay BIT (2018)										16
Cambodia - Turkey BIT (2018)										12
Ethiopia - Qatar BIT (2017)										11
Turkey - Uzbekistan BIT (2017)										12
Colombia - UAE BIT (2017)										15
Singapore Qatar BIT (2017)										9
Chile HK (2016)										22
Morocco - Nigeria BIT (2016)			Defined							14
State of Palestine - Russia BIT (2016)									level of treatmen	5
Argentina- Qatar BIT '16										15
Japan- Oman '15		2								14
Denmark- Macedone FYR '15		2								8
Canada- Burkina Faso BIT '15		6								22
Cambodia- Russia BIT '15		0							3.5. Not committe	6
Canada- Cote d'Ivoire BIT '14		4								17
Japan- Kazakhstan BIT '14		2								11
Colombia- Turkey BIT '14		3								17
Russia- Azerbaijan BIT '14		1							3.5. Not committe	7
Japan- Myanmar BIT '13		2							Temporary Safegu	15
India- UAE BIT '13		2							IL & laws prevail	8
Guatemala- Russia BIT '13		1							3.5. Not committe	7
Colombia- Singapore BIT '13		3								15
Bahrain- Mexico BIT '12		2							IL & laws prevail	10
Canada- China BIT '12		5							Reaffirm TRIMS of	20
Iraq- Japan BIT '12		1							Multilateral IP Ag	12
Kazakhstan- Macedonia FYR '12		1								9
Canada- Kuwait BIT '11		4							Art IX waiver	20
Colombia- Japan BIT '11		3								18
Kenya- Slovakia BIT '11		1								10
India- Nepal BIT '11		1								8
Switzerland- Trinidad BIT '10		0							Contracts and IL p	7
Canada- Slovakia BIT '10		0							Art IX waiver "Any	12
Austria- Tajikistan BIT '10		1							Contracts and IL p	9
Congo- Germany BIT '10		0							7.4. compatibility	6
Germany- Pakistan BIT '09		0							Ref to full respec	7
St Vincent & the Grenadines- Taiwan		0	2 (establishment NT & Est							10
Ethiopia- UK BIT '09		0								8
Czech Republic- Saudi Arabia BIT '09		1								8
Congo- Spain BIT '08		2							Ref to full respec	10
BLEU- Oman BIT '08		0							Laws and IL preva	7
Japan- Peru BIT '08		2							Ref to full respec	14
China- Colombia BIT '08										11
Libya- Spain BIT '07		2							8.3. Nothing affec	11
Djibouti- France BIT '07		0							If there is a contr	6
BLEU- Korea BIT '07		0							Laws and IL preva	7
Oman- Singapore BIT '07									If there is a contr	5
India- Jordan BIT '06		0								6
Canada- Peru BIT '06		6							Art IX waiver, ND	21
Switzerland- Kenya BIT '06		0							if legislation or i	6
India- China BIT '06										7
Jordan- Thailand BIT '05		2							Contracts and IL c	9
Guyana- Switzerland BIT '05		0							Contracts and IL p	6
China- Portugal BIT '05		0							Contracts and IL p	7
Serbia- Switzerland BIT '05		0							Contracts and IL p	7
Number of provisions	58	58	31	59	57	28	59	58	15	10.55813953

Printed by Printforce, the Netherlands